THE SEVENTY-EIGHTH ANNUAL MEETING OF THE AMERICAN ACADEMY OF POLITICAL AND SOCIAL SCIENCE

APRIL 5 AND 6, 1974
THE BENJAMIN FRANKLIN HOTEL
PHILADELPHIA, PENNSYLVANIA

The Annual Meeting will be addressed at each session by prominent scholars and officials and will be devoted to

USA: USSR Agenda for Communication

Approximately 1,000 persons will be in attendance sometime during the two days of sessions, representing a wide variety of cultural, civic and scientific organizations.

Members are cordially invited to attend and will automatically receive full information.

- Proceedings of this 78th Annual Meeting will be published as the July issue of THE ANNALS

- FOR DETAILS WRITE TO: THE AMERICAN ACADEMY OF POLITICAL AND SOCIAL SCIENCE • BUSINESS OFFICE • 3937 CHESTNUT STREET, PHILADELPHIA, PENNSYLVANIA 19104

Kindly mention THE ANNALS *when writing to advertisers*

Kindly mention THE ANNALS *when writing to advertisers*

VOLUME 411   JANUARY 1974

THE ANNALS

of The American Academy *of* Political
and Social Science

RICHARD D. LAMBERT, *Editor*

ALAN W. HESTON, *Assistant Editor*

CHANGING CONGRESS: THE
COMMITTEE SYSTEM

Special Editor of This Volume

NORMAN J. ORNSTEIN
Assistant Professor of Political Science
The Catholic University of America
Washington, D.C.

PHILADELPHIA

The articles appearing in THE ANNALS are indexed in the
Reader's Guide to Periodical Literature, the *Book Review
Index*, the *Public Affairs Information Service Bulletin*,
and *Current Contents: Behavioral, Social, and Management Sciences.* They are also abstracted and indexed in
*ABC Pol Sci, Historical Abstracts, International Politi-
cal Science Abstacts* and/or *America: History and Life.*

International Standard Book Numbers (ISBN)

ISBN 0-87761-172-6, vol. 411, 1974; paper—$3.00

ISBN 0-87761-173-4, vol. 411, 1974; cloth—$4.00

*Issued bimonthly by The American Academy of Political and Social Science at Prince and
Lemon Sts., Lancaster, Pennsylvania 17604. Cost per year for individuals: $15.00 paper-
bound; $20.00 clothbound. Institutions: $15.00 paperbound; $20.00 clothbound. Add
$1.00 to above rates for membership outside U.S.A. Second-class postage paid at Lancaster
and at additional mailing offices.*

Editorial and Business Offices, 3937 Chestnut Street, Philadelphia, Pennsylvania 19104.

CONTENTS

BOOK DEPARTMENT

INTERNATIONAL RELATIONS

ASIA, AFRICA AND LATIN AMERICA

EUROPE

UNITED STATES HISTORY AND POLITICS

POLITICAL THOUGHT

SOCIOLOGY

PREFACE

For the first time in twenty-eight years, since the landmark Legislative Reorganization Act of 1946, Congress is taking a serious look at reform of its committee systems. The House Select Committee on Committees, chaired by Richard Bolling—Democrat, Missouri—will soon release a committee report with recommendations for restructuring committees in the House of Representatives. The Senate, following a series of 1973 ad hoc hearings conducted by Senators Charles McC. Mathias—Republican, Maryland— and Adlai Stevenson III—Democrat, Illinois—will probably establish a select committee of their own.

Undoubtedly, movement by Congress toward major internal reform, after years of inactivity, was spurred by the series of Nixon vetoes and impoundments which followed his 1972 landslide reelection. Watergate, with its resulting reduction in presidential challenges to congressional legislative prerogatives, has slowed down the momentum for reform. Nevertheless, it appears that Congress' inertia in the area of committee reform has been reduced enough to bring about significant changes, especially in the House.

It is this prospect which, on the suggestion of Terence Finn of the House Select Committee on Committees, engendered this volume. However, we are concerned with more than the specifics of committee reform. Although many of the selections deal directly with concrete proposals, essays in the volume focus, as well, on: the possible forums for committee change; the importance of the internal congressional environment for committee operations; and committees as seen by nonlegislators who interact with Congress. We are especially attempting to put committee system reform in a larger context which recognizes that committees, while terribly important, are merely one variable in a complex, interactive legislative process.

One interesting feature of this volume is that several of the essays have independently arrived at similar conclusions about the direction reform should take in Congress, particularly in the House of Representatives. Elements such as a regularized rotation of committee assignments, a major reduction in the number of standing committees and a strengthened party leadership structure, are mentioned by numerous authors. For example, Davidson's essay on representation on committees mentions rotation as a possible cure for unrepresentativeness; Brenner's article on the scope of conflict in the committee process notes the impact of both rotation and committee reduction on conflict and policy formation in the House; Jones' essay focuses on the need for strengthened leadership; Peabody details a revamped House committee system involving only ten committees; and essays by Gardner and Ornstein discuss all three of these recommendations. These reforms are the least likely to be enacted by the contemporary Congress—which makes their ubiquitousness even more surprising. They point to the broader, more general perspectives on committee system reform which this collection of essays by legislators, journalists and academicians reflects.

NORMAN J. ORNSTEIN

Committees in the House

BY RICHARD BOLLING

ABSTRACT: The committee system in the House of Representatives contributes directly to the House's failure to provide vigorous national leadership. By denying the Speaker necessary tools of leadership, by using inadequate informational resources, by abdicating macroeconomic responsibilities and by employing outmoded jurisdictions, House committees clearly reveal the need for significant reorganization. Such reorganization is not impossible to achieve, however; the House of Representatives has changed in the past and, with self-discipline and hard work, can do so again. Signs of change already exist: procedural changes affecting the role of the Speaker, creation of the Office of Technology Assessment and the House Information Systems Office, consideration of fundamental budgetary reform proposals and establishment of the Select Committee on Committees, all point to a climate of reform. The select committee, after debating organizing principles of a committee system within a legislative body, can contribute significantly to this reform by its examination of committees in the House. Several schemes of committee reorganization within the mandate of the Select Committee illustrate generally the parameters of change.

Richard Bolling is United States Representative from the Fifth District of Missouri. A member of the House of Representatives since 1948, he is a member of the Committee on Rules and the Joint House-Senate Economic Committee. Long an advocate of congressional reform, Bolling served as Chairman of a special Rules Committee Subcommittee, whose work led to the creation of the Committee on Standards of Official Conduct and to the first code of ethics adopted by the House of Representatives. In 1973 Speaker Carl Albert named Bolling Chairman of the House Select Committee on Committees, which is to propose changes in the committee system. Representative Bolling is the author of House Out of Order *(1965) and* Power in the House *(2d ed., 1974), two critical studies of the House of Representatives.*

THE United States House of Representatives should be the most vigorous institution of the federal government. Its election every two years provides a representative form of government. Its Constitutional authority to raise revenues offers a means of control over federal activity and keeps the historic power to tax in a body responsive to the people. Its legislative responsibilities enable the House to set national policy objectives and to determine that which is legal or illegal. Its large membership enables the country's legislature to develop the issue expertise a smaller body cannot. Finally, the diversity and humanity of the House—its common touch—provide citizens with access to the federal establishment and remind us all that our national government is made up of real people, not simply white buildings and tax returns. The House of Representatives should be the forge of democracy.[1]

Yet, today, the House is not the vigorous institution it should be. It does not occupy, as it once did, a commanding place in the American scheme of government. Hampered by decentralized authority, lacking informational resources, stymied by obsolete rules and denying the Speaker his rightful tools, the House of Representatives cannot do its job. It is still, sadly, out of order.

THE COMMITTEES

Central to the operation of the House is the committee system. The ranking Republican member of the Rules Committee and Vice-Chairman of the Select Committee on Committees, Representative Dave Martin of Nebraska, called committees "the heart and soul of the legislative process."[2] Woodrow Wilson's famous dictum that the House of Representatives sits not for serious discussion, but to sanction the conclusions of its committees, remains generally true.[3] At present the House conducts its business via twenty-one standing committees. These committees—which vary in size but average thirty-three members—enable the House to split up its work and concentrate on a variety of issues. Such division of labor and its accompanying specialization have helped the House meet modern legislative demands. They also have helped to keep the institution from becoming captive of the executive branch. In addition, committees have created entry points or gateways to the House of Representatives for those wishing to affect government. They have become vehicles for the advancement of members' interests and careers.

As does the House, itself, committees have had a long and fascinating history. In the earliest Congresses the House relied upon select committees for the consideration of legislation. At that time the House would resolve itself into the Committee of the Whole to decide upon a bill's general principles, whereupon a select committee would be established to settle details and draft the final product. By 1800, after five Congresses had met, only four standing committees existed; of these,

1. The phrase is Neil McNeil's; see his *Forge of Democracy: The House of Representatives* (New York: David McKay Company, 1963); and Richard Bolling, *Power in the House* (New York: E. P. Dutton, 1968).

2. U. S., Congress, House, *Congressional Record*, 93rd Cong., 1st sess., 31 January 1973, daily ed., H 592.

3. Woodrow Wilson, *Congressional Government* (Cleveland, Ohio: Meridian Books, 1956, originally published in 1885), p. 69.

only one was a legislative committee. This committee—Interstate and Foreign Commerce—was established in 1795 and is now the oldest standing committee in the House of Representatives.

The Ways and Means Committee was created in 1802, the Judiciary Committee in 1813 and the Agriculture Committee in 1820. The Appropriations Committee was not established until 1865, nor the modern Rules Committee until 1885. By 1900 the House had fifty-eight standing committees; by 1930 it had sixty-seven such committees. Some of these, such as the Committee on Pacific Railroads and the Committee on Woman Suffrage, have disappeared. Others, such as the Committee on Public Buildings and Grounds and the Committee on Naval Affairs, have become subcommittees of committees or have merged with other committees. In 1946, when the House last reorganized its committee system, forty-eight committees were reduced in number to nineteen. In 1958 the Committee on Science and Astronautics was created; nine years later the Committee on Standards of Official Conduct was established. This raised the number of standing committees in the House to twenty-one.

The present committee system, however, fails the House of Representatives in four ways: (1) the system cripples the Speaker by denying him operational leadership of the House; (2) the system neither receives, utilizes nor generates adequate information; (3) the committee system does not consider the economy from a macroeconomic point of view; and (4) it does not facilitate coordinated policies, nor does it coordinate emerging issues, because the jurisdictions of House committees are outdated. The fail-

ure of the modern House to provide vigorous national leadership stems directly from these four shortcomings. No corporate board of directors would permit a company to operate with outmoded organization or without central direction, adequate information or economic integrity. Yet, that is what the House of Representatives is doing. Who is to blame for the disarray? The 435 men and women who sit in the House as representatives. They are responsible for the resulting drift and decay of the House. These individuals—who, by and large, are honest, diligent and capable people—must now restore the institution in which they serve. What is needed is self-discipline and hard work.

A HOUSE IN TRANSITION

The House of Representatives has changed before; it can do so again. No immutable rules or customs exist, because the House is a dynamic institution. In times past Speakers have appointed committee chairmen; legislative committees have appropriated funds; seniority has been discarded—indeed, the system of seniority was not fully developed until after the turn of the century; a freshman member has been named Speaker;[4] and party caucuses have ruled supreme. Precedents such as these indicate that the House is capable of significant change.

For example, the Speaker, when a Democrat, now sits on his party's committee which makes committee assignments for Democratic members. This party committee is a focus of power in the House. Moreover, the Committee on Rules no longer obstructs the Speaker, who also benefits from new Democratic

4. Representative Henry Clay, in 1811.

Caucus rules which strengthen subcommittees at the expense of full committees and their chairmen. Thus, the present Speaker, Carl Albert of Oklahoma, occupies a stronger post than his predecessor, Representative John McCormack of Massachusetts.

The Speaker

A strong Speaker is necessary if the House of Representatives is to regain its proper place in government. The only officer of the House mentioned in the Constitution, the Speaker is both coach and quarterback. Under such Speakers as Henry Clay, Thomas Reed, Nicholas Longworth and Sam Rayburn, the House of Representatives received firm leadership. Goals were set, strategy devised and tactics employed. The result was a record of achievement, a sense of purpose and public recognition for the whole House. No institution can obtain these results without such leadership.

Currently, the Speaker lacks the institutional tools of leadership. He must rely upon personal persuasiveness, as Longworth and Rayburn did. The Speaker cannot establish an agenda for the House. He cannot nominate—much less designate —its lieutenants, the committee chairmen. He cannot discipline the unfaithful, and he has little with which to reward the deserving. The Speaker is but titular head of the organization. His power is personal; thus, House leadership is dependent upon the rare fortune of finding an exceptional man.

Informational resources

In the area of informational resources, the House of Representatives operates at a disadvantage in comparison with the executive branch and the business community. The treatment of information by the House is archaic. An appropriate analogy is one of quill pens versus electronic computers. The House has overtaxed its committee staffs, misused its slender research facilities, distrusted automatic data processing systems and ignored the potential for contract research. Most important of all, the House has not realized that, in a society dependent upon technology, information must necessarily be viewed as a valued resource. Solutions to a legislative problem depend on the right kind of information; so, in fact, does the very perception of the problem.

Quite recently the House has shown signs of recognizing the importance of informational resources. It has established an office for automatic data processing and an office for contract research with the Senate. The first office, the House Information Systems, has installed an electronic voting device and is supporting the Clerk of the House with administrative services. It has also developed a bill status system and is planning a system for the preparation of committee calendars. The second office, the Office of Technology Assessment, will hopefully increase the congressional evaluation of technology's impact on society. While neither office is comparable to the informational resources of the executive branch nor equal to the House's potential, they are a start.

Macroeconomic role

The House of Representatives has also been operating at a disadvantage in the area of macroeconomics. The president and his advisors, the Office of Management and Budget and the Council of Economic Advisors are in charge. The federal budget is called the president's budget, and it is he who determines the amounts to be spent. The House does not coordinate the work of its taxing and spending committees. Its Appropriations Committee reviews less than half of the annual federal expenditures and does not report legislation on time—often because the authorizing committees fail to act in time in authorizing appropriations. Its members have no means of debating economic priorities. For a body with macroeconomic responsibilities, the situation is absurd. Unless the House of Representatives gets a handle on the federal budget, it will continue to be the economic mistress of the executive branch.

Late in 1972 the House began at last to reform the committees' consideration of the federal budget.[5] In cooperation with the Senate, the House established a Joint Study Committee on Budget Control to recommend procedures which would improve "Congressional control of budgetary outlay and receipt totals" and would assure "an overall view of each year's budgetary outlays."[6] Spurred on by the president's unprecedented impoundment of appropriated funds in 1972 and 1973, the joint study committee met and recommended additional committee structure: new House and Senate committees which would set a budgetary ceiling and attempt to sponsor a true debate over priorities. These proposed budget committees would be comprised of members from the respective taxing and appropriating committees, with additional members appointed by the majority leadership—in the case of the House, by the Speaker. Moreover, the new committees would have an enlarged professional staff with access to more data without which the House of Representatives simply cannot regain its macroeconomic role.

Unfortunately, the recommendations of the joint study committee had serious defects. For example, no provision was made for committee consideration of tax expenditures; no safeguards existed to prevent the new budget committees from predetermining the priorities debate; and, of great significance, no potentially powerful committee should be created in the House without greater participation of the Speaker.

Jurisdiction

The last area in which the committee system fails the House is jurisdiction. At present, the jurisdiction of the twenty-one standing committees is spelled out in Rule XI of the House rules. Last revised more than twenty-five years ago in the Legislative Reorganization Act of 1946, Rule XI is now unsatisfactory. House committee jurisdictions are unclear and duplicative. They are also full of omissions and antiquated or irrelevant listings.

Rule XI is unclear as to which committee in the House of Representatives has jurisdiction over the control of dangerous drugs; several committees have claimed jurisdiction.[7] Clarity is also lacking in

5. On December 5, 1973 the House of Representatives passed a budget reform measure, "The Budget and Impoundment Act of 1973."

6. See, U.S., Congress, Joint Study Committee on Budget Control, *Improving Congressional Control Over Budgetary Outlay and Receipt Totals: Interim Report* (Washington, D.C.: Government Printing Office, 7 February 1973), p. 1.

7. The Committee on Education and Labor, the Committee on Interstate and Foreign Commerce and the Committee on Judiciary.

the area of water resources, in which three committees of the House are involved.[8] The rule is also duplicative. For example, it designates two committees with jurisdiction over national forests, the Committee on Agriculture and the Committee on Interior and Insular Affairs. Rule XI is particularly deficient in omitting some subject categories. In 1946 these subjects were not national issues, thus, understandably, they were not covered by the rule. Today, categories such as energy and crime need a focal point within the House of Representatives. This is possible only by explicit designation of committee jurisdiction. As Representative John Culver of Iowa stated on the House floor:

Our first obligation is to see that there is a coherent, realistic, and contemporary setting for the consideration of all legislation and to be sure that the most commanding and imminent issues of public policy are mirrored and realized in the organizational structure of Congress.[9]

The inadequacies of Rule XI, however, have not meant that the House fails to act in areas of jurisdictional uncertainty. Acting on behalf of the Speaker, the Office of the Parliamentarian refers all bills to committee, whether or not the subject is specifically listed in the rule. When Rule XI is silent or unclear, the office is guided by precedent, logic or political advantage. Over a period of time such a process inevitably leads to confusion and inconsistency. House committees acquire jurisdiction by accretion. Different commit-

tees receive similar subject matter. Procedural uncertainty frequently results. Public policy often suffers.

The same outcome sometimes occurs when House committees compete with one another for jurisdiction over emerging national issues. Often, bills are drafted so that they will reach a certain committee. Different committees sometimes end up with similar legislation and identical jurisdiction. Take, for example, the current fascination with energy. Three committees of the House have created subcommittees on energy, while a fourth committee considers itself the appropriate site of energy legislation.[10] A coherent, sensible national energy policy is difficult to achieve under the best of circumstances; when several committees vie for control, it is next to impossible. At times, of course, overlapping jurisdiction is desirable because differing points of view which may be suppressed in one committee receive fair consideration in another. However, a diversity in communication patterns does not warrant conflicting legislation and this, too, can result from such overlap.

A further disadvantage with the present system of committee jurisdiction is imbalanced workload. Some House committees do not have much to do. Others are so busy that they must neglect urgent public business within their jurisdiction. In 1973 a member of the Committee on Ways and Means indicated that the committee had to postpone consideration of tax reform in order to take

8. The Committee on Interior and Insular Affairs, the Committee on Merchant Marine and Fisheries and the Committee on Public Works.

9. U.S., Congress, House, *Congressional Record*, 93rd Cong., 1st sess., 31 January 1973, daily ed., H 602.

10. The Committee on Interstate and Foreign Commerce, the Committee on Public Works and the Committee on Science and Astronautics have created subcommittees on energy. The Committee on Interior and Insular Affairs considers itself to be the logical focus of energy legislation in the House.

up trade legislation.[11] A critical issue was delayed because Ways and Means which has jurisdiction, under Rule XI and the precedents of the House, over taxes and the public debt, social security, national health programs, such as medicare and medicaid, revenue sharing and trade was too busy.

A final disadvantage of the present configuration of committee jurisdiction is that subject areas or issues without a committee to call their own lose focus and protection. Committees in the House afford a subject a sense of place, a home in which its constituency can centralize strategy, develop friends and rebuff foes. Issues which are orphans usually do not fair well in the House. Prestige is involved too. National issues need a legislative point of convergence which only committees can provide.

THE SELECT COMMITTEE ON COMMITTEES

In January of 1973 the House acted to remedy the problem of committee jurisdictions. At the initiation of the Speaker and with the support and encouragement of the minority leader, Representative Gerald Ford of Michigan, the House approved creation of a select committee to recommend changes in Rule XI, as well as in Rule X which designates the names and numbers of standing committees.[12] The Select Committee on Committees, as the new body is called, consists of ten members of the House, five Democrats and five Republicans. The balance between

Democrats and Republicans is unusual because the makeup of congressional committees traditionally reflects the ratio of the majority and minority parties in each house. An exception was made in this case because the success of the Select Committee is dependent upon bipartisan support.

During the debate on the resolution creating the Select Committee, the question of why a select committee was required was raised. Could not the Joint Committee on Congressional Organization, the Committee on House Administration or the Rules Committee—which has legislative jurisdiction over changes in House rules—examine Rules X and XI? Any of these alternatives, it was argued, could do the job and save the time and expense of assembling a new committee and staff.

However, each of these alternatives presented serious difficulties. The Joint Committee on Congressional Operations would involve United States senators in the determination of House committees—an involvement for which they were neither qualified nor welcome. The Senate and the House are fundamentally different and need not be involved in each other's internal organization. Moreover, the joint committee is specifically prohibited from recommending changes in the rules, parliamentary procedures or precedents of either house.[13] Also, it is not a bipartisan committee, but one in which Democrats currently outnumber Republicans. The absence of bipartisanship was again compelling in considering the Committee on House Administration as an alternate to the select committee. In addition, an obvious need existed for the body conducting the

11. U.S., Congress, House, Select Committee on Committees, *Committee Organization in the House, Hearings*, 93rd Cong., 1st sess., volume 1 of 3, part 1 of 2, May and June, 1973, p. 283.

12. House Resolution 132, 93rd Cong., 1st sess., 15 January 1973.

13. P. L. 91–510, section 402(d).

study to be as free as possible of present committee structure. As one of the twenty-one standing committees of the House, the Committee on House Administration could not be neutral. It would have had an unfair advantage were it responsible for the study. A similar conflict of interest would occur were the Rules Committee to conduct the study of Rules X and XI. Moreover, partisanship could be acute, as the majority outnumbers the minority on Rules two to one. Furthermore, the committee's staff is small and would be unable to assume the necessary added responsibilities. The legislative recommendations of the select committee, however, will be subject to clearance by the Rules Committee before they are debated and acted upon in the House, itself. Finally, the Select Committee on Committees is a nonexclusive body whose members serve on ten of the other standing committees. Such diversity gives the select committee a useful perspective on various aspects of the committee system.

CRITERIA FOR CHANGE

In examining Rules X and XI the select committee must keep in mind that any operating process in the House of Representatives must be democratic. This means that any reorganization of committees must be consistent with the underlying values of our political system. Committees in the House, regardless of their number or jurisdiction, must therefore function openly and with deliberation. The legislative process must be visible to the public. Moreover, democracy does not always operate best behind closed doors, and neither do committees. The process must also be delibera-

tive. Committees are a place to think things through. Goals should be stated, premises revealed, alternatives explored and conclusions questioned. After all, the House is a legislative body, and the unique function of a legislature is to provide a forum for the debate of public issues.

To be democratic, House committees must also function responsibly. Here, again, a constraint has been placed upon the select committee. Its recommendations must enable the committees of the House to be held accountable for their actions; this means, simply, that credit or blame can be affixed. Such responsibility is vital to the political integrity of the House, particularly now when Americans' faith in their institutions of government is unusually low.

Another criterion for the reorganization of committees is representation, which means that affected interests are given an opportunity to be heard. The House of Representatives should not operate without hearing those who wish to be heard, as some committees have at times done. Representation means that committees must listen to those upon whom committee actions have an impact. Such listening is essential to fair play.

A further requirement for the democratic operation of committees is responsiveness. The House and its committees must be responsive to national needs. The criterion is an illusive one, of course, because people's perceptions of problems and remedies vary greatly. Yet, committees should not ignore that which generally seems to be a real problem, and committee structure should not prevent the House from working its will.

Two other criteria serve as additional guidelines for the select committee in reorganizing the committee structure of the House. The first is to maintain the relative equality of all members. A committee system should not make some members of the House feel that they are backbenchers. Every member of the House is important. Each has a vote equal to the other, and each should have a committee role of some importance. While the need for leadership in the House and the quirks of personality mean that some representatives are more influential than others, House committees should be structured to give all 435 a piece of the action.

QUESTIONS ABOUT COMMITTEES

In contemplating significant changes in Rule X and XI, the Select Committee on Committees—or anyone else planning a reorganization of House committees—must first ask some basic questions about the committee system. These questions should precede any rearrangement of committee jurisdictions. Their answers will comprise a necessary framework upon which to base reorganization. They also will heavily influence the committee arrangement which occurs. Four of these basic questions are discussed below.

An appropriate first question concerns the budget. Will reorganization include committee consideration of the federal budget? If so, several questions follow: (1) should the appropriation and authorization functions continue to be separated? Is the setting of a budget ceiling by the House desirable or practical? At what level of funding, and where in the committee process, does the priorities debate occur? Does a budget ceiling make an appropriations committee superfluous? What

mechanism will guarantee coordination between spending and taxing?

A second basic question concerns the scope of jurisdiction. Should the jurisdiction of committees in the House cover several different areas of public policy or be limited to one such area? Are single interest committees, such as the Committee on Agriculture whose jurisdiction is pretty much confined to agriculture, preferable to multiple interest committees, such as the Committee on Public Works whose jurisdiction includes water resources, transportation and public buildings? Additional questions include: do single interest committees develop greater expertise than multiple interest ones; do multiple interest committees become less susceptible to capture by lobbying groups; do single interest committees really function as a single unit rather than as a grouping of subcommittees? Should the interests of multiple interest committees be related or deliberately different?

Another basic question to ask before reorganizing committee jurisdictions concerns oversight—the monitoring of the executive branch. Is the oversight function best served by having a separate committee in the House perform most, or nearly all, of the oversight or should oversight be divided among the legislative committees, the Appropriations Committee and a Government Operations Committee, as is now the case? Should the party not in the White House direct oversight in the House? What mechanism will guarantee coordination of oversight activity with the House's appropriation of funds?

A fourth basic question concerns the size of committees. How many members should House committees have? Currently, the average size of the twenty-one standing committees is thirty-three members. Committee size, of course, affects a committee's jurisdiction and internal procedures. Committees of thirty-three members tend to be unwieldy if everyone attends, to discourage equal participation of members and to encourage the use of subcommittees. They also allow committees to have multiple interest jurisdictions, although the House presently has two larger committees which are single interest: the Committee on Agriculture and the Committee on Foreign Affairs. Committees smaller than thirty-three members would most likely increase the number of single interest committees in the House. Larger committees would enhance the subcommittee system and enable members to serve on several committees. Whether House committees should be exclusive assignments is itself another basic question which directly relates to the size of committees.

Having answered basic questions such as these and, thus, devising a framework upon which to base a reorganization of House committees, the next step is to restructure committee jurisdiction. This is not easy, because policy areas are interrelated. It is not usual either, because those scholars and other observers who have commented on the committee system have neglected to present alternatives.

SCHEMES OF REORGANIZATION

What follows in the tables below is thus unusual: three schemes of committee organization—preceded by the existing scheme of House committees and their jurisdiction. The new schemes vary considerably, and no preference is expressed or implied. Each of the schemes reduces the number of committees; each provides a separate committee for oversight, although these are not inevitable. However, the schemes differ in scope of committee jurisdiction. Scheme A provides multiple interest, exclusive committees of similar subject matter which would enjoy equal legislative significance. Scheme B provides a sharp reduction in the number of committees which again would be multiple interest and exclusive, but with greater diversity of subject matter than in Scheme A. Scheme C provides a mix of single interest and multiple interest committees. These committees would not necessarily be exclusive, but would be far larger in number than those in the other new schemes.

The three new committee schemes also differ in their consideration of the federal budget. Scheme A grants the present Appropriations Committee—which receives a new name—jurisdiction to set a budget ceiling, but retains the distinction between authorizing and appropriating committees. Scheme B creates a new Committee on Budget and Revenues which combines the spending and taxing functions and requires the other committees to appropriate, as well as to authorize funds. Scheme C creates a new Budget Committee and also reunites the appropriating and authorizing functions. However, the scheme does not combine the spending and taxing jurisdictions.

CONCLUSION

These schemes represent an effort to portray what different committee systems could be. As a key component of the House, committees must

TABLE 1

THE PRESENT SCHEME OF COMMITTEE JURISDICTION

COMMITTEE	JURISDICTION
1. Agriculture	Agriculture, forestry and rural development
2. Appropriations	Appropriation of funds
3. Armed Services	Military affairs and national security
4. Banking and Currency	Wage and price controls, banking, international banking, deposit insurance, currency and coinage, housing, urban affairs, generally, and urban mass transit
5. District of Columbia	Washington, D.C. affairs
6. Education and Labor	Education, fine arts, manpower and labor relations
7. Foreign Affairs	International relations and disarmament
8. Government Operations	Budget and accounting measures, executive branch reorganization, intergovernmental relations, the efficiency and economy of government
9. House Administration	Administrative matters of the House and federal elections
10. Interior and Insular Affairs	Forestry, national parks, American Indians, water supply, mining, public lands, land-use planning, environment and territorial matters
11. Internal Security	Subversive activity
12. Commerce	Public health, air pollution, civil aviation, interstate oil compacts, railroads, commerce, generally, communications, interstate power transmission, securities and exchanges and the weather
13. Judiciary	The judiciary, bankruptcy, espionage, crime, civil liberties, constitutional amendments, interstate compacts, immigration and naturalization, patents, national penitentiaries, antitrust matters and federal holidays
14. Merchant Marine and Fisheries	The merchant marine, fisheries and wildlife, environment, oceanography and the Panama Canal
15. Post Office and Civil Service	Census, national archives, postal service and the civil service
16. Public Works	Flood control, river and harbor improvement, highways, public buildings and grounds, regional economic development, the Capitol Building, water pollution and water power
17. Rules	Changes in the House rules and regulation of floor debate
18. Science and Astronautics	Space exploration, science and technology, weights and measures and astronautical research and development
19. Standards of Official Conduct	Official conduct
20. Veterans' Affairs	Veterans' affairs
21. Ways and Means	Taxes and the public debt, social security and welfare, national health programs—medicare and medicaid—revenue sharing and trade between nations

TABLE 2

COMMITTEE JURISDICTION SCHEME A

COMMITTEE	JURISDICTION
1. Agriculture and Rural Affairs	Agriculture and rural development
2. Armed Services	Military affairs and national security
3. Economic Affairs	Wage and price controls, banking, deposit insurance, currency and coinage, economic affairs, generally, regional economic development, bankruptcy, securities and exchanges and small business, commerce, and labor relations
4. Budget and Appropriations	Budget ceiling, budget and accounting measures and appropriation of funds
5. Ethics (nonexclusive)	Official conduct
6. Foreign Affairs	International relations, disarmament, Panama Canal, international banking and trade between nations
7. Government Operations	Executive branch reorganization, intergovernmental relations, the efficiency and economy of government, public buildings and grounds, the Capitol Building, civil service, national archives and the postal service
8. Judiciary	The judiciary, espionage and internal security, crime, civil liberties, federal elections, Constitutional amendments, interstate compacts, immigration and naturalization, patents, copyright and trademarks, national penitentiaries, antitrust matters, territorial affairs and federal holidays
9. Natural Resources and the Environment	Forestry, national parks, water resources, mining, public lands, land-use planning, environment, fisheries and wildlife, pollution, weather, flood control and energy
10. Human Resources	Education, fine arts, manpower, public health, national health programs, American Indians, consumer affairs, social security and welfare, veterans' benefits and the elderly
11. Space, Science and Technology	Space exploration, science and technology, weights and measures, astronautical research and development, census, oceanography and communications
12. Transportation and Urban Affairs	Civil aviation, highways, railroads, merchant marine, rivers and harbors, urban mass transit, Washington, D.C. affairs, housing and urban affairs, generally
13. Ways and Means	Taxes, revenue sharing and the public debt
14. Office of the Speaker	Changes in the House rules, regulation of floor debate and the administrative matters of the House

be reorganized if the House of Representatives is to regain its role in government. Yet, this reorganization requires a searching examination of the concepts underlying committees in a legislative body. Changing committees is an exceedingly difficult task, both intellectually and

TABLE 3

COMMITTEE JURISDICTION SCHEME B

COMMITTEE	JURISDICTION
1. Budget and Revenues	Spending ceiling—other committees appropriate via special subcommittees—budget and accounting measures, taxes, revenue sharing and the public debt
2. Economic Affairs	Wage and price controls, banking, deposit insurance, currency and coinage, economic affairs, generally, housing, urban-rural affairs, regional economic development, bankruptcy, securities and exchanges, small business, antitrust matters and commerce and labor relations
3. Human Resources	Education, fine arts, manpower, public health, national health programs, American Indians, consumer affairs, social security and welfare, veterans' benefits and the elderly
4. International Relations	Military affairs and national security, international relations, disarmament, Panama Canal, international banking and trade between nations
5. Judiciary	The judiciary, espionage and internal security, crime, civil liberties, federal elections, Constitutional amendments, Washington, D.C. affairs, interstate compacts, immigration and naturalization, patents, copyright and trademarks, national penitentiaries, territorial affairs and federal holidays
6. Natural Resources	Forestry, national parks, water resources, public lands, land-use planning, environment, fisheries and wildlife, pollution, flood control, mining, oceanography and energy
7. National Policy Planning	Planning, generally
8. Government and Program Review	Executive branch reorganization, intergovernmental relations, public buildings and grounds, civil service and the economy and efficiency of government
9. Rules and Agenda	Changes in the House rules, regulation of floor debate, administrative matters of the House and referral of bills
10. Science and Space	Space exploration, science and technology, weights and measures, astronautical research and development, communications, national archives, census, postal service and weather
11. Transportation	Civil aviation, highways, railroads, merchant marine, rivers and harbors and urban mass transit

practically. It is also a risky one. For, as the experience with the provisions of the Legislative Reorganization Act of 1946 shows, the appearance of change is not necessarily the reality of reform. Today's gleaming reorganization is tomorrow's out-of-date organizational inadequacy. Hopefully, the articles in this issue of THE ANNALS will throw some light on the road ahead, wherever it may lead.

TABLE 4

COMMITTEE JURISDICTION SCHEME C

COMMITTEE	JURISDICTION
1. Agriculture and Consumer Affairs	Agriculture and consumer affairs
2. Armed Services	Military affairs and national security
3. Budget	Spending ceiling—other committees appropriate via special subcommittee, as well as authorize
4. Commerce, Banking and Labor	Wage and price controls, banking, deposit insurance, currency and coinage, economic affairs, generally, labor relations, commerce, securities and exchanges, federal holidays, bankruptcy and small business
5. Communications	Communications, copyright and trademarks, national archives, census and the postal service
6. Community Development	Rural development, housing, urban affairs, generally, land-use planning, public buildings and grounds, revenue sharing, regional economic development, Washington, D.C. affairs, American Indians and veterans' housing
7. Education	Education and manpower
8. Energy	Mining, power and energy
9. Government Review	Budget and accounting measures, executive branch reorganization, intergovernmental relations, the efficiency and economy of government, civil service and review of military procurement
10. Health	Public health, health research, veterans' hospitals and national health programs
11. House Administration	Administrative matters of the House, Library of Congress and the Smithsonian Institution
12. International Affairs	International relations, disarmament, Panama Canal, international banking and trade between nations
13. Judiciary	The judiciary, espionage and internal security, crime, civil liberties, federal elections, Constitutional amendments, interstate compacts, immigration and naturalization, national penitentiaries, territorial affairs and federal holidays
14. Natural Resources and the Environment	Forestry, national parks, water resources, public lands, land-use planning, environment, fisheries and wildlife, pollution, weather and flood control
15. Rules and Jurisdiction	Changes in the House rules, regulation of floor debate and referral of bills
16. Science and Technology	Space exploration, science and technology, weights and measures, astronautical research and development, oceanography, patents, copyright and trademarks
17. Standards of Official Conduct	Official conduct
18. Social Services	Social security, welfare and veterans' pensions
19. Transportation	Civil aviation, highways, railroads, merchant marine, rivers and harbors and urban mass transit
20. Ways and Means	Taxes and public debt

Committees in the Senate

BY BILL BROCK

ABSTRACT: Senators are dependent on groups of their peers—committees—for consideration of Senate business. In addition, committees are both vital to the legislative process and varied in their structure. In this paper, attention is focused on some of the major problems: committee organization, procedure, activities and realignment. The framework for discussion of the Senate committee system is colored by what has been called the Constitutional balance approach to government. Reforms in the committee system must promote both coequal status of the branches of government and committee responsibility in decision making. If Congress is to assume its proper Constitutional role, it must regain the authority which it has abdicated to the executive branch and must exercise influence in ways which are now neglected by all government. Committee reform can be an important means for achieving this objective; the time for committee reform is now. A strong committee system means a strong Congress.

Senator Bill Brock, now serving his first term in the Senate after eight years in the House of Representatives, was the first Republican elected in his home House district in forty-two years. A leader in the fight for congressional reform, Brock serves on the Senate Committee on Government Operations, Committee on Housing and Urban Affairs, Republican Policy Committee, the Republican Senatorial Campaign Committee—of which he is Chairman— and as Co-Chairman of a bi-partisan group of forty-two senators–who were elected in 1968, 1970 and 1972. Throughout his career, he has been a civic leader. In Chattanooga he was active in work with handicapped children and spearheaded an adult literacy movement. Brock is a Navy veteran and a graduate of Washington and Lee University.

S INCE 1789, when the Standing Committee on Enrolled Bills— now part of the Rules and Administration Committee—was established, senators have been dependent on groups of their peers to consider the business of the Senate. Senators are assigned to be members of specific committees which have a defined membership and jurisdiction. Such groupings are essential to the legislative process; they are varied in their structure, according to the attributes of their members, the nature and scope of their activities and the legal and political environment in which they operate.

INTRODUCTION

This essay will focus on some of the major problems which I have encountered in the Senate committees, particularly with respect to their organization, procedure and activities. Where appropriate, I have proposed reforms which would, in my view, improve our committee system.

In many ways, my framework for discussion of the Senate committee system is colored by what has been called the Constitutional balance approach[1] to government. Two assumptions of this approach are that the branches of government are presumed to be inherently coequal and that congressional committees are important in refining policies for decision by congressional majorities. In other words, committees are a management tool of the Congress and are valuable to the extent that they promote the strength of the legislative branch relative to the other branches, particularly the ex-

ecutive. If Congress is to assume its proper Constitutional role, reforms in the committee system must, in the final analysis, promote the coequal status of the branches of government. I firmly believe that Congress must regain the authority which it has abdicated to the executive and that it must exercise influence in many ways which are now neglected by all government. I do not advocate more government, but I do know we need a more responsive and responsible government. Committee reform can be an important vehicle for meeting that objective.

COMMITTEE ORGANIZATION AND PROCEDURES

Jurisdiction

From the standpoint of their jurisdiction, the standing committees of the Senate are a hodge-podge of incongruous arrangements, more the result of precedent—or accident —than design. For example, many committees deal with wholly unrelated fields of legislation; worse yet, there is incredible overlapping. The Committee on Aeronautical and Space Sciences has jurisdiction to study and report on space activities "which are peculiar to or primarily associated with the development of weapons systems or military operations," but the Armed Services Committee has jurisdiction over "aeronautical and space activities peculiar to or primarily associated with the development of weapons systems or military operations."[2] Furthermore, the Armed Services Committee has jurisdiction over the

---

1. George Goodwin, Jr., *The Little Legislatures* (Boston, Mass.: University of Massachusetts Press, 1970), p. XI.

2. The Aeronautical and Space Sciences Committee may survey and review, but may not receive legislation, whereas the Armed Services Committee has legislative jurisdiction.

maintenance and operation of the Panama Canal; yet, the Commerce Committee also has jurisdiction over the Panama Canal. And so it goes. The Committee on Veterans' Affairs reports legislation on soldiers' and sailors' civic relief, while the Armed Services Committee deals with soldiers' and sailors' homes. The Committee on Agriculture covers forestry and forestry reserves other than those created from the public domain; the Committee on Interior and Insular Affairs handles forest reserves created from the public domain. The Committee on Public Works has jurisdiction over flood control and river and harbor improvement; the Committee on Interior and Insular Affairs has jurisdiction over irrigation and reclamation.

Conflicts do exist and are a major source of committee inefficiency. However, value judgments based on this fact are not uniform. At least one respected political scientist, Heinz Eulau of Stanford University, argues that jurisdictional overlap is a salutary feature of committee organization;[3] he adopts the position that jurisdictional conflicts "maximize congressional bargaining operations." Organizational purity for the sake of purity is, of course, a questionable principle. It seems to me, however, that any advantages gained by jurisdictional conflict are greatly outweighed by one obvious disadvantage: with so many different committees covering the same field of public policy, the chances of developing a coherent, integrated program are substantially reduced. Moreover, jurisdictional conflict works to impede the committees oversight function—everybody's responsibility is nobody's responsibility, as the saying goes.

Another aspect of this problem is the establishment of subcommittee jurisdiction. Senate subcommittees should have well established areas of jurisdiction. Jurisdictional disputes among subcommittees of the same committee could often be avoided if areas of jurisdiction were well defined.

Intercommittee coordination

Another basic issue is that of intercommittee coordination within the Senate. Some coordination is deemed desirable in order to avoid jurisdictional disputes—and no matter how carefully constructed the definitions of jurisdiction are, there will always be legislation which cuts across committee boundaries. Such coordination can generally be accomplished by four methods: (1) realignment of committee jurisdictions; (2) interlocking committee memberships; (3) intercommittee bill referrals; and (4) joint committees and joint staffing. The question is: how much coordination is desirable? Taken to the extreme, it might dangerously speed up the legislative process and increase majoritarian control at the expense of minority rights and interests.

It is important to note that four of the seventeen standing committees of the Senate are formally identified as exclusive committees. Both parties have established rules limiting a senator's membership to one of these exclusive committees.[4] Thus, fully

3. Heinz Eulau, "The Committees in a Revitalized Congress," in *Congress: The First Branch of Government*, ed. Alfred de Grazia (Garden City, New York: Doubleday Anchor Books, 1967), pp. 212–216.

4. These rules implemented sections of the Legislative Reorganization Act of 1970 and Rule XXV of the United States Senate. A grandfather clause in Rule XXV allowed those senators serving on more than one exclusive committee to remain on those committees.

three-fourths of the Senate has an opportunity to serve on an exclusive committee. These exclusive committees are Appropriations, Armed Services, Finance and Foreign Relations.[5]

Despite the major reduction of the number of House and Senate standing committees accomplished by the Legislative Reorganization Act of 1946, there is, nevertheless, dissatisfaction with the committee system. This dissatisfaction stems from the fact that there has been a proliferation of subcommittees. As a result of the 1946 act, members were sitting on fewer committees; however, the total number of assignments— committee and subcommittee—is still regarded by many as excessive.

Not all members, however, have regarded this proliferation negatively. Senator Metcalf once remarked that: "I don't think it's entirely bad and it has been a pragmatic approach to the complete control and power of the chairman in the seniority system."[6] An excessive number of subcommittees, then, might tend to weaken the standing committee chairman. This is especially true if subcommittees are autonomous and independent of the standing committee.

Joint committees

Do we need more joint committees? In the 1946 hearings on legislative reorganization there was very little enthusiasm expressed for joint committees. House members, in particular, complained that senators dominate joint committee meetings; in turn, senators argued that joint committees impaired their appellate jurisdiction.[7] In the 1965 hearings, however, the mood of Congress was different, and there was widespread and vocal support for more joint committees.

George Galloway has offered these arguments in support of joint committees:

—They are more economical of the time and energy of legislators and administrators, substituting a single inquiry for two separate studies or investigations.
—They speed up the legislative process.
—They help to maintain coordinate equality with the executive branch, by preventing it from playing one house off against the other.
—When measures are matured by joint actions, differences between the House are not likely to arise and require subsequent adjustment in conference.[8]

Galloway's case is less than convincing if it is analyzed in light of bicameralism and the check and balance system. Former Senator A. S. Mike Monroney made this clear in 1945, when he responded to Harvard Professor Arthur N. Holcombe's

---

5. In the 93rd Congress, Appropriations membership is fifteen Democrats and eleven Republicans; Armed Services is split nine to six; and both Finance and Foreign Relations are split ten to seven, making a grand total of seventy-five exclusive committee assignments.

6. U.S., Congress, Joint Committee on the Organization of the Congress, *Hearings,* 89th Cong., 1st sess., August 1965, part 10, pp. 1604–1605.

7. See, for example, U.S., Congress, Joint Committee on the Organization of the Congress, *Hearings,* 79th Cong., 1st sess., April 1945, part 2, p. 276; George Galloway, "The Operation of the Legislative Reorganization Act of 1946," *American Political Science Review,* 45, no. 1 (March 1951), p. 45.

8. U.S., Congress, Senate, Committee on Expenditures in the Executive Departments, *The Organization of Congress: Some Problems of Committee Jurisdiction,* 82nd Cong., 1st sess., July 1951, document number 51, p. 4.

suggestion that more joint committees be created: "Doctor, don't you
agree that 90 percent of all the legislative work in Congress is done in
committees? Wouldn't we then be
moving toward a 90 percent unicam-
eral system?" "No doubt you are correct," replied Professor Holcombe,
"but that would be a movement in
the right direction."[9] This is letting
the cat out of the bag.

The various proposals to establish
new joint committees—and dozens
have been suggested—should be
viewed with skepticism. An excessive number of joint committees
—particularly if they are given full
legislative powers—might tend to
weaken bicameralism.[10] On the
other hand, joint committees performing investigatory, advisory and
oversight functions does not raise so
many objections. Certainly, joint
hearings before two or more House
and/or Senate committees to receive
testimony should be encouraged as
this practice would simply save time
without changing the organizational
structure of the Congress.

Select committees

Arguing that select committees
often duplicate the efforts of the
standing committees, Senator
LaFollette urged, in 1945, that select
committees be abolished.[11] The act
of 1946, as originally passed in the
Senate, prohibited select committees, but this provision was stricken
in the House. Even so, according to

Monroney, "the spirit of the Act
clearly indicated that . . . this special work should be done by the
regularly constituted standing
committees."[12] Of course, it is obvious that Congress has, in this respect, continued to violate the spirit
of the act, even to the present. Oddly
enough, little concern over this problem was expressed in the thousands
of pages of hearings in 1965. Accepting the fact that Congress will continue to create these temporary
committees, the point that they
should be held to a minimum is
well-taken by Monroney. He said:

On special committees you never get to
a point where you can do without them,
but the law of diminishing returns
applies. For instance, if we have two
or three special committees in the House
working, they will have the spotlight
of public interest; but if you spread
that to ten or fifteen committees, you undermine the value of the special committee weapon, and you destroy the very
effective use of special committees' prerogatives and equipment.[13]

Select or special committees
should be discouraged, but not prohibited. In duplicating regular
committee efforts, they tend to
weaken the standing committees.
Perhaps a limit should be established for the number of special
committees which can exist in any
one Congress under the rules of the
Senate.

Standing committees

Standing committees differ to
some extent from one another in the
nature of their membership. For instance, attorneys serve on the
Judiciary Committee. Businessmen

9. U.S., Congress, Joint Committee on the
Organization of Congress, *Hearings*, 79th
Cong., 1st sess., May 1945, part 3, p. 623.
10. The Joint Committee on Atomic
Energy now has legislative authority.
11. U.S., Congress, Senate, Committee on
Expenditures in the Executive Departments,
*Evaluation of the Legislative Reorganization
Act of 1946, Hearings*, 80th Cong., 2nd sess.,
February 1948, p. 69.

12. Ibid., p. 81.
13. U.S., Congress, Joint Committee on the
Organization of Congress, *Hearings*, 79th
Cong., 1st sess., May 1945, part 3, p. 635.

may be attracted to the Government Operations Committee. The Interior Committee is generally made up of Senators from the western states in which federal land policy is vital to the interest of many citizens. The only easterner currently sitting on the Interior Committee is Senator James Buckley of New York. However, the most important factor in determining committee membership is seniority;[14] the senator's background, previous elective experience, interests, ideology, state and personal goals are minor factors.[15]

Committee resources include staff, office space, printing, consultants and direct assistance from the General Accounting Office, Congressional Research Service, legislative counsel and, soon, the Office of Technological Assessment. The quality and quantity of these resources determine, to some extent, the success of committees. An extensive study needs to be made of the resources available to committees and of the manner in which they can make use of technological advances in fields such as information retrieval and program analysis and evaluation.

Staffs are vital to the responsible functioning of committees.[16] Not only must staffs be of high quality, but they must be supportive of all senators on the committee. It is not unreasonable to expect this kind of

14. Senate Rule XXIV; Goodwin, *Little Legislatures*, pp. 83–94.

15. Barbara Hinckley, *The Seniority System in Congress* (Bloomington, Ind.: Indiana University Press, 1971).

16. Harrison W. Fox, Jr., and Susan Webb Hammond, "Congressional Staffs and Congressional Change" (Paper delivered at the 1973 Annual Meeting of the American Political Science Association, New Orleans, La., September 4–8, 1973). To be published in *Comparative Legislative Staffs* (Beverly Hills, Cal.: Sage, 1974).

support from a centrally hired staff; thus, to assure various perspectives, the minority should be guaranteed at least one-third of the committee staff to support its work. In addition, each senator should be assigned at least one professional staff member for every standing committee on which he serves.

The most notable characteristic of the rules adopted by the seventeen standing committees of the Senate is their remarkable diversity. Some allow proxy votes, others do not; some apparently allow the chairman to cancel meetings on his own authority, others do not; some encourage open hearings, others do not. The differences in rules are almost limitless. Perhaps the best method for dealing with this problem is the preparation of a model rule which would be applicable to all committees, with the understanding that all committees could add to this model as their special needs demanded.

For the present, I urge the adoption of the following rules for *all* committees:

—The statement of rules should include word for word, rules contained in the Legislative Reorganization Acts of 1946 and 1970 and all amendments thereto. One reason for the confusion caused by the present book of rules compiled by the Joint Committee on Congressional Operations is that some committee rules contain the above information, other committee rules allude to the above and still other committee rules make no mention of them at all.

—All hearings and executive sessions should be open to the public, unless a majority of the members vote to close them.

This applies to the meetings of the subcommittees, as well as of the full committees.

—In any phase of committee procedure all votes should be recorded and made available to the public upon the request of three members. The identity of any member making a motion or offering an amendment and the nature of that motion or amendment shall also be made a part of the record upon the request of three members.

—One-third of the committee members should be able to obtain hearings on any bill under consideration by the committee or any subcommittee thereof.

—All committees should, to the maximum extent feasible, establish the same meeting schedule as their parallel committees in the House to facilitate the receiving of joint testimony.

—When consultants are hired to advise a committee, the minority members should be entitled to one-third of the funds.

COMMITTEE BUSINESS

The actual workload of a committee depends on the number of bills referred to a committee, the quality and quantity of work demanded by these bills and the substance of legislation considered. Table 1 contains a numerical count of all bills referred to, and reported by, the standing committees of the Senate from the first day of the current session through July 20, 1973. Although these statistics are incomplete and do not cover the whole session, they at least establish *prima facie* evidence that the workload varies drastically from one committee to the next.

The quality of a committee's legislative effort is more difficult to measure. Yet, in the final analysis, it is

TABLE 1

WORKLOAD OF STANDING COMMITTEES IN THE UNITED STATES SENATE, 93RD CONGRESS, 1ST SESSION*

COMMITTEE	SIZE OF COMMITTEE	PUBLIC BILLS REFERRED	REPORTED	PRIVATE BILLS REFERRED
Aeronautical and Space Sciences	11	4	1	0
Agriculture and Forestry	14	75	10	0
Appropriations	24	2	0	0
Armed Services	16	68	4	0
Banking, Housing and Urban Affairs	15	138	24	0
Commerce	18	249	25	0
District of Columbia	7	16	1	0
Finance	16	233	1	0
Foreign Relations	16	70	9	0
Government Operations	18	91	7	0
Interior and Insular Affairs	16	286	16	399
Judiciary	16	717	21	0
Labor and Public Welfare	17	212	24	0
Post Office and Civil Service	9	73	4	0
Public Works	16	78	12	0
Rules and Administration	9	90	12	0
Veterans' Affairs	9	51	4	0

* As of July 20, 1973.

probably the most important factor, calling to mind Aesop's fable of "The Lioness":

A great rivalry existed among the beasts of the forest over which could produce the largest litter. Some shamefacedly admitted having only two, while others boasted proudly of having a dozen.
At last the committee called upon the lioness.
"And to how many cubs did you give birth?" they asked the proud lioness.
"One," she replied sternly, "but that one is a lion![17]

Arguments on quality notwithstanding, it is clear from quantitative analysis that committee workloads vary greatly. Setting aside the Appropriations Committee—which is in a category by itself—the committees with the heaviest workloads are Judiciary, Interior and Insular Affairs, Commerce, Finance and Labor and Public Welfare.

The size of the committee seems to have little relationship to the committee's workload. Thus, the Judiciary Committee, the busiest committee in terms of bills referred to it, has sixteen members—the same number as Armed Services, which handles not even one-tenth the legislation. Of course, number of bills is not a true indicator of workload in the qualitative sense. Armed Services does deal with intricate legislation, but, clearly, so does Judiciary. In any case, more detailed study is needed to determine the real workload of the committees.

Some committees handle so little legislation that it is difficult to justify their existence. Included here would be Aeronautical and Space Sciences. The figures would also seem to suggest that the recent creation of the Veterans' Affairs Committee was unjustified. Because the workload of the twin District of Columbia Committees is so light in each house, it would seem that the suggestion, made by members of Congress during the 1945 Legislative Reorganization Act hearings, to establish a joint committee on the District of Columbia may have been a valid proposal.

The range of committee business can be viewed as a continuum: ideas—research—policy development—goals, objectives and substance—legislation—oversight. This continuum might reasonably be bent into a circle, as oversight clearly leads to new ideas. Much emphasis has been placed, within and outside the committee, on the legislative aspect of its work. Within committees, the major portion of senatorial and staff time is devoted to considering legislation. Civics texts and works by students of committees and the Congress have focused mainly on this aspect of committee work. In my view, the other stages in the above noted process have been neglected and even ignored by those both within and outside the committee. Congress as a whole will not have assumed its place as a coequal branch of government until committees: participate actively in the development of ideas; encourage and utilize ongoing research to develop these ideas; formulate policy statements identifying goals and objectives based on this research, which in turn can be used as a framework for formulating proposed legislation; and perform the oversight activities which are necessary to ensure continuation of successful legislation and the elimination of wasteful programs.

The process denoted by the continuum is complex; however, committee members must become mas-

17. *Aesop's Fables,* (New York: Grosset and Dunlap, 1947).

ters of diverse ideas, as well as overseers of their legislative output. Ideas today are haphazardly drawn from senators, themselves, committee hearings, a few experts and the executive branch. Where can we look for these ideas? In addition to the sources noted above, ideas should come in greater degree from: committee staff, legislative branch support personnel in the Congressional Research Service and the General Accounting Office, experts and scholars, Senate office casework, regulatory agencies, special commissions and research institutions, such as the American Enterprise Institute and the Brookings Institution. Good ideas are the base upon which committee work rests. A more systematic effort must be undertaken by committees to catalog and evaluate ideas which could possibly result in legislation.

Committees—senators and staff—cannot do very much primary research themselves. Yet, they can utilize and encourage others within the administration or experts and scholars to engage in primary research upon which written policy statements can be based. In other words, committees should be mostly involved in secondary analysis of the research of others.

Committee analysis leads to policy development. Here Congress should concentrate its resources. Committee staff, the General Accounting Office and the Congressional Research Service should develop material upon which extensive debate among senators could be based. Policy statements setting forth the goals and objectives of impending legislation would then be formulated.

Legislative efforts of committees are very well discussed in the press, civics textbooks and social science literature. This is part of the how-a-bill-becomes-a-law syndrome which has taken hold of most of us in committees. I do not want to discount the importance of the legislative process. It is vital. However, it should be put in the perspective of overall committee business. Committee work in the legislative area includes: receiving newly introduced bills; referring these bills to subcommittees, in most instances; holding committee hearings on legislation; drafting legislation; and reporting out bills for Senate consideration.

Under the Legislative Reorganization Acts of 1946 and 1970 each of the standing committees is charged with the duty of overseeing the operation of the departments and agencies which come within its jurisdiction. Senator LaFollette, one of the principal architects of the First Reorganization Act, explained the reasoning upon which this stipulation was based:

It was felt it was desirable to have that oversight made by the standing committee which was responsible for the original jurisdiction of legislation affecting a department, so that its members would be more intimately brought into contact with the operation of the department or agency.[18]

Experience under the Legislative Acts indicates that, in large measure, the committees have not lived up to the oversight duties assigned to them. Can committees better perform their oversight duties? I think so.

A most perceptive and informative analysis of oversight is provided by Walter Oleszek, of the Congressional Research Service, in his working paper recently presented to the House Select Committee on

18. *Evaluation of the Legislative Reorganization Act of 1946,* p. 76.

Committees.[19] Taking a broad view of the oversight function, Oleszek distinguishes two types of review: legislative and investigatory. The former involves committee review of programs and agencies, with an eye toward new legislation; the latter refers to the more exploratory and wide ranging effort to uncover incompetence and wrongdoing in the administration of public policy. Regardless of whether the review is legislative or investigative, however, Congress, its committees and individual members possess many techniques to determine whether bureaucrats are complying with congressional directives and whether agencies are properly administered. These techniques may also be used to block executive waste and dishonesty, to prevent agency usurpation of legislative authority and to ensure that executive policies reflect the public interest. More specifically, these techniques of oversight involve casework, legislative veto, committee veto, hearings and investigations, the appropriations process, nonstatutory controls, statutory controls, reporting requirements, control through audit, ad hoc groups, the confirmation process and studies by experts in the legislative branch.

Committee Realignment

Generally speaking, there are four ways to align the standing committees of Congress: (1) by the function performed; (2) by the internal organization of the executive branch; (3) by clientele served—special interest government; (4) by geographical area of operations—regional government. Congress relies principally

19. Walter Oleszek, "Congressional Oversight Methods and Reform Proposals" (Paper presented to United States House Select Committee on Committees, June, 1973).

on the first two, although certain elements of three and four are also to be found. If functional classification is accepted as the basis for a committee system, it follows that closely related functions should be combined in the same committee and that totally unrelated functions should not be combined in the same committee. By grouping related functions together, overlaps can be minimized.

A classification of the major functions of the United States government—formerly used in the executive budget—groups federal programs into twelve functional fields:

1) international affairs and finance,
2) national defense,
3) veterans services,
4) social welfare, health and security,
5) housing and community development,
6) education and general research,
7) agriculture and agricultural resources,
8) natural resources,
9) transportation and communication,
10) finance, commerce and industry,
11) labor,
12) general government.

Another alternative for committee configuration would be the present six major categories utilized by the administration:

1) national defense,
2) international affairs and finance,
3) space research and technology,
4) physical resources,
5) human resources,
6) general government.

Of course, each of the two alternatives would have to encompass tax and expenditure committees, as well as housekeeping committees: rules, administration and ethics.

Another alternative is to organize the committee system so that it will closely parallel the organization of the executive branch. It is often considered desirable that similar grouping standards be used for legislative and executive branch organization in order to facilitate their working relations and the performance of the oversight function. If both congressional committee and executive agency jurisdictions are based upon subject matter grouping criteria, then there will be greater correspondence between the primary responsibilities of committees and agencies. This will facilitate surveillance of the administrative branch by the legislative committee; particularly if parallel standing committees in each house are organized with identical jurisdiction and terminology, they will be correlated with the administrative activities. There is already a fairly close parallelism between the legislative and administrative structures, but it could well be brought more in line with current changes in the organization of the administrative branch.

Organizing the committee system to parallel the organization of the executive branch may seem to be preferable to functional organization for the simple reason that it better facilitates legislative review. This is not to say, however, that functional organization should be rejected *in toto*. For example, it can usefully be employed in the establishment of a congressional budget by the Budget Committee. No matter which alternative is followed, there seems to be no way of avoiding the present problem of vested interest legislation, which results from the fact that members of Congress naturally

gravitate towards committees which are concerned with the same issues as their constituents. This is natural and inevitable, for representing the interests of constituents is one of the major congressional functions. For example, a rural legislator's rejecting the Committee on Agriculture may well be an act of political suicide.

One speculative idea, raised by Senator Case,[20] does warrant some consideration: abolishing the Appropriations Committees and reverting back to the practice of allowing the regular standing committees to report appropriations bills.[21] Under the present scheme, this would not be practicable, of course; with the development of a legislative budget and budget committees giving Congress some general standard to follow other than the executive budget, Senator Case's suggestion may be worthy of careful scrutiny.

In sum, my own preference would be that we lead the executive branch—reorganizing the Congress first along largely functional lines and then reorganizing the executive so that its patterns would be subject to the same efficiency and scrutiny. This would more closely respond to our Constitutional mandate. Under no circumstances can we long tolerate a continuation of the existing situation in which neither efficiency nor oversight are achieved.

CONCLUSION

In defense of Congress it can be said that most congressmen hold at-

20. U.S., Congress, Joint Committee on the Organization of the Congress, *Hearings*, 89th Cong., 1st sess., June 1965, part 4, p. 647.

21. Previous to 1867 the Finance Committee handled all appropriation bills. During the period 1867 to 1898 the Appropriations Committee reviewed these bills. Many, but not all, appropriation bills were given to the standing committees in 1898 and then reassembled in the Appropriations Committee in 1921.

titudes and have identified goals which encourage committee reform for a more responsive and responsible Congress. Thus, the time seems right for a thorough consideration of these reforms.

In looking at the various committee reform proposals, we should remember the warning of Edmund Burke—that not all change is reform—and ask the following question: does the proposal tend to weaken or strengthen the committee system? That is, does it promote bicameralism, independence of the executive, Senate control over its committees, deliberation, protection of the minority and compromise? If the answer is no, such a proposal should be viewed with skepticism. It may actually be no reform at all.

Committee reform must be considered by the Senate. Perhaps the best vehicle for consideration of this matter is a temporary Select Committee on Committees. With the support of Senator Mathias and nine others I have recently introduced a Senate resolution, S.R. 89, which would create such a committee.[22]

The Select Committee on Committees, in addition to reviewing the topics discussed in this essay, would consider seniority, committee hearings, committee meetings, committee assignments, the budgetary process, the committee and the news media, the impact of committee on party and administration leadership on committees, the proper role and authority of committee chairmen, the number of committee assignments per Senator and the authorization appropriations process and its implications for committee structure. The time for committee reform is now. A strong committee system means a strong Congress. The people deserve a peoples' branch which can be heard.

22. Introduced on April 3, 1973 and referred to the Committee on Rules and Administration.

Evolution of the Senate's Committee System

BY WALTER KRAVITZ

ABSTRACT: After a quarter century's reliance on select committees, the Senate established a system of legislative standing committees in 1816. Whereas select committees had been subordinate creatures of the Senate, the standing panels acquired prerogatives which almost completely reversed this relationship. Eventually, the political parties evolved procedures which ensured majority control of the committees, but also granted the minority equitable representation. The seniority system emerged shortly thereafter; however, it differed somewhat from modern usages because of the large number of standing committees. After precipitous increases at the turn of the twentieth century, the Senate drastically reduced the number of committees in 1921 and again in 1946, forcing a change in seniority practices and contributing to the growth of subcommittees. Fewer committees also enhanced the influence of the remaining chairmen. In part, that enhancement provoked moves both to limit the chairmen's authority within their committees and to disperse other positions of power among more members. Other recent trends include more equitable distribution of assignments to important committees, attempts to reduce the overall committee burden of members, growth of committee staff and the evolution of a formal code to regulate committee procedures.

Walter Kravitz is Acting Assistant Director and Senior Specialist in American Government and Public Administration of the Congressional Research Service (CRS) of the Library of Congress. He attended New York University and American University. An employee of the Library since 1951 and of CRS since 1957, he has been detailed to assist numerous congressional committees, most notably the House Committee on Rules when it produced the Legislative Reorganization Act of 1970. A frequent lecturer and author of several articles on congressional reorganization, he is currently writing a history of the Senate.

O N THE day after its first quorum finally arrived, the first Senate of the United States appointed its first two committees and entrusted the chairmanships of both to Oliver Ellsworth of Connecticut.[1] Even at that early date Ellsworth was apparently one of the chamber's most respected and influential men; one of his committees wrote the Senate's first rules, many of which endure to this day.

Were that master-builder to return to the Senate today, its modern committee system would surely astonish him; it is so vastly—indeed, so radically—different from the one he helped to establish. Most often, the system changed slowly, incrementally and, at times, almost imperceptibly; the Senate has rarely consented to sudden comprehensive rearrangement of its internal mechanisms. Occasionally, however, the evolutionary pattern has been punctuated by some fundamental alteration or by some decisive event.

FROM SELECT TO STANDING COMMITTEES

The first radical change occurred in 1816. On December 10 the Senate suddenly turned from its overwhelming reliance on select committees and established a standing committee system whose basic structural philosophy has remained un-

changed to this day.[2] Until 1816 the Senate had relied on select committees almost exclusively.[3] Literally hundreds of these ad hoc, temporary panels were raised during those first twenty-seven years—more than forty in the first session of the first Congress, between ninety and one hundred in the session of 1815–1816.[4] Each was formed for a specific and usually narrow purpose, and each ordinarily expired once its mission was completed.

The early Senate made remarkably flexible use of its select committee system. Some committees were limited to the technical job of legislative drafting; others were directed to make policy recommendations; still others were told to do both. These jobs were assigned either before or after, or both before and after, initial floor consideration. Furthermore, the Senate of the period had no compunction about disposing of measures or nominations without committee referral at all. In short,

1. *Annals of Congress*, 1st Cong., 1st sess., 7 April 1789, pp. 18–21. Swanstrom calculated that Ellsworth served on twenty-two of the forty committees formed in the Senate's first session, compared to twenty for the next busiest committee appointee, Robert Morris of Pennsylvania, and a far lesser number for most other senators. Roy Swanstrom, *The United States Senate: 1787–1801*, 87th Cong., 1st sess., 26 September 1961, Sen. doc. 64, p. 231.

2. *Senate Journal*, 14th Cong., 1st sess., 10 December 1816, p. 38. Eleven committees were created on December 10: Foreign Relations, Finance, Commerce and Manufactures, Military Affairs, Militia, Naval Affairs, Public Lands, Claims, Judiciary, Post Office and Post Roads and Pensions. A twelfth, on the District of Columbia, was added a week later on December 18.

3. The four standing committees established before 1816—Enrolled Bills (1789), Engrossed Bills (1806), Library (1806) and Audit and Control of the Contingent Expenses of the Senate (1807)—were purely housekeeping rather than legislative committees; see, Henry H. Gilfry, *Precedents: Decisions on Points of Order . . .*, 62nd Cong., 3rd sess., 1914, Sen. doc. 1123, p. 267.

4. Swanstrom, *United States Senate*, p. 226; William Hickey, *Statement of the Rules and Practice of the Senate of the United States in the Appointment of Committees from March 4, 1789, to March 14, 1863*, 38th Cong., spec. sess., 14 March 1863, Sen. misc. doc. 42, p. 4.

the early Senate treated its select committees as convenient tools to be employed in any manner most appropriate to the matter at hand.

This rather improvisational approach had several impressive attractions. We have seen how flexible it was. In addition, the select committees invariably responded to the will of the Senate's majority, since by the very act of creating a committee for some purpose the Senate offered *prima facie* evidence that it favored the purpose. Because committee members were usually appointed anew for each measure, the chamber could, and did, pack each group with senators sympathetic to the majority's view.[5] Therefore, it was virtually inconceivable that a committee might defy the Senate by delaying or by refusing to report.

Precisely why the Senate abandoned this system is not clear. One scholar believed it happened because "the needless inconvenience of the frequent choice of select committees taxed the Senate's patience."[6] Perhaps senators were unhappy about the tendency of the old system to distribute the Senate's workload unevenly.[7] Perhaps they

also noticed that the vagaries of elections sometimes excluded expert members from committees on which they could have made a valuable contribution.[8] Part of the incentive to change may have been the fact that by 1816 the House of Representatives had already created more than a dozen legislative standing committees. Implicit in this suggestion is the thought that the Senate was either merely imitating the House or tacitly acknowledging that similar committee systems in the two houses would facilitate relations between them.[9]

The research of other scholars has thrown considerable doubt on at least the first two of these possible explanations. George Lee Robinson found that during the decade before 1816 the Senate was already treating many of its select committees as if they were standing committees, keeping them alive through most of a session by referring to them all or most matters concerning the subjects within their initial jurisdictions.[10] Some have also suggested that both houses established standing committee systems to counteract the influence of presidents. Until James Madison's administrations, the legislature habitually relied upon the chief executive and his associates for the initiative on much significant legislation. Congress lost its traditional agenda-maker—so the theory goes—because of the deep

---

5. "Following the British precedent, a Senator who opposed the basic purpose of a bill was not to be appointed to the committee considering it, on the theory that a 'child is not to be put to a nurse that cares not for it.' However, this rule did not extend to a Senator who merely took exception to some detail in the bill." Swanstrom, *United States Senate*, p. 228.

6. George H. Haynes, *The Senate of the United States: Its History and Practice* (Boston, Mass.: Houghton, Mifflin, 1938), I, p. 272.

7. Swanstrom found that 30 percent of the members held almost 95 percent of the total number of committee assignments during the Third Congress' second session and that this pattern, in greater or lesser degree, was typical of the entire 1789 to 1801 period. *United States Senate*, pp. 230–231.

8. Ibid., p. 230.

9. Lauros Grant McConachie, *Congressional Committees: A Study of the Origins and Development of Our National and Local Legislative Methods* (New York: Crowell, 1898), pp. 253, 315.

10. George Lee Robinson, "The Development of the Senate Committee System" (Ph.D. diss., New York University, 1955), pp. 27–28, 50.

and bitter estrangement between Madison and his Congresses and turned to standing committees to fill the vacuum.[11]

Although the Senate's creation of a standing committee system evoked little public discussion at the time, it was nonetheless a decisive moment in the institution's history. The system created an environment which eventually fostered profound changes in the chamber's working habits, floor practices and structure of internal authority.

Unlike their ephemeral predecessors, permanent standing committees, by the very fact of their permanence, could acquire the prestige and expertise upon which influence is based. Gradually, there evolved in rule and custom the idea that, except under the most extraordinary circumstances, all measures should be referred to committees before the Senate considers them. Instead of the Senate telling its committees what to put into legislation, the committees assumed the prerogative of determining which substantive provisions the Senate should consider. Thus, the standing committees became policy-making bodies instead of merely technical aids to the chamber.

Eventually, the standing committees acquired exclusive jurisdictional privileges over certain subjects and the right to pigeonhole measures referred to them. With these prerogatives the committees, in effect, became the Senate's agenda-maker. In short, with their growing authority, prestige and expertise, the standing committees al-

11. Wilfred E. Binkley, *President and Congress*, 3rd ed. rev. (New York: Vintage Books, 1962), p. 72; McConachie, *Congressional Committees*, pp. 218–221; Robinson, "Senate Committee System," pp. 20, 32.

most completely reversed the earlier relationship in which the ad hoc panels had been the Senate's subordinate creatures. At times, thereafter, it appeared that the Senate was little more than a collection of committees and its chamber merely a convenient meeting place for the routine ratification of committee decisions. Finally, the standing committee system created suitable conditions for the eventual emergence of the seniority system.

FROM INTERMITTENT TO PERMANENT PARTY CONTROL

Today's Senate punctiliously adheres to two unwritten rules concerning the party composition of its committees. One dictates that on every standing committee—and on most select committees—each party is entitled to a number of seats roughly proportional to its strength in the whole chamber. The second concedes to the majority party control of all full committee chairmanships. These practices obviously flow from the acceptance of two underlying principles: (1) the majority party should control all committees; and (2) the minority is entitled to an equitable voice on every committee, not at the whim of the majority, but as a matter of hallowed and unbreachable custom. Although now taken for granted, the Senate did not adopt this pattern as a consistent practice until the mid-1830s and did not complete its evolution until 1921.

In the select committee era senators evidently did not hesitate to pack a committee entirely with the majority party's members. During the period 1789 to 1801, many important committees consisted entirely of Federalists. "Excluding the minority from important committees was not considered unsportsmanlike or unobjective," Swanstrom observed, "because committees were regarded merely as instrumentalities to accomplish the purposes of the Senate majority."[12] The Federalists did not invariably exclude Democratic Republicans from committees. Sometimes they even gave chairmanships to opposition members. On the whole, however, Swanstrom found that minority party senators were usually assigned to committees "considering questions on which party lines were not strictly drawn—which often meant questions of secondary importance."[13]

From 1816 through the early 1830s, party control of the standing committees was notably haphazard. Although the Democratic Republicans far outnumbered all others in the chamber during this period, it was not at all uncommon for minority members to chair important committees and even to hold most of the seats on some. Because of the often hazy party affiliation of many senators during this period, exact overall figures are difficult to compile. It appears that, from 1819 through 1832, minority members chaired approximately 25 percent of the Senate's committees and held a majority of the seats on about 20 percent of them. On the other hand, many committees were entirely composed of majority members: Military Affairs in 1816 and 1823, Finance in 1821 and 1829, Commerce and Manufactures and the Committee on the Militia in 1821.

This state of affairs mirrored the then fluid—indeed, chaotic

—condition of the nation's political parties. However, when recognizable Democratic and Whig parties emerged in the 1830s, the impact of sharper party conflict was soon reflected in the Senate's committee system. For example, in the first session of the 23rd Congress, 1833 to 1834, senatorial Democrats and Whigs were just about evenly divided; so was the party composition of the standing committees; and exactly half the panels were chaired by each party.

In the next Congress—the 24th—the Democrats held only a slim majority of the chamber's seats, but the organization of the committees underwent a startling change. Gone was the old easy generosity to the minority; Democrats occupied 85 percent of the committee chairmanships and an absolute majority of the seats on all but one panel. This dominance continued during the 25th and 26th Congresses, 1837 to 1841. The Whigs, returning to power in the 27th Congress, enthusiastically emulated the practices of their opponents. They, too, held virtually every chairmanship and a majority of the seats on all but the most insignificant committees—and did the same in the 28th Congress. The Democrats, in the 29th Congress, once more in the majority, also took firm and complete control of the committees.

Systematic majority party domination of the system was thus first introduced in 1835 and, with rare exceptions, has persisted to this day. Not until the mid-1840s, however, did the Senate finally settle on a convenient, equitable and amicable procedure for doing so. During the most crucial years of change, 1833 to 1837, the chamber went through the tedious process of balloting for each

12. Swanstrom, *United States Senate*, p. 229.

13. Ibid., pp. 227, 228, 229.

chairman and for the members of every committee at the beginning of every session.[14] Obviously, there had to be a more convenient way. The sheer waste of time was annoying enough. Beyond that, the tenuousness of party discipline, the opportunity for factions to strike bargains and the personal popularity of some members sometimes combined to produce committee rosters of the most bizarre political composition.

The Senate had tried some other methods in previous years, but all had turned out badly for one reason or another. During the select committee era, the rule required balloting; evidently, senators often avoided it simply by incorporating the names of members to serve on a committee into the motion to establish it.[15] In 1823 the Senate authorized its presiding officer to appoint all committees unless the chamber ordered otherwise. Vice-President John C. Calhoun temporarily discredited this method in 1825 when he blatantly packed all the important committees with President John Quincy Adams' enemies. Even the president's opponents thought this went too far; the Senate overwhelmingly voted to return to balloting on April 15, 1826.

Two years later the chamber gave the appointing power to its president pro tempore. Unlike the vice-president, this official was one of the Senate's own and, presumably, could be trusted to act more temperately. In December 1833, however,

the pro tempore in the chair—elected during the previous session —was a minority senator. So, the chamber once more readopted the balloting rule.

After the events of 1833 to 1837, the Senate left the rule untouched, but took to evading it. From September 1837 through March 1845 it regularly waived the rule by unanimous consent and let the presiding officer make all or most of the appointments. Thomas H. Benton and a few friends, feuding with their fellow Democrats, joined the Whigs on December 4, 1845 to force a vote on the resolution to suspend the balloting rule. Their defection from the majority's ranks defeated the resolution by a single vote, and the Senate was back to balloting again.

Benton did it again in December of 1846. Evidently, extensive private negotiations then occurred; for, on December 14 leading Democrats and Whigs indicated that party committee lists were available. By unanimous consent the rule was thereupon suspended and these lists adopted. With rare exceptions, the Senate has continued to accept such party lists without balloting since that year.[16]

THE SENIORITY SYSTEM EMERGES

Once the parties established control of the committees and eliminated the election process, the stage was at last set for the appearance of a seniority system in the Senate. While the chamber had often tended to favor some of its more senior members for chairmanships prior to that time, there seemed to be no sys-

14. Before 1884 the Senate chose its committees at the beginning of every session instead of at the beginning of every Congress. McConachie, *Congressional Committees*, p. 323.

15. Swanstrom, *United States Senate*, p. 223; Hickey, *Rules and Practice of the Senate*, p. 29.

16. For a more detailed description of the evolution of this process, see, Hickey, *Rules and Practice of the Senate*, passim; and Haynes, *The Senate of the United States*, pp. 273–277.

tematic movement in this direction. Indeed, during the 1820s members awarded several chairmanships to freshmen in their first year in the Senate. The most notable case was the elevation of Maryland's Samuel Smith to the leadership of Finance as soon as he entered the Senate in 1823. In the mid-1830s James Buchanan became chairman of Foreign Relations only two years into his first Senate term and with no previous service on that committee. David Sturgeon of Pennsylvania immediately stepped into the chairmanship of the Patents Committee upon his entrance into the Senate in 1840.

However, seniority practices developed rapidly during the half dozen years following the events of December 1846. By 1859 Democrat George E. Pugh of Ohio could declare that these practices consisted of two usages: "first, never to displace a Senator from a committee without his own consent; and, second, never to promote any one else over him."[17] Although the latter practice was not always honored between 1846 and 1852, from 1853 to the present exceptions have been quite rare.

Pugh neglected to mention two additional facets of the system. The first was the understanding that no senator should chair more than one legislative—as contrasted with housekeeping—standing committee. From this it followed that a junior member of a committee could move into a chairmanship over his seniors if they already headed other panels. The other usage permitted any senator to become chairman of a committee on which he had never before served if his party colleagues on that committee either preferred

not to chair it or already led other committees. In such situations preference evidently was given on the basis of seniority of service in the Senate rather than tenure on a particular committee. Both parties had to resort to these usages with increasing frequency as the number of standing committees expanded. By the early 1900s there were so many committees that almost every member of the majority could be a chairman.

EXPANSION AND CONTRACTION OF THE SYSTEM

The Senate's overall pattern of standing committee creation and destruction falls rather neatly into two eras. The first, from 1789 to 1920, was one of accelerating creation and ever larger numbers. The second began with a cataclysmic destruction of committees in 1921, followed by a further reduction in 1946.

During its first quarter century the Senate established only four standing committees. After the twelve births of 1816, the total grew at a slow, but almost even, pace until 1844, when the total stood at twenty-seven. Thereafter, the chamber created no additional standing committees until 1863 and actually abolished a few in 1857. Between 1863 and 1898, however, the number more than doubled—from twenty-two to forty-nine. Then, in 1899 and again a decade later, the Senate indulged itself in two bursts of creation—or rather of conversion, since most of the twenty-three new standing committees formed in those years had been select committees. By 1914 the total number of simultaneously existing standing committees stood at seventy-four—actually seventy-five, if one counts the Senate members of the Joint Commit-

17. *Congressional Globe*, 36th Cong., 1st sess., 19 December 1859, p. 178.

tee on the Library who sometimes appeared to enjoy standing committee status.

The fierce constancy with which the Senate clung to its committees, no matter how obsolete their jurisdictions or how negligible their activities, was quite remarkable. Of the eighty-two standing committees created between 1789 and 1915, it is true that no fewer than seventy-four were still alive in 1920, but many were alive only in the most generous sense of the word. A considerable number of them were sinecure committees which, as Missouri's Senator George G. Vest bluntly put it in 1884: "have never had a bill, or a resolution or a particle of business before them within the memory of a living man that I know of."[18] In 1909 Senator Elmer H. Burkett of Nebraska counted thirty-six of these "graveyards to the great body of the senators."[19]

Many of these sinecure committees were allocated to the minority party, a custom already established in the 1840s. Senior minority senators chaired them, and often a majority of the committee's members were also recruited from minority party ranks. While the total number of these remained small before the Civil War, the Senate nevertheless continued to assign one, two and sometimes as many as three committees per session to minority chairmen. The custom lapsed during the Civil War for lack of Democrats, but it was revived shortly thereafter and was steadily expanded, by both Republican and Democratic Senates, during the decades which followed.

At first only the most senior minority party senators were accommodated in this fashion. However, as the Senate gradually increased the number of its committees, even relatively junior minority members could be chairmen. By 1920 the sinecure committees numbered more than forty, of which no fewer than twenty-five were minority fiefs.

The Senate tolerated this situation for several reasons. Devotion to traditional practices may have been one. The desire to enhance the prestige of colleagues, even those on the minority side, with a chairman's title may have been another. Motives of party courtesy were also involved; the Senate refused to abolish the Committee on Revolutionary Claims in 1884 because its large room was the traditional meeting place for the minority party's caucus.[20] Party leaders also found sinecure committees handy dumping grounds for members they preferred to keep off the more important panels.

However, the dominant reason for keeping sinecure committees alive was that a chairmanship entitled a senator to certain substantial privileges denied to others: office space, clerical staff, a larger stationery allowance and even some small printing privileges. Theoretically, these perquisites adhered to the committee; in practice, they belonged to its chairman.[21] When the Senate eventually began to provide every senator with reasonable clerical staff, office space and other allowances, the chief *raison d'être* for sinecure committees vanished.

18. *Congressional Record*, 48th Cong., 1st sess., 11 January 1884, p. 308.

19. *Congressional Record*, 60th Cong., 2nd sess., 25 February 1909, p. 3069.

20. *Congressional Record*, 48th Cong., 2nd sess., 1 January 1884, p. 232.

21. See, for example, *Congressional Globe*, 42nd Cong., 1st sess., 10 March 1871, p. 50; *Congressional Record*, 47th Cong., 1st sess., 16 December 1881, p. 144; 48th Cong., 2nd sess., 1 January 1884, p. 308. See, also, Charles W. Thompson, *Party Leaders of the Time* (New York: Dillingham, 1906), pp. 100–101.

In April 1921 a Republican-controlled Senate did away with forty-one committees, thereby hacking off in a single stroke the encrustation of a century. Down went the venerable Committee on Engrossed Bills, created in 1806, and that ancient anachronism, the Committee on Revolutionary Claims. With the exception of Interoceanic Canals and Banking and Currency, down went every standing committee created between 1892 and 1914. The total now stood at thirty-four.

During the next quarter century no additional standing committees were created, and one disappeared. Nonetheless, dissatisfaction with the total number continued. In the 1930s Vice-President John N. Garner reportedly declared he saw only "one glaring need" for reform in the Senate: fewer committees with smaller memberships.[22]

World War II revealed how exasperating it could be to have more than thirty committees whose jurisdictions largely depended on their names and on outdated precedents. One executive branch official, for example, had to discuss the rubber shortage with about seventeen different congressional committees.[23]

Feeding on these and other complaints, the spirit of congressional reform waxed strongly during the war. At its end, Congress drastically reorganized the committee structures of both houses through the Legislative Reorganization Act of 1946 which reduced the number of Senate standing committees to fifteen and, for the first time, defined the jurisdiction of each.[24] In 1958 the Senate added a

Committee on Aeronautical and Space Sciences, and the Legislative Reorganization Act of 1970 created another, the Committee on Veterans' Affairs.[25]

One of the most immediate consequences of the 1921 contraction of committees was a concomitant change in seniority customs. With fewer committees and, therefore, fewer chairmanships to fill, the need to appoint a senator as chairman of a committee on which he had never served virtually disappeared. The custom of filling such chairmanships on the basis of seniority of service in the Senate lapsed. Thereafter, length of service on a particular committee, rather than in the Senate, became the invariable usage.

Although the reorganizations of 1921 and 1946 reduced the number of standing committees, the basic character of the two consolidations was somewhat different. In 1921 the Senate rid itself of many groups which were fundamentally irrelevant to current public policy concerns. The 1946 contraction, on the other hand, created conglomerates of panels which had generally been active and working entities.

The Senate discovered that reducing the number of standing committees under these circumstances was like squeezing a fistfull of water: out squirted a stream of subcommittees. Although the use of subcommittees was not at all uncommon in the Senate before 1921, we are not sure just how many of them existed at any given moment.[26] Figures for the period 1921 to 1945 are also unavailable; evidently, there was some in-

22. Irving G. Williams, *Rise of the Vice Presidency* (Washington, D.C.: Public Affairs Press, 1956), p. 159.

23. Roland A. Young, *Congressional Politics in the Second World War* (New York: Columbia University Press, 1956), p. 230.

24. Act of 2 August 1946, 60 Stat. 814–820.

25. P.L. 91–510, 26 October 1970, 84 Stat. 1164.

26. Swanstrom, *United States Senate*, p. 227; McConachie, *Congressional Committees*, p. 153; Burton L. French, "Sub-Committees of Congress," *American Political Science Review* 9 (February 1915), pp. 71, 73.

crease. Sixty-eight were counted in 1945.[27] However, we do know what happened after the 1946 consolidation. Within a decade the number of subcommittees jumped to about one-hundred-fifteen. They have remained at approximately that level, give or take a dozen or so in any given session, ever since.

RECENT TRENDS

Several other recent trends in the Senate's committee system are also attributable, at least in part, to the 1921 and 1946 committee contractions. The fewer the number of committees, the fewer the chairmanships, and the longer a member could expect to wait before succeeding to one. The frustrations this situation generated were compounded both by the enhanced prestige chairmen acquired as their number dwindled and by the additional influence they wielded as committee consolidations expanded the range of public policy areas in their domains. More than ever before, it seemed, influence in the chamber had become the prerogative of a relatively small group of privileged senior members. Dissatisfaction with this constricted circle of power inevitably produced a reaction. It took several paths.

One involved attempts to limit the chairmen's authority within their committees. By law—and occasionally in rules adopted by particular committees, themselves—regulations were devised to circumscribe a chairman's discretion in internal committee affairs and to give committee members some formal means for controlling committee activities. The Legislative Reorganization Acts

of 1946 and 1970 contained a few of these kinds of provisions, most of them aimed at diluting the obstructive powers of chairmen. These required regular committee meetings, permitted a majority of a committee to force special meetings, commanded the chairmen to report promptly measures approved by their committees and provided a committee's majority with a procedure for enforcing that command. The 1946 act also required that a majority be physically present before a committee reported any measure or recommendation, and the 1970 act somewhat limited the use of proxies in such situations.

A second trend involved initiatives to disperse positions of power among more members. For example, in some committees subcommittees achieved virtually autonomous stature and consequently heightened influence for their chairmen—a development the Joint Committee on the Organization of the Congress thought inadvisable.[28] As a result of the joint committee's initiative, one section of the 1970 reorganization statute sought to curb such autonomy by reenforcing full committee control over all subcommittee funds.

In other provisions, however, the 1970 act distinctly leaned toward dispersion of formal authority. It embodied in law what had long been an informal Senate practice: no member was to hold more than one full committee chairmanship. A more innovative clause limited senators to no more than one subcommittee chairmanship on any major standing committee. In 1971 the Senate's Republican Party responded to the pressures for disper-

27. U.S., Congress, Joint Committee on the Organization of Congress, *Hearings*, 79th Cong., 1st sess., May 1945, pp. 1039–1043.

28. U.S., Congress, Joint Committee on the Organization of the Congress, *Final Report*, 89th Cong., 2nd sess., 28 July 1966, Sen. doc. 1414, pp. 13–14.

sal by decreeing that none of its members was to occupy the ranking party position on more than one standing committee. The resulting shuffle brought promotions to three Republicans.[29]

Several other developments during the past three decades deserve at least a brief mention. One saw both Senate parties relax their seniority practices in a limited way to provide a more equitable distribution of assignments on important committees. In 1953 the Democratic minority leader, Lyndon B. Johnson, persuaded his party to withhold a second major committee assignment from any Democrat until every other party member, no matter how junior, also had one.[30] Republicans adopted their own version of the Johnson rule on January 12, 1965. The Javits rule—Jacob K. Javits of New York chaired the party panel which recommended it—provided that no Republican sitting on one of the big four—that is, Appropriations, Armed Services, Finance and Foreign Relations—could be assigned to another of the four until other Republicans were offered the opening.[31]

With some minor modifications, the 1970 reorganization act applied both party regulations to the entire Senate. In effect, the act created a class of major standing committees—thirteen of them—and specified that every member must be assigned to two, but no more than

two. The same section also contained the essence of the Javits rule, making exclusive committees of Appropriations, Armed Services, Finance and Foreign Relations.

Another notable feature of the 1970 act was its attempt to reduce and equalize the burden of committee assignments for senators. The Joint Committee on the Organization of the Congress found that a similar provision in the act of 1946 had been inadequate: in 1965 some senators sat on as many as five full committees.[32] In a rather complex formula based on the joint committee's recommendations, the 1970 act imposed a series of regulations intended, over a period of years, to reduce the average senator's committee burden to no more than three or four assignments.

The 1970 statute also reenforced the modern trend towards larger committee staffs. The Senate had permitted some committees to employ clerks as early as 1855.[33] Most committee staffs, however, remained quite small until the Legislative Reorganization Act of 1946 authorized four professional and six clerical employees for each committee. The 1970 act added two professional staff to each committee's basic permanent authorization. At the same time, it granted to the minority party on each committee—upon request, but as a matter of right—the authority to choose two of the professional, and one of the clerical, staff authorized to committees. This feature formalized and regularized a practice many committees had adopted in one form or another during the decade prior to 1970.

29. *Congressional Quarterly Weekly Report*, 5 February 1971, p. 340. In 1973 the Republicans gave their members on each committee the right to choose the ranking member. Ibid., 13 January 1973, pp. 57–58.

30. Rowland Evans and Robert Novak, *Lyndon B. Johnson: The Exercise of Power* (New York: New American Library, 1966), pp. 63–64.

31. *Congressional Quarterly Weekly Report*, 15 January 1965, p. 86.

32. U.S., Congress, Joint Committee on the Organization of the Congress, *Final Report*, p. 19.

33. Hickey, *Rules and Practice of the Senate*, p. 20.

The 1970 act expanded the code of formal committee regulations in several additional directions. To the minority party it granted a formal right to call witnesses during at least one day during a committee hearing and to have three days in which to file minority or additional views on committee reports. In a series of antisecrecy provisions, the act encouraged open business meetings and hearings, required the disclosure of all rollcall votes in committee, asked for at least one week's public notice of hearings and required every committee to adopt rules of procedure and to publish them annually. Finally, the statute revised and clarified the definition of legislative oversight first enacted into law by the act of 1946 and added to the functions of all committees a responsibility for including five-year cost estimates in their reports on authorizing legislation.[34]

34. For the provisions of the Legislative Reorganization Act of 1946, see, 60 Stat. 812; the Legislative Reorganization Act of 1970 appears at 84 Stat. 1140.

Committee Reform in the House of Representatives and the Subcommittee Bill of Rights

By David W. Rohde

ABSTRACT: Prior to 1971 committee-related reforms in the House were primarily changes in the House rules, which had to be voted on by the full membership. After 1971 most committee reforms were in the form of resolutions passed by the Democratic Caucus. The post-1970 reforms dealt primarily with the selection of committee chairmen and the make-up and powers of subcommittees. The most recent of these reforms was the Subcommittee Bill of Rights which established the method of selection of subcommittee chairmen and members and defined powers and duties of subcommittees. One short run result of the reforms has been the strengthening of the liberals within the House. A possible long run consequence both of the use of the Democratic Caucus as a vehicle for reform and of the reforms, themselves, is the creation of a milieu in which the Democratic leadership can exert a substantially greater influence over outcomes within the House.

David W. Rohde is Associate Professor of Political Science at Michigan State University. Educated at Canisius College and the University of Rochester, he is the author of a number of articles on decision making in the Supreme Court and the Congress. The events relating to the proposal and passage of the Subcommittee Bill of Rights occurred while he was serving as an American Political Science Association Congressional Fellow in the office of Representative Benjamin S. Rosenthal of New York from December, 1972 to April, 1973.

CONGRESSIONAL reform is a subject which has come to be of great interest in recent years. It has captured the attention of journalists, academics, public and private interest groups, attentive citizens and, most especially, members of Congress. The purpose of this article is to describe committee-related reforms passed in the last few years by the House of Representatives and to discuss in some detail the genesis, substance and impact of one of these reforms passed early in the 93rd Congress.

COMMITTEE REFORMS, 1961 TO 1970

Committee reforms in the House have followed two different tracks. Before 1971 most of the reforms relating to committees had been changes in the House rules, which had to be considered by the full House on the floor. From 1971 to the present, most of the reforms occurred through resolutions passed by the Democratic Caucus. The shift from the House floor to the Democratic Caucus as the arena for reform was dictated, as one might expect, by changes in the distribution of power within the House which affected the likelihood of passage of reform measures. In addition, there was a change in the nature of the reform proposals which made the Caucus a more appropriate vehicle.

The reforms considered by the full House before 1971 fall into two categories: (1) those relating to the Rules Committee and (2) those relating to committees in general, passed as part of the Legislative Reorganization Act of 1970. One of the reforms relating to the Rules Committee was the twenty-one-day rule.

Virtually all major bills must be cleared—that is, granted a rule—by the Rules Committee before they can be considered on the House floor. By refusing to grant a rule, the committee has often been a roadblock to liberal legislation, and many varied attempts have been made to curb its power.[1] The twenty-one-day rule was one of these. The rule, first adopted by the House in 1949, provided the Speaker with the authority to call on a member of the committee from which the bill was favorably reported to call up a rule for consideration of the bill, if the Rules Committee did not grant a rule for a bill within twenty-one days of a request. The twenty-one-day rule was repealed in 1951, when Democrats lost twenty-nine seats in the House; enacted again in 1965, after the Johnson landslide; and repealed again in 1967, after the 1966 elections when the Democrats lost forty-seven seats. A modified—thirty-one-day—rule was proposed in 1971, but was defeated.

Another reform relating to the Rules Committee was the enlargement of the committee in 1961 from twelve to fifteen members. Before 1961 the committee, although divided eight to four along party lines, was divided six to six on ideological lines. Speaker Rayburn supported a move to add two Democrats and one Republican to the committee to create an eight to seven majority in favor of the "national Democratic" or "liberal" position. The expansion was successful by a vote of 217 to 212.[2]

1. For a general treatment of the Rules Committee, see, James A. Robinson, *The House Rules Committee* (Indianapolis, Ind.: Bobbs-Merrill, 1963).

2. An excellent journalistic account of the fight to expand the Rules Committee is contained in, Tom Wicker, *JFK and LBJ:*

TABLE 1

VOTES ON THE TWENTY-ONE-DAY RULE, 1965 AND 1967

	1965			1967		
	TOTAL VOTES	SUPPORT*	PERCENT SUPPORT	TOTAL VOTES	SUPPORT*	PERCENT SUPPORT
Northern Democrats	188	185	98.4	148	141	95.3
Southern Democrats	98	23	23.5	87	18	20.7
Republicans	139	16	11.5	173	26	14.2
All Members	425	224	52.7	418	185	44.3

* Support equals number of votes cast in favor of twenty-one-day rule.

The other set of committee reforms—relating to committees in general—passed by the House as a whole before 1971 were contained in the 1970 Legislative Reorganization Act. Among these reforms were provisions which: (1) somewhat limited closed committee meetings; (2) required that roll calls in committee be made public; (3) limited proxy voting in committee; (4) provided at least one-third of committee staff funds to the minority;[3] and (5) permitted radio and television broadcasting of committee hearings.

COMMITTEE REFORMS, 1971 TO 1973

Beginning in 1971 the focus for committee reform shifted from the House at large to the Democratic Caucus. The primary reason for this shift was simply that the Caucus offered a greater chance of success for reform efforts. All of the reforms discussed above—except minority staffing—received more support from Democrats than Republicans.

Table 1 compares support among Northern Democrats, Southern Democrats and Republicans for the twenty-one-day rule in 1965 and 1967. We can see that the proportion of each group supporting the rule was approximately the same in both years. The difference in outcome between the two votes was simply caused by the fact that there were many more Northern Democrats in 1965 than in 1967.[4] In addition, the nature of the issues raised in 1971 by Democratic reformers—seniority, an internal party matter, and subcommittee chairmanships, all of which are held by Democrats—made the Caucus the most appropriate vehicle for change.[5]

4. The size of the vote in support of the rule should not be taken as an index of the number of proreform members in each group, because the twenty-one-day rule involves questions of the division of power between the two parties in the House and ideological matters unrelated to reform. It is, however, indicative of the difference in reform orientation between the parties and within the Democratic party.

5. For a detailed account of the politics of the Democratic committee reforms of 1971 and 1973, see, Norman J. Ornstein, "Causes and Consequences of Congressional Change: Subcommittee Reforms in the House of Representatives, 1970–1973" (Paper de-

The Influence of Personality Upon Politics (Baltimore, Md.: Penguin Books, 1969), chap. 1 to 5. The expansion in 1961 was a temporary one, made permanent in 1963.

3. This provision was repealed in January of 1971.

In March, 1970, as a result of a Caucus resolution sponsored by the Democratic Study Group (DSG),[6] the Committee on Organization, Study and Review was formed. Made up of eleven Democrats, it was divided relatively evenly among liberals, moderates and conservatives and was chaired by Julia Butler Hansen, a moderate member of the Appropriations Committee from Washington. The Hansen committee was charged with considering reform proposals and making recommendations to the Caucus. The committee met a number of times

during 1970, and in December it issued its report unanimously recommending a dozen resolutions to the Caucus. In January 1971 the Caucus accepted all of the Hansen committee recommendations.

The 1971 resolution which was considered most important by the DSG and by reform advocates outside the Congress was one which provided that, upon demand of ten members, a separate vote could be had on any committee chairman or member recommended by the Democratic Committee on Committees. Thus, House Democrats were, for the first time, presented with the opportunity of bypassing the seniority system in the selection of committee chairmen if the votes of a majority of the Caucus could be mustered in favor of that course.[7]

The other major committee reform recommended in 1971 by the Hansen committee placed limits on the number of subcommittee chairmanships a member could hold. The resolution stated that: "No Member shall be chairman of more than one legislative subcommittee." This reform had far greater immediate impact than the seniority reform. It brought subcommittee chairmanships to a group of liberal activists who would otherwise have had to wait a number of years for such positions.[8]

In 1973 the Caucus produced two more committee-related reforms;

---

livered at the Annual Meeting of the American Political Science Association, New Orleans, La., 4–8 September 1973). Ornstein points out another reason for shifting the focus to the Caucus and for the success of this strategy: a sharp change in the balance between pro- and antireform forces within the Democratic membership in the House. In the 1970 elections the Democrats gained twelve seats over those they had after 1968. Ornstein estimates, however, that there was a net gain of twenty proreform votes. In 1972 the Democrats lost thirteen seats, but—according to Ornstein's estimate—the reform forces gained about a dozen votes.

6. The DSG is a group of liberal and moderate Democratic representatives originally formed in 1959 to press for liberal legislation in the House. It has grown in strength over the years—its membership numbered over 160 in 1973—and is now the dominant force in the Democratic Caucus. For a discussion of the DSG and its role in reform, see, "Democratic Study Group: A Winner on House Reforms," *Congressional Quarterly Weekly Report*, 2 June 1973, pp. 1366–1371.

One of DSG's actions, which set the stage for the use of the Democratic Caucus as a reform vehicle, was its sponsorship of a resolution, accepted in 1969, calling for monthly meetings of the Caucus. Before 1969 the Caucus met only once at the outset of each Congress for organizational purposes. The press of business at these organizational caucuses made almost impossible the consideration of reform proposals. See, Ornstein, "Causes and Consequences," p. 3.

7. The first test of the new system was not long in coming. At the February, 1971 caucus an attempt was made to reject John McMillan of South Carolina as chairman of the District of Columbia Committee. The move was defeated 126 to 96.

8. The changes effected by this reform are detailed in Ornstein, "Causes and Consequences," pp. 10–14. In addition, the resolution stated that each subcommittee chairman was entitled to select one staff member, another important gain for the liberals.

again, one dealt with chairmen and seniority, the other with subcommittees. Dissatisfied with the requirement in the 1971 reform which required ten members to openly challenge a committee chairman before a vote could be had, the DSG proposed that votes on chairmen be made automatic.[9] Olin Teague of Texas, chairman of the Caucus, ordered the Hansen committee—of which he was a member—to reconvene and consider this and other reform proposals. The committee approved the automatic vote proposal, but failed to specify a procedure for taking the votes. The DSG feared that if a voting procedure were not specified, votes would be taken in the open, thus, destroying any hope of defeating a chairman. Therefore, Frank Evans of Colorado, a member of DSG, proposed an amendment to the Hansen committee resolution which would have required that the vote on each chairman be taken separately and by secret ballot. The Evans amendment was defeated, but the substance of the reform was saved when the Caucus approved a resolution offered by Thomas P. O'Neill, Jr., of Massachusetts—the new majority leader—which authorized a secret ballot vote if 20 percent of the Caucus members demanded it.[10] The other major committee reform

in 1973 involved a set of proposals termed the Subcommittee Bill of Rights, which we will now consider in detail.

PROPOSING THE REFORM

Early in December, 1972, Peter Barash—a young lawyer and legislative assistant to Representative Benjamin S. Rosenthal of New York —was commenting on the impending Caucus consideration of the proposal for an automatic vote on committee chairmen. His position was that while this reform may have been important symbolically, it was not very important substantively. It was unlikely that any chairman would be rejected; in any event, the real problem in regard to committee chairmen was not so much who occupied the position, but the fact that in most committees the rules invested the chairman with almost total power.[11] The most liberal representative could become as autocratic as the most conservative Southerner when he assumed a chairmanship.[12] Therefore, a more important reform initiative would be

---

9. The Republican Caucus had adopted a system of automatic votes on ranking minority members of committees in 1970.

10. The reformers were easily able to muster the requisite 20 percent for every committee chairman. No chairman was rejected; the level of opposition ranged from 31.2 percent—Richard Ichord of Missouri, Internal Security—to 1.3 percent—Melvin Price of Illinois, Standards of Official Conduct. For the votes on all chairmen, see, *Congressional Quarterly Weekly Report*, 27 January 1973, p. 136.

11. Two notable exceptions were Education and Labor and Post Office and Civil Service. Both of these committees, as a result of committee member revolts against unsatisfactory chairmen, had rules which strictly limited the chairman's powers. See, Richard Fenno, *Congressmen in Committees* (Boston, Mass.: Little, Brown, 1973), pp. 130–133 and 135–137.

12. In addition, too much tampering with the seniority system seemed dangerous on ideological grounds. The system, which over the years had worked to put committee chairmanships in the hands of Southern conservatives in both House and Senate, was now bringing Northern liberals to power. For a detailed analysis of this point, see, Norman J. Ornstein and David W. Rohde, "Seniority and Future Power in Congress," in *Change in Congress*, ed. Norman J. Ornstein (New York: Praeger, forthcoming, 1974).

one which reduced the autocratic powers of chairmen and distributed such powers to subcommittee chairmen or to the committee as a whole. After a detailed examination of the rules of House committees, a meeting was arranged with Richard Conlon, the staff director of the DSG, to whom such a course was proposed.[13]

The DSG leadership accepted the idea of the reform, modified and extended the proposals and offered them in a resolution. It was referred to the Hansen Committee, further modified and unanimously approved. On January 23, 1973, the Subcommittee Bill of Rights was approved by the Democratic Caucus.

THE SUBSTANCE OF THE REFORM

The Bill of Rights required that each committee establish a caucus of its Democratic members. The caucus was required to meet at the beginning of each Congress and approve and secure the adoption of committee rules incorporating certain principles.[14]

(1) All subcommittees would have fixed jurisdictions determined by the full committee.

(2) Each subcommittee would be authorized to meet, hold hearings, receive evidence and report on all matters referred to it.

(3) All legislation and other matters referred to a committee would be referred to the subcommittee of appropriate jurisdiction within two weeks, unless a majority of the Democratic members of the committee voted to consider a measure in the full committee. This provision, in conjunction with provision (1), would halt the practice of some committees, such as Armed Services and Judiciary, which had only numbered subcommittees. In such a situation, the chairman could send a bill to any subcommittee he chose, often determining its fate by that choice.

(4) Each subcommittee would be required to have a ratio of Democrats to Republicans at least as favorable to the Democrats as the ratio on the full committee. As we shall see, this was not true on about one-third of the subcommittees.

(5) Each subcommittee would have an adequate budget, and subcommittee chairmen would select all staff of the subcommittee.

(6) Each Democratic member of the committee would have the right, in order of full committee seniority or seniority on the subcommittee concerned—whichever the Democrats on the committee chose—to bid for vacant subcommittee chairmanships. Such requests would be subject to the approval of the committee caucus.

(7) Each Democratic member—other than the committee and subcommittee chairmen—would have the right, in order of full committee seniority, to membership on one subcommittee of the member's

---

13. At approximately the same time, Representative Hanna of California was making similar proposals to the DSG.

14. The text of the Subcommittee Bill of Rights—or the resolution on "Committee and Subcommittee Organization and Procedure," as the Hansen committee termed it—may be found in Ornstein, "Causes and Consequences," appendix II.

TABLE 2

COMPLIANCE BY COMMITTEES WITH THE PROVISIONS OF THE
SUBCOMMITTEE BILL OF RIGHTS

PROVISION	NUMBER OF COMMITTEES WITH RULES WHICH COMPLIED WITH THE PROVISIONS*	
	92ND CONGRESS	93RD CONGRESS
(1) Fixed jurisdictions	7	11
(2) Powers of subcommittees	5	7
(3) Reference of legislation	3	11
(4) Ratios	3	6
(5) Staff	5	8
(6) Subcommittee chairmanships	2	5
(7) Subcommittee memberships	2	3

* See footnote 16.

choice if a vacancy were available. No member could retain more than two of his old subcommittee assignments until every member had made his one choice. This would prevent a chairman from stacking a subcommittee with members whose views he shared.

COMPLIANCE WITH THE REFORM

The discussion here must begin with a caveat: substantive compliance with the requirements listed above could only be determined by extensive interviewing with members of all committees—which was not done. Nevertheless, formal compliance with the reform can be measured by comparing the rules of various committees in the 92nd and 93rd Congresses. This can, however, be misleading. The fact that a committee has a rule which complies with the requirements does not mean that the rule is being followed. Conversely, the absence of such a rule does not mean that the substance of it is not being obeyed.[15]

With this in mind, one can assess formal compliance with the reform. As can be seen from table 2, compliance varies a great deal.[16] The greatest compliance—eleven committees—was with the rules on fixed jurisdictions and reference of legislation. Since these two rules afford the greatest protection of subcommittee autonomy, such widespread compliance is important.

15. See, for example, the discussion of subcommittee ratios, below. As another example, the Appropriations Committee does not have a rule which complies with the required procedure for appointment of members to subcommittees. However, the procedure was followed in 1973.

16. Since, in many instances, committee rules are not worded in precisely the same way as the Bill of Rights, judgments had to be made in a number of cases whether a rule was in compliance. Two general cases of this should be noted here: (1) committees which named their subcommittees in the rules were counted as being in compliance with the rule on fixed jurisdictions, because a number of committees did fix jurisdictions of such named subcommittees, but not in the rules; (2) committees which stated in their rules that subcommittee chairmen were entitled to choose "at least one" staff member were counted as being in compliance with the provision on staff. Compliance is only examined for those seventeen committees which have subcommittees. Thus, four committees—Ways and Means, Rules, Internal Security and Standards of Official Conduct—are ignored.

Furthermore, most of the committees which are not in compliance—four of the six in regard to each of the provisions—are in that position because they have no explicit rule on the subject, not because they have a contrary rule vesting powers in the chairman.

The lowest level of formal compliance was in the case of the rules on selection of subcommittee chairmen and members. I am not, however, aware of a single committee which did not follow the procedures specified in the Subcommittee Bill of Rights in these matters. This should not be surprising since these procedures are reinforcements of the seniority system and are the procedures which many committees had traditionally followed.

Some committees were little affected by the reform. Education and Labor and Post Office and Civil Service, as I have noted, already had strong protections in their rules for subcommittees; however, other committees were greatly affected. In the 92nd Congress the rules of Science and Astronautics vested power over all of the matters covered by the provisions of the Subcommittee Bill of Rights in the chairman. In the 93rd Congress, on the other hand, the committee got a new chairman—Olin Teague, Caucus chairman and member of the Hansen committee. The committee rewrote its rules, bringing them into full compliance with the requirements.

Finally, I want to emphasize again that substantive compliance often can take place, even if the committee does not formally reflect compliance in its rules. The case of the provision on party ratios reflects this well. In the 92nd Congress on only five committees was it the case that every sub-

committee had a party ratio at least as favorable as that on the full committee. Indeed, fully 36.7 percent of the subcommittees—forty-four of one hundred twenty—had less favorable ratios. In the 93rd Congress this level fell to 16.7 percent—twenty-one of one hundred twenty-five—of the subcommittees, with ten committees having all of their subcommittees in compliance.[17] This strengthening of Democratic control on subcommittees may be the greatest long run effect of the reform.

CONCLUSIONS

The implications of two events should be addressed here: (1) the shift in the primary arena for reform from the House floor to the Democratic Caucus and (2) the reforms, themselves. It appears that the revitalization of the Caucus and its use as a vehicle for policy making may have profound implications for the future. The continued growth in the relative strength of both liberal and reform groups within the Caucus may lead not only to the continued use of the Caucus for instituting further structural reform, but also to attempts to employ it as a vehicle for dictating substantive outcomes. In

17. The information on subcommittee memberships on which these calculations are based were taken from *Congressional Quarterly Weekly Report,* 23 April 1971, pp. 891–905; and 28 April 1973, pp. 973–989. In the 93rd Congress the Interior Committee set subcommittee ratios in its rules. While all of these were at least as favorable as the full committee ratio, the memberships listed in *Congressional Quarterly* do not reflect these ratios. On the basis of the membership lists, none of the seven Interior subcommittees are in compliance with the requirement. If they were, the overall level of noncompliance would fall to 11.2 percent—14 of 125.

January 1971 the Caucus was used to bind Democrats to voting for the repeal of the minority staffing provisions of the 1970 Legislative Reorganization Act. In 1972 the Caucus ordered Democratic members of the Foreign Affairs committee to draft and report a resolution to terminate the Indochina War. While this might have some import for Democratic liberals, it may be even more important in that it offers the Democratic leadership the possibility of exerting greater control over committees should they choose to exercise it.

The implications of the reforms, themselves, have already been discussed generally. Clearly, by making committee chairmen dependent for their position on the acquiescence of the Caucus and by affording protections in Caucus and committee rules for subcommittee chairmen and committee members, the powers of the committee chairmen have been reduced. Again, the potential for stronger influence by the Democratic leadership appears to have been created. If the leadership desires a particular outcome, the committee chairmen are less capable of blocking it, and the newly strengthened subcommittee chairmen would seem less likely to resist. On the other hand, if the leadership chooses not to attempt to exert influence, the result may be simply the creation of one hundred twenty plus baronies, instead of the previous twenty-one. However, this would depend on the nature of the subcommittee chairmen and would seem unlikely in the short run, given that they are more liberal and activist, in general, than their chairmen.

In any event, final conclusions about the impact of the reforms must await the passage of more time.[18] It does seem fair to say, however, that committee reforms have produced a real and important redistribution of power in the House of Representatives within but a few years.

18. For some other comments on the impact of the Subcommittee Bill of Rights see, Ornstein, "Causes and Consequences," pp. 16–19.

Representation and Congressional Committees

By Roger H. Davidson

ABSTRACT: Congressional committees are not little legislatures because they do not accurately reflect the full range of interests articulated in the political system or even in the parent houses. Legislators tend to seek assignments on committees which offer them career advancement; committees, in turn, are most vulnerable to interests with direct stakes in their decisions. More generalized interests are thus underrepresented—a fact which reflects the broader biases of pluralist decision making. Shifts in committee control lag behind social and political changes affecting the electorate at large. Reformers should devise measures to make committee membership more responsive to diverse political viewpoints and to subject the committees to stronger countervailing forces by exposing committee work to closer scrutiny and control by other legislators. Ultimately, intensified social and economic interdependencies may reduce this problem by equalizing the impact of any given problem upon individual constituencies.

Roger H. Davidson is Professor of Political Science at the University of California, Santa Barbara. He is presently on leave, serving as Professional Staff Member for the Select Committee on Committees of the United States House of Representatives. Educated at Colorado and Columbia Universities, he is author of The Role of the Congressman *and* The Politics of Comprehensive Manpower Legislation, *as well as of numerous articles. His co-authored works include* Congress in Crisis, *a study of the political dynamics of congressional reform. He has also served as consultant to the National Commission on the Causes and Prevention of Violence, the National Commission on Population Growth and the American Future and the White House.*

COMMITTEES are the instruments by which Congress defines public problems and shapes policies. Here, the political soundings are taken, the delicate compromises worked out and the technical language of bills drafted and redrafted. Floor debate may illuminate problems, and crucial questions may even be resolved in the clash of voting in the chamber. However, it is quite impossible for a large body of legislators to write complex pieces of legislation during floor debate. Thus, Congress—as any large legislature faced with a burgeoning workload—has been forced to delegate its work to specialists.

Committees, however, are not little legislatures, replicating in miniature the full range of articulated interests in our political system. It is no secret that committees tend to attract members intimately concerned about their subject matter—sometimes to the point of serious conflicts of interest. In turn, committees are most responsive to those interests with the most direct stakes in committee decisions. All this is perfectly natural, but it does not promote a clash of ideas or competition among policy approaches. The general public— which includes interests peripheral to the committee's work, as well as those which are simply unarticulated—has little or no inkling of what goes on in most committee hearings or mark-up sessions. Except for an occasional investigatory spectacle, committees labor outside the spotlight thrown by the mass media. Even if their work were adequately covered by the press, there is little reason to think that the average citizen would pay much attention.

One issue which has received little attention from reformers is the relationship between committees and external constituencies—to legislators' geographically based electorates and to de facto clientele groupings. Nothing is more natural than the clustering of interested parties around committees whose decisions affect them directly. Yet, it if is true that war is too important to be left to generals, it follows that it is unwise to leave agricultural policy to the farmers, banking regulation to the bankers and communications policy to the broadcasters—or, for that matter, to entrust the environment to environmentalists. In this article this fundamental dilemma will be explored, some possible counterweights to committee biases will be described and an explanation as to why the problem so evades real solution will be given.

WHY COMMITTEES ARE UNREPRESENTATIVE

Legislators view their committee assignments in terms of career goals and aspirations. As Richard Fenno explains in his perceptive book on committees, legislators have at least three motivations in their committee work: to enhance their chances for reelection, to influence policy making and to exert influence within the legislative body.[1] Such goals are quite understandable. The problem is that not all legislators harbor these motives in equal proportions, and not all committees offer equal opportunities for fulfilling these goals.

1. Richard F. Fenno, Jr., *Congressmen in Committees* (Boston, Mass.: Little, Brown, 1973).

Legislators' goals

Legislators from electorally competitive districts and other members unsure about their political future tend to see their committee assignments in terms of the next election. First termers typically frame their approach to the committees on committees to emphasize the "significance of the assignment for constituency service and reelection."[2] For their part, party leaders cater to this need by keeping constituencies firmly in mind in making assignments. As former Minority Leader Gerald Ford put it, "We like to give people committee assignments because they want them and because it broadens their political appeal."[3] No doubt this is comforting to those who have experienced, or expect to experience, difficulty at the polls. Even veteran legislators buttress their campaigns by pointing to the committee seniority they have accumulated.

Not all committee assignments pay off at the polls. Available evidence suggests that the public is more interested in the legislator's concrete service to the district than in the substance of policy making. In a 1968 survey a national sample were asked to discuss their reasons for evaluating their representatives the way they did.[4] The vast majority of the answers dealt with the representatives' personality or their ability to serve the district in a material way. About three out of every five responses concerned some aspect of the representatives' service to the district; one in every five cited the legislators' personal characteristics or reputation. The entire range of policy issues—foreign, domestic and defense—accounted for no more than one out of every ten responses. In contrast, Congress as a collective institution is evaluated largely on the basis of overall policy preferences. Thus, it would appear that committee assignments benefit legislators at the polls mainly when they influence the material well-being of the electorate—through government projects, contracts, targeted programs and the like.

Legislators harbor other goals in seeking a particular committee assignment. Most of them sincerely want a meaningful role in shaping public policies. Of course, people differ in their backgrounds, interests and calculations of where the highest payoffs lie; however, everyone presumably wants to feel that they are a significant part of the enterprise. Some legislators, at least, aspire to positions which maximize their influence over their House or Senate colleagues.

The committee pecking order

Committees differ in the opportunities they offer for realizing these goals; hence, they differ in overall attractiveness. As a rough measure of the phenomenon known as the committee pecking order—at

---

2. Robert Healy, "Committees and the Politics of Assignments," in *To Be A Congressman: The Promise and the Power*, ed. Sven Groennings and Jonathan Hawley (Washington, D.C.: Acropolis Books, 1973), p. 117.

3. U.S., House of Representatives, Select Committee on Committees, *Committee Organization in the House* (Washington, D.C.: Government Printing Office, 1973), vol. I, part 1, p. 32. See, also, Nicholas A. Masters, "Committee Assignments in the House of Representatives," *American Political Science Review* 55 (June 1961), pp. 345–357; and Healy, "Politics of Assignments," pp. 111–112.

4. Louis Harris and Associates, Study No. 1900 (under contract from the author).

least in the House—I have arranged the standing committees in order of the average seniority of their members in the 93rd Congress (table 1). Although it would be risky to interpret this as a perfect prestige ranking, it illustrates quite vividly the differential attractions of various committees.

The most senior committee, Standards of Official Conduct, is a small body whose most critical function is adjudication of ethics cases— a factor which explains its member-

TABLE 1

AVERAGE SENIORITY OF HOUSE COMMITTEE MEMBERS, 93RD CONGRESS*

COMMITTEE	AVERAGE SENIORITY OF MEMBERS— NUMBER OF TERMS
Standards of Official Conduct	9.42 terms
Ways and Means	8.00
Appropriations	7.94
Rules	7.53
Foreign Affairs	6.41
Government Operations	5.85
Average of all House members	5.59
Armed Services	5.58
House Administration	5.38
Banking and Currency	5.26
Veterans Affairs	5.23
Interstate and Foreign Commerce	4.93
Public Works	4.74
Merchant Marine and Fisheries	4.63
Post Office and Civil Service	4.58
Education and Labor	4.46
Interior and Insular Affairs	4.28
Agriculture	4.14
Science and Astronautics	4.14
Internal Security	4.00
Judiciary	3.86
District of Columbia	3.76

SOURCE: Terms of service for members of the 93rd Congress are listed in: *Congressional Directory*, 93rd Cong., 1st sess., 1973, pp. 244–255.

* As of March 10, 1973.

ship of respected House elders. Those committees generally regarded as most prestigious—Ways and Means, Appropriations and Rules—rank next in the mean seniority of their members. First-term representatives, although not unknown on these committees, are extremely rare. Despite their importance, these committees deal with relatively complicated topics and offer members few opportunities for public exposure. Thus, the leadership tends to recommend members whose seniority and electoral invulnerability frees them for hard work and for making unpopular—responsible is the usual term—choices.

Most committees offering direct constituency payoffs are accessible to junior members. These include the so-called pork and interest committees—most notably, Agriculture, Interior, Merchant Marine and Fisheries and Public Works. To be sure, each of these committees is responsible for a significant segment of public policy, for example: agricultural policies, transportation—Public Works—and environmental questions—Interior and Merchant Marine. It is fair to say, however, that these committees are initially sought by legislators because of their promise of direct constituency payoffs.

Some committees hold limited attraction for members. These are committees whose workloads promise neither glamour nor constituency payoffs nor great influence within the legislature. The District of Columbia committees, for example, have little direct relevance to legislators whose districts lie outside the Washington metropolitan area; this is also the case with housekeeping committees, such as Senate Rules and Administration and

House Administration. Generalizations are risky, of course. Some members can parlay their work on such committees into the coin of influence over their colleagues, as House Administration Chairman Wayne Hays has vividly demonstrated. Other examples of legislators who have made the most of seemingly unattractive assignments could be cited. As an overall proposition, however, a committee's prestige is reflected in its ability to attract and hold high seniority members.

Biases of the committee system

The marriage of these factors—legislators with different goals and committees of varying attractiveness—produces congressional committees which are often unrepresentative of the chamber, not to mention the political system at large. Representativeness can be defined in many ways, but it seems reasonable to begin with a simple measure of ideological coloration, such as the "liberalism" rankings displayed in table 2.

TABLE 2

"LIBERALISM" RANKINGS OF HOUSE COMMITTEE MEMBERS, 92ND CONGRESS, 1971 TO 1972

COMMITTEE	ALL MEMBERS (PERCENT)	DEMOCRATS (PERCENT)	REPUBLICANS (PERCENT)	NUMBER
Education and Labor	56	79	25	38
Judiciary	55	76	27	37
Government Operations	52	65	35	39
Foreign Affairs	51	67	31	38
Banking and Currency	49	63	27	37
House Administration	46	62	22	25
Science and Astronautics	45	56	28	29
Merchant Marine and Fisheries	44	50	34	36
Rules	44	59	14	15
Interior and Insular Affairs	43	60	17	38
Average for entire House	43	58*	21	432
Public Works	41	56	15	37
Interstate and Foreign Commerce	41	63	11	43
District of Columbia	40	51	25	24
Ways and Means	40	58	12	25
Post Office and Civil Service	39	57	14	26
Veterans' Affairs	39	50	22	26
Appropriations	38	50	19	55
Internal Security	32	57	7	8
Agriculture	30	42	12	36
Armed Services	29	36	18	41
Standards of Official Conduct	21	31	12	12

SOURCE: "Liberalism" rankings for individual members are drawn from *Congressional Quarterly's* "Opposition to Conservative Coalition" scores, with the figures recomputed to eliminate the effect of absences from the House floor. *Congressional Quarterly Weekly Report* 30 (18 November 1972), pp. 3022–3027.

* For the 168 northern Democrats, the "liberalism" score was 76; for the 87 southern Democrats, the score was 25.

Some committees are notably out of tune with the House as a whole, if measured by the ideological rankings of their members. For example, Armed Services and Internal Security are far more conservative than the parent body, mainly because such subjects appeal to conservatives; in contrast, liberals have tended to shun these committees—to their eventual sorrow. Also, leaders of these committees have resisted bids to infuse the membership with people they deemed insufficiently committed to national security. Appropriations members are also more conservative than the House as a whole. This is mainly the result of a conscious decision by party leaders to restrict the committee to members whose views would lead them to a budget-cutting posture and whose safe constituencies would give them the independence to resist pressures for higher spending.

At the liberal end of the spectrum, Education and Labor reigns supreme. Northern liberal Democrats generally control the committee, as indicated by the fact that its Democrats are more liberal even than northern Democrats as a whole. Because its jurisdiction embraces many of the ideological issues which have divided liberals and conservatives since the New Deal era, the committee attracts liberals who want to frame strong legislation in these fields or those who have working class constituencies. Moreover, the AFL-CIO informally clears prospective Democratic committee members, thus, ensuring that such members have the "right" views on labor-management problems. In contrast, Republicans on the committee are only slightly more liberal than their colleagues as a whole.

Education and Labor has been at odds with the parent House on numerous occasions. Bills emanating from the committee are closely scrutinized and are frequently heavily amended during floor debate. Republicans complain heatedly that committee Democrats fail to support the House position in conferences with the Senate. Unhappiness with the committee is probably the real source of the oft-heard proposal to split the committee's jurisdiction—although such a move might well be justified in the interests of equalizing the workload.

Almost as unrepresentative is Judiciary, which has had its own problems relating to the House. Judiciary's technique has been to bury major legislation desired by conservatives who are restless with the federal courts and the problem of crime. In the 92nd Congress the committee managed to get itself discharged from the school prayer amendment after it had pigeonholed the measure. The committee's lassitude on the crime issue was one reason for the creation of the Select Committee on Crime in 1969.

With the exception of Appropriations, the so-called prestige committees are not ideologically unreflective of House sentiment. For more than a generation the Rules Committee was controlled by a bipartisan conservative coalition, oftentimes frustrating the Democratic leadership. As a result of efforts by three successive Speakers since 1961 to appoint cooperative Democrats, Rules is now near the center of the ideological spectrum.

Other types of malrepresentation can be cited. Geographic biases—westerners on Interior, farm representatives on Agriculture, coastal areas on Merchant Marine and Fisheries—are obvious and of long standing. For example, no less than 63 percent of Interior's members come from districts west of the Mississippi River; only 35 percent of the all House members come from the same region. No doubt, such members find irresistible the committee's jurisdiction in national parks, public lands, reclamation and natural resources.

Urban legislators' indifference to Agriculture assignments is legendary. Occasionally, very junior urban representatives find themselves placed on the committee; invariably, they are quick to transfer to another assignment. Arriving in Washington in 1969, Brooklyn's Shirley Chisholm was slated for the committee, but promptly asked the Democratic Caucus to remove her from the committee list and to direct the Committee on Committees to recommend another assignment. "I think it would be hard to imagine an assignment that is less relevant to my background or to the needs of the predominantly black and Puerto Rican people who elected me . . ." she told the Caucus. As she explained later: "I was simply mad at being put where I would be wasted, and I could not keep quiet about it."[5]

Although extraordinary, Representative Chisholm's action followed the venerable principle that committee assignments should have career payoffs. As a result, no legislators from predominantly urban districts now serve on the House committee, and no more than a handful have done so in the past

generation. In the twelve states represented on the Senate Agriculture Committee, only 37.6 percent of the population resides within metropolitan areas (SMSAs); for the twenty-five states represented on the House committee, the figure is 51.6 percent. Nationally, 68.6 percent of the people are metropolitan dwellers.

Other committees have porkbarrel aspects which prove an irresistible temptation to constituency-minded legislators. Armed Services Committee members—labelled as "the Pentagon's lobby on the Hill" by a junior representative—support military spending not only out of ideological conviction, but because of the economic advantages of military installations and contracts. It is perhaps no accident that the forty-three members of the House committee have no less than 108 military installations in their districts.[6] Of the 108 senators and representatives who hold reserve commissions in the military services—a practice of dubious constitutionality—seven are on the Senate Armed Services Committee, ten are on the House Armed Services Committee, five are on the House Defense Appropriations Subcommittee and nine are on the House Veterans' Affairs Committee.

Sometimes the attractions are more subtle. As a result of repeated contacts with federal administrators, private contractors and interest-group representatives, even the most conscientious and unbiased member finds it hard to escape the blandishments of clientele

5. Shirley Chisholm, *Unbought and Unbossed* (Boston, Mass.: Houghton Mifflin, 1970), pp. 98, 100.

6. According to Defense Department lists of April 1973, there were 482 military installations scattered in a total of 204 congressional districts. See, *Congressional Quarterly Weekly Report* 31 (9 June 1973), pp. 1433–1437.

interests. The process is aided if the subject matter is glamorous or politically fashionable—as is, for example, space flight, international diplomacy, civil aviation or military preparedness.

These committee biases, whether dictated by imbalanced membership or induced by gradual identification with the policy area, are a manifestation of the larger phenomenon of pluralist policy making, in which lawmaking is, in a sense, delegated to the interests most closely affected through preferential access to the government decision makers.[7] The ingrown relationships which result in various policy fields have been described as "subgovernments" by Douglass Cater, "policy whirlpools" by Ernest S. Griffith or "cozy little triangles" by Dorothy B. James. Congressional committees form a crucial element in these triads, which also embrace the relevant administrative agencies and appropriate clientele groups outside the government.[8]

In the long run such arrangements encourage abdication of legislative responsibilities. Biased policy makers tend to act as lobbyists for the interests supposedly under their purview. As one representative observed:

It has generally been regarded . . . that the members of the committees should almost be partisans for the legislation that goes through the committee and for the special interest groups that are affected by it.[9]

Legislation is all too often ill-advised or sloppily drafted because the committees assume that administrators or private interested parties will clear up the ambiguities or because the laws, themselves, aim at protecting the rule-making prerogatives of these decision makers.

Although committees are enjoined by the 1946 Legislative Reorganization Act to maintain "continuous watchfulness" over the programs within their purview, more often than not the legislative committees give little thought to the programs once the legislation has been enacted and the presidential pens passed around. Considering the membership and disposition of many committees, asking them to maintain watchfulness is like expecting the fox to guard the henhouse. If the House Agriculture Committee were to engage in thoroughgoing review of the Department of Agriculture, Chairman W. R. Poage said,

About all we would accomplish, as I see it, is to create hard feeling, a loss of confidence on the part of our farmers that the Department of Agriculture could render them a service, because we can be so critical of the Department . . . that there won't be any farmer in the nation that will have any confidence.[10]

No doubt these sentiments are widely shared in the committee rooms; therefore, it is hardly surprising that legislative review is one of Congress' most glaring deficiencies.

STRATEGIES FOR MAKING COMMITTEES MORE REPRESENTATIVE

Whether they intend it or not, House and Senate reformers will

---

7. This approximates the concept of "interest group liberalism," as described by Theodore J. Lowi in *The End of Liberalism* (New York: W. W. Norton, 1969), pp. 71–72.

8. See, J. Leiper Freeman, *The Political Process*, rev. ed. (Garden City, N. Y.: Doubleday, 1965).

9. *Committee Organization*, vol. I, part 1, p. 38.

10. Ibid., p. 66.

find it hard to avoid the consequences of committee representation. A number of strategies have been suggested for making committees more representative or, failing that, more responsive to the broader political complexion of the parent houses.

Balanced committees

One approach would be to encourage the membership of each committee to mirror, insofar as possible, the membership of the parent house. This principle, at least in the abstract, has long been recognized. As Richard Bolling has written:

The committees, creatures of the House, should be more representative of the membership of the whole House. This is particularly true today when a committee's proposed legislation is often passed or rejected on the floor with little substantive modification.[11]

Actually, some standards of balance are already applied to committee memberships. Partisan ratios are maintained on all committees; geographic balance is a consideration for appointments to Ways and Means and certain other committees. This principle would simply be extended to embrace other variables—for instance, ideology or type of district represented. Whether these rather simplistic variables would yield truly representative committees is open to question, for, as has been noted, more than demographic factors are at work. Moreover, rigid adherence to a quota system would certainly be resisted by the caucuses.

No such scheme would be feasible if it did not accord with individual

legislators' political needs and career aspirations. Past attempts by the parties' assignment committees to promote better balanced committees have often been foiled by the overriding pressures to cater to applicants' preferences. It is futile to conscript urban legislators for the Agriculture Committee as long as they consider the assignment unrewarding or irrelevant. Morale would suffer and with it committee performance. Representativeness might be achieved, but at the cost of member and committee effectiveness.

To avoid this objection, committee jurisdictions might be rearranged so that a diverse group of legislators would naturally find the committee's work attractive. This would imply a relatively small number of committees with broad jurisdictions, in order to combine topics of interest to competing or disparate groups. Committee workloads would be equalized, insofar as possible, so that legislators would find any of the committees meaningful and challenging. Although it is impossible to balance precisely the interests reflected in each committee's jurisdiction, the basic objective of the plan would be to internalize within each committee the checks and balances of divergent interests—for example, business and labor; farmers and consumers; urban and rural development. Such a plan would offer the prospect of lively confrontation and dissent during the committee deliberations.

A serious drawback of this plan is that such committees might be unwieldy. To achieve the desired broad jurisdictions, the number of committees would probably have to be reduced. Larger committees would only intensify the current tendency to push the real legislative work down into the subcommittees.

11. Richard Bolling, *House Out of Order* (New York: E. P. Dutton, 1965), p. 108.

The largest of the current committees, the fifty-five-member House Appropriations Committee, already operates almost wholly in its subcommittees, with little coordination among them. Other broad jurisdiction committees would undoubtedly follow this pattern. Unless steps were taken to control subcommittee composition and to mandate committee-wide review, no gains would have been registered over the present system.

Advocacy committees

An alternative tactic would be to create a large number of narrow jurisdiction committees with the frank intention that they become advocates of the interest and programs within their purview.[12] This would maximize the chances for any interest to grasp control of a committee and get its viewpoint articulated and would encourage policy entrepreneurship on the part of individual legislators or groups of like-minded members. Do-your-own-thing would be the rule of the day, with a premium placed on airing diverse interests and generating flexible new solutions to problems.

Such committees would obviously attract groups of legislators who were intensely interested in segments of public policy. With such a large number of committees, however, multiple assignments and the attendant scheduling problems

12. Interestingly, Theodore J. Lowi has proposed a similar plan, in order to "provide incentives for creative leadership in Congress." It would have such an effect, but it would also increase the likelihood of capture of individual committees by relevant interests, thus, intensifying the phenomenon of interest group liberalism. See, Lowi's "How to Make Congress Work," New York Times Magazine, 27 May 1971, p. 39.

would be likely. Policy innovations would percolate from the committees, with few hindrances from unsympathetic chairmen or opposing committee members. However, with all these advocacy-type committees generating policies responsive to their own clienteles, where would be the mechanism to balance opposing interests and to coordinate policies? Could we rely upon the process of floor deliberation to moderate committee initiatives and to coordinate them with the initiatives of other committees? The answer is probably in the negative, and if we could not rely on the parent houses to coordinate these committees' activities, the excesses of interest-biased policy making would only be magnified.

Membership rotation

A third device to control the membership biases of the committees would be to limit legislators' service on a given committee to a certain number of years. Enforced rotation of membership, it is argued, would ensure a steady inflow of young tigers on each committee and would minimize cozy relationships which flourish in the wake of long committee tenure. It would also broaden the horizons and skills of legislators—just as management trainees in private industry gain perspective by transferring among the firm's several departments. Such an approach would also moderate the firm hand of seniority by limiting eligibility for chairmanships on a given committee.

Rotation of membership raises the issue of the value of prolonged committee service in conferring expertise. Students of legislatures agree that expertise is a valuable resource for the legislature and that

Congress has profited by cultivating a cadre of highly skilled and knowledgeable committee leaders whose tenure often exceeds that of the executive branch officials with whom they deal. This expertise has helped Congress minimize the natural disadvantages which busy legislators encounter in dealing with bureaucratic specialists.

However, how much expertise is enough? Or, rather, how long does a legislator have to serve on a committee to learn the ropes? There is no doubt that a committee leader of twenty-five-years tenure should have learned a lot, but a dedicated legislator could learn as much in half, or a quarter, of the time. As Representative John Culver of Iowa recently noted: "It seems to me you don't have to be twenty years in a particular environment to learn anything."[13] Often, the long term veteran has lost the critical capacity or the creative edge which would allow him to bring an extra dimension of leadership to his post. In pointing out the obvious advantages of legislative expertise, observers of Congress have overstated the amount of seniority necessary to gain these advantages.

Control by the parent house

If committees are biased or unresponsive, so the traditional view holds, the remedy lies in supervision by the parent house. As former Minority Leader Gerald Ford recently put it:

As long as the House can work its will, I think that is the crux of the matter. Any overemphasis of one committee toward a particular subject or a particular problem, I think, can be overcome.[14]

In an ultimate sense, of course, this is true. Members of the full body can modify committee bills, can pressure the committee to take certain actions and can ultimately resort to such sanctions as discharge petitions. Over time a committee's behavior may lead it into disrepute, and the leadership will seek to alter its coloration through the appointment of new members.

At least in the short run, however, the full house is an imperfect counterweight to committee biases. Floor amendments can bring committee bills into line, but it is often futile to challenge committee members' expertise. Indeed, disparities of information are sometimes such that legislators not on a particular committee may be quite unaware of the biases hidden in committee bills. It is even harder to cope with the nondecisions of the committees. When a committee chooses not to pursue a given line of inquiry, there is little the parent house can do. Committee specialization is a cherished norm on the Hill, and an extreme sanction, such as the discharge petition, is invoked only rarely. "The role of the House," wrote George B. Galloway in 1962, "is now largely limited to ratifying decisions made by its committees."[15] This judgment was perhaps a bit overdrawn—and would not apply so strongly to the Senate— but it indicates the trend.

Nonetheless, procedural changes can affect outcomes by making it easier for noncommittee legislators to challenge a committee's monopoly. Broad gauged legislation could be referred to two or more committees to encourage a clash of

13. *Committee Organization*, vol. I, part 1, p. 43.

14. Ibid., p. 38.

15. U.S., House of Representatives, Committee on Administration, *History of the United States House of Representatives*, prepared by George B. Galloway, 87th Cong., 1st sess., 1962, H. Doc. 246, p. 87.

viewpoints. This practice is common in the Senate, but not in the House—a matter of precedent rather than rule. Procedures which publicize the committees' work—for example, requirements for open mark-up sessions, publicized committee votes and computerized information on the status of bills—help to reduce the committees' control over information and encourage other legislators to make a contribution. In the House the rules under which major bills are considered on the floor can weight the advantages either for or against the committee offering the bills. In the latter category would be: open rules; rules permitting certain points of order; and rules granting privileged status to motions from other committees with an interest in the legislation.

Even voting procedures have an impact. Prior to 1971 most House votes on key amendments to bills were taken in Committee of the Whole and were unrecorded. Members of the sponsoring committee tended to dominate debate and to prevail in these votes, largely because it was difficult to induce large numbers of legislators to the House floor. With the rise in recorded votes—because of the recorded teller vote provision of the 1970 Legislative Reorganization Act and, since 1973, the electronic voting system—more members are attracted to the floor for votes; the committees' control over vote outcomes has been diluted.

Control by external forces

According to Constitutional theory, Congress is uniquely exposed to the pulling and hauling in the political system at large. Unfortunately, external political checks on committees are not reliable. Con-

sider several potential checks upon committee activities: (1) the electoral process; (2) political parties; (3) interest groups; and (4) the communications media.

Voters wield the ultimate sanction upon an unresponsive or out-of-touch legislator, but this is a blunt instrument, indeed. As noted earlier, legislators are not evaluated primarily for their committee work, but for their district service—which, admittedly, may be facilitated by service on an appropriate committee. If, as Aaron Wildavsky has suggested, there are actually "two presidencies"—a constricted one for domestic problems and an expansive one for foreign affairs—there are in effect two dimensions to the elected legislator's job: one district oriented and one policy oriented. Because legislators are judged by voters primarily on the first dimension, the capture of committees by special interests is not likely to be remedied at the polls. For, if the legislator joins a committee for constituency reasons, he is in all probability a partner in the special interests controlling the committee; if his committee work is unrelated to his district, the voters are unlikely to restrict him, no matter what his behavior in committee.

Many commentators have advocated stronger political parties as an antidote to rampant pluralism. "The parties do very little to discipline or defend their members," E. E. Schattschneider observed, which permits groups to "trade on the fears and the confusion of individual members of Congress."[16] In recent years several steps have been taken towards the goal of more responsible parties. Caucuses have

16. E. E. Schattschneider, "Pressure Groups Versus Political Parties," THE ANNALS 259 (September 1948), pp. 18–19.

been strengthened, party steering groups have been created or revitalized and control over certain committee activities has been exerted. No doubt, these steps have fortified the parties' authority over committee activities. However, the parties' ability to assert themselves is limited by their own cohesion. It is hard to believe that party mechanisms on Capitol Hill can be strong if the parties, themselves, are incoherent at the grassroots level.

Interest groups best provide a check when they are in conflict and fairly evenly matched. The recent history of environmental legislation is a good example of conflicting interests which approximated equilibrium. Environmental sentiment swept the nation; public attitudes were strongly supportive of measures which would check the long-standing dominance of producer interests. This equilibrium may well be short lived and, in any event, is probably a rarity. More typical is the cozy relationship which develops when a few interest groups dominate a policy area and reach agreements among themselves as to how to divide up the pie, while tangentially interested parties look the other way. The pluralist system, then, produces competition of interests less frequently than monopolistic, or at least oligopolistic, control of policies.

By casting light on decisions and helping countervailing interests to mobilize and participate, the press is potentially a check upon biased decision making. Inevitably, however, the committee rooms of Congress are virtually ignored by the general circulation press. "Dark dungeons of silence" is the term used by the Nader organization to describe the committees. This leaves committee deliberations to be reported by the specialized trade press or by information services hired by the interested parties. Needless to say, such specialized media tend to be biased in favor of their clienteles and, in any event, do not normally reach the potentially countervailing interests. Although in theory the activities of committees should be subject to the pressures generated by the political system as a whole, in fact, there are few dependable external checks on the activities of the committees and their associated interests.

CONCLUSIONS

At a time when legislatures and other institutions must divide up their workload to survive, it is understandable that congressional committees reflect those interests which are most directly affected by certain policies and programs. To dictate otherwise would be to disturb the natural affinity of individual legislators for committees which will aid their careers and to dampen the natural desire of interested parties to exercise control over policies which affect them. To attain a truly representative division of labor in Congress may be as difficult as defying the law of gravity.

This conclusion may seem overly pessimistic. However, as with the larger phenomenon of pluralistic policy making—of which committee bias is merely a manifestation—it is easier to recite the evils of the system than to propose remedies. For, pluralistic decision making and its accompanying biases are direct products both of the complicated society in which we live and of the specialized modes of decision making we have adopted to deal with complexity.

Still, there are some grounds for

believing that committee deliberations can be made more representative. The increasing nationalization of political issues will help to ease the problem. The decline of regionalism in American politics means a decrease in the uniqueness of particular constituencies. Already, the distinctions between urban and rural constituencies have become somewhat blurred as more and more territory is taken up by multiuse, megalopolistic areas. In the Senate, with its statewide constituencies, this trend is already well advanced; House districts, which are less heterogeneous, have been slower to change. Yet, heterogeneity should decrease the constituency-based motivations for legislators to prefer one committee assignment over another. Although this will not eliminate the problem of similar birds flocking together, it may moderate its effects.

These demographic changes are accompanied by increasing interdependencies of social and economic life. No longer is it possible for citizens to ignore entirely the effects of events which may seem thousands of miles away. We have reached a point at which concrete political realities are forcing the urban legislator to be knowledgeable about agricultural policies; New Englanders to be as concerned about energy policy as legislators from oil-producing areas were a generation ago; and all of them to feel acutely the effects of international monetary and trade developments which would not have interested their predecessors. Brooklyn legislators of the future should strive to serve on an agriculture committee—or, for that matter, a committee dealing with foreign policy or monetary affairs—because their constituents are likely to be as affected by such issues as by so-called urban legislation. Increased efficiency of communications will heighten our awareness of these interdependencies.

Significant changes in committee composition have taken place in recent years, although such changes lag far behind the evolution of new public issues. Since 1971, for example, Speaker Carl Albert—responding to pressures within his party—appointed a limited number of liberals to conservative-dominated committees. Appropriations, Armed Services and Internal Security now have small, but vocal, liberal factions which have succeeded in raising, if not always winning, issues which had previously been given short shrift. An urban minority has built up considerable seniority on the Interior Committee; an activist minority on Foreign Affairs, including four subcommittee chairmen, is campaigning for a more vigorous congressional role in foreign policy making.[17] Oftentimes, the appointment of nonconforming members meets with stout opposition from committee chairmen, and the slow workings of the seniority system mean that committee shifts may trail political and social changes by a decade or more.

In the shorter run, therefore, reformers would do well to consider structural or procedural changes which would encourage a clash of interests and viewpoints within and between the committees. Such innovations take a variety of forms, and none are free of problems of implementation. A promising package would include: recasting juris

17. John Maffre, "New Leaders, Staff Changes Stimulate House Foreign Affairs Committee," *National Journal* 3 (19 June 1971), pp. 1314–1322.

dictions to embrace conflicting interests; encouraging of lateral mobility among committees, perhaps through membership rotation; and more sparing use of rules which discourage floor challenges to committee measures. Such steps might help dissolve some of the excess rigidities of the committee system, not to mention its encrustation by special interests.

The common goal of such innovations would be to reduce as much as possible the costs of decision-making involvement by tangentially or distantly related interests. Only then will legislative decision making be able to counteract particularistic pressures, so that the interests of the rest of us—what E. E. Schattschneider called "the remote, general, and public considerations" —can have an adequate voice in public policy.

Committees and the Norm of Specialization

By HERBERT B. ASHER

ABSTRACT: The need for congressmen to specialize and acquire expertise in a limited number of policy areas is so universally conceded as to be labelled a norm of legislative behavior. Specialization is intimately tied to the ability of Congress to make informed voting decisions on a wide range of issues; congressmen often rely upon expert colleagues for information and advice on bills beyond their own expertise. More importantly, specialization, especially as facilitated by the committee system, is an adaptive response to the resource advantages possessed by the executive branch; specialization facilitates congressional performance of the oversight function. In order to determine why and in what areas a congressman will specialize, attention must be given to the member's goals, personal and professional background and electoral situation. Levels of specialization differ across the House and Senate, between national and state legislatures, across committees, and over time. Specialization, particularly as manifested through the committee and subcommittee systems, has both intended and unintended consequences. Foremost among the latter is the differential access to government specialization provides various groups. Finally, the extent of specialization will be affected by changes in the committee system.

Herbert B. Asher is Assistant Professor of Political Science at Ohio State University. He received his B.S. from Bucknell University (1966) and his Ph.D. from the University of Michigan (1970). He is the author of a number of articles on the socialization of freshman congressmen and on methodological problems of survey research. His fields of interest include American legislative and electoral behavior and methodology.

THE need for congressmen to specialize in a limited number of policy areas and thereby, presumably, to develop expertise has been recognized by observers of, and participants in, the legislative process. In a study of the United States Senate, Matthews wrote that a senator was expected: "to specialize, to focus his energy and attention on the relatively few matters that come before his committees or that directly and immediately affect his state."[1] Clapp's work on the House of Representatives also affirmed the necessity of specialization; he wrote:

The structure of the House and the expectations and duties of members dictate reliance on the specialist; congressmen accomplish their business largely by relying on the judgment of others.[2]

The importance of specialization is so universally conceded that it is commonly referred to as a norm of legislative behavior—that is, a standard of conduct governing the behavior of the representative within the legislative arena. As a norm, specialization describes a type of behavior deemed appropriate by most other legislators; failure to comply with the norm may lead to the invoking of sanctions against the deviant member. That specialization is still a viable norm is evidenced by the work of Asher, who found that sizable majorities of nonfreshman and freshman representatives agreed to its necessity.[3]

Given the existence of a norm of specialization, the question becomes: why? The basic answer is that the volume and complexity of congressional business is too much for any single legislator to master. Rather, members must carve up the domain of legislative activity into manageable units, thereby placing a heavy reliance on fellow legislators for information and advice in areas in which the member has not acquired expertise. Indeed, the norm of specialization is intimately tied to the ability of congressmen to make informed decisions at the voting stage of the legislative process. Observers have often argued that congressmen cannot possibly be fully informed on all the bills on which they must vote. Hence, the reliance on fellow legislators for information and advice has been posited as an economizing device whereby the legislator can make reasonably informed decisions without tremendous investments of his scarce resources.[4] This reliance often depends upon specialization—that is, members often turn to colleagues who are recognized as experts in various policy fields.

Hence, at the very least, specialization is functional for the legislative system in that it serves as a partial underpinning for an efficient mode of congressional decision making. However, this says little about the

1. Donald R. Matthews, *U. S. Senators and Their World* (New York: Vintage Books, 1960), p. 95.

2. Charles L. Clapp, *The Congressman: His Work As He Sees It* (Garden City, N.Y.: Anchor Books, 1963), p. 27.

3. Herbert B. Asher, "The Learning of Legislative Norms," *American Political Science Review* 67 (June 1973), pp. 499–513.

4. Donald R. Matthews and James A. Stimson, "Decision Making by U.S. Representatives: A Preliminary Model" (Paper prepared for Conference on Political Decision Making sponsored by the Sperry-Hutchinson Foundation and the Department of Political Science of the University of Kentucky, Lexington, Ky., 10–11 April 1968); and Donald R. Matthews and James A. Stimson, "The Decision Making Approach to the Study of Legislative Behavior: The Example of the U.S. House of Representatives" (Paper prepared for the Sixty-Fifth Annual Meeting of the American Political Science Association, New York, N.Y., 2–6 September 1969).

quality or content of the decisions made. One can argue whether decisions made by specialists are necessarily wise decisions in the public interest, however it is defined. It is possible that specialization—however necessary it may be—may have some undesirable, unintended consequences. Before turning to a discussion of these consequences, some conditions conducive to the development and maintenance of specialization must be considered.

THE REASONS FOR SPECIALIZATION

Specialization in coping with the external environment

External constraints, such as the heavy demands placed upon the Congress, are certainly conducive to the development of a division of labor organized around substantive policy areas. The expansion of the federal government in the 1960s into such areas as health care, space exploration and education makes it even more difficult for the legislator to be a policy generalist. Also promoting specialization is the need for Congress to respond and adapt to an executive branch whose resources far exceed its own. It is not uncommon for high ranking administration officials to bring to a congressional committee hearing an army of aides which exceeds in size the committee's membership and staff. The comparison is often made between the meager personnel and informational resources available to the Congress and the abundant resources available to the executive.

Hence, the Congress must cope with a powerful executive branch, and the most frequently cited coping mechanism is clearly the congressional committee and subcommittee

system. As Morrow has observed, a basic purpose of the committee system was to create a division of labor which would facilitate "some means of expertise in policy review and legislative oversight."[5] It is not entirely clear that the structure of the contemporary committee system is simply a response to executive branch advantages. While Morrow has asserted that the Legislative Reorganization Act of 1946 "provided for major committee consolidation to accomodate organizational changes accomplished within the executive branch,"[6] Neustadt, on the contrary, argued that the shape of the bureaucracy was a reflection of the jurisdiction of the committees and subcommittees—although he recognized that the relationship between the legislative and executive structures might be reciprocal.[7] However the relationship goes, it is clear that specialization is an adaptive response to some external constraints impinging upon the Congress.

Lest the above discussion leave the impression that committee-related specialization is solely a response to the presence of the powerful executive branch of today, the reader should keep in mind the words of Hasbrouck, who wrote at a time when legislative-executive relations were far different:

Touching any proposal of new legislation in so diverse a country as the United States, there are a multitude of technical problems. A committee facilitates the use of experts. It forms a means of com-

5. William L. Morrow, *Congressional Committees* (New York: Charles Scribner's Sons, 1969), p. 13.
6. Ibid., p. 9.
7. Richard E. Neustadt, "Politicians and Bureaucrats," in *The Congress and America's Future*, ed. David B. Truman, 2nd ed. (Englewood Cliffs, N.J.: Prentice-Hall, 1973), p. 120.

municating with the executive departments, and may call technical officials or members of the cabinet before it. Drafting experts of the Legislative Counsel are available to perfect the form of the bill, to delve into the constitutional problems which it involves, and to provide material for the report. The committee system had the advantages of high specialization.[8]

This suggests that the very existence of a committee system has an independent impact on the development of specialization, regardless of the state of legislative-executive relations. Of course, the degree to which the committee system is institutionalized is affected by the shape of the external environment.

Specialization and the individual legislator

The discussion can now move from the macro level—the functions which specialization serves for the congressional system at large—to the micro level. Here the question is: given that specialization is a desirable goal, how does one guarantee that the individual legislator will specialize? Why should a representative expend scarce resources to acquire expertise in a relatively narrow area? One possible answer is that failure to comply with the norm of specialization would lead to sanctions, perhaps in the form of less desirable committee assignments or lowered effectiveness in getting pet legislation passed. Yet, internal legislative sanctions are not readily invoked; furthermore, even if imposed, they may be largely ineffective in influencing the behavior of certain legislators. For example, the senator or representative with aspi-

rations toward another office may feel safe in ignoring his colleagues; the entrenched member from a safe district may feel secure from any possible legislative sanctions. One must look beyond the threat of sanctions to the positive advantages and rewards available to the member who specializes.

Certainly, a plausible general proposition is that members will specialize if such an activity promotes the achievement of goals important to them. Such goals may range from: avoiding sanctions to achieving genuine influence in the legislature; winning reelection to moving on to another office, or promoting benefits for the district to solving major national problems by the formulation of sound policies. Obviously, these goals can be highly interdependent: career advancement may be furthered by policy initiatives; policy initiatives may be furthered by the acquisition of influence in the legislature. It is clear that representatives with serious legislative objectives and concerns for accruing seniority will be more likely *ceteris paribus* to specialize than members with progressive ambitions and without major policy goals.[9]

While a member's goals will help explain whether or not he will specialize, other factors must be considered as well in accounting for the areas in which he chooses to specialize. Matthews cites three such factors: (1) personal and professional background; (2) perceptions of the concerns of present and future constituents; and (3) committee assignment.[10] One's background, district

8. Paul D. Hasbrouck, *Party Government in the House of Representatives* (New York: Macmillan, 1927), pp. 69–70.

9. Joseph A. Schlesinger, *Ambition and Politics* (Chicago, Ill.: Rand McNally, 1966).

10. Matthews, *U.S. Senators and Their World*, p. 250.

and even one's committee assignment(s) may determine the fields in which a member specializes. This is clearly illustrated in the comments of former Mississippi Congressman Frank Smith:

When I came to the House of Representatives, I wanted to be a responsible member, with both a voice and a vote in historic decisions made by Congress. If my constituents were to give me this freedom, I felt that I had to render them special service in areas of major concern to the district. This called for specialization in flood control and water resource development. . . .The interest of my district dictated my field of specialization in the House, but the decision to specialize in some legislative field is automatic for the member who wants to exercise any influence.[11]

With respect to committee assignments, Fenno discusses the ways in which congressmen are assigned to various committees.[12] Quite clearly, legislators who received their desired assignments and members who were coopted onto more prestigious committees are more likely to perform the activities required by specialization than members who were placed on a committee they did not seek. In short, specialization need not automatically follow simply because the legislator is assigned to a committee; individual goals and situations must also be taken into account.

Modifications in the criteria used to assign members to committees may facilitate specialization. For example, Masters states that, compared with criteria such as reelection prospects, seniority and geography, a representative's professional background is seldom the major determinant of his committee assignment.[13] A better matching of the member's background with his committee and subcommittee assignments would undoubtedly make specialization more attractive to him. Similarly, a greater attention to the needs and problems of the legislator's constituency in assigning him to a committee would most likely provide stronger incentives for the member to become expert in the work of the committee. However, a greater reliance on background and constituency criteria may have negative consequences for the policy decisions adopted—a theme to be developed in a later section of this paper.

VARIATIONS IN LEVELS OF SPECIALIZATION

House-Senate differences

The assertion that membership on committees and subcommittees is likely to lead to policy specialization and expertise is acceptable enough, although one should recognize that there are variations across committees and over time, as well as differences between the House and the Senate. With respect to the latter, Fenno has written:

Senators do not specialize as intensively or as exclusively in their committee work as House members do. Since decision-making is less committee-centered, there is less reward in committee-based specialization. Since committees are more permeable, it is easier for the committee nonmember to involve himself in

11. Frank E. Smith, *Congressman from Mississippi* (New York: Capricorn Books, 1964), pp. 129–130.

12. Richard F. Fenno, Jr., *Congressmen in Committees* (Boston, Mass.: Little, Brown, 1973), pp. 19–20.

13. Nicholas A. Masters, "House Committee Assignments," in *The Congressional System: Notes and Readings,* ed. Leroy N. Rieselbach (Belmont, Cal.: Wadsworth, 1970), p. 65.

TABLE 1

MEAN NUMBER OF COMMITTEE AND SUBCOMMITTEE ASSIGNMENTS IN THE 93RD CONGRESS*

HOUSE		SENATE	
Committee	Subcommittee	Committee	Subcommittee
1.6	3.5	2.6	9.7

* The figures include all subcommittees—standing, special and ad hoc—of only the standing committees. Committee chairman and ranking minority members are included in the subcommittee tallies only when they have specific assignments; automatic ex officio memberships on subcommittees are not counted.

TABLE 2

SUBCOMMITTEE CHAIRMANSHIPS IN THE 93RD CONGRESS

NUMBER OF SUBCOMMITTEES CHAIRED	NUMBER OF DEMOCRATIC SENATORS	PERCENT OF SENATE DEMOCRATS	NUMBER OF DEMOCRATIC REPRESENTATIVES	PERCENT OF HOUSE DEMOCRATS
0	2	3.5	124	52.1
1	16	28.1	107	44.9
2	24	42.1	7	3.0
3	8	14.0	0	0.0
4	6	10.5	0	0.0
5	1	1.8	0	0.0
Totals	57*	100.0	238†	100.0

* The total includes Harry Byrd of Virginia.
† The total excludes the Speaker and Majority Leader. In addition, there were three vacancies at the start of the 93rd Congress in seats which had been held by Democrats.

any committee's subject matter. And, since he serves on so many committees and subcommittees, the average Senator must, perforce, spread his efforts over a greater span of subjects than the average Representative.[14]

Support for Fenno's argument is given in table 1 which presents the mean number of committee and subcommittee assignments for House and Senate members at the outset of the 93rd Congress.

More striking evidence of House-Senate differences is provided by an examination of the number of subcommittee chairmanships held by Democratic members in both bodies at the outset of the 93rd Congress;

14. Fenno, Congressmen in Committees, p. 172.

the appropriate data are given in table 2. While almost all Democratic senators have at least one subcommittee chairmanship, fewer than half of the House Democrats are in the same position. When a Democratic senator chairs an average of two subcommittees in addition to his membership on others, then, quite clearly, the degree to which he can become a specialist in one particular area is limited.

National-state differences

A focus on state legislatures—while not our central concern here—would reveal major differences in the importance of specialization and would provide additional insights into the conditions which facilitate it. In their four-state study, Wahlke and his colleagues compiled a list of forty-two rules of the game perceived by state legislators.[15] Nowhere on the list was specialization explicitly mentioned, although one might view some of the items far down on the list, such as ability and intelligence—number 24—and commitment to job—number 31—as at least approximations of a norm of specialization. One fact of state legislative life which contributes to the lesser importance assigned to specialization is the high turnover of personnel characterizing many state legislatures— a situation which contrasts sharply with the career-oriented Congress. Obviously, if tenure in office is shorter, the likelihood of developing expertise is less.

Numerous reasons for higher turnover at the state level can be cited: (1) the electoral properties of the districts; (2) the personal goals of the state legislators;[16] and (3) the lower levels of legislative professionalism in many state bodies. Professionalism is commonly measured by legislators' salaries, the length of legislative sessions and the availability of staff resources.[17] More highly professionalized legislatures are presumed to be more attractive to the member and, therefore, characterized by lower turnover. As the report of the Citizen Conference on State Legislatures notes, in 1970 legislative salaries ranged from $200 per two year session in New Hampshire to $19,200 per year in California.[18] Finally, if one combines the turnover rate in a legislature with the degree to which the committee system has become institutionalized in that legislature, an even greater diversity in the development and significance of specialization at the state level can be envisaged. It seems likely that legislatures with high turnover and weak committee systems will experience difficulties in dividing up their workloads efficiently. This suggests that other actors will move in to fill the void created by low levels of specialization and expertise: gubernatorial initiatives and interest group inputs are likely to be particularly influential.

Committee differences

If the committee system tends to facilitate specialization, then the presence of subcommittees is likely to produce additional specialization. Even here there is great diversity among congressional committees. In the 93rd Congress Ways and Means, Rules and Internal Security in the House had no standing subcommittees, as did Aeronautical and Space Sciences in the Senate. The absence of subcommittees is reflected in low levels of specialization, at least on Ways and Means. Manley asserts that there is no norm of specialization on Ways and Means, that "in keeping with the organizational structure of the Committee, the division of labor on the Committee is not spelled out in any detail."[19] In a similar vein, Fenno

15. John C. Wahlke, et. al., *The Legislative System* (New York: John Wiley, 1962), pp. 146–147.

16. James D. Barber, *The Lawmakers* (New Haven, Conn.: Yale University Press, 1965).

17. John Grumm, "The Effects of Legislative Structure on Legislative Performance," in *State and Urban Politics*, ed. Richard Hofferbert and Ira Sharkansky (Boston, Mass.: Little, Brown, 1971), pp. 298–322.

18. John Burns, *The Sometime Governments: Report of the Citizen Conference on State Legislatures* (New York: Bantam Books, 1971), p. 137.

19. John F. Manley, *The Politics of Finance* (Boston, Mass.: Little, Brown, 1970), p. 94.

notes that "so long as there are no subcommittees, specialization will remain at a low level on Ways and Means."[20] This is not to argue that the existence of subcommittees is a necessary and sufficient condition for specialization; Fenno cites the case of Education and Labor as a committee with subcommittees, but with a low level of specialization.[21] It is probably accurate to conclude, as does Fenno,[22] that the existence of subcommittees is simply a necessary, but not sufficient, condition of specialization.

In contrast to those committees which operate without subcommittees are the Appropriations Committees of the House and the Senate, each of which had thirteen subcommittees in the first session of the 93rd Congress. Fenno asserted that the House committee approached its decision-making tasks by a heavy reliance on subcommittees and specialization. He wrote:

Each subcommittee was given jurisdiction over a group of budget estimates, and each group of estimates formed the basis of an appropriation bill. In large part, the subcommittee structure parallels the structure of the executive branch . . . The Committee at work is the Committee compartmentalized . . . for the ordinary committee member, compartmentalization does mean that 90 to 95 per cent of his committee time and energy will be expended in the work of his subcommittees.[23]

Temporal differences

Finally—in addition to differences between committees in the same branch of Congress and variations across the House and Senate—diversity appears also along a temporal dimension, with the most significant trend being a proliferation of the number of subcommittees since the Legislative Reorganization Act of 1946. Morrow states that in 1945 there were 97 standing subcommittees in the House and 34 in the Senate,[24] while the comparable figures for 1967 were 101 and 80, respectively. For the 93rd Congress the numbers are 119 and 120, clearly indicating a continuing growth in the number of subcommittees. This proliferation is probably understated by excluding from consideration special and ad hoc subcommittees of which there can be a substantial number.[25] Hence, the opportunity for specializing, as reflected in the number of subcommittees extant, appears to be increasing.

THE CONSEQUENCES OF SPECIALIZATION

Intended consequences

Some of the end results of specialization are quite clearly desirable and intended, but others may, in fact, be undesirable and unintended. A number of consequences in the former category have already been mentioned. For example, at the system level specialization enables the Congress to handle increasingly complex business and to cope, in part, with an executive-dominated environment. In addition, Eulau argues that specialization, as reflected in committee proliferation, produces committees and

20. Fenno, *Congressmen in Committees*, p. 105.

21. Ibid., p. 103.

22. Ibid., p. 105.

23. Richard F. Fenno, Jr., *The Power of the Purse* (Boston, Mass.: Little, Brown, 1966), pp. 130, 135.

24. Morrow, *Congressional Committees*, p. 39.

25. Donald G. Tacheron and Morris K. Udall, *The Job of the Congressman* (Indianapolis, Ind.: Bobbs-Merrill, 1966), p. 169.

subcommittees accessible to conflicting interests, which is functional
for the resolution of conflict.[26] At
the individual level the need for
specialization, particularly as manifested through the subcommittee
structure, provides opportunities for
"less senior legislators to gain prestige and to follow their interests and
exploit their abilities as they could
not in a seniority-governed committee system which tolerated no
subcommittees."[27] Along this line,
Ornstein states that one result of recent House Democratic reforms will
be to distribute subcommittee chairmanships among a wider number
of relatively junior Democratic representatives.[28]

Unintended consequences

Of course, there are drawbacks to
specialization for both the individual legislator and the congressional
system, particularly to the extent
to which specialization is tied to
the subcommittee structure. For example, the many subcommittee
assignments of a congressman
—mainly a senator—are certainly
counterproductive to the development of member expertise. At the
system level there is the danger of
overspecialization and overcom-
partmentalization of legislative activity. Morrow cites the case of Representative John Brademas who

warned about the "minimum of
facilities we have for integrating policy in a comprehensive fashion."[29]
Certainly, recent proposed reforms
dealing with the budgetary process
represent a response to the undesirable consequences of congressional
overspecialization and overcom-
partmentalization. For example, in
early 1973 a bipartisan joint committee recommended that a new committee on the budget be formed in
each house. As described by *Congressional Quarterly*, the "committee would set an annual ceiling on
spending, appropriations, and the
national debt, and recommend a
target for revenue to be raised."[30]
This proposed reform is obviously a
reaction to the fragmented, uncom-
prehensive fashion in which Congress handles the budget and undoubtedly reflects the fragmentation
of congressional responsibility for
the budget: revenue measures origi-
nating in certain committees, appropriations in others and authorizations in yet others.

A more subtle consequence of
specialization, particularly as linked
to the subcommittee system, concerns the access of public and private groups to legislative decision
makers. For example, Ripley talks
of subgovernments[31] which may
"dominate policy-making in individual subject matter areas," and describes these subgovernments as:

ordinarily composed of a few key
bureaucrats, a few key interest group
representatives, and a few key committee members (typically subcommittee
chairmen and ranking minority mem-

26. Heinz Eulau, "The Committees in a
Revitalized Congress," in *Congress: The First
Branch of Government*, ed. Alfred de Grazia
(Garden City, N.Y.: Anchor Books, 1967), p.
210.

27. George Goodwin, Jr., "Subcommittees:
The Miniature Legislatures of Congress," in
*The Congressional System: Notes and Read-
ings*, ed. Leroy N. Rieselbach (Belmont, Cal.:
Wadsworth, 1970), p. 93.

28. Norman J. Ornstein, "Change in the
House: Prospects for '73 and Beyond,"
mimeographed.

29. Morrow, *Congressional Committees*, p.
21.

30. "The Budget: A Legislative Strategy
Begins To Unfold," *Congressional Quarterly
Weekly Report* 31 (10 February 1973), p. 261.

31. Douglass Cater, *Power in Washington*
(New York: Random House, 1964).

bers). Critical decisions are made at the subcommittee level and routinely ratified in full committee and on the floor. Thus the few individuals in the subgovernment essentially make policy, particularly on matters that are seemingly routine.[32]

In a similar fashion McConnell discusses the phenomenon of clientelism or what he more critically labels the capture of segments of public power by private interests;[33] Fenno discusses the "interest-sympathy-leniency syndrome," which refers to the situation in which appropriations subcommittees charged with jurisdiction over agency budgets, in fact, become advocates for the agencies and the particular clientele which the agencies serve.[34] What Ripley, McConnell and Fenno are all asserting is that small, specialized governmental structures, such as subcommittees, may be coopted by the very groups they were supposed to oversee or, at the very least, may provide differential access to government for certain groups, often at the expense of others.

While McConnell cites numerous instances in which the policies adopted by coopted decision-makers benefit private groups, it is not the case that the public interest must necessarily be adversely affected by the marriage of public power and private groups. However, what is clear about subgovernmental decision making is that the subgovern-

ments "cannot be expected to consult more than a narrow range of interests in making their decisions."[35] Hence, the serious possibility exists that groups with legitimate interests will be excluded from the decision-making process and thereby suffer from, or fail to profit by, the policies adopted.

This exclusion of a diversity of inputs and viewpoints might well be exacerbated by giving greater attention to the criteria of professional background and constituency needs in the assigning of congressmen to committees and subcommittees. Greater reliance on these criteria, as suggested by some, might facilitate specialization and expertise; however, it would also guarantee that certain groups would receive sympathetic hearings at the expense of others and that certain basic questions would remain unasked and underlying assumptions, unchallenged. For example, when many members of the House Agriculture Committee are themselves in agriculture and serve on subcommittees which deal with commodities of interest to their local constituents, it is not likely that concern about the national impact of farm programs will outweigh the need to protect local, agricultural interests. Since the preponderance of the membership of the House Interior and Insular Affairs Committee comes from the western United States, it is not surprising that "the Committee remains an arena in which commercial user groups (as opposed to conservationist groups) are likely to obtain their most favorable governmental treatment."[36]

32. Randall B. Ripley, "Party Leaders and Standing Committees in the House of Representatives," *Working Papers on House Committee Organization and Operation* (Washington, D.C.: Government Printing Office, 1973), p. 9.

33. Grant McConnell, *Private Power and American Democracy* (New York: Alfred A. Knopf, 1966).

34. Fenno, *Power of the Purse*, p. 141.

35. Ripley, "Party Leaders," p. 9.

36. Fenno, *Congressmen in Committees*, p. 64.

SPECIALIZATION AND COMMITTEE REFORM

The structure of the congressional committee system is currently undergoing close scrutiny, particularly by the Bolling Select Committee on Committees. Numerous reforms have been proposed—some likely to be adopted and others less so. The key point is that change in the committee structure has consequences for the levels of congressional specialization. For example, one proposed reform is to reduce the number of committees, the size of the reduction differing across proposals. Such a reform would be accompanied by an increase in the number of subcommittees, and this would have differential consequences for the House and Senate. As tables 1 and 2 indicate, the number of subcommittee assignments and chairmanships per House member is not that great; it would be feasible to distribute additional subcommittee assignments and chairmanships to a relatively unburdened House membership. This would probably be functional for specialization since it would give a greater number of members a vested interest in the influence of their subcommittees, thereby probably increasing oversight—particularly if subcommittee chairmen acquired additional prerogatives in areas such as subcommittee staffing and investigations. In the Senate, however, an increase in the number of subcommittees may be dysfunctional for specialization since senators are already overburdened by subcommittee assignments. In fact, one may argue that no matter how the committee system is restructured, the Senate, because of its smaller size, is confronted with a work overload. This might lead to an increasing Senate reliance on committee and personal staff, as well as a willingness to expand the informational resources available to senators.

Another proposed reform involves the rotation of committee chairmanships and even of committee assignments—that is, a limit would be placed on the number of years a member could chair or serve on a committee. If becoming a specialist requires years of committee experience, then such a reform could be dysfunctional for specialization —especially if, in conjunction with electoral defeats, it led to a sudden, high turnover on a committee. Of course, modifications in the proposal could prevent such a situation. On the other hand, an enforced, but limited, circulation of congressmen across committees could lead to the Congress taking a more comprehensive view of issues while preserving the advantages of specialization. Again, one should recognize that changing the committee structure will affect the extent of specialization.

CONCLUSION

As is often the case in discussing Congress, one cannot offer a straightforward, unqualified conclusion. While specialization, particularly as related to the committee system, is obviously a necessity if Congress is to perform its lawmaking and oversight functions, the end results of specialization are not uniformly positive. The fragmentation of decision making, the differential access encouraged by the committee and subcommittee system and the norm of specialization may prevent the Congress from taking a comprehensive view of major issues.

Yet, no one is suggesting that Congress could perform without the division of labor encouraged by the committee system and maintained by the norm of specialization. One might argue that, within the general requirement for a division of labor, one can make incremental adjustments which will lessen the chance of undesirable consequences. For example, the assignment of members of subcommittees where no clientele interest exists is a strategy used by the House Appropriations Committee to develop expertise and to avoid the pitfalls of the "interest-sympathy-leniency" syndrome discussed by Fenno. Recent proposals, such as additional congressional staff and the creation of congressional assessment and evaluation agencies, may enable Congress to engage in specialization more effectively, while minimizing its potential disadvantages. But, certainly, the need for committee-related specialization will remain unchallenged for the foreseeable future.

House-Senate Relationships: Comity and Conflict

By Walter J. Oleszek

ABSTRACT: Although equal in power, the national House and Senate differ in more ways than they are similar. They differ in size, rules and procedures, policy biases, customs and traditions, terms of office, constitutional responsibilities, constituencies and in numerous other ways. Moreover, each chamber is jealous of its powers and prerogatives and generally suspicious of the other body. Despite their differences, the two houses must still work together if policy recommendations are to be enacted into law. Two principal legislative devices serve to join senators and representatives together on matters of common concern: conference committees and joint committees. In this analysis, two important aspects of conference procedure are explored: the conferee selection process and the question of who wins in conference, the House or the Senate. Joint committees, although used since the First Congress, are viewed negatively by many members. Given both the variety and uses of joint committees, it is worth identifying some of the factors which facilitate their creation. Finally, two principal suggestions are offered to better facilitate interhouse cooperation—more contact between respective party leaders of each house and the development of parallel committee jurisdictions. Of course, the goal of interhouse cooperation needs to be balanced against the requirement that each house present and defend different and conflicting points of view on the issues of the day.

Walter J. Oleszek is Professional Staff Member of the House Select Committee on Committees, on leave from the Congressional Research Service. He is also Lecturer at the University of Maryland, Associate Director of the Washington Semester Program of the State University of New York and author of several articles on the national legislative process.

TO SPEAK of the Congress implies a unity between the House and Senate which is often lacking, given their different sizes, terms of office, constitutional responsibilities, constituencies and rules and procedures. Moreover, each legislative body has developed different customs and traditions, and this affects their relationships with one another. For example, even though the Constitution grants the House authority for initiating all revenue-raising measures, by custom, the House also initiates appropriation measures. Over the years the Senate has sometimes challenged the House's prerogatives in this area, only to have the House vigorously defend what it considers a fundamental right.

Each chamber, too, is thought to play different roles. For example, scholars have claimed that the contemporary Senate is the forum in which innovative ideas and policies are often first introduced and communicated to the nation.[1] This, combined with the generally greater media coverage accorded its members, helps to explain why, in recent years, the Senate has become a rich source of aspirants to the presidency. The House, on the other hand, is expected to be more thorough in its committee and floor work—that is, representatives are expected to be better informed specialists than senators who are usually less expert in the technical details of many bills. As one representative has written: "if the Senate has been the nation's great forum, the House has been its workshop."[2]

Finally, the House and Senate reflect different political and policy biases. Recent evidence has shown that the contemporary Senate is more liberal than the House on various issues.[3] Thus, the House, for example, will often view suspiciously legislation enacted by the other body. Fresh evidence of the jealousy, suspicion and rivalry which exist between the chambers occurred on May 23, 1973, when the House failed to override President Richard Nixon's veto of a measure—S. 518—which would require Senate confirmation of the director and deputy director of the Office of Management and Budget. One of the arguments offered to sustain the president's veto was that presented by a representative who argued that the bill "would have a negative and destructive effect on the leadership of the House in fiscal affairs. As you know, our leadership in this field is already being eroded by back-door appropriations procedures that have been invoked in the other body." Another member added that if the bill were enacted the budget director would become the "Senate's man," something the House would not want.[4]

Despite all their differences, the two houses still have to work together if measures are to be enacted into law. The question, then, which serves as the central focus of this paper is: how do the two houses reconcile their differences? In exploring this question two devices will be examined—conference committees and joint committees. Both devices represent the principal formal means for joining together members from

1. See, for example, Nelson Polsby, "Strengthening Congress in National Policymaking," *Yale Review* 59 (Summer 1970), pp. 481–497.
2. Quoted in Charles Clapp, *The Congressman* (Garden City, N.Y.: Doubleday, 1963), p. 39.

3. Sam Kernell, "Is the Senate More Liberal Than the House?" *Journal of Politics* 35 (May 1973), pp. 332–363.
4. 119 *Congressional Record*, 23 May 1973, daily ed., pp. H3913, H3916.

each chamber to resolve common problems. Given that each is a separate and complex topic in its own right, this analysis will focus only on selected aspects of each: for conference committees, problems regarding the selection of conferees and the respective influence of each chamber in conference; for joint committees, an examination of several factors which have led to their creation. Finally, several suggestions will be offered as possible methods for improving relationships between the two chambers.

CONFERENCE COMMITTEES

A bicameral legislature requires some means to resolve disagreements over legislation. Conference committees serve that function for the Congress. Although nowhere mentioned in the Constitution and hardly known outside Capitol Hill, conference committees are a vital part of the legislative process. As one representative concluded:

When I came to Congress I had no comprehension of the importance of the conference committees which actually write legislation. We all know that important laws are drafted there, but I don't think one person in a million has any appreciation of their importance and the process by which they work.[5]

Used since the first Congress, conference committees are composed invariably of legislators from the committees of jurisdiction in each house, but are accountable to their respective chambers. Their importance stems from two key factors: (1) conferees make important policy decisions which are usually accepted by each house; and (2) the most important bills usually involve conferences, for example, appropriations,

taxes and defense. Hence, as key participants in an important stage of legislative policy making, it is important to know (1) how conferees are selected; (2) the problems of the selection process; and (3) what reforms have been proposed to resolve them.

For both houses, three rules or precedents govern the selection of conferees: (1) the Speaker or Presiding Officer, as the case may be, is formally to appoint conferees—although in actual practice committee chairmen, usually in consultation with their ranking minority members, select them; (2) they are to be named from the committee or subcommittee of jurisdiction; and (3) at least a majority of the conferees are to represent the majority view of their chamber. Although the last precedent is of long standing duration, it has sometimes been violated on controversial measures, such as antibusing and the supersonic transport (SST).

For example, on December 18, 1970, Senator William Proxmire of Wisconsin charged that four of the seven conferees on the Department of Transportation appropriation bill—H.R. 17755—were supporters of the SST, even though the Senate had voted to defeat this proposal. Proxmire said:

They stacked the conferees. It is no secret that the real controversy in the transportation appropriation bill is the SST. Sure, there are differences of opinion on other matters, but the controversial issue that really divides the country and the Senate, on which there was so much debate, is the SST. There is no secret that the conferees were appointed who would vote for the SST, which is a direct and express violation of the rules of the Senate.[6]

5. Clapp, *The Congressman*, p. 276.

6. 116 *Congressional Record*, 18 December 1970, p. 42402.

Senator Warren Magnuson of Washington rejected Proxmire's contention, noting that "conferees on the Department of Transportation appropriation bill are not appointed simply on the basis of their position on the SST. That is only one minor part of the bill."[7]

A question, then, that has never been fully answered in either house is: which criteria shall determine whether a senator or representative has supported the majority position of his chamber? The usual practice has been that a member's vote on final passage is indicative of his overall position on a measure. Hence, a member's position on final passage outweighs any antecedent vote on a particular amendment(s). However, other legislators argue that conferees should be selected according to their stand on the principal matters of disagreement between the two houses. Yet, still unanswered is the question of who is to determine the principal matter(s) in disagreement.

To help resolve this dilemma, legislators in both houses have proposed various reforms. On January 6, 1973, Representative Pierre du Pont of Delaware offered the following amendment to the rules of the House:

A majority of the House members of a conference committee shall have indicated by their votes their support of the bill as passed by the House of their concurrence in the prevailing opinion of the House on matters of disagreement with the Senate. The responsibility to insure that a majority of the House members of a conference committee are in agreement with and intend to support the significant provisions of the bill as passed by the House shall rest with the Speaker.[8]

The effect of the latter sentence would be either to require or to permit the Speaker in his discretion to ask each member he is about to appoint whether that member supports the measure as adopted by the House. This approach would avoid the confusions inherent in both the examination of how individual members voted on the different parts of a bill and the determination of which part of the bill is the most crucial. It relies on the word of individual members, which is an accepted practice in the House. Furthermore, it would imply that the Speaker may go beyond the membership of the reporting committee, if necessary, in appointing conferees.

As another example of a reform proposal, Senator Fred Harris of Oklahoma recommended in 1972 that: "committee chairmen should present recommendations [regarding conferees] to the majority leader who would then forward them to the presiding officer of the Senate unless he found that they were not consistent with . . . the position of the Senate on the bill in question."[9] Senator Harris' proposal failed to win the support of his colleagues, although a variation of it did. On April 13, 1972, the Senate Democratic Conference adopted a resolution which states that committee chairman shall make certain that at least a majority of the Senate's conferees support the majority position of an issue.[10] Some of the factors governing a chairman's decision include: seniority on a committee or subcommittee, special knowledge or familiarity with the subject matter and particular interest a measure represents to a senator's state.

7. Ibid.
8. 119 *Congressional Record*, 6 January 1973, daily ed., p. E38.

9. 118 *Congressional Record*, 19 April 1972, daily ed., p. S6387.
10. Ibid.

The conferee selection process is important, for that procedure often determines the contents of the final legislative product. Also, the report resulting from a conference is not always the product of conflict between two opposing chambers, as one might infer from reading the literature on conferences or the floor remarks of conferees who usually state how vigorously they defended the position of their chamber against opposing arguments of the other.[11]

For example, it seems clear that conflict between the chambers generally occurs in most appropriation conferences.[12] The House, with its strong budget-cutting ethos, views the Senate as generally more irresponsible on fiscal matters. The House Appropriations Committee usually reduces agency funding requests and leaves the Senate Appropriations Committee in the position of an appellate body which listens to federal officials argue for restoration of funds eliminated or cut by the House. However, the traditional appellate function of the Senate in appropriation matters may be changing, at least in defense matters. In a study of congressional actions on defense budgets from 1960 to 1970, Arnold Kantor found that the Senate was even more critical than the House in reducing budget requests and no longer played its traditional

role of "dependably restoring House cuts."[13] Given this development, conferees from the respective appropriations committees are now likely to clash not only about policy and program considerations, but over which chamber is really after economy in government.

Moreover, given that the contemporary Senate is said to be more liberal than the House, conferees from liberal House committees often agree more with a bill passed by the Senate than with their own chamber's version. For instance, the House Education and Labor Committee often reports out legislation more liberal than that which the full House will accept, yet closer to that which the Senate will propose. Nevertheless, the House's conferees will be appointed from the Committee on Education and Labor; thus, when they meet with their counterparts from the Senate, the conference often resembles more a session of like-minded legislators who share similar ideas and values than one group of united antagonists pitted against another. The Republican conferees from Education and Labor may later accuse their Democratic counterparts of selling out to the Senate.

Knowing which conferences considering the various types of measures are most likely to produce conflict or cooperation in decision making is difficult to determine, mainly because conferences are traditionally shrouded in secrecy. There is no record of their proceedings nor of votes taken. Yet, the question of conference conflict or cooperation is important, for it illustrates both how well each legislative

11. See, David L. Paletz, *Influence in Congress: An Analysis of the Nature and Effects of Conference Committees Utilizing Case Studies of Poverty, Traffic Safety, and Congressional Redistricting Legislation* (Ph.D. diss., University of California, Los Angeles, Cal., 1970).

12. See, for example, Richard Fenno, *The Power of the Purse: Appropriations Politics in Congress* (Boston, Mass.: Little, Brown, 1966), chap. 12; and Jeffrey Pressman, *House vs. Senate: Conflict in the Appropriations Process* (New Haven, Conn.: Yale University Press, 1966).

13. Arnold Kantor, "Congress and the Defense Budget: 1960–1970," *American Political Science Review* 65 (March 1972), p. 143.

branch reflects contrary points of view on policy matters and how well each chamber's conferees present and defend their house's position on legislation—that is, the framers of the Constitution created a bicameral legislature as part of our checks-and-balances system. How well this works in conference committees is unclear, however. For example, it is often contended that the House has greater influence in conferences because representatives, having fewer committee assignments than senators, are more knowledgeable about the substance of legislation.[14] Representative Jamie Whitten of Mississippi noted that appropriations conferences are periodically interrupted because senators are always "in and out, in and out," attending other committee meetings.[15] Assuming the truth of this argument, the House should predominate over the Senate in conferences by having its position on bills accepted more than the Senate's. Is this, then, an effective system of checks and balances?

Scholars who have examined the question of who wins in conference are not in agreement. In 1898 Lauros McConachie opined that the Senate frequently prevailed in conferences.[16] Writing in 1923, Paul Hasbrouck observed that House con-

ferees will likely prevail in conference "if their position has been won after free discussion and decision by the House."[17] In 1951, after examining fifty-six conferences on various measures from the 70th to the 80th Congresses, Gilbert Steiner concluded that the House prevailed in thirty-two and the Senate in fifteen; the remaining nine were split between them.[18] Then, in 1966 Richard Fenno—who examined appropriation bills only—concluded that the Senate is stronger than the House in conference.[19] Five years later, another political scientist argued that the Senate dominates the House in conferences.[20]

This suggests the need for a better definition of winning; otherwise, that notion serves more to hide, than to reveal, the complexities of the conference process. For example, which criteria should be developed to define winning: (1) assessing the objectives of the respective conferees, which may change from one day to the next; (2) determining the real policy preferences of a chamber; or (3) examining the reactions of outside groups, including the executive branch. Moreover, given the gamesmanship that occurs in conference, who wins cannot be inferred simply by counting the number of times that one house gave in to the other; for, that process does not distinguish the important from the unimportant for each house. House conferees, as an example, may feel

14. In 1973 each senator served on an average of 15.9 committees and subcommittees as compared to 5.6 per representative. See, Charles O. Jones, "Congressional Committees and the Two-Party System," *Working Papers on House Committee Organization and Operation,* House Select Committee on Committees, 93rd Cong., 1st sess., p. 4.

15. U.S., Congress, *Organization of Congress, Hearings before the Joint Committee on the Organization of the Congress,* 89th Cong., 1st sess., p. 655.

16. See, Lauros McConachie, *Congressional Committees* (New York: Thomas Crowell, 1898), p. 252.

17. Paul Hasbrouck, *Party Government in the House of Representatives* (New York: Macmillan, 1927), p. 231.

18. Gilbert Steiner, *The Congressional Conference Committee* (Urbana, Ill.: University of Illinois Press, 1951).

19. Fenno, *The Power of the Purse,* p. 669.

20. David Volger, *The Third House: Conference Committees in the United States Congress* (Evanston, Ill.: Northwestern University Press, 1971).

intensely about an issue and regard as relatively unimportant ten other matters on which they would adopt the Senate's position. If in this instance the House's position were to be adopted, can it be said that the House really lost the conference to the Senate? It is clear that much more needs to be known about conference committees, especially since their reports are so difficult to defeat. With more information about conferences—including advance notice of who the conferees shall be—some minimal conditions can be established for promoting better public understanding of each chamber's ability to make independent, informed policy judgments.

It should be noted that while elected representatives are often uninformed about conference meetings, certain federal officers participate in certain sessions as a matter of course. As Senator Hubert Humphrey of Minnesota noted in discussing the conference report on the 1972 debt ceiling bill—H.R. 16810:

In fact, in the instance of this conference report, the Secretary of the Treasury, the Deputy Under Secretary of the Treasury, and the Director of the Office of Management and Budget sat in the conference. May I say that within itself is something Senators around here did not have a right to do.[21]

Hence, it also seems necessary to provide information to members and staff about the extent of executive involvement in conference sessions. For just as it is important to determine the respective influence of each chamber in various conferences, the same obtains for executive involvement. Their participation in conferences may require regulation or more publicity to insure that Congress does not lose control to the president over this vital part of the legislative process.

JOINT COMMITTEES

A device which has been proposed as a means either to minimize the use and influence of conferences or, alternatively, to increase understanding between the House and Senate is joint committees. For example, the Joint Committee on Internal Revenue Taxation (JCIRT) functions mainly as a holding company for staff. This highly regarded staff works closely with the respective tax-writing committees of each house, pointing out areas of common ground and interpreting the intent of one committee to the other. As a result, the JCIRT staff helps facilitate decision making during conferences between the two committees.

Joint committees are of various types. As noted above, some are mainly staff operations, while others perform housekeeping functions—for example, the Joint Committee on Printing—or have study and investigative responsibilities—for example, the Joint Economic Committee. Another, the Joint Committee on Reduction of Federal Expenditures even has two members of the executive branch, Treasury and Office of Management and Budget, as statutory members. Only one committee, the Joint Committee on Atomic Energy, is authorized to report legislation.

Several advantages are associated with joint committees. First, they provide the insights of each chamber on how to resolve national and international questions. Second, they economize the time of legislators and administrators by avoiding the repetition of testimony before similar committees of the two houses. In

21. 118 *Congressional Record,* 17 October 1972, daily ed., pp. S18514–15.

addition, they facilitate an integrated approach to problem solving. Finally, joint committees better focus responsibility for oversight; thus, executive agencies cannot play off one chamber's committees against the other's.

Even with these and other advantages, generally, joint committees are not popular devices. Several factors account for this. Probably the most important issue is jurisdictional encroachment. Legislators are very sensitive to the powers and responsibilities of the committees of which they are members and will very often oppose the formation of committees which may become rival centers of power and prestige. Senators and representatives often perceive that a proposed joint committee represents an attack on their committee's jurisdiction. Another factor involves the rivalries of House and Senate members. Many House members regard senators as prima donnas who only seek publicity and do as little committee work as possible. Moreover, House members are irritated when senators send their staff to represent them in negotiations with representatives. A final factor discouraging the use of joint committees involves the constitutional powers of each chamber. As Senator John Bricker of Ohio noted: "It seems to me joint committees should be held to a minimum or, putting it the other way, if we go too far in creating joint committees we get away from the bicameral makeup of the Congress."[22] For example, although Senator John McClellan's—of Arkansas—oft-repeated proposal for a Joint Committee on the Budget has passed the Senate several times, it has never been enacted by the House—mainly because that body views the measure as an intrusion by the Senate into its prerogative of initiating appropriation bills.

Even with these alleged disadvantages, many legislators still introduce proposals calling for the creation of joint committees. For example, from 1971 to 1973 members introduced recommendations for joint committees in the following areas: information and intelligence, foreign trade, causes and origins of United States involvement in Vietnam, aging, environment, energy, national security, individual rights and the Central Intelligence Agency (CIA). Not one was enacted. A brief look at the creation of three joint committees—Internal Revenue Taxation, Economic and Atomic Energy —may illuminate some of the common factors instrumental in their establishment. Quite obviously, "historical causation is infinitely complex and elusive," and these brief sketches are only suggestive of those conditions which may enhance joint committee formation.[23]

The Revenue Act of 1926—P.L. 69–20—established a "joint congressional committee on Internal Revenue Taxation." According to John Manley, the "primary stimulus for this action was the sensational revelations of tax evasions aided by misconduct on the part of Internal Revenue Bureau employees, revelations which stemmed from the work of a select committee headed by Michigan Senator James Couzens."[24] Both chambers accepted

---

22. *Organization of Congress*, p. 1281.

23. Stephen Bailey, *Congress Makes A Law* (New York: Columbia University Press, 1950), p. 14.
24. John Manley, "Congressional Staff and Public Policy-Making: The Joint Committee on Internal Revenue Taxation," *Journal of Politics* 30 (November 1968), p. 1049.

the idea that some joint committee should monitor the work of the agency. Certain factors helped facilitate its enactment. First, the joint committee dealt with an agency involved in a technical and arcane subject area familiar to only a very few legislators. Moreover, since the committee was granted only limited advisory authority, problems regarding jurisdictional encroachment did not develop, either between the chambers or from the committees in each house. In addition, the policy of rotating the chairmanship between the chambers eliminated a source of friction between the House and Senate.

The Joint Economic Committee, originally known as the Joint Committee on the Economic Report, was established by the Employment Act of 1946. The bill, whose origins can be traced to the economic depression of the 1930s, charged the federal government with the responsibility of ensuring maximum employment, production and purchasing power; the joint committee device was the legislative mechanism to ensure congressional participation in that process. As Senator Joseph O'Mahoney of Wyoming said on the floor of the Senate: "Mr. President, this is a bill to vest in Congress the power and responsibility of meeting the issue, instead of continually delegating the power to the executive branch of the government. This, Mr. President, is a bill to restore the functions of Congress." It should also be noted that a constituency had developed to give support to the joint committee idea, the liberal Union for Democratic Action.[25]

Following World War II Congress

enacted an atomic energy measure which established a Joint Committee on Atomic Energy. The committee apparently stemmed from secret relationships between certain House and Senate members during the war years involving funding for construction of the atomic bomb. As Harold Green and Alan Rosenthal have pointed out:

The legislative history of the 1946 Act does not provide a clear picture of the origin of this uniquely armed committee. One possible precedent for the establishment of a Joint Committee may be found in the informal practice that prevailed during the Second World War. During that time, the entire atomic program developed by the Manhattan Engineer District was kept from general Congressional scrutiny. Requests for appropriations were hidden in the budgets of a number of Executive Agencies and were passed on by the chairmen of the Senate and House Appropriations and Military Affairs Committees, who constituted an informal joint committee. At the same time, these four men were necessarily privy to secret developments in the atomic program. The proven feasibility of this arrangement and its success in preserving security during the war may have influenced the draftsmen of the 1946 Act in suggesting a joint committee.[26]

Of course, atomic energy was a new field then and not within any committee's jurisdiction. Hence, no committee could claim that atomic energy belonged under its jurisdiction—as would likely be the case today, given the existence of space and science committees in each house.

Though certainly not prerequisites, several factors or condi-

25. Bailey, *Congress Makes A Law*, p. 120.

26. Harold Green and Alan Rosenthal, *The Joint Committee on Atomic Energy* (Washington, D.C.: George Washington University Press, 1961), p. 4.

tions increase the probability that joint committees will be formed to deal with specific problems. Some of these factors include:

(1) crisis, national or international, which both houses seek to resolve jointly;

(2) a constituency which will support the creation of a joint committee as a mechanism to give visibility and attention to a problem;

(3) the need for both houses to act together to oversee the executive;

(4) the emergence of an issue which is not directly within any existing committee's jurisdiction or one which involves so many committees that a joint committee acts to facilitate shared decision making among members selected from the concerned committees;

(5) a previous or existing pattern of cooperative relationships between senators and representatives in a particular area;

(6) enactment of procedures to insure that members from each house are accorded equal rights and privileges on a joint committee;

(7) granting a joint committee only limited authority.

CONCLUSIONS

It is important that the policy positions of the House and Senate be forcefully articulated. Yet, it is equally important for the general welfare that internecine clashes between the House and Senate be kept to a minimum while actions are taken to strengthen the legislative branch in general through intercameral cooperation, particularly in this era of presidential prominence.

Quite obviously, party control of the houses is a factor which may help or hinder intercameral relationships, as will the degree of unity experienced by Democrats and Republicans in each house. For example, party disunity may limit the potential for interhouse cooperation on matters of mutual interest and concern.

Bicameral cooperation can take many forms, although only two will be described here: (1) party relationships and (2) committee parallelism. Party relationships can take diverse patterns—for example, the "Ev and Charlie show," after reports to the press by former Senate Republican Leader Everett Dirksen and former House Republican Leader Charles Halleck; the formation of joint party policy committees; informal contacts among House and Senate leaders; and more regular, continuing liaison between House and Senate leaders. For example, in 1931 the Democratic leaders of each house established a Joint Policy Committee with Speaker John Nance Garner of Texas as chairman. The purpose of the joint committee, as outlined by Speaker Garner, was "to coordinate the work of the majority in the House and the minority in the Senate. It is unofficial and advisory only. It is for the purpose of our people in the House and in the Senate to talk over legislative measures and coordinate and harmonize legislative policies, which is good strategy."[27] Information regarding the work of the Joint Policy Committee is scant, although one commentator wrote "there has been inclination to question the success and value of its work."[28]

More recently, Senate Majority Leader Mike Mansfield of Montana

27. W. H. Humbert, "The Democratic Joint Policy Committee," *American Political Science Review* 26 (June 1932), p. 553.
28. Ibid., p. 544.

and Speaker Carl Albert of Oklahoma have met several times or exchanged letters regarding legislative and party matters. In a January 1973 statement before the Democratic Conference, Majority Leader Mansfield informed his colleagues of several meetings with the House leadership:

Together with the Speaker and his associates, we are seeking ways to promote effective unity between the democrats in the two Houses of Congress. In turn, the joint congressional leadership is establishing regular contact with the Democratic governors of the nation and with the Chairman of the Democratic National Committee.[29]

In another January 1973 address to his colleagues, Mansfield questioned the wisdom of Congress adjourning *sine die* ever again, since it would then be unable to reassemble except by call of the president. That concern was reflected in an arrangement worked out by Mansfield and Speaker Albert to recall Congress from its 1973 summer recess if action on the economy, energy problems, the bombing of Cambodia or some other matter was necessary. Under their arrangement, the president pro tempore of the Senate or the House Speaker, the majority leaders of the House and Senate, acting jointly, or the two minority leaders could reassemble the Congress during this period.[30] Thus, efforts to coordinate the common concerns of each house—for example, the budgetary process—through various leadership arrangements can both maintain and strengthen the institutional powers of Congress.

Another proposal which has been made to facilitate intercameral cooperation is the creation of parallel committee structures—that is, the respective committees of each house should be similar so far as number and jurisdictional responsibilities are concerned. Although the committees of the contemporary House and Senate have somewhat paralleled each other, jurisdictional problems still result because committees in one house may not have the same authority as those in the other chamber. For example, certain scientific matters are thus referred in each house:

A bill to create a Commission on Science and Technology is referred in the Senate to the Committee on Government Operations which has jurisdiction, among other things, over organizational matters in the government; the same bill in the House is referred to the Committee on Science and Astronautics which has jurisdiction in science matters. The Senate Committee on Aeronautical and Space Sciences does not have the same jurisdictional reach as the House committee. The bill to amend the National Science Foundation Act went to the House Committee on Science and Astronautics and was approved, but in the Senate it went to the Committee on Labor and Public Welfare.[31]

A negative consequence of this situation is that confusion sometimes results in conference committees. The 1965 Joint Committee on the Organization of the Congress, for example, recommended that the jurisdiction of House and Senate committees be as nearly parallel as possible because the "practice requiring one committee of one body to meet with

---

29. 119 *Congressional Record*, 31 January 1973, daily ed., p. S1528.

30. Ibid., 30 July 1973, daily ed., p. H6850. See, *Congressional Quarterly Weekly Report*, 28 July 1973, p. 2060.

31. Herbert Roback, "Congress and the Science Budget" (Paper presented at the Meeting of the American Association for the Advancement of Science, New York, 28 December 1967), p. 6.

four or five committees in the other body, in order to iron out differences that usually involve the same overall programs, results in chaos and confusion and prevents or severely hampers review of total policy programs."[32] Moreover, committee parallelism would likely facilitate more interhouse consultation and coordination of the type illustrated by the floor remarks of Senator Henry Jackson of Washington: "The only reason my amendment is being offered to this bill is that we discussed it with the [Senate] leadership and with the House Committee on Interstate and Foreign Commerce, and they are willing to accept it."[33] Thus, the political and procedural delays attendant to passage of various measures might be minimized through improved consultations between the concerned committees of each chamber.

The need to maintain a relatively close degree of parallelism is evidently perceived as important by many senators and representatives. The Legislative Reorganization Act of 1970—P.L. 91–510—for example, established a new Senate Committee on Veterans' Affairs to parallel the already existing Veterans committee in the House. As another example, just as the new Select Committee on Committees is examining the committee system of the House, resolutions have been introduced in the Senate to create a similar select committee. Senator Adlai Stevenson argued for the creation of such a committee by noting that "if the Senate fails to take action and the House study results in major changes in its committee jurisdictions, the net result could be to reduce the effectiveness of the Congress, rather than to strengthen it."[34]

Other arrangements, such as joint rules or the establishment of a mediation board to resolve procedural disputes, might also facilitate bicameral cooperation. It is also likely that what really counts toward the development of productive associations between the chambers is the goodwill binding together various senators and representatives. Yet, there is the problem of how far to go in institutionalizing chamber cooperation, given the imperative of having the House and Senate present and defend different and conflicting points of view. Too much efficiency or cooperation between the chambers may lessen the chance for a full exchange on the issues of the day. Moreover, it is important to recognize that certain issues require cooperation if the position of Congress is to be sustained on matters opposed, for example, by the president. However, on other issues, vigorous interhouse advocacy is necessary to ensure that national laws are the product of careful, critical and copious analysis.

32. U.S., Congress, *Organization of Congress, Final Report of the Joint Committee on the Organization of the Congress,* Senate Rept. No. 1414, 89th Cong., 2nd sess. (1966), p. 15.

33. 119 *Congressional Record,* 31 July 1973, daily ed., p. S15205.

34. Ibid., 9 May 1973, daily ed., p. S8674.

Committee Conflict in the Congressional Arena

By PHILIP BRENNER

ABSTRACT: When congressmen engage in conflict can their behavior be explained by their objective interests as elite decision makers in our society? Congressional conflict can have the consequence of encouraging participation by outsiders, because conflict is contagious. As decision makers, congressmen eschew uncontrollable interference with their deliberations. Conflict can also arouse an interest which is antagonistic to the hierarchic structure of American society, and such arousal is resisted by congressmen. The nature of the conflict over the Higher Education Act of 1972 indicates that, although these considerations alone did not govern congressmen's behavior, they were significantly involved in structuring the conflict. In the first instance one finds that, while the interests at stake were not likely to generate mass arousal, some congressmen did attempt to curtail conflict in order to discourage the involvement of outsiders. In the second instance one finds that congressmen shaped the conflict in a particular way, seemingly, in order to avoid consideration of how education is used to buttress the structure of our society and, thus, to avoid the awakening of mass interests which they recognized were real, though unarticulated. The structure of the committee system significantly contributes to the legislators' abilities to control conflict in at least five ways. In considering reforms of the system, congressmen will take into account the extent to which the reforms alter the committees' role in structuring congressional conflict.

Philip Brenner is Instructor of Political Science at Trinity College, Washington, D.C. A member of the editorial board of Politics and Society, *he has been a coordinator of seminars for congressional assistants through the Institute for Policy Studies and has worked as a staff member in Congress. Mr. Brenner has co-edited books on American politics and is the author of articles on the politics of education. He is completing a doctoral dissertation on Congress at Johns Hopkins University, from which this essay is adapted.*

AFTER eight weeks of a House-Senate stalemate over the Higher Education Act of 1972, Representatives John Brademas—Democrat-Indiana—and Al Quie—Republican-Minnesota—rushed into the conference on May 16, huddled with some of their House colleagues, and a majority of the House delegation quickly voted to recede to a compromise proposed by Senator Claiborne Pell—Democrat-Rhode Island. The conference still had to resolve a major dispute over the busing of school children for the purpose of desegregation, but with a sudden burst it had resolved a principal conflict which had prevented a bill from passing.

This fight in conference over the Higher Education Act provides us with a useful case to understand the political implications of changes in the committee system. As congressmen are political elites, they necessarily see conflict, in part, in political terms. When they choose to avoid a conflict, to end one quickly or to extend a conflict over time, what do they expect the various political consequences to be? What consequences do they attempt to avoid? In what ways do committee operations affect the nature of conflict? The purpose here is to understand how the functioning of the committee system, vis-à-vis conflict, is consistent with the interests of congressmen as political elites. This will help to suggest some of the political calculations congressmen might make in deciding to support or oppose reforms in the committee system.

Education legislation is a good vehicle for such an inquiry, because education can be seen from at least two perspectives. As a pork barrel concern, it focuses on how much money is to be distributed to each district. As a concern which relates to the fundamental processes of our society, educational conflicts touch on questions of social mobility—and the legitimating of the lack of mobility, the training of personnel for our economy and the imbuing of succeeding generations with the basic values of the society. Landmark education legislation—which is what the Higher Education Act was called[1]—thus allows us to consider how congressmen's calculations about conflict relate to policy at several levels.

THE HIGHER EDUCATION ACT

In August of 1971 the Senate passed a higher education bill, and in November the House followed suit. However, it produced a very different bill from that of the Senate. The Senate, in turn, took up the House version in December, and passed a new bill in March, 1972, still different from the House's.

Much attention has been focused on the busing provisions of both bills and the laborious efforts to work out a compromise busing plan during an election year. Here, I will avoid the busing issue—as congressmen were wont to say—and refer only to the two principal education provisions of the act which were in dispute: those which provided for institutional aid and for student aid.

In the House bill colleges and universities were to receive federal aid on the basis of their total full time enrollment. Two-thirds of the aid was to go to colleges simply on the basis of enrollment. One-third was to

1. "Senate Passes Landmark Aid to Higher Education Bill," *Congressional Quarterly Weekly Reports,* 28 August 1971, p. 1844. The official title of the act is: Education Amendments of 1972.

be differentially allotted to schools on the basis of the total amount of federal student aid students at a school were receiving.[2] Student aid provisions in the House bill would have essentially left the then current programs intact.

In contrast to the House, the Senate keyed its landmark legislation to student aid, with institutional aid based solely on the number of students at a school who were receiving student aid.[3] Under the Senate bill the federal government would have declared, as a matter of policy, that it had a responsibility for assuring that every college age student would not be prevented from attending a post-secondary institution because of a lack of funds. The bill provided that every student would be eligible for a grant of up to $1,400, depending on the student's costs and the ability of his family to contribute to these costs. Existing student aid programs would have been renewed, as well.

Aid to colleges and universities under the Senate bill was to be based on the new program of student grants, called basic opportunity grants. Institutions were to receive a cost-of-instruction allowance for enrolling a student who received any amount from a basic opportunity grant. There was no provision for general institutional aid.[4]

2. H.R. 7248, 92nd Cong., 1st sess. Also, see, Joel Havemann, "Education Report: Pending Bill Could Revolutionize Federal Programs for Higher Education," *National Journal*, 18 March 1972.

3. S. 659, 92nd Cong., 1st sess. Subsequent revisions of this bill by the Senate pertained to the question of busing students for the purpose of desegregation.

4. Both the House and Senate bills did provide emergency general aid to institutions which were facing immediate financial crises. However, the Senate bill made clear that the emergency aid was only temporary.

In mid-March, 1972 a conference committee convened, with seventeen members from the House and nine from the Senate. In a conference each body has one vote, with a majority of the members from a particular house determining the position of that house in conference. Eight weeks later, when a compromise was reached, the bill was decidedly similar to the Senate version with regard to institutional and student aid.[5] In effect, the compromise paid little deference to the House Education and Labor Committee, which had rejected the Senate's provisions, or to the House, which had also rejected the Senate's emphases. The bill's focus on student aid and rejection of general institutional aid had been denounced by a coalition of higher education associations. Furthermore, the bill was anathema to the chief House sponsor of the Higher Education Act, Representative Edith Green—Democrat-Oregon—who had labored for three years to bring out a bill. How did the Senate prevail in such a situation and bring off this upset?

The genesis of the so-called compromise lay in actions which had occured two years earlier. In the 91st Congress—1969 to 1970—Mrs. Green had been adamant about

5. Under the act as finally passed there is a program of basic opportunity grants entitling all students up to $1,400, each. Institutions are to receive money according to a tripartite formula: (1) the first 45 percent of institutional aid is to be distributed to schools on the basis of the amount of money students at a school receive from federal student aid programs; (2) the second 45 percent is to be distributed on the basis of the number of students receiving basic opportunity grants at a school; (3) the last 10 percent is to be based on enrollment of graduate students—with any school receiving $200 for each graduate student who is enrolled. Only the last provision corresponds to the House version.

punishing student rioters. She was very concerned about campus disorders, and she sponsored a higher education bill that included a section which would have required strong punitive action to be taken against students involved in disorders.[6]

In 1969 and 1970 Congressman Brademas led a group of Education and Labor Committee members who opposed a strong punitive section. These members proceeded to boycott the meetings of the Special Subcommittee on Education in an effort to deny Mrs. Green a quorum and, thus, to prevent a bill from being reported out of the subcommittee. Mrs. Green was chairwoman of the subcommittee, and it is this subcommittee which considers higher education legislation.

Mrs. Green prevailed sufficiently to have the bill reported to the full committee, where it died in September, 1970 by one vote. The conflict engendered antagonisms which did not die. Several sources reported that Representatives Brademas and Green were personally hostile to each other in all subsequent encounters.[7]

Shortly after the committee shelved the 1970 bill, representatives from the major college associations allegedly approached Brademas and proposed that he sponsor a new bill. He rejected this plan, arguing that it was too late in the session to bring up new legislation. They then turned to Mrs. Green and in February, 1971 she announced hearings on a new higher

education bill. The associations never went back to Brademas, nor did they make an effort to work closely with the ranking Republican on the committee, Al Quie. One spokesman for the associations contended that they ignored Brademas and Quie because the positions of the two congressmen were antithetical to that of the associations, and any effort would have been to no avail.[8] Understandably, the associations favored an across-the-board institutional aid formula, based on a per capita amount for each student enrolled. They tended to represent institutions with large student bodies which would stand to gain the most under a general aid formula. Brademas and Quie, however, maintained that they were not fixed in their positions and they would have been open to suggestions.[9]

At this point, a new lobby entered the picture—academic policy advocates located in such havens as the Carnegie Commission on Higher Education and the Brookings Institution. They had had long-standing, close relations with Congressman Brademas, and now they turned to the Senate. The academic lobbyists—as distinguished from the administrator-dominated higher education associations—favored a cost of instruction approach to federal aid, coupled with aid to needy students. This approach also corresponded to an approach the Nixon administration had advocated in 1969, although by 1971 the administration had abandoned an active

6. Mrs. Green said that she did not strongly advocate such a provision in 1972 only because the incidence of campus riots had decreased.

7. Other House sources, while corroborating the hostility between Green and Brademas, said that their mutual antagonism dated back farther than 1969.

8. This is an example of a general approach which Dexter discerned among lobbies. See, Lewis Anthony Dexter, "The Representative and His District," in The Sociology and Politics of Congress, ed. Dexter (Chicago, Ill.: Rand McNally, 1969), pp. 166–168.

9. For Brademas' position, see, Havemann, "Education Report," p. 474.

effort to pass a higher education act. Congress perceived little pressure from the Office of Education to bring out a particular bill.[10]

In spite of the apparent predisposition of leading members of the House conference to support the Senate position, they were still faced with the fact that the House had clearly rejected the Senate bill, and the nominal leader of the House conference was Mrs. Green. Protocol, if not political sensitivity, demanded that some compromise be reached which did not abandon, in toto, Mrs. Green's position. Yet, reports indicated that Mrs. Green was adamant in refusing to compromise at all.

At some point Brademas and Quie made a breach of protocol and in a secret set of meetings with Senator Pell, the principal sponsor of the Senate bill, they arranged for the compromise which finally emerged.[11] They then convinced a majority of their House colleagues that a workable solution had been reached, and the stage was set for the upset vote.

ANALYZING COMMITTEE CONFLICT

Two elements of interest emerge from this necessarily brief sketch of the conference committee conflict. The first serves to affirm that one way in which political scientists have studied conflict in Congress does provide us with a mode of analysis which can be useful. However, the second element suggests that another dimension should be added to the study of conflict in Congress.

In the first instance we find that personality differences were a significant factor in this dispute. Personal relationships between key actors can forge alliances or prevent them, with quite substantive consequences. For example, Congressmen Brademas and Quie were willing to break with protocol and meet with Senator Pell, according to several participants who were interviewed, because the chairman of the full committee, Carl Perkins—Democrat-Kentucky—had approved of their move. Congressman Perkins, it was said, gave his approval because of his antagonism toward Mrs. Green.[12] For Mrs. Green's part, it is important to understand the discrimination she has felt as a woman in Congress. For example, a few sources suggested that some male members of the committee saw her as an aggressive female, a woman who was deflating their egos, and that were she a man, their reactions to her behavior would have been different. Mrs. Green partly confirmed that she felt hamstrung because she is a woman member of Congress. When asked in an interview to what extent she felt excluded from decision making because some business discussions occur in the House gymnasium, she said: "I try not to think about that. I get very angry when I do."

10. While I have distinguished here between the approaches of the academics and the administrators in theory, the impact of the two bills in practice may have been quite similar. The associations argue, for example, that even with $1,400 a needy student would still not be able to afford the costs of private institutions in which tuition ranges from $2,000 and upwards. These students are likely to attend the state schools which would have benefited the most from the Green formula.

11. Congressman John Dellenback—Republican-Oregon—the ranking Republican on the Higher Education Subcommittee, was also closely involved.

12. Congressman Perkins was said to be miffed for the following reasons: (1) Mrs. Green had voted in the House to instruct the conferees, which he saw as a vote of no confidence for his committee members; (2) she strongly favored busing, which he felt should not be dealt with in this bill, because it would hurt the bill's chances of passing.

That personality differences might be significant was a fact to which we were alerted by previous studies of congressional committees. Fenno pointed to the hostilities he noticed among members of the Education and Labor Committee in explaining the committee's behavior; Manley noted, in contrast, the efforts of the Ways and Means Committee to avoid hostility and to work in a friendly atmosphere.[13]

The second element, however, is more interesting: the awareness members of Congress had of the scope of conflict. That is, congressmen were concerned about both the duration of a conflict and the number of participants involved. I had expected that the scope of conflict would be one concern of partisans, as they must take it into account in planning their legislative strategies. What I found suggested that a new set of questions must be raised about the nature of conflict in Congress.

One learns from Schattschneider that the duration of a conflict is critical because the longer a conflict ensues, the more likely is a change in the balance of forces. Those in a stronger position thus favor a speedy resolution of conflict, while the weaker forces seek delay. Schattschneider also explains that one strategy for the weaker side is to increase the number of participants in a conflict in an effort to gain adherents to its side. Conversely, the stronger side attempts to limit the number of participants to those already involved. One way to do this is to keep proceedings secret: con-

flict is contagious and publicity is likely to arouse interested parties to join the fray.[14]

Mrs. Green, it seems, was pursuing a strategy of expanding the scope of conflict by keeping it going. She appears to have had a two-fold purpose in being unyielding. First, she hoped that if the conflict continued, it would arouse college presidents and middle class parents to bring pressure on her opponents. She needed time for these forces to become mobilized, especially since conference committee proceedings take place in secret. Second, she was hoping—it was said—that Senator Pell would capitulate because he was anxious to begin his campaign for reelection in what was assessed to be an uphill fight.

Congressmen Brademas and Quie were pursuing a strategy of limiting the number of participants in the conflict. Though they recognized —by their own admission—that their behind-the-scenes maneuvering might upset some members because these members were excluded, they argued that time was a factor and that the work had to be done quickly. Moreover, it was suggested that if more members had been involved, a compromise would have been more difficult to achieve, because there would have been more views to reconcile.

So far, the political science literature prepares one to expect such considerations about conflict. However, one member of the committee provided some unexpected reflections, when he said in an interview: "You know, it's ironic which people were involved in this fight. The bill intimately affects students

13. Richard Fenno, "The House of Representatives and Federal Aid to Education," in New Perspectives on the House of Representatives, ed. Robert L. Peabody and Nelson Polsby (Chicago, Ill.: Rand McNally, 1963); John F. Manley, The Politics of Finance (Boston: Little, Brown, 1970), pp. 65-70.

14. E. E. Schattschneider, The Semi-Sovereign People (New York: Holt, Rinehart and Winston, 1960), chap. 2 and 4.

and faculty members—it affects the way they will lead their lives. But only presidents were here to talk to us, and they speak for the administration at a college or university." This member recognized that not all of those who would be affected—who had an interest at stake—were involved in the process in any way. When asked why he did not try to involve students and faculty members, he first indicated that he did not have the time to do this. Then he said, "It was a very complex bill which meant that we really couldn't involve too many people. It was too complicated for students to get into. I'm not running a political science seminar here— I'm trying to pass legislation." In short, this congressman recognized that there was an interest at stake, but he was going to be the guardian of this "objective" interest. Similarly, another member remarked, "I feel like a parent to *all* children, looking out for their welfare."

Their attitude is not explained by traditional pluralist theory—which informs most of the scholarly research on Congress. Students were not a potential interest group because their interest was unarticulated;[15] thus, their interest should not have been even recognized. Yet, some congressmen felt as if they

were representing a real student interest or that they were at least cognizant of this interest. They made reference to it in discussing their behavior, but what was their behavior? They were engaged in a conflict among elites, in which some attempted to expand the conflict to other elites and others tried to confine the conflict to the elites in the conference or in Congress. The question to be asked, therefore, is whether one can explain this behavior in terms of the objective interests involved and in terms of congressmen's positions as elites. In order to do this one must rise above the din of battle and abstract our congressmen a bit.

RULING INTERESTS AND THE LIMITATION OF CONGRESSIONAL CONFLICT

On one level the story of the conference committee conflict would have been described adequately by reference to personal motivations, interest group miscalculation and the cunning strategy of Congressmen Brademas and Quie and Senator Pell. Such is the stuff which daily journalism provides us. Journalists report their stories in this way because they come to know congressmen and interest group leaders as persons, not as abstractions. To be sure, this adds a dose of realism to accounts of what happens in Congress. However, abstraction can help us to understand what underlies a congressman's decision to engage in conflict in a particular way.

Certainly, it is fair to abstract congressmen to a point at which they may be called societal decision makers. They do make significant decisions which intimately affect us all. The budget of the federal government passes through their hands,

15. The assumption that a felt need—that is, an articulated interest—is required as part of the definition of potential groups is based on Truman's discussion of potential groups; see, David B. Truman, *The Governmental Process* (New York: Alfred A. Knopf, 1951), p. 34. Isaac Balbus provides an illuminating critique of this assumption in arguing that pluralist analysis suffers from the lack of a conception of "objective" interest—and so is at pains to explain the systematic development of interests; see, Isaac Balbus, "The Concept of Interest in Pluralist and Marxian Analysis," *Politics and Society* 1, no. 2 (February, 1971).

and this accounts for one-quarter of our gross national product. Tax laws which they make affect the distribution of the nation's income, the types of industries which are encouraged and discouraged and the concentration of land and of productive enterprises—that is, the degree of capital monopolization. They also decide on the types of services which the government will provide the economy, from communication and transportation networks, to training and general education and to the subsidy of technological research which private companies cannot afford to support if they are to maintain high levels of profit.[16] All of this is to say that congressmen are key actors in a federal government which does these things. Whether we accept C. Wright Mills' contention that congressmen are merely at the middle levels of power[17] or see them as members of a power elite, the fact remains that the federal government does make significant decisions which relate to the structure of American society; this means that Congress takes a part in making these decisions.[18]

Does this role tend to encourage a type of behavior unique to it? Not necessarily, because congressmen are not the only decision makers we have in our society. Another large group of decision makers is professionals. Indeed, congressmen do exhibit many of the characteristics which sociologists have used to identify professionals. For example, Baker and Carper have explained that a professional's work-based identity becomes associated with: (1) occupational title and an area of endeavor represented by the title; (2) commitment to specific kinds of work—the I'm-here-to-write-legislation syndrome; and (3) social position—the person's status in the larger society leads him to see himself as appropriately suited only to work with others of a similar status.[19] We can take the analogy even further, to the point at which Carr-Saunders and Wilson explain that the development of specialized skills is a critical component of professionalism:

We have found that the application of an intellectual technique to the ordinary business of life, acquired as a result of prolonged and specialized training, is the chief distinguishing characteristic of

---

16. For a discussion of these governmental services, see, James O'Connor, *The Fiscal Crisis of the State* (New York: St. Martin's Press, 1973), chap. 1 and 2. Also, see, J. Kenneth Galbraith, *The New Industrial State*, 2nd rev. ed. (Boston, Mass.: Houghton Mifflin, 1971), chap. 26 through 28. Gordon Adams provides a useful categorization of services which the state provides in capitalist societies; see, Gordon Adams, "Public Ownership and Private Benefits: The Case of Rolls Royce," in *Exploring Contradictions: Political Economy in the Corporate State*, ed. Philip Brenner, Robert Borosage and Bethany Weidner (New York: David McKay, forthcoming).

17. C. Wright Mills, *The Power Elite* (New York: Oxford University Press, 1959), p. 256.

18. Lowi would disagree, arguing that congressmen give up their decision making to administrators by writing broad, unspecific legislation; see, Theodore J. Lowi, *The End of*

Liberalism (New York: W. W. Norton, 1969). Yet, the decision to give up the power to decide must be related to congressmen's policy preferences. As Arrow argues, while a "rule for social decision making is not the same as a welfare judgment," a person chooses a rule through which he can realize his welfare judgment; see, Kenneth Arrow, *Social Choice and Individual Values*, 2nd ed. (New York: John Wiley and Sons, 1963), p. 106. As the rule is repeatedly applied in the case of congressmen, they have ample feedback by which to judge whether they approve of the welfare judgment rendered through the rule.

19. Howard Baker and James Carper, "Professional Identification," in *Professionalization*, ed. Howard Vollmer and Donald Mills (Englewood Cliffs, N.J.: Prentice-Hall, 1966), pp. 102–107.

the professions. . . .Where a technique is specialized, the rise of a profession is inescapable.[20]

Congressmen do seem to be coming into focus ever more clearly as we list the characteristics of professionals. The norm of specialization is readily acknowledged as a pervasive one in the House. The specialization in question, it has been argued, comes from long association with the subject matter and technical questions—technique—which confront a committee. Indeed, proposals for change in the committee system always have the potential for running into the argument that the change would weaken the House because it would diminish the specialization of its members. Whether this is true or not, it would seem that some of the hostility towards change might stem from the member's fear that with decreased specialization their status as professionals would be diminished.

The argument that there is a relationship between specialization and the members' sense of being professional is buttressed by the nature of the specialization which the members emphasize: specialization of person. Thompson usefully distinguishes for us two types of specialization: that of task and that of person. In cases of the former, a job becomes progressively smaller so that each task can be done by a different person; the task becomes so unskilled that virtually anyone can perform it. In cases of specialization of person, the worker "is adapted or changed. He can do things . . . other people cannot do."[21] Con-

gressmen, understandably, think in terms of the latter kind of specialization, because their work would be difficult to specialize in terms of task. Moreover, specialized persons acquire some power because of their partial monopoly over knowledge or services which other people desire.

Although members think in terms of person specialization, the arguments which they make for specialization sometimes confuse the issue. When they cite the need for efficiency and the organizational need of the House and Senate for a strict division of labor as reasons for encouraging specialization, they are suggesting that the specialization involved is akin to that in a factory—of the task. In fact, specialization of person may even be inefficient in some cases, as knowledge becomes widely scattered. Similarly, when political scientists point to the need for cooperation, in contrast to conflict, in Congress—citing its highly specialized character—they too imply that task specialization is involved. Thompson explains that cooperation must be emphasized with task specialization in order to coordinate activities of people who are essentially automatons.[22]

The impulse for specialization, then, would seem to be related in part to the professional status and power which professionalization provides congressmen. This same impulse would also seem to affect the way in which congressmen regard people who are not in their profession, who are not congressmen or who are not, at least, elites—that is, the public at large. There is a tendency among specialists, whether professional or not, to deny to a com-

20. A. M. Carr-Saunders and P. A. Wilson, *The Professions* (Oxford: Oxford University Press, 1933), pp. 491–492.

21. Victor A. Thompson, *Modern Organization* (New York: Alfred A. Knopf, 1961), pp. 25–27.

22. Ibid., p. 29.

parable specialist the right to accept or reject decisions he makes or even to be involved in making the decisions.[23] In a like manner, professionals tend to eschew the participation of laymen whom they are affecting with their decisions. As Everett Hughes remarks, a most common complaint of professionals "is that they are somehow prevented from doing their work as it should be done."[24] This was the attitude displayed by the congressman who did not want to involve students in the battle over the Higher Education Act. Moreover, he was not atypical, as the prevailing orientation on Capitol Hill is that congressmen are there to make decisions for people.[25] Congressmen are willing to accept advice at times, but, ultimately, they know what is best. Thus, they attempt to limit participation in their conflicts as best they can.

It follows, then, that congressmen make a sort of calculation before they engage in a conflict whether the conflict is likely to encourage outsiders to meddle in congressional affairs—that is, congressmen recognize that conflict can be contagious. When they weigh, in each case, the benefits to be gained from a conflict and the costs that would be incurred, they include the cost of outside participation. Of course, one option open to them is to engage in conflict,

but to limit the scope through mechanisms such as secrecy. Closed committee hearings, for example, are used to prevent conflict from spreading.

Crucial to their calculation is an understanding that what impels a group, or individual, to enter a conflict in Congress is its interest. If conflicts can be arranged in such a way that the issues are narrowly defined, the number of groups aroused tends to be small, or at least disparate, and—from a congressman's perspective—manageable. Most importantly—unlike the pluralists—congressmen recognize the existence of objective interests and concern themselves not only with existing groups and articulated interests, but also with unarticulated, structurally defined interests, such as those of the students in this study. The congressmen try to avoid conflicts which might involve the objective, unarticulated interests of a large number of people for fear that the conflict will awaken an unmanageable interest which would place pressure on them.

In this regard, the case of the Higher Education Act suggests a further reason that congressmen might want to avoid issues which involve objective interests of a large number of people. Congressmen may want to preserve not only their prerogatives as professionals, but also to preserve the hierarchic structure of American society which could be threatened by people whose class interests are antagonistic to the existing structure. Therefore, it is notable that, despite the disagreements in the House over the formula for spending money on higher education, every congressman in a sample of sixty-one interviewed in 1972 agreed with the

23. Ibid., p. 76.

24. Everett C. Hughes, *Men and Their Work* (Glencoe, Ill.: Free Press, 1958), pp. 75–76.

25. This point should not be confused with various discussions of the representational role of congressmen. I am not referring to the source to which congressmen look in making their decisions. Regardless of whether they consider themselves to be trustees or delegates, congressmen tend to see themselves as people whose job it is to shape the world of other people.

statement that "Congress should help to maintain or expand our present system of higher education."[26] Most elaborated on the statement by saying that higher education was an important means of providing for social mobility and that everyone should have an equal opportunity to rise up.

While higher education may provide mobility for some, it has not been a mechanism for altering the structure of society. Recent data indicate that the distribution of income and wealth in the society has remained unchanged since, perhaps, the turn of the century.[27] Some may rise up, but the distribution suggests that the overall impact of higher education has been minimal. Rather, higher education may have served to reproduce the structure of our society, albeit under new circumstances.[28] With each age, new requirements are found through which some become anointed and others do not. At a time when the society needs college-trained people, a college degree is a *sine qua non* for success.

Equally important is the legitimating function of education. Though there may be gross inequality, people tend to accept the inequality as legitimate if they feel there is a rational basis for it. Inequality rooted in meritocracy, rooted in education, provides that basis.[29] In this sense, the Pell-Brademas-Quie group was acting to reinforce the structure of society by attempting to increase the rationality of the reward system. They were attempting to allow anyone to go to post-secondary school— or make it seem as if anyone could go if they wanted to go—so that in the future it could be said that there were no bars to anyone's success. Under the Green formula there would have remained the hint of irrationality, as the bill favored the children of those who already had some measure of success.

Congressmen's own elite status is legitimated by the overall legitimacy of inequality in our society. When inequality comes into question, the legitimacy of all elites becomes questionable. In avoiding the larger question of the functions of education, congressmen avoided arousing the objective interest shared by all nonelites. Thus, there may have been no conflict in Congress over the social function of education because, in part, there was no disagreement in Congress as to what the function should be. Even if there were disagreement, which the study did not detect, there was little interest in the issue. After all, the congressmen were not "running a political science seminar."

CONFLICT AND THE COMMITTEE SYSTEM

Theory has it that Congress functions to keep societal conflicts in check by acting as a surrogate bat-

26. The sample was stratified according to party and seniority, although it included most of the thirty-seven members of the House Education and Labor Committee.

27. Letitia Upton and Nancy Lyons, *Basic Facts: Distribution of Personal Income and Wealth in the United States* (Cambridge, Mass.: Cambridge Policy Studies Institute, 1972).

28. For a cogent explanation of this phenomenon, see, Samuel Bowles, "Unequal Education and the Reproduction of the Social Division of Labor," in *Schooling in a Corporate Society*, ed. Martin Carnoy (New York: David McKay, 1972).

29. For a fuller discussion of this point, see, Ralph Miliband, *The State in Capitalist Society* (New York: Basic Books, 1969), chap. 6. Also, see, Alan Wolfe, *The Seamy Side of Democracy* (New York: David McKay, 1973), pp. 159–165.

tleground for these conflicts, as an arena for the adjustment of competing interests in the society. The nature of conflicts in the arena, however, are shaped by congressmen, not by the society. Furthermore, congressmen do not simply translate societal conflicts into congressional conflicts by rote.

What I have tentatively explored here is one perspective from which one might try to understand how congressmen choose to shape their conflicts. I have argued that congressmen are concerned about the impact the conflict will have on those outside of Congress in terms of arousing the outsiders to action. It seems that they will make a decision to engage in a conflict—or will attempt to structure the issues in conflict—in part, on the basis of their calculation as to the extent of this impact on outsiders.

The committee system plays an important part in these calculations. Whatever other functions committees serve, they are an important mechanism for controlling the impact which conflict can have. In considering the ways in which they serve this function, one can suggest the acceptability of certain proposals for change in the committee system to congressmen. That is, if a change would affect the utility of a mechanism which the legislators use to control the consequences of conflict, then the degree to which the change diminishes the utility of the mechanism will also diminish the acceptability of the change.

Consider five characteristics of committees or of the committee system which relate to the control of conflict. The ways in which some prominent proposals for change would affect the capability of committees to control conflict can be indicated.

Limited participation

At most stages during which a committee considers a bill the number of members involved is small. Even at the final point of committee deliberation there will be at most—in the case of the House Appropriations Committee—13 percent of the total membership of the House or—in the case of the Senate Appropriations Committee—26 percent of the Senate involved in a conflict. Limited participation in a conflict engenders quick resolution, because there are fewer positions to reconcile and, as we noted earlier, quick resolution is an obvious way of preventing a conflict from spreading.

In this light, a proposal to decrease the number of standing committees might be seen as a proposal to increase the number of participants involved in critical stages of conflict over legislation. If there were fewer committees, then the membership on each committee would concomitantly increase; thus, during final deliberation there might be a tendency to generate uncontainable conflict. Of course, as with the House Appropriations Committee today, subcommittees might make the key decisions and, again, only a few members would be involved.

Secrecy

If those who might have an interest in a conflict are kept from knowing that a conflict is occuring or what it entails, they are less likely to join in the fight.[30] Committee secrecy through closed hearings—and particularly conference committee secrecy—tends to keep out of a conflict everyone but those whom members specifically invite to join the

30. Schattschneider, *The Semi-Sovereign People*, p. 16.

conflict. Secrecy in the case of conference committees also keeps non-conference members in the dark about details of a bill, so that once a bill reaches the floor the members of the conference remain in control of the debate.[31] Open hearings would remove an element of secrecy from these proceedings and, thus, remove an element of control from the hands of members. Open hearings could encourage noncommittee members, as well as the public at large, to become involved in internal committee fights.

Close interaction

Committees tend to generate friendships among their members through close interaction. Although congressmen may be on several subcommittees—which divides their attention and loyalty—over many years, members do come to see each other as friends with common problems rather than as representatives of a position. This is a general tendency in Congress, but is particularly engendered by the size of most committees.[32] Close interaction thus encourages members to avoid intense conflict in order to maintain

cordial relations with their friends. It further discourages the congressman who might fight for a position which is antagonistic to prevailing interest from continuing his fight, because in doing so he tends to alienate himself from people with whom he works closely. One such congressman commented in an interview that he had helped to form an informal group of like-minded congressmen because he was so frustrated and isolated in his committees.

Two proposed changes in the committee system would tend to take away from committees this element of close interaction and, thus, would remove a characteristic which discourages conflict. The first, noted above, would be a decrease in the number of committees. By virtue of the increased size of each committee, members would not be as close with each other. While subcommittee work would probably remain confined to a few members, the whole committee would have less leverage in controlling the conflictual tendencies of disagreeable members. A second change would be the rotation of members so that a congressman could serve on a committee only a fixed number of years. Clearly, this change would work against the development of friendships which are built over several years of continuous effort together.

Seniority

The automatic ascension of a member to the coveted chairman's post as a result of longevity works to mitigate conflict within a committee by removing an issue over which there can be a fight. Perhaps as important as the avoidance of tension is the fact that the choosing of committee chairmen by seniority takes away

31. David Vogler, *The Third House: Conference Committees in the U.S. Congress* (Evanston, Ill.: Northwestern University Press, 1971), p. 5. Also, see, Jeffrey Pressman, *House vs. Senate: Conflict in the Appropriations Process* (New Haven, Conn.: Yale University Press, 1966), p. 56.

32. Miliband vividly portrays this tendency in the British Parliament: "David Kirkwood, one of the 'wildmen' wrote later that, before he entered the House of Commons in 1922, he knew little of the 'Great Ones,' but felt that 'they and the world they represented were crushing my fellows down into poverty . . . and death.' But when he entered the House he was 'full of wonder' in finding 'them all so simple and unaffected and friendly.'" Ralph Miliband, *Parliamentary Socialism* (London: George Allen and Unwin, 1961), p. 95.

a focal point for outsiders. Were there biannual fights over the selection of chairmen in each committee, outsiders would be encouraged to pressure members, and candidates might be encouraged to campaign on the basis of their positions on upcoming issues. While Polsby has argued that the attempt to use outsiders in a conflict which members consider to be an internal matter is likely to be a losing strategy,[33] this fact is unlikely to deter the outsiders from trying to influence a conflict if they see an interest at stake. The election of committee chairmen by members of a committee would, therefore, be a change which could encourage participation in congressional conflicts by nonmembers of Congress.

Specialization

As was maintained earlier, specialization may be emphasized in Congress because it works to diminish conflict and to discourage the participation of nonspecialists. The greater the extent to which committees are responsible for narrow issue areas, the more they provide the aura of committee members as specialists. Indeed, members may not be specialists. The overwhelming ease with which Representative Wilbur Mills—Democrat-Arkansas—reportedly contends with most of his Ways and Means Committee colleagues—who are supposed specialists, too—suggests that specialization may be more apparent than real and that the appearance is conveyed by the mask of committee specialization.

33. Nelson Polsby, "Two Strategies of Influence: Choosing a Majority Leader, 1962," in *New Perspectives on the House of Representatives*, ed. Peabody and Polsby (Chicago, Ill.: Rand McNally, 1963), pp. 267–270.

Were the number of committees decreased so that each committee was less specialized and covered a large area of concern or were members rotated from one committee to the next, the apparent specialization of committee members would be less convincing. Committee assignment rotation further would tend to provide several noncommittee members with knowledge of a committee's area of concern, thus, mitigating the ability of committee members to control floor conflict by virtue of their supposedly unique knowledge. Members who had previously served on a committee could reasonably claim, in floor debate, that they had gained a knowledge of the subject at hand while they had been on the committee. This is rarely the case now with committees, such as Appropriations or Ways and Means, as members tend to leave these committees only through death or retirement.

CONCLUSION

The way which committees function to contain conflict is probably not the consequence of a congressional conspiracy. I have not intended to suggest that congressmen consciously designed the committee system so that it would tend to limit conflict. However, as it does function in this way, congressmen are reluctant to change a system which serves their needs as political elites.

Congressmen may not always want to contain a conflict. As with the case of Mrs. Green and the Higher Education Act, a representative may seek to bring in outsiders in order to win a fight and, thus, may favor the prolongation of the conflict. In part, the hostility to the House Rules Committee in 1961 and 1965—which led, respectively, to the enlargement of the committee and to the twenty-one-day rule—was generated by the overbearing limitation on conflict which the committee commanded. On balance, however, congressmen will favor mechanisms which have a bias towards limiting the scope of conflict.

To be a congressman is a difficult way of earning $42,500 a year. Even considering the fact that their position can allow them to earn more than their congressional salary, national legislators must choose their profession because of their interest in affecting governmental decisions and the shape of our society. This means that they do care about policy. When an organizational change affects their ability to shape policy as they would like to, particularly when it may affect their ability to keep the mass public out of their deliberations, their calculations of the desirability of change will go beyond mere organizational questions of harmony and efficiency. They will undoubtedly consider the political effects of the change, and these effects are closely related to the way in which conflict can be controlled in the legislature.

Congress, the Executive and the Budget

By Louis Fisher

ABSTRACT: During the autumn months of 1972 President Nixon and Congress engaged in a prolonged and bitter struggle over a spending ceiling. The president wanted a limit of $250 billion for fiscal 1973, with complete discretion to cut wherever needed to preserve the ceiling. Congress refused to grant him such broad discretion. This single incident tells one many valuable things about the relative advantages available to the two branches. While factually wide of the mark, the president's offensive against a big-spending Congress proved to be overpowering in the political arena. Congress lacked the capability—and, probably, also the will—to defend itself. The result was a serious collapse in informed and responsible policy making.

Louis Fisher received his doctorate in political science from the New School for Social Research. After teaching for three years at Queens College, he joined the Congressional Research Service of the Library of Congress in 1970. His book, President and Congress: Power and Policy (The Free Press, 1972), was issued in paperback in 1973. He has also published widely in professional journals and national magazines.

The views expressed here are Dr. Fisher's and not those of the Congressional Research Service.

RECENT budget conflicts between Congress and the president have centered on impoundment and spending ceilings. The
two issues reached a climax in 1972
when President Nixon asked Congress to establish a spending ceiling
of $250 billion for fiscal year 1973.
If outlays threatened to go above
that ceiling, the president wanted
complete discretion to decide which
programs to curtail or eliminate.
After weeks of floor debate and conference activity—with intense jost-
ling over the politics and Constitutionality of the proposal—the
spending ceiling was rejected by
Congress. This controversy, by itself, yields important insights into
the strengths and weaknesses of the
two branches in their struggle for
budget control.

TAKING THE INITIATIVE

In his message of July 26, 1972
calling for a spending ceiling, President Nixon claimed that the budget
crisis had been precipitated by the
"hoary and traditional procedure of
the Congress, which now permits action on the various spending programs as if they were unrelated and
independent actions."[1] In his
nationwide radio address of October
7, the president warned that "excessive spending by the Congress might
cause a congressional tax increase in
1973." Not only did Congress fail
to consider the total financial picture when it voted on individual appropriation bills, it could not do so
even if it wished. It had no
mechanism to act responsibly.[2] John
D. Ehrlichman, the president's
domestic adviser, blasted the

"credit-card Congress" for adding
billions to the budget; he likened the
lawmakers to a spendthrift brother-
in-law "who has gotten hold of the
family credit card and is running up
big bills" without thought of paying
them.[3]

A large number of representatives
and senators from both parties
agreed with this assessment. Rather
than defending the record of their
own institution, they agreed that
Congress was, indeed, as irresponsible as the president said it was.
Members told their colleagues—and
the public—that there was no way to
return the country to fiscal sanity unless Congress radically revised its
procedures and organization.

While traveling around the country with ten members of the House of
Representatives, Richard Fenno observed this same pattern. The general approach was to downgrade
Congress. Each representative criticized Congress and portrayed himself, in contrast: "as a fighter against
its manifest evils. Members run for
Congress by running against Congress." On the spending ceiling
issue, the representatives castigated
the House from two different directions: (1) for giving away its power
of the purse—that is, letting the
president decide which programs
to curtail or eliminate; and (2) for
behaving in such irresponsible fashion as to force the president to
make the request in the first place.[4]

The president's attack did not go

3. *Wall Street Journal*, 27 July 1972, p. 3.
4. Richard D. Fenno, Jr., "If, as Ralph
Nader Says, Congress is 'The Broken Branch,'
How Come We Love Our Congressmen So
Much?" (Paper presented to the Harvard
Club, Boston, Massachusetts, 12 December
1972, as part of the Time, Inc. editorial project
on "The Role of Congress"). Reprinted in 119
Congressional Record, 8 March 1973, daily
ed., H1582.

1. *Weekly Compilation of Presidential
Documents* 8, no. 31 (26 July 1972), p. 1176.
2. Ibid., 8, no. 41 (1 October 1972), p. 1498.

altogether unchallenged. Writing for the *Washington Post* on October 31, 1972, Hubert H. Humphrey charged that after four years of fiscal mismanagement the Nixon administration was preparing an "election year argument to tell the American people that a Democratic Congress is to blame." If members of Congress refused to grant the president the spending ceiling, he would call them spendthrifts. In an election year, this was the same as being blamed for inflation, budget deficits and high taxes. On the House floor on October 10, Representative Hale Boggs sounded the same note:

We are told that these unprecedented budget deficits are the result of wanton, reckless spending by the Congress, but this, Mr. Speaker, is not true. It is part of a cynical, election year scheme to escape responsibility for the worst economic failure in forty years.

Gaylord Nelson propounded a similar theme during Senate debate on October 13:

Mr. President, the Nixon Administration, having lost all control of the Federal budget, is desperately looking for a scapegoat. President Nixon has decided that Congress must be blamed for the failure of his economic game plan and its consequences.

These voices, however, were few and far between.

After a stormy and emotionally charged session, the House of Representatives voted for the $250 billion ceiling, giving the president total discretion to cut where he pleased to preserve the ceiling. The Senate also voted for the ceiling, but placed restrictions on where and how the president could cut. When the two houses failed to reconcile their differences in conference, the statutory spending ceiling was dropped.

Phoenix-like, the spending ceiling emerged from the ashes, this time in the form of an administratively imposed spending ceiling. Secretary of the Treasury Shultz announced that the president had reviewed the budget and "now feels sure that he can hold the outlays in the fiscal 1973 budget to $250 billion, and he is determined to do so."[5] And, indeed, he did; he impounded funds for housing, agriculture, water pollution control and other programs.[6] The logic was hard to follow. President Nixon asked Congress for authority to cut spending; rebuffed, he announced through his treasury secretary that he had the power to do so, anyway. Then, why come to Congress in the first place? Speaker Carl Albert reacted by saying that the president had made a "monkey out of the legislative process."[7]

WHO IS THE BIG SPENDER?

The Nixon administration, boldly alerting the nation to a fiscal crisis, was rather loath to admit that it had contributed anything to it. When Secretary Schultz was asked if half of the blame was the president's, he protested: "Oh, nowhere near it. You would have to use a low number."[8]

Although the spending ceiling was rejected, the premise of legislative irresponsibility led to the creation of the Joint Study Committee on Budget Control. In its final report —dated April 18, 1973—the joint

5. *Weekly Compilation of Presidential Documents* 8, no. 51 (11 December 1972), p. 1752.
6. Louis Fisher, "Impoundment of Funds: Uses and Abuses," *Buffalo Law Review* 23, no. 1 (Fall 1973).
7. *Washington Post*, 7 March 1973, p. A4.
8. U.S., Congress, House, *The Federal Budget for 1974, Hearings before the House Committee on Appropriations*, 93d Cong., 1st sess., 1973, p. 148.

committee associated congressional inadequacies with the increasing size of budget deficits:

The constant continuation of deficits plus their increasing size illustrates the need for Congress to obtain better contorl over the budget. The Joint Study Committee has concluded that the failure to arrive at congressional budget decisions on an overall basis has been a contributory factor in this picture.[9]

Does it follow that large deficits, by themselves, demonstrate the need for better congressional control? Surely, something more than a *prima facie* case is needed. Why were the deficits excessive; by what amount; and during which years? The joint committee did not answer such questions. As to the source of these deficits, statistics in the committee report do not support the assumption of legislative irresponsibility. On the contrary, for in pointing out that the federal budget had been in a deficit position thirty-seven times since 1920, the committee noted that in thirty-two of those years the budgets were submitted to Congress with a deficit.[10]

For the Nixon years, table 6 of the committee report showed that the net effect of congressional action on budget authority—money available to be spent—was a stand-off. During fiscal years 1969 to 1973, Congress reduced the president's requests for appropriations by a total of $30.9 billion. At the same time, it increased spending authority on legislative bills—backdoor spending, or mandatory programs—by $30.5 billion. As for outlays—money actually spent—table 6 shows the following impact of congressional action for the five-year period: $10.5 billion

reduced from appropriation bills and $17.3 billion added to legislative bills. The difference of $6.8 billion is a rough index of the amount Congress had added to the public debt.[11]

Compare this to the budget deficits proposed by President Nixon during the same period. Stated in terms of the federal funds budget, which excludes trust funds, table 1 of the committee report shows the following proposed deficits: fiscal 1969, $11.8 billion; fiscal 1970, $6.8 billion; fiscal 1971, $7.3 billion; fiscal 1972, $23.1 billion; and fiscal 1973, $36.2 billion. The proposed deficit for the five-year period comes to $85.3 billion. The actual deficit was worse: more than $100 billion. That clearly overshadows the contribution made by Congress.

Actual deficits were higher partly as a result of the 1970 recession. The Joint Economic Committee has said that the subsequent recovery "represents a return from a recession that should never have taken place and that has cost the United States some $180 billion in lost output. As pointed out in earlier reports of the Committee, it was a recession resulting from economic mismanagement by the [Nixon] Administration."[12]

As a conservative estimate, the federal government takes 20 percent of national output, the state and local

11. This can be augmented, somewhat, by speculating on what federal deficits might have been in the absence of presidential impoundment. See, my study, reprinted in *Improving Congressional Control of the Budget, Hearings before the Senate Committee on Government Operations*, 93d Cong., 1st sess., 1973, part 2, pp. 318–319. This study also discusses the difficult statistical problems of measuring congressional impact on the budget, such as the ripple effect of add-ons and reductions on subsequent years.

12. H. Rept. no. 93–90, 93d Cong., 1st sess., 1973, p. 7.

9. H. Rept. no. 93–147, 93d Cong., 1st sess., p. 1.

10. Ibid., p. 7.

governments an additional 10 percent. Therefore, the loss of $180 billion meant a revenue loss of $36 billion for the federal government and $18 billion for state and local governments. Not only did the recession reduce tax receipts, it increased such federal outlays as unemployment compensation and welfare benefits. Moreover, by decreasing revenues to state and local governments, the recession made them more dependent on federal funds. An inflow of $18 billion to state and local budgets should have reduced the feeling of urgency for the $30 billion general revenue sharing proposal put forth by the Nixon administration.

On the tax side, the Nixon administration acted on several fronts to decrease revenues and, thus, added to the size of budget deficits. An administrative regulation on accelerated depreciation, as originally proposed and implemented by the administration, contemplated revenue losses of $10.9 billion for fiscal years 1972 through 1974. Congress revised the regulation, in the Revenue Act of 1971, to reduce the three-year loss to an estimated $5.6 billion.[13] Other receipts were lost as a result of the Revenue Act of 1971, a tax-reduction effort for which the administration took substantial credit.[14] As a final note, at the same time that the Nixon administration was impounding funds for various education programs, it was proposing a tax credit to assist sectarian schools. The estimated cost was $300 million the first year and $450 million each year, thereafter.[15]

From these statistics, one would conclude that the basic thrust behind budget deficits in recent years has been administrative, not legislative. The next issue is to decide whether those deficits were responsible for inflation.

DEFICITS AND INFLATION

For all the concern expressed about budget deficits, linking their growth and size to inflationary conditions, it has never been demonstrated that deficits in the last five years have been inadvisable or harmful to the nation. The only recent correlation between deficits and inflation is the 1966 to 1968 period, a time when the economy was operating near the gross national product (GNP) potential and also sustaining sizable deficits. However, the period since 1969 has been marked by recession, high unemployment and unutilized plant capacity.

Since the unemployment rate in the economy hovered between 5 and 6 percent, it is difficult to see why Congress should have substantially reduced the size of budget deficits. It could have done so in the name of fiscal integrity; fortunately, it did not. Paul A. Samuelson—professor of economics at the Massachusetts In-

13. *The Budget of the United States Government, Fiscal Year 1974*, p. 62.

14. Ibid.; see, also, *Economic Report of the President*, January 1972, pp. 69–72.

15. U.S., Department of the Treasury, *Proposals for Tax Change*, 30 April 1973, p.

82. For litigation in 1973 seeking release of impounded education funds, see *National Ass'n of Collegiate Veterans* v. *Ottina* (Civ. Action No. 349–73, D.D.C.); *Minnesota Chippewa Tribe* v. *Carlucci* (Civ. Action No. 175–73, D.D.C.); *Commonwealth of Pennsylvania* v. *Weinberger* (Civ. Action No. 1125–73, D.D.C.); *State of Alabama* v. *Weinberger* (Civ. Action No. 4101–N, 4103–N, 4104–N, M.D. Ala.); *State of Oklahoma* v. *Weinberger* (No. Civ–73–425–C, W.D. Okla.); *Commonwealth of Massachusetts* v. *Weinberger* (Civ. Action No. 1308–73, D.D.C.); and *District of Columbia* v. *Weinberger* (Civ. Action No. 1322–73, D.D.C.).

stitute of Technology—offered this perspective, on July 27, 1972:

Congress has responsibly insisted upon budget deficits that by historical standards would have been considered large, but which the anatomy and physiology of the GNP accounts have shown to be vitally necessary to turn an anemic expansion into a vigorous one.[16]

The same attitude was shared by the Joint Economic Committee on the fiscal 1974 budget. The committee supported a policy of an approximate balance on a full employment budget basis—that is, a $27.8 billion federal funds deficit.[17]

How much did the Nixon administration want to cut from fiscal 1973? When—on September 27, 1972—the administration's spending ceiling proposal was first reported out of the House Ways and Means Committee, it was estimated that in the absence of such a limitation the "level of expenditures could, on the basis of appropriations bills passed to date in this session, be expected to approximate $256 billion . . . your committee was advised that if such a limitation is not imposed upon budget outlays, either inflationary pressures can be expected to be significantly greater —with their detrimental effects on the domestic economy and international trade—or a tax increase would appear necessary."[18]

This $6 billion estimate was probably too high. Yet, to be enacted were the Labor-Health, Education and Welfare (HEW), foreign assistance, defense, military construction and State Justice appropriation bills. The first Labor-HEW bill, vetoed by President Nixon, was $1.8 billion higher than his request. When Congress passed the bill again, section 409 authorized the president to withhold as much as $1.2 billion. Of the other outstanding bills, State Justice was enacted with a slight reduction from the president's request. Defense was cut heavily: a $5 billion cut in budget authority which reduced fiscal 1973 outlays by $1.5 billion.[19] More than $300 million was cut from military construction. For foreign assistance, the House had already reduced the president's request by a billion dollars; on the same day that Ways and Means reported out the spending ceiling proposal, the Senate cut foreign assistance by another $1.3 billion. Congress was also about to pass the Clean Water Bill, a huge $18 billion, three-year package which far exceeded the president's request. However, only $250 million was expected to be spent in fiscal 1973.[20]

Ironically, at the same time that the president was accusing Congress of going on a spending binge, the administration was letting out all stops to ensure passage of the five-year, $30 billion revenue sharing program. Representative James A. Burke exclaimed: "To me, it is the epitome of hypocrisy for the same administration to pressure us on the need for cutbacks that only a few weeks ago was working with us to add another $5.3 billion to the deficit in the form of revenue sharing."[21]

16. U.S., Congress, *The 1972 Midyear Review of the Economy, Hearings before the Joint Economic Committee,* 92d Cong., 2d sess., p. 153.

17. H. Rept. no. 93–90, 93d Cong., 1st sess., p. 21.

18. H. Rept. no. 92–1456, 92d Cong., 2d sess., p. 2.

19. The outlay estimate for defense appears in U.S., Congress, House, *The Federal Budget for 1974, Hearings before the House Committee on Appropriations,* 93d Cong., 1st sess., p. 85.

20. 118 *Congressional Record,* 17 October 1972, daily ed., S18547.

21. Ibid., 10 October 1972, daily ed., H9371.

The impact on fiscal 1973 was even greater. Since the administration proposed that revenue sharing be made retroactive by moving it back to January 1, 1972, total outlays for fiscal 1973 were actually $6.8 billion.[22] In short, the cost of general revenue sharing was about the same amount that the president wanted to cut to stay within the $250 billion ceiling. This strongly suggests that the motivation behind the spending ceiling was not to fight inflation; rather, it was a means of protecting a presidential initiative at the expense of congressionally enacted programs.

The privileged status of revenue sharing was never in doubt. In September 1972 members of the House Ways and Means Committee tried to elicit from the administration a list of programs which would be exempt from spending cutbacks. The administration declined to supply such a list, but did indicate three areas which would be protected: interest on the public debt, social security payments and revenue sharing.[23]

Even if we were to accept the figure of $256 billion anticipated by Ways and Means, would an excess of $6 billion in a trillion-dollar economy have caused "significantly greater" inflationary pressures? The committee report offered no analysis or statistics to sustain that proposition. When the president resorted to impoundment, was that effective in curbing inflation? A 1973 study by the University of Florida Law School examined that claim. After carrying out economic model computations,

the study concluded that the withholding of funds did not significantly prevent or reduce inflation. The only measurable economic effect was an increase in unemployment.[24]

OTHER INFLATIONARY FACTORS

The administration's proposal to withhold about $6 billion in fiscal 1973 for the purpose of combating inflation was an oversell of fiscal policy. That is obvious now; it should have been obvious then. Despite all the impoundments toward the end of 1972, the situation with inflation dramatically worsened in 1973.

The inability of the federal government to control inflation solely by fiscal and monetary policy had been well recognized. In his economic report of 1968, President Johnson called attention to a number of industries in which prices had climbed persistently because of: (1) supply bottlenecks in labor, materials or capacity; (2) backward technology; (3) inefficient distribution systems or trade practices; or (4) other, so-called structural reasons. President Johnson concluded: "Existing Government organization is not effectively suited to dealing with the full range and dimensions of the problem of prices."[25]

A November 1970 study by the Committee for Economic Develop-

22. *The Budget of the United States Government, Fiscal Year 1974*, p. 163.

23. U.S., Congress, House, *Administration Request to Increase Debt Ceiling, Accompanied by a Spending Ceiling, Hearings before the House Committee on Ways and Means*, 92d Cong., 2d sess., 1972, pp. 20, 52.

24. See, 119 *Congressional Record*, 27 November 1973, daily ed., S21120–26, especially the sections on "Macroeconomics" and "Unemployment" on p. S21124.

25. *Economic Report of the President*, February 1968, p. 20. A Cabinet Committee on Price Stability—established by President Johnson—issued a report on the job market and manpower policy, industrial structure and competition policy, the performance of the construction sector and the trade-off between unemployment and inflation. See, *Studies by the Staff of the Cabinet Committee on Price Stability*, January 1969.

ment (CED) noted that while "appropriately stabilizing fiscal and monetary policies are clearly essential for the containment of inflation, it seems doubtful that these policies *alone* can fully succeed in reconciling price stability with high employment." CED observed that the pressure on prices stemmed from cost-push elements and longer term structural factors which were not readily influenced by changes in aggregate demand.[26]

On March 26, 1973 the Joint Economic Committee charged that the administration's economic programs had failed to cope with structural rigidities, such as import quotas, monopoly restraints, bad regulatory practices and poorly managed government procurement. The administration had done "nothing to initiate the economic reforms which would strengthen competition, make labor markets more efficient, and thereby make possible over time the achievement of genuinely full employment without inflation."[27]

If the administration's fight against inflation had been as robust as its campaign pronouncements, action would have been taken across a broad front. Instead of criticizing Congress for "throwing dollars" at social programs, the administration might have spent some time preventing the tens of billions in cost overruns on weapons systems—many of them technically incapable of meeting contract specifications. It might have lifted import quotas to bring in less expensive goods and raw materials from abroad, acted vigorously in

antitrust matters and pursued expanded manpower policies rather than the impoundment of funds in that area.

The president was also in a position to make the regulatory agencies more responsive to the consumer. He selects the chairmen—except for the Interstate Commerce Commission (ICC). By appointing commissioners he is able to change, within a few years, the composition of a commission into a majority of his own liking. The effect on prices by such agencies as the Civil Aeronautics Board, the Federal Power Commission and the Federal Trade Commission is direct and profound.

Wage-price controls were also at the command of the president. Empowered to exercise those controls in August 1970, six months later he was still declaring his firm faith in free markets:

Free prices and wages are the heart of our economic system; we should not stop them from working even to cure an inflationary fever. I do not intend to impose wage and price controls which would substitute new, growing and more vexatious problems for the problems of inflation.[28]

His game plan awry, the president radically shifted course on August 15, 1971, bringing wage-price controls to life in the form of his new economic policy. The record after that was characterized by ideological swings within the administration —oscillating between controls one moment and free enterprise the next, starting off with phase 1 and replacing that periodically, amidst considerable confusion and uncertainty of purpose, with phase 2, phase 3 and phase 4.

---

26. Committee for Economic Development, *Further Weapons Against Inflation: Measures to Supplement General Fiscal and Monetary Policies* (November 1970), p. 12.

27. H. Rept. no. 93–90, 93d Cong., 1st sess., p. 8.

28. *Economic Report of the President*, February 1971, p. 7.

A SYSTEM OF DUAL STANDARDS

Budget disputes continually remind us that the executive branch possesses certain natural advantages, while Congress is surrounded by pitfalls. The development of the full-employment budget concept illustrates that point. President Nixon's first budget to Congress in February 1970 advocated a balanced budget: "I have pledged to the American people that I would submit a balanced budget for 1971 . . . The budget I send to you today—the first for which I bear full responsibility as President—fulfills that pledge."[29] Less than six months later, facing a deficit of spectacular dimensions, he embraced the full-employment budget concept:

In raising the issue of budget deficits, I am not suggesting that the Federal Government should necessarily adhere to a strict pattern of a balanced budget every year. At times the economic situation permits—even calls for—a budget deficit. There is one basic guideline for the budget, however, which we should never violate: Except in emergency conditions, expenditures must never be allowed to outrun the revenues that the tax system would produce at reasonably full employment.[30]

Thus, instead of a $29.8 billion federal funds deficit for fiscal 1971, President Nixon was able to exhibit a $1.4 billion full-employment surplus.[31] Outlays were to be matched against the revenues which would have been generated by corporations and individuals in a full-employment economy.

29. *Public Papers of the Presidents*, 1970, p. 46.
30. Ibid., p. 601.
31. The federal funds deficit is taken from H. Rept. no. 93–147, 93d Cong., 1st sess., p. 34. The $1.4 billion estimate appeared in *The Budget of the United States Government, Fiscal Year 1972*, p. 10.

What would have happened had this policy innovation come from Congress? Let us imagine the tax and appropriations leaders, flanked by party leaders, announcing at a press conference the adoption of a new budget concept. Merely by calculating the amount of additional revenues which would have been available if the economy were operating at full employment, the congressional leaders declared that the previous $30 billion deficit had been replaced by a small surplus. Congress would have had an awkward time satisfying the press and the public on that score; yet, the president made the conceptual shift with only minor embarrassment.

Furthermore, he continues to make capital out of the full-employment budget concept, with unflattering effects on Congress. In his October 7, 1972 radio message, he likened the president's budget to the family budget:

In our economy, the President is required by law to operate within the discipline of his budget, just as most American families must operate within the disciplines of their budget.

Both the President and a family must consider total income and total out-go when they take a look at some new item which would involve spending additional money. They must take into account their total financial situation as they make each and every spending decision.

In the Congress, however, it is vastly different. Congress not only does not consider the total financial picture when it votes on a particular spending bill, it does not even contain a mechanism to do so if it wished.[32]

32. *Weekly Compilation of Presidential Documents* 8, no. 41 (7 October 1972), p. 1498.

The uninitiated would have concluded that the president was required to operate within the "discipline of his budget" by matching outlays with available revenues. Not so. The president was operating on the basis of the full-employment budget concept, matching outlays with revenues which the federal government would have had if times had been more prosperous. In essence, then, there was no difference at all between a "credit-card Congress"—voting funds in excess of available revenues—and the president acting within the "discipline of his budget."

Still, the president retains the image of a tightfisted budgeter while Congress has the reputation of spending like drunken sailors. As Senator Humphrey remarked: "Isn't it interesting that we get scolded because we appropriate more than the President asks for and the President asks for more than there is money to pay for. Who is lacking in what we call integrity or responsibility?"[33]

During hearings in the fall of 1972, Secretary Shultz defended the president's reliance on budget deficits to stimulate the economy as a "good thing and a courageous thing." Senator Ribicoff wondered about that:

I am still puzzled. If it is courageous for the President to build in a deficit in his budget, why is it less than courageous for Congress to build in a deficit in its budget? Why is it right for the President and wrong for Congress?[34]

Shultz replied vaguely that it was right for the president or Congress to use the budget to stimulate the economy "in a responsible manner, and wrong for either to do it in what I will call an irresponsible manner." That falls somewhat short of economic analysis. When this type of generalization is translated into real world terms, it becomes more concrete: it is responsible if the president recommends it; irresponsible, if Congress recommends it.

This is a strange commentary to make on a democratic system, but Congress remains at a disadvantage because its process is open, at least when compared to that of the executive branch. The public and the press can listen to floor debates, sit in on committee hearings and even observe some of the committee markup sessions. In contrast, little is known about executive proceedings. Log-rolling and vote-trading persist on the executive side, but we do not see it.[35]

As a consequence, the process and product of the executive branch appears to be more rational than the hurly-burly activities of Congress. We soon begin to treat that appearance as though it were reality, itself. A mystique of technical competence grows up, dignifying each recommendation of an executive official. The policy results can be disastrous and the predictions grotesquely in error. Yet, no one from the administration will concede that a mistake was made. Members of Congress, on the other hand, are continuously apologizing for the shortcomings of their institution.

The budget process is no exception. As Aaron Wildavsky has writ-

33. U.S., Congress, *Improving Congressional Budget Control, Hearings before the Joint Study Committee on Budget Control,* 93d Cong., 1st sess., 1973, pp. 87–88.

34. U.S., Congress, Senate, *$465 Billion Debt Limit, Hearing before the Senate Committee on Finance,* 92d Cong., 2d sess., 1972, p. 42.

35. Louis Fisher, *President and Congress: Power and Policy* (New York: Free Press, 1972), pp. 206–212.

ten, the executive budget is "announced by trumpet blasts from on high," while the legislative budget "sounds more like the Tower of Babel instead of the Heavenly Chorus." Congressmen are all too familiar with what went into their own budget and, like sausage makers, are somewhat disgusted by the product. They respect the executive budget more "because they know the ingredients less."[36]

CONGRESSIONAL BUDGET CAPABILITY

Congressional rejection of the spending ceiling proposal, together with presidential discretion to cut where he pleased, was not based on economic analysis or sober reflection of the facts on hand. It was more of a visceral reaction against delegating that kind of power. With its reputation damaged in the public mind because of Vietnam, Congress was not about to pass a domestic Gulf of Tonkin Resolution.[37] Members of Congress did not want to give credence to the view—promoted by Ralph Nader—that its institution was the "broken branch."[38]

However, in winning this particular skirmish, Congress demonstrated that it was ill-prepared for the longer war. Even when a few members of Congress were able to discredit the administration's argument, they had no effective way to transmit that information to the American people. The president's edge in public debate was too formidable. There was no center, no solid core within Congress to do battle. During debate on the spending ceiling, Senator Humphrey asked:

How many of us could find time on television; how many of us could get a chance to get up and explain our point of view? We might get three minutes on the Today Show and six minutes on the Tonight Show just before it goes off the air. But when the President, whoever he is, wants to put his ideas across to the people, the eagle has its wings up, and the whole Nation is called to attention.[39]

The press could have filled this slack by analyzing the facts available on the spending ceiling, but its coverage was spotty and often superficial. After Senator Humphrey finished another speech on the spending ceiling, Senator Hart expressed dismay that few people in the country—or even in Congress— were familiar with the points Humphrey was making. Hart had a "terrible feeling that some in the Chamber do not understand it, because I hear the suggestion made that we are the fellows who bundle up the money and throw it out the window. I look up at the gallery, and there is one correspondent there. How can we make it clear?" A few minutes later Hart had to correct his remarks by saying that the person he thought to be a member of the press media was actually a Senate staffer. Senator Mansfield added that Congress was a "sitting duck, a pigeon, easy to criticize."[40]

Congress is easy to criticize because it cannot, or will not, defend itself. It prefers to depend on infor-

36. Aaron Wildavsky, "The Annual Expenditure Increment," reprinted in *Improving Congressional Control of the Budget, Hearings before the Senate Committee on Government Operations*, 93d Cong., 1st sess., 1973, part 1, p. 494.

37. See, dissenting views of Congressmen James A. Burke, Richard Fulton and James C. Corman, opposing the spending ceiling; H. Rept. no. 92–1456, 92d Cong., 2d sess., 1972, pp. 15–21.

38. Ralph Nader Congress Project, *Who Runs Congress?* (New York: Bantam Books, 1972); see, chap. 4.

39. 118 *Congressional Record*, 13 October 1972, daily ed., S18044.

40. Ibid., 10 October 1972, daily ed., S17349.

mation from the executive branch, information which is often self-serving and manipulated to satisfy administrative goals. Congress delegates awesome power to the executive branch, but shrinks from delegating power or responsibility to party leaders, party caucuses, policy committees or internal staff support.

Dozens of budget reform proposals have been put forth since the fall 1972 dispute. Acting defensively to President Nixon's attack, Congress established a Joint Study Committee on Budget Control. The committee's report of April 18, 1973 recommended that budget committees be established in each house to fix spending ceilings and allocate spending quotas to the various committees. Complex floor procedures were devised to assure that subsequent floor amendments for increasing the allocations would have to specify the source of the funds, either by an equivalent decrease in another area, increased debt or additional revenue.

The thrust of these recommendations ran directly counter to two basic themes of congressional reform: (1) a stronger role for party leaders and party caucuses and (2) an increased sense of participation on the part of individual members. The April 18 recommendations were substantially revised by the Subcommittee on Budgeting, Management and Expenditures of the Senate Government Operations Committee. Membership on the budget committees was now made open to any member of Congress, without favored treatment for those from the tax and appropriations committees. The revised approach still continued to call for initial spending ceilings and budget allocations to committees.

On what basis can budget committees—regardless of their membership—decide allocations early in a session without first holding hearings and examining budget estimates in detail? On what grounds would budget committees decide the balance to be struck between domestic spending and defense spending? What special expertise would enable the members of those committees to choose between highways and mass transit, between space and education? For the sake of producing a legislative budget, there is risk in fundamentally impairing the participation of individual members.

Congress needs an in-house capability to strengthen its role in budget policy. The fall 1972 debate stands as a clear reminder of this. There is need of a joint budget staff to provide professional, nonpartisan assistance—a staff independent of any of the existing committee structures, free to serve Congress as a whole. Part of the duties of a joint budget staff would be to act as a clearinghouse for studies now prepared by the Joint Economic Committee, Joint Committee on Internal Revenue Taxation, Joint Committee on Reduction of Federal Expenditures, the General Accounting Office and the Congressional Research Service. The duties and functions of the Joint Committee on Reduction of Federal Expenditures could even be transferred to the joint budget staff.

Unless Congress can improve its budget capability it will remain a patsy, forever being bulldozed around by executive assaults and encroachments—no matter how factually unsound or spurious in design they are. Such capability is needed not merely to restore a balance between the two branches and to protect congressional spending prerogatives, but to raise the level of public debate and the quality of public policy.

The Press and the Committee System

ABSTRACT: Committees rely on the press to inform the public about their proceedings and decisions; the press relies on committees, their members and staffs as sources of information. Committee members expect their committee work to further their career and to enhance their reputation. Reporters, in addition to competing for the news, feel they have a critical function to perform. What results is a complicated relationship with ambivalences on both sides. An unholy alliance between the press, committee and staff can exist, with the advantage that issues and facts are brought to light, publicized and needed action is taken. However, newsmen may be used by the staff to float an idea or they may become coopted by the committee point of view and report the story less than fairly. Similarly, committees may be seduced into going for headlines rather than doing less sensational, but equally important, work. Both committees and the press tend to take shortcuts because of the limits on their time. The system the press uses to cover Congress favors attention to subjects and issues rather than to the workings of Congress, itself; Congress, preferring that the press know only that which it wants to disclose, has institutionalized the attitude by closing the doors to some committee hearings. This brings about a conflict in the relationship, as does criticism from the press. In the end, the mutual interdependence of Congress and the press contributes to the good points and the failings of each. While reform would help, the relationship is ultimately based on human values of trust, fairness and responsibility—which rest with the individual.

Mary Russell is a reporter for The Washington Post, *currently covering Congress.*

BEGIN with the basic premise that committees rely on the press to inform the public about their proceedings and decisions. Add to that the hope of committee members and staffs that their words and actions will be reported in a favorable light, thus, possibly furthering careers or, in rare instances such as those of the Kefauver committee and the Watergate Committee, making the members' names a household word. Begin with the premise that reporters must rely on committee staffs and members for information. Add to that the fact that newsmen can feel a certain responsibility to exercise a critical function in their coverage. Add, also, the fact that newsmen—as do congressmen—have ambitions and exist in a competitive world in which they are rewarded for scooping their colleagues or uncovering the big story. A complicated relationship between committees and the press emerges; it is full of pitfalls, dangers and opportunities for abuse—a form of love-hate relationship around which principles and egos swirl.

Media reports can be an important source of information to a committee and may even lead to a congressional inquiry. Watergate is the most recent and obvious example, although there are a number of others. Similarly, a committee investigation or hearing can develop issues or uncover scandals, causing the press to rely on the committee as a source of information. Obviously, the committee is one of the most important sources of information about the form and status of legislation under consideration. These situations can lead to a kind of unholy alliance between the press and the committee and its staff, one which can work to the advantage of both or to the detriment of both.

THE UNHOLY ALLIANCE

The advantages of this alliance are obvious: issues and situations which otherwise might not be brought to light are publicized, and needed action may be taken through mutual cooperation. The public is informed, the press fulfills its function and Congress has a forum for its proceedings and its individual members. The disadvantages of the system are somewhat less obvious. A newsman eager to get a story may be less critical than he should be towards the committee he is covering. He may become coopted by the committee point of view in his eagerness to remain on the good side of the members or staff. He may be used to float an idea, or he may become the type of reporter Warren Weaver, Jr., of the *New York Times* describes in his book, *Both Your Houses;* he describes members of the press who are so assimilated into the congressional scene that they become adjuncts rather than critical observers.

Weaver calls this phenomenon "institutional reporting." He claims that the Congress, itself, cooperates in the institutionalization of reporters by providing them with handouts, galleries from which to work, access to congressional leaders on a daily basis and a host of committee reports, bills and digests. They occasionally allow, in Weaver's words, "acolytes of the Establishment" to peek inside, or even to gain full admission to, the inner circle. "Protecting in print a source of important information through anonymity is one thing," Weaver says, "but withholding important information because it involves a valued source is another."[1]

1. Warren Weaver, Jr., *Both Your Houses* (New York: Praeger, 1972), p. 12.

The most serious result of this phenomenon is that the public never hears the bad news, nor does it get a picture of that which is wrong with the system. "There is rarely even any inference in this that there might be a better way to make laws than the closed rule and the filibuster, that an appropriation bill is five months past deadline, that a committee chairman is gently sliding from seniority into senility."[2]

While reporters can become coopted by Congress, Congress, just as surely, can become coopted by the press. The possibility of headlines may seduce committees into dealing with the sensational rather than slogging through more important, but less sensational, hearings or oversight matters. For example, when the Kefauver crime committee showed Frank Costello's hands as he mumbled over and over, "I refuse to answer on the grounds that it might incriminate me," they produced good drama; however, the legislation which resulted from the hearings failed to make very much of a dent in the activities of the Mafia or organized crime. Without implying criticism of the consumer movement, it provides one of today's opportunities for headlines. It is easier to find a dangerous drug and to hold hearings which emphasize its alarming consequences through the dramatic tales of the victims than it is to look carefully at the Food and Drug Administration in order to determine whether it is doing its job and, if not, what needs to be done about it. Alan L. Otten, in his article in the *Wall Street Journal*, notes that thorough studies of the shortcomings of an agency or program frequently do not pay: "Truly productive oversight can be dull, time-consuming,

thankless work, disregarded by colleagues, press and public alike."[3]

DEFINING NEWS

The problem can be partly attributed to the very definition of news. Although journalism students often spend a whole semester on this definition, a practical guideline might be that the importance of a news item is relative to: (1) the importance of people involved, (2) the effect it will have or (3) the magnitude of what happened. When applied to Congress, the definition means that a Judiciary Committee hearing on prison reform during which Jimmy Hoffa testifies will attract more media attention than will a hearing on the marking up of the farm bill—in spite of the fact that Hoffa's testimony will not greatly affect the outcome of the bill, while the farm bill will have an impact on more people in a much more basic way by affecting the amount of food produced and the price consumers will pay for it.

Thus, the press may by-pass certain committees no matter how valuable their work. Also, they may by-pass committees handling certain subjects, if those subjects are obscure, abstract or complicated—that is, too hard to explain in a single column of type. In a September column of the *Washington Star* William Safire referred to subjects which editors call MEGOS. These subjects are important, but so heavy, dull and abstract to the reader that an editor says of a story about them: "My Eyes Glaze Over."[4]

David Broder, a *Washington Post* political columnist, pointed out that

2. Ibid., p. 12.

3. Alan L. Otten, "Politics and People," *Wall Street Journal*, 6 September 1973, p. 14.
4. William Safire, "The Mego News Era," *Washington Star*, 6 September 1973, p. A15.

few stories were written about Senator Henry Jackson's Land Use Bill passed by the Senate, despite the potential impact of such a bill on the whole nation. The bill—which amounts to the first attempt the nation has made to get a handle on the way it will grow and to order land use according to some reasonable plan—has been touted by Jackson as "the most important bill" before Congress. As Broder said:

At the very least, I am now persuaded that the issue with which Jackson has been struggling for three years is as important to the future of this country as Watergate. And it is a matter of some chagrin that, except for the excellent coverage of the Christian Science Monitor's Robert Cahn, those of us in journalism have let it go largely unreported.[5]

Probably, one of the reasons that this is true is that theoretical long range planning has only a minimum amount of the proverbial "who, what, when, where or why" which makes for action or sex appeal in a story; thus, the bill made reporters' "eyes glaze over." Bad or sensational news, such as scandals, kickbacks, junkets, cost overruns or such charges as those made during the Joe McCarthy era, tend to be looked on as more newsworthy than calm, long range planning for the future.

How Congress operates—its procedures, rules and internal set-up —often falls into the dull category, also. It is a relatively sure bet that a poll of the public would turn up few correct answers if it asked what a conference committee does, what the difference between authorizations and appropriations is, what the Rules Committee in the House does

5. David Broder, "Land Use Bill: 'Important as Watergate,' " *Washington Post*, 1 August 1973.

or what closed rule, suspension of the Calendar and back door spending mean. It may not be essential for the public to understand such matters in order to understand an issue, but I think a case can be made that understanding procedures and protocols, as well as knowing the personality of key members of Congress, would help the public to understand the institution.

Understanding such matters might well lead to a public reaction against the way Congress works; yet, on the other hand, the general public's lack of familiarity with how Congress operates may account, in part, for the low esteem in which it is currently held. Thus, when President Nixon states that Congress is so involved in Watergate that other duties are being neglected, it may have some credence for a public unfamiliar with the fact that there are over one hundred committees and subcommittees functioning as usual.

Congress bears some responsibility for the lack of knowledge, since Congress exhibits an understandable ambivalence about press coverage. Members of Congress would prefer the press to know only that which they want to disclose. In many cases, the wheeling-dealing, the trade-offs, the manipulation of the process or the candid explanation of a bill's passage or demise are matters which congressmen would prefer not to have reported. This, of course, is precisely what most enterprising reporters would like to know; during this past year, the question of open committee meetings has vividly illustrated the clash of interests.

THE OPEN HEARING QUESTION

Rules which permit committees to close their doors to the public and the press have come under attack in recent years. Reforms by the House Democratic Caucus earlier this year have gone a long way towards opening committee sessions to the press. Now, a majority of a committee must vote to close a session to the press and public; furthermore, the vote must be taken in open session before the meeting begins. Even mark-up sessions—during which the real work of deciding what will or will not be in a bill takes place—are theoretically open in the House. Still, some committees—notably Appropriations and Ways and Means—have voted to close their doors on important occasions; Ways and Means recently decided to close its doors while marking up the Trade Bill. The Senate rules call for a majority vote to open the doors for mark-up and some other sessions.

There are many rationales for keeping the press and public out, for example: (1) senators and congressmen will not speak freely while considering the mark-up of bills if the doors are open; (2) deals formerly made in committee rooms behind closed doors will still be made, but simply pushed further back from public view; sensitive matters affecting national security are discussed, which the press and public should not hear.

In the minds of most members of the press, not one of these considerations—except, possibly, that of national security—overrides the consideration that a Congress elected by the public to represent the people should be willing to perform its work in public. That can happen only if all sessions, including House-Senate conferences to iron out differences in the versions of bills, are open to the public and press.

Warren Weaver, in *Both Your Houses,* goes further and insists that sessions should be open to television coverage, as well as press coverage.[6] He feels that this would create "instant familiarity" between people and their Congress and might lead to improvement in the system. The idea is worth considering, although the pitfalls—the grandstanding to which it might lead and, in a political campaign, the enormous advantage of incumbents, who have received that much free television time, would have to be carefully weighed.

CRITICIZING CONGRESS

If Congress resists letting the public find out what it does not want the public to know, what happens when a reporter goes on a search for just this kind of information? The press, exercising its legitimate role of criticism, does this in many ways. It looks at sweetheart relationships between committees and their special interests—between large cotton interest and the members of the Agriculture Committee, for instance; it looks at bills and how much money is spent, for what and whether congressmen are putting through pet projects; it looks at the effectiveness of committee chairmen and the way they run the committee; it looks at inaction on bills or failure to conduct oversight hearings. In all of these instances, the relationship between the reporter, the committee and the staff changes drastically.

Once the possibility that a reporter might be coopted or used by members of the staff no longer exists, it is likely that he will be cut off from information he cannot obtain in a public session. In such a situation the partisanship of Congress often plays into his hands. A minority member or minority staffer may be willing to leak the information to him; a disgruntled majority member

6. Weaver, *Both Your Houses,* pp. 15–17.

or staffer might do the same. In conferences it is sometimes possible to play the Senate members off against the House members.

However, none of this is quite as easy as it sounds. Staffers are naturally fearful that they may lose their jobs if they are found out. Committee members often feel more loyalty to their colleagues and the committee than they do to the press. Even if they think the press can help them prevail on an issue, they must take into consideration the fact that they are likely to need the committee's help on a different issue.

Outside sources, lobbyists and the executive branch can then become helpful. Yet, this normally leads to stories attributed to unnamed sources—a practice even newsmen deplore, since they feel their credibility goes down in proportion to the number of unnamed sources in a story. If it is necessary to protect a source, or if there is no other way to print a story, reporters will use the device. Since members of Congress often prefer the veil of anonymity when discussing anything controversial, the practice is increasing. Only agreement throughout the press corps not to use anything "off the record" could stop it; if only one paper or reporter adopts such a rule, they are merely cutting themselves off from stories. In fact, competition for news makes any such agreement unlikely.

Critical stories are less likely to be written by reporters who must come back and cover the beat or the committee again, since losing sources could cost stories. Some would say the answer is to rotate Hill coverage or to start independent investigative reporting teams, beholden to no one and not likely to have to return to those sources. Others would say that, in a negative way, the system imposes honesty on both press and the committee: a committee member who lies to a reporter risks being dropped as a source—for a story not absolutely accurate is not worth the risk to a beat reporter, while nothing will stop that reporter from printing a story he is sure is true.

MUTUAL INTERDEPENDENCE

In the end, then, the committee system and the press contribute to one another's good points and failings through their mutual interdependence. Some reforms of the committee system could be mutually beneficial. More openness in committee hearings would obviously contribute to better reporting. More and better oversight hearings would lead to more and better reporting of them. Placing more time, money and attention on the coverage of Congress would probably lead to a better Congress and a better informed public. Willingness to concentrate on those issues which are dull but important might spur Congress to do the same. Basically, the relationship between committee members and the press is based on human values of trust, fairness and responsibility. These values can be built into the system to an extent; however, ultimately, they rest with the individual.

Assessing the Congressional Committee System: Contributions from a Comparative Perspective

By GARRISON NELSON

ABSTRACT: The study of American congressional committees has flourished in recent years, but two major perceptual problems have limited the utility of this research for students of legislatures. One problem—the Washington bias—which deems Congress, and Congress alone, as the only legislature worthy of study has led to an overemphasis on minor intercommittee differences and away from an examination of the entire committee system as it relates to other institutions of the government. The other problem—the bifocal inference—has resulted in American political scientists focussing on only two elements in the legislative process, the committees and the parties, and concluding from the atypical American and British experience that their power positions are inversely related. Both problems can be alleviated through a comparative perspective which enables us to see that the American congressional committee system is the most powerful one in the world and that it derives part of its strength from the weakness of American legislative parties. While there is no necessary connection between party weakness and committee strength, this is the case in the United States, and it provides Congress with the protective mechanism which it needs to overcome the often fatal combination of an exertive presidential executive and a nonarticulative party system.

Garrison Nelson, who received his Ph.D. from the University of Iowa, is Assistant Professor of Political Science at the University of Vermont and the Director of its Political Data Laboratory. He has contributed articles to journals of opinion and has co-authored laboratory manuals in political analysis.

THE continuing interplay between a political institution and the society of which it is a part often obscures the fact that throughout the world there are many similar institutions performing similar operations in very different national contexts. What is lost in this obscuration is the sense of a comparative perspective which links these institutions to one another and provides an understanding of how these institutions shape behavior in a way unique to them and separated, somewhat, from the social fabric of their nations. The presidents of the United States and Honduras have more in common with one another in terms of what they do in office than either has with the chief justices of their respective Supreme Courts. To ignore this simple fact is to foster the illusion that all political institutions are indigenous to their native soils and that they are incapable of being compared across national boundaries.

This particular point is stressed because of the seeming indifference which many students of the American Congress have toward studies done on the legislatures of other nations. By depriving themselves of this rich area of research, many congressional scholars are unable to place the American Congress in its world context and to see what non-American legislative analysts have come to appreciate about its uniqueness.

It will be the purpose of this study to examine the American congressional committee system from two comparative perspectives: direct observation of the American committees by foreign scholars and assessments of the role played by committee systems in other parts of the world. Hopefully, these perspectives will help to liberate American writing about committees from two basic perceptual problems: the Washington bias and the bifocal inference.

CONGRESSIONAL COMMITTEES AND THE WASHINGTON BIAS

Ironies often accompany great intellectual advances. The serendipitous discovery, the accidental combination of chemicals and the insightful observations randomly encountered have deepened our understanding of the world. One of the ironies of American political science is that the classic analysis of Congress in the nineteenth century was written by a young scholar who never traversed the forty miles between Baltimore's Johns Hopkins University and the Capitol in Washington while he was writing his book. The book is, of course, Woodrow Wilson's *Congressional Government*.[1] Whatever deep and mysterious motives may have kept Wilson from Capitol Hill[2] did not obscure the truth of his observation that the government of the United States had, in the eighteen-eighties, become "a government by the Standing Committees of Congress."[3]

One major contribution of Wilson's book was that it blended the descriptive talents of a reporter with the prescriptive assessments

1. Woodrow Wilson, *Congressional Government* (Boston, Mass.: Houghton, Mifflin, 1885). The edition used here is the 1956 reprint published by Meridian of New York.
2. Sigmund Freud and William C. Bullitt described this occurrence as a "shrinking from actual contact with men and events," in their *Thomas Woodrow Wilson: A Psychological Study* (Boston, Mass.: Houghton, Mifflin, 1967), p. 27.
3. Wilson, *Congressional Government*, p. 56.

derived from a comparative perspective. His microlevel observations convinced him that Congress and its committees had abrogated the checks and balances created in the Constitution, while his macrolevel perspective suggested that the variance between actual American practice and the formal separation of powers could be eliminated by restructuring the governmental framework along the lines of the British parliamentary model. Perhaps because he was outside the ambiance of Washington, he was able to transcend mere reportage and to discern not only how the committees operated within Congress, but how they affected the role of Congress, itself, within the national governmental structure. Thus, he was able to analyze the distribution of influence on two levels.

Wilson's emphasis upon committees continues to shape much of that which has been written about Congress. In the past decade more than a dozen of the House and Senate committees have been examined in numerous books and articles.[4] There is no question that the academic study of congressional committees has flourished. However, with few exceptions, this vast abundance of material has been confined to only one level of analysis: that of microlevel concerns about specific chairmen, membership transfers, floor success and internal harmony or lack of it. The conclusions reached from this sizeable outpouring of academic contributions have been succinctly stated by Richard Fenno

in the closing chapter of his book, *Congressmen in Committees:* "Congressional committees differ from one another. And House committees differ from Senate committees."[5]

My purpose here is not to debate whether or not incremental benefit can be derived from more studies of more committees, but to suggest that, in pursuit of situation-specific pieces of information, the studies have lost sight of the American congressional committee system as a whole. This is a natural consequence of the Washington bias of most studies of congressional committees. Too often, congressional scholars have seemed to believe that Congress, and Congress alone, is worthy of study. This bias has led to an understandable exaggeration of differences between the various committees wherein minor personnel and jurisdictional changes have been enlarged beyond their actual impact. A case in point is the 1961 Rules Committee vote. All the House did in that vote was to add three seats to the committee, but each successive retelling of the story makes the event take on meaning beyond its actual consequences. The chairman retained his leadership post on the committee; the seniority system, which made it possible for him to occupy it, was left unchanged.

In any case, the most important fact of the American committee system is that it is the most powerful one in the world. Despite this fact, three major book-length studies dealing with congressional committees in recent years contain only one reference to the operations of committee systems in other national legislatures and none to those in the Ameri-

---

4. A short history of this development is recounted in Robert L. Peabody, "Research on Congress: A Coming of Age," in *Congress: Two Decades of Analysis,* ed. Ralph K. Huitt and Robert L. Peabody (New York: Harper and Row, 1969), pp. 17–25.

5. Richard F. Fenno, Jr., *Congressmen in Committees* (Boston, Mass.: Little, Brown, 1973), p. 280.

can states.[6] Perhaps it is the uniqueness of the congressional committee system which makes this level of comparison unnecessary, but it is this peculiar phenomenon of virtually autonomous, stable and seemingly omnipotent committees which fascinates most foreign observers of Congress.

PERSPECTIVES OF FOREIGN OBSERVERS

Twice during the past decade the Inter-Parliamentary Union has issued surveys of the structure and functions of the world's national legislatures. The most recent—in 1966—compares the American congressional committee system to those of fifty-four other legislatures and shows no hesitancy in placing the American system at the powerful "end of the scale."[7] Not since the collapse of the Fourth French Republic has the committee system of another nation been mentioned in a similar context.[8]

The greatest contrast exists between the American committee system and that within legislatures patterned on the British Parliament. As Kenneth Bradshaw and David Pring point out in their book, *Parliament and Congress*, "In no way is the difference between Parliament and Congress more marked than in the use each makes of committees."[9] They make their case with an industrial metaphor:

A picture of Congress today is of a great number of self-contained machines operating independently of each other. Parliament is itself one machine, of which its committees form a component part—a vital part, but one which has little utility except when fitted into place.[10]

Committees in these legislatures have little power to investigate executive actions or initiate legislation, unless the executive so wills it. Seriously handicapped by their lack of specialization, membership continuity and research staffs, most of the legislative committees of Great Britain and the Commonwealth traditionally could not challenge the authority of their parliamentary executives. The reason for this state of affairs was the belief, as enunciated by Peter Campbell, that:

Effective government in a parliamentary system seems to demand the virtual fusion of executive and legislative powers in the cabinet and the maintenance of the cabinet by a durable and obedient majority.[11]

Specialist committees were presumed to lead to the creation of crosscutting membership loyalties

6. The three books are William L. Morrow, *Congressional Committees* (New York: Charles Scribners' Sons, 1969); George Goodwin, Jr., *The Little Legislatures: Committees of Congress* (Amherst, Mass.: University of Massachusetts Press, 1970); and Fenno's *Congressmen in Committees*. Morrow's book contains one observation of Ralph Huitt's on the British system, p. 117.

7. Inter-Parliamentary Union, *Parliaments: A Comparative Study on the Structure and Functioning of Representative Institutions in Fifty-Five Countries* (London: Cassell, 1966), p. 164. See, also, K. C. Wheare, *Legislatures*, 2nd ed. (New York: Oxford University Press, 1968), p. 93; and Jean Blondel, *Comparative Legislatures* (Englewood Cliffs, N. J.: Prentice-Hall, 1973), pp. 66–70.

8. See the 1962 edition of *Parliaments*, p. 144. See, also, D. W. Brogan, "Comparison with American and French Parliamentary Systems," in *Parliament: A Survey*, ed. Lord Campion, *et al.* (London: George Allen and Unwin, 1952), pp. 72–88.

9. Kenneth Bradshaw and David Pring, *Parliament and Congress* (London: Constable, 1972), p. 207.

10. Ibid.

11. Peter Campbell, "Some Aspects of Parliamentary Government in Europe," *Parliamentary Affairs* 12 (Summer-Autumn 1959), p. 416.

which would erode this durability and obedience. Often cited in this regard was the Fourth French Republic with its strong committees and legislative *immobilisme*.[12]

Despite the cross-channel proximity of this particular horror, individuals who wish to reform Parliament have continued to look to a standing committee system as the type of legislative arrangement which can give the membership more control over their parliamentary leaders. As *The Times* of London reported after a 1966 survey of thirty-seven new members of Parliament (MPs):

Eight of those questioned supported the fashionable idea of specialist backbench committees, on the American model, able to question Ministers about defence and finance, and to influence them before policy was evolved.[13]

Not all of the British reformers have desired an undiluted American version of committees for the House of Commons;[14] however, references to the congressional committee system have been so frequent that a monograph on just this subject was issued in 1967, because the debate on specialized standing committees was "not always based on an accurate knowledge of the way in which these foreign committees work."[15] With interest mounting in some new form of committee arrangement, experiments with specialized committees have been conducted in Parliament and in other legislatures of the Commonwealth. The British experiment launched in 1966 by the Labour government was less than whole-hearted.[16] As Professor John P. Mackintosh, a disenchanted Labour member from Scotland, stated in a 1970 paper:

The Government decides what committees it will have, it dispenses with some as soon as they are becoming effective (as happened to the Agriculture Committee), it sets up others which no one wants (Scottish Affairs), it chooses the chairmen, and it nominates the majority of the members, while the power to send for persons and papers means exactly what the Government or the Department in question chooses it to mean. Almost every chairman or committee member would far prefer a post in the Government to his position on a committee, and even if, at the end of all this, there is criticism of the Government, it can be

12. Martin Harrison, "The Composition of the Committees in the French National Assembly," *Parliamentary Affairs* 11 (Spring 1958), pp. 172–179.

13. "New MPs Have Kept Their Zeal for Reform," *The Times*, 6 June 1966; reprinted in *The Backbencher and Parliament: A Reader*, ed. Dick Leonard and Valentine Herman (London: Macmillan Press, 1972), pp. 209–210.

14. Positions against the adoption of standing specialized committees for Parliament may be found in Herbert Morrison, *Government and Parliament* (London: Oxford University Press, 1954), pp. 155–159; and Brogan, "Parliamentary Systems," pp. 83–84. Positions for adopting these committees may be found in Bernard R. Crick, *The Reform of Parliament* (London: Weidenfeld and Nicolson, 1964), pp. 161–170; and Michael Ryle, "Committees of the House of Commons," *Political Quarterly* 36 (July-October 1965), pp. 295–308. Reflections on the entire debate may be found in the Hansard Society for Parliamentary Government, *Parliamentary Reform, 1933–1960* (London: Cassell, 1961), pp. 43–55; and A. H. Hanson and H. V. Wiseman,

"The Use of Committees by the House of Commons," in *Readings on British Politics and Government*, ed. Robert Benewick and Robert E. Dowse (London: University of London Press, 1968), pp. 258–276.

15. H. V. Wiseman's introduction to John D. Lees, *The Committee System of the United States Congress* (London: Routledge and Kegan Paul, 1967), p. v.

16. See, C. J. Boulton, "Recent Developments in House of Commons Procedure," *Parliamentary Affairs* 23 (Winter 1969–1970), pp. 61–71. An update may be found in Rt. Hon. Sir Robin H. Turton, "Reform of Parliamentary Procedure," *Parliamentarian* 53 (January 1972), pp. 69–74.

ignored or set aside by the use of the ministerial majority.[17]

Experiments in Australia and Canada have apparently been more sincere.[18] The initial evidence is incomplete concerning the success of these specialist committees, but the fears of parliamentary authority being eroded appear to have been muted by the benefits derived from committees with some degree of membership continuity and specialization. Even in parts of the world, such as Latin America and the Soviet bloc, where legislatures have not enjoyed the longevity or the influence of those in the Anglo-American democracies, legislative committees have expanded in number, activities and importance.[19] Here, again, it is the American committees which have served as the model.[20] Whether damned for frag-

menting power and responsibility or praised for providing specialized and institutionalized scrutiny of executive actions, virtually all of the comparative students of legislatures would agree with Winfried Steffani's judgment that the American congressional committee system is a "tremendous power which is not found in any other parliament of the world."[21]

COMMITTEE POWER VERSUS PARTY POWER: THE BIFOCAL INFERENCE

Despite their world prominence, the committees of the House and Senate are not in sole command of the legislative output of the American Congress. Internally, their major rivals for influence are the party floor leaders. As described in Stephen Bailey's recent study of Congress, the committees are "centrifugal forces" dispersing power throughout both chambers, and the party leaders are "centripetal forces" desirous of establishing coherent and cohesive voting blocs.[22]

The one area of congressional research which has not suffered appreciably from the Washington bias is that dealing with legislative party voting. While debates continue over the actual degree of variance in vot-

17. John P. Macintosh, "Reform of the House of Commons: The Case for Specialization," in *Modern Parliaments: Change or Decline?* ed. Gerhard Loewenberg (Chicago: Aldine-Atherton, 1971), p. 53.

18. The Australian example is recounted in R. E. Bullock, "The Australian Senate and Its Newly-Expanded Committee System," *The Table* 40 (1971), pp. 38–53. Canada's increased use of specialist committees may be found in Thomas A. Hockin, "The Advance of Standing Committees in Canada's House of Commons: 1965 to 1970," *Canadian Public Administration* 13 (Summer 1970), pp. 185–202.

19. On the increased strength of the committees in one Latin American legislature, see, Weston H. Agor, *The Chilean Senate: Internal Distribution of Influence* (Austin, Tx.: University of Texas Press, 1971), chap. 2. For references to Soviet bloc countries, see, Blondel, *Comparative Legislatures*, p. 67n; Vincent C. Chrypinski, "Legislative Committees in Polish Lawmaking," *Slavic Review* 25 (June 1966), pp. 247–258; and D. Richard Little, "Soviet Parliamentary Committees After Khrushchev: Obstacles and Opportunities," *Soviet Studies* 24 (July 1972), pp. 41–60.

20. Agor, *The Chilean Senate*, contains over twenty references to the United States Congress and indicates that Chilean senators

are very aware of the role of American committees; see, p. 69. Chrypinski, in "Polish Lawmaking," compares the Soviet area legislative committees to the American system on pp. 248–249.

21. Winfried Steffani, "Congress and Bundestag," in *Public Seminar Course in Comparative Government* (Berlin: Colloquium Verlag, 1965), pp. 24–41; reprinted in *Comparative Political Parties: Selected Readings*, ed. Andrew J. Milnor (New York: Thomas Y. Crowell, 1969), p. 302.

22. Stephen K. Bailey, *Congress in the Seventies* (New York: St. Martin's Press, 1970), chap. 4 and 5.

ing which is explained by members' party affiliations,[23] there is a general awareness of the fact that American congressional parties are less cohesive than those in other industrialized nations of the world. The high cohesion levels attained by the British parliamentary parties are the best known in this regard.[24]

The visible tension which exists within Congress between its powerful committee system and its often fragmented legislative parties has led some observers to conclude that these two forces are irreconcilable. Some support for this position can be found in the recent studies which have examined the relative floor success of individual congressional committees. These studies indicate that the committees most able to get legislation enacted were those which were the least divided internally along partisan lines.[25] With a full awareness of this tension, Malcolm Jewell and Samuel Patterson articulated a "middle-range" theory about the general relationship between legislative parties and committees:

There is an inherent contradiction between party and committee leadership. Party leadership is centralized; committee leadership is decentralized. Where committees are strong and independent, party leadership is weak. Where party leadership is strong, the committees are either weak or simply agents of the party.[26]

When the American convergence of weak parties and strong committees is compared to the British Parliament with its strong parties and weak committees, the causal link almost shouts for recognition: committee strength is inversely related to party strength. If Great Britain and the United States possessed the only two legislatures in the world, this inference might be true. But they do not, and the inference is not true. There are legislatures which possess both strong party leaders and strong committees, while there are other legislatures which possess neither.

The major problem with the inference is that it is bifocal in that it only considers two actors in the legislative process and uses only two legislatures to sustain its validity. By limiting the inference to only two actors in the process, one loses sight of the fact that there are circumstances when the committees may unite with the parties to protect the legislature's autonomy from encroachments by an expansionist executive. Furthermore, by being built on only two cases, the vast panorama of legislative experience throughout the world is dramatically reduced to

23. Compare two recent entries in the debate: Cleo H. Cherryholmes and Michael J. Shapiro, *Representatives and Roll Calls* (Indianapolis, Ind.: Bobbs-Merrill, 1969), pp. 106–110 on the importance of party influence; and Aage R. Clausen, *How Congressmen Decide: A Policy Focus* (New York: St. Martin's Press, 1973), pp. 91–100, for a caveat.

24. The earliest comparison appeared in A. Lawrence Lowell, "The Influence of Party Upon Legislation in England and America," *Annual Report of the American Historical Association for 1901*, vol. 1 (Washington, D.C.: American Historical Association, 1902), pp. 321–542—especially pp. 538–541. The best-known comparison appeared in Julius Turner, *Party and Constituency: Pressures on Congress* (Baltimore, Md.: Johns Hopkins Press, 1951), p. 24.

25. James W. Dyson and John W. Soule, "Congressional Committee Behavior on Roll Call Votes: The U.S. House of Representatives, 1955–64," *Midwest Journal of Political Science* 14 (November 1970), pp. 626–647; see, also, Fenno's case analyses of the House Appropriations and Education and Labor Committees in *Congressmen in Committees*, pp. 83–94 and pp. 226–242.

26. Malcolm E. Jewell and Samuel C. Patterson, *The Legislative Process in the United States* (New York: Random House, 1966), p. 203.

ideal types. This is not to deny the truth of the inference as it applies to present-day Parliament and Congress, but to suggest that the relationship between legislative parties and committees is much more complex. The simple beauty of the inference may be fatal to our understanding.

REASSESSING THE RELATIONSHIP BETWEEN PARTIES AND COMMITTEES

In an article on the seniority system of the United States House, Polsby, Gallaher and Rundquist gave recognition to the fact that strong legislative party leaders and strong committees are not mutually exclusive.[27] The authors categorized six national legislatures on the basis of two dimensions: (1) the internal division of labor through the committee system and (2) the centralization of party leadership control over the policy output of the legislature.

While the Houses of Representatives and Commons fell into their expected antithetical slots, four legislatures emerged in cells which counter the exclusivity assumption. Italy and Japan were cited as nations possessing both strong leaders and strong committees within their legislatures, while Colombia and Ecuador were presumed to possess neither within theirs. In the latter two countries, they point out that "decentralization of power without division of labor leads to parliamentary ineffectiveness."[28] Polsby's recognition of the relative lack of influence of these two legislatures

receives some confirmation from the Banks and Textor panel of area authorities who classified both nations as possessing "partially effective legislatures."[29] Later research confirms the marginality of the Colombian Congress, while consigning that of Ecuador to total ineffectiveness.[30]

Other examples of legislatures without influence can be found in the Middle East, Africa and in Communist nations.[31] Banks and Textor have asserted that seventy-two of the one hundred nations which they could reliably classify had legislatures which were less than "fully effective" in 1963.[32] Clearly, in these nations meaningful political power is absent from the legislature, and the question of whether the party floor leaders or the committees have

27. Nelson W. Polsby, Miriam Gallaher and Barry Spencer Rundquist, "The Growth of the Seniority System in the U.S. House of Representatives," *American Political Science Review* 63 (September 1969), pp. 789–790.

28. Ibid., p. 789.

29. Arthur S. Banks and Robert B. Textor, *A Cross-Polity Survey* (Cambridge, Mass.: Massachusetts Institute of Technology Press, 1963); see, "finished characteristics" 174 and 175.

30. Polsby, Gallaher and Rundquist, "Growth of the Seniority System," p. 789n. On Colombia, see, Ernest A. Duff, "The Role of Congress in the Colombian Political System," in *Latin American Legislatures: Their Role and Influence*, ed. Weston H. Agor (New York: Praeger Publishers, 1971), pp. 369–402. On Ecuador, see, Carlos Alberto Astiz, "The Decay of Latin American Legislatures," in *Legislatures in Comparative Perspective*, ed. Allan Kornberg (New York: David McKay, 1973), p. 115.

31. On the Middle East, see, Dankwart A. Rustow, *Middle Eastern Political Systems* (Englewood Cliffs, N.J.: Prentice-Hall, 1971), pp. 90–92. The African experience is recounted in Newell M. Stultz, "Parliament in Former British Black Africa," *Journal of the Developing Areas* 2 (July 1968), pp. 479–493. For the Soviet Union, see, Jeremy R. Azrael, "The Legislative Process in the U.S.S.R.," in *Lawmakers in a Changing World*, ed. Elke Frank (Englewood Cliffs, N.J.: Prentice-Hall, 1966), pp. 83–100; and John S. Reshetar, Jr., *The Soviet Polity* (New York: Dodd, Mead, 1971), pp. 198–208.

32. Banks and Textor, *Cross-Polity Survey*, p. 110.

more influence is not a very relevant one.

A more fascinating set of cases involves the legislatures which have been able to thrive with both strong party floor leaders and strong committees. Polsby's contentions in the cases of Japan and Italy are both sustained by subsequent research.[33] Committees and parties can be compatible within legislative bodies.

Further evidence for this assertion may be found in Sweden and West Germany. The five political parties in Sweden's Riksdag had a mean score of 93.4 on Rice's Index of Cohesion in the years 1964 to 1966.[34] This score compares favorably to the combined Rice score of 61.9 recorded for the House Democrats and Republicans during the same years.[35] While the party cohesion scores are much higher in Sweden, this apparently did not affect the operations of its important committee system. It is within the committees that Sweden's famous politics of compromise occur,[36] and their long-standing bicameral memberships were an essential component in bringing about the 1970 integration of the two chambers into one.

The West German case is also supportive of committee and party compatibility. The mean Rice score for the four parties in the Third Bundestag—1957 to 1961—was 93.6,[37] which is thirty-six points higher than the 57.6 score compiled by the House parties of the 85th and 86th Congresses.[38] With party scores at this level, the bifocal inference would lead us to expect a very weak committee system. This is not the case in the Bundestag in which, as Steffani notes, "a good proportion of parliamentary power and work is to be found and performed in standing committees."[39]

From an examination of these four cases it can be argued that in parliamentary systems with a number of well-disciplined legislative parties a

33. See the sources cited in Polsby, Gallaher and Rundquist, p. 789n. Later research indicates that the Italian committees are becoming even stronger; see, F. Consentino, "Parliamentary Committees in the Italian Political System," Journal of Constitutional and Parliamentary Studies 1 (April-June 1967), pp. 1–12. The categorization of strong legislative parties and committees in the Japanese Diet is also confirmed by more recent research; see, Robert E. Ward, Japan's Political System (Englewood Cliffs, N.J.: Prentice-Hall, 1967), pp. 87–92.

34. This score is a recomputation of 726 roll calls presented in Nils Stjernquist and Bo Bjurulf, "Party Cohesion and Party Cooperation in the Swedish Parliament in 1964 and 1966," Scandinavian Political Studies 5 (Oslo: Universitetsforlaget, 1970), pp. 129–164.

35. This is based upon the Congressional Quarterly's "party score," corrected for average party attendance in the 89th Congress; see, Congressional Quarterly Almanac 22 (1966), pp. 1028 and 1038.

36. On the role of Swedish committees, see, Neil C. M. Elder, "The Parliamentary Role of Joint Standing Committees in Sweden," American Political Science Review 45 (June 1951), pp. 464–473; and Dankwart A. Rustow, The Politics of Compromise (Princeton, N.J.: Princeton University Press, 1955), pp. 180–187; and, more recently, Joseph B. Board, Jr., The Government and Politics of Sweden (Boston, Mass.: Houghton, Mifflin, 1970), pp. 131–135.

37. Recomputed from data in Gerhard Loewenberg, Parliament in the German Political System (Ithaca, N.Y.: Cornell University Press, 1967), p. 357.

38. Recomputed from data presented in Congressional Quarterly Almanac, 14 (1958), pp. 123 and 117; and 16 (1960), pp. 139 and 101.

39. Steffani, "Congress and Bundestag," p. 301. See, also, Loewenberg, Parliament in the German Political System, pp. 191–202; and a critical view of the power of the committees in Wilhelm Hennis, "Reform of the Bundestag: The Case for General Debate," in Modern Parliaments, Loewenberg, ed., pp. 65–79.

strong committee system fulfills a crucial, integrative function by providing a less visible meeting ground for members. In the relative obscurity of a committee hearing, subject matter expertise is likely to overtake partisan rhetoric as a vehicle for generating legislation.

Whatever the case may be, two things should be apparent. The first is that the bifocal inference is of little help in explaining the relationship of parties to committees in most legislatures of the world. The second is that the United States does not possess either a parliamentary system or well-disciplined legislative parties; thus, the existence of its strong legislative committees must be explained in a different way.

THE CONGRESSIONAL COMMITTEE SYSTEM AS A PROTECTIVE MECHANISM

Banks and Textor listed the United States as one of the twenty-eight countries with a fully effective national legislature in 1963. Since this distinction is shared by 24.3 percent of all the nations studied and by 28 percent of those whose status could be reliably determined, this is not a particularly unique designation. Nor is it a surprising one in view of the fact that forty-five of the fifty-six other characteristics—that is, 80.4 percent—associated with the United States were positively correlated with other nations possessing fully effective legislatures. This indicates that Congress and its committee system operate within a sociopolitical atmosphere which is mostly, but not wholly, conducive to legislative effectiveness.

Of the eleven American characteristics negatively correlated with

legislative effectiveness only three were explicitly political and statistically significant. These three characteristics and their Yule's Q correlations with legislative effectiveness were: negligible interest articulation by political parties— $-.861$; the presidential system— $-.856$; and a significant degree of interest aggregation by the executive— $-.675$.[40]

Thirteen other nations shared these legislature-weakening characteristics in 1963.[41] According to Banks and Textor, the legislatures in these countries were classified as: fully effective—one; partially effective—one; largely ineffective—nine; and wholly ineffective—two. Quite clearly, these characteristics can be fatal to the effective use of legislative power unless some type of protective mechanism is available within the political system.

As an example of the need for protective mechanisms one can cite the recent history of the Philippines —the only nation other than the United States possessing a fully effective legislature in 1963 in spite of sharing the three debilitating characteristics. At the time of the designation the Philippines Congress had neither strong legislative parties nor strong legislative committees to

40. The technique matched two dichotomies: (1) nations with fully effective legislatures vs. nations with less than fully effective legislatures and (2) characteristics shared by the United States vs. characteristics not shared by the United States. The computational formula is explained in Lee F. Anderson, Meredith Watts, Jr., and Allen R. Wilcox, *Legislative Roll-Call Analysis* (Evanston, Ill.: Northwestern University Press, 1966), pp. 50–51.

41. The countries were: Central African Republic, Congo—Braazaville, Dahomey, Gabon, Ghana, Guinea, Ivory Coast, Mexico, Niger, the Philippines, Senegal, Tunisia and Upper Volta.

counter executive power, but it did possess a highly competitive electoral system which manifested itself in the legislature.[42] The two key parties, the Liberals and the Nacionalistas, alternated in their control of the presidency until the 1969 reelection of Ferdinand Marcos. In addition to this high rate of party alternation, the politics of the Philippines were "nationalized" by the fact that most of its presidential and vice-presidential candidates came from its Senate, which was elected at large. Ambition theory would suggest that a legislature so constituted will spawn public figures whose constituencies and interests would be congruent with those of the president, thereby checking the ambitions of an expansionist executive with the competing ones of its own members.[43]

The rhythmic alternation of power in the Philippines was halted by Marcos' reelection, and in 1972 the quarter-century experiment with American-style democracy came to an end. The fatal combination of the legislature-weakening variables undercut its existence. This can be seen quite dramatically in the official justification put forth by Marcos' new regime:

At the national level, the political parties were merely shifting coalitions of the local factions. Beneath their surface frictions, the platforms of the Nacionalistas and the Liberals were as interchangeable as their memberships. The balance of power among the factions prevented national leadership from innovating or making hard decisions about major problems. . . . The inevitable outcome of this democracy of stalemate was the decaying of society and the increasing impotence of political authority.[44]

It is apparent that the three legislature-weakening characteristics of the United States can jeopardize an effective legislature without a protective mechanism. Because the United States has an independently elected president, the conventional safeguards of a parliamentary system are denied to Congress. Also, as we know from roll call studies, the legislative parties lack internal cohesion. It is within this particular vacuum that the congressional committees function.

Article I of the Constitution enumerates the powers of Congress in section 8, but as Constitutional authorities continue to tell us, the executive branch has inserted its own authority within areas presumed to be reserved for the Congress.[45] However, also within Article I there is section 9, wherein is located the "power of the purse" which does, in

42. Jean Grossholtz, *Politics in the Philippines* (Boston, Mass.: Little, Brown, 1964), pp. 145–148 on weak party discipline and p. 122 on weak legislative committees. Confirming evidence on the parties may be found in Carl H. Landé, *Leaders, Factions, and Parties: The Structure of Philippine Politics* (New Haven, Conn.: Yale University Southeast Asia Studies, 1965), pp. 57–69. However, a more sanguine assessment of the legislative committees appears in Robert B. Stauffer, "Congress in the Philippine Political System," in *Legislatures in Development Perspective*, ed. Allan Kornberg and Lloyd D. Musolf (Durham, N.C.: Duke University Press, 1970), pp. 352–353.

43. This follows the logic of Joseph A. Schlesinger in *Ambition and Politics* (Chicago, Ill.: Rand McNally, 1966), pp. 127–129. Supporting evidence for the Philippines may be found in Grossholtz, *Politics in the Philippines*, pp. 119–120; and in Stauffer, "Philippine Political System," pp. 353–355.

44. "Building the New Society," in *Philippine Prospects*, a supplement to *New York Sunday Times*, 10 June 1973, sec. 11, p. 4.

45. See, Louis Fisher, *President and Congress: Power and Policy* (New York: Free Press, 1972).

fact, empower Congress to appropriate funds for the entire governmental apparatus and to inquire as to
their disposition. Recent writing on
the subject indicates that the executive oversight function associated
with the "power of the purse" has
become far more important to Congress' role within the American
political system than the policy-
initiation function which was envisioned by the authors of the
Constitution.[46] This is the vehicle by
which the committees can exercise
their influence.

Herein we see the role of the congressional committees in maintaining the effectiveness of Congress
vis-à-vis the president. Through the
appropriations process and the oversight function, the congressional
committees can take advantage of
their specialization and membership
continuity to shape the administration of government. In this way the
committees can safely abandon partisanship and adopt a stance of institutional protection. In an assertive
presidential system, such as our
own, there may be no other alternative for the legislature which wishes
to maintain its institutional integrity.

46. The best known statement of this view
is in Samuel P. Huntington, "Congressional
Responses to the Twentieth Century," in *The
Congress and America's Future*, ed. David B.
Truman (Englewood Cliffs, N. J.: Prentice-
Hall, 1965), pp. 5–31. A detailed examination
of both pre- and postlegislative control by
Congress may be found in Joseph P. Harris,
Congressional Control of Administration
(Washington, D.C.: The Brookings Institu-
tion, 1964). Contrary views expressing belief
in Congress' continuing role in policy initia-
tion appear in Ralph K. Huitt, "Congress: The
Durable Partner," in *Lawmakers in a Chang-
ing World*, Frank, ed., pp. 9–29; and Ronald
C. Moe and Steven C. Teel, "Congress as
Policy-Maker: A Necessary Reappraisal,"
Political Science Quarterly 85 (September
1970), pp. 443–470.

SUMMARY

By shedding the Washington bias
we can see that the standing committee system of the American Congress
is the most powerful one in the
world. Non-American legislative
analysts have been uniformly im-
pressed by its strength and resili-
ence in contrast to the weak legislative parties which inhabit the Capitol. While there is no necessary
connection between party weakness
and committee strength as the bifocal inference asserts, this is apparently the case in Congress and
may be a key source of its institutional power. Weak party discipline
may strengthen the overall position
of the Congress, much as it has
strengthened its individual committees.

Congress operates within an atmosphere which is mostly, but not
wholly, favorable to the effective use
of legislative power. The preponderance of favorable characteristics
does not fully negate the impact of
three crucial legislature-weakening
characteristics which manifest
themselves in the American political
system: a presidential executive, a
high degree of interest aggregation
by that executive and negligible interest articulation by its political parties. Institutional survival in such
an atmosphere depends upon a
unique solution to the dilemma
posed by the convergence of these
characteristics.

The apparent solution worked out
in the United States was the expansion of the power of congressional
committees and their shift from
policy-initiating bodies into executive oversight ones. This shift has resulted in a change of reference
groups. The most effective committees in Congress are those which
have most successfully subdued the

spirit of partisanship. Thus, congressional effectiveness has depended upon sending united committees to oversee the operations of the executive branch and not upon united parties. It is the committee government, which Woodrow Wilson so deplored a century ago, that has kept the American Congress from suffering the fate of other national legislatures. It is the American model of standing committees which legislative analysts of the world now see as a route to institutional salvation.

Committees from the Leadership Perspective

By ROBERT L. PEABODY

ABSTRACT: Party leaders and committee leaders in the
United States Congress, while sometimes adversaries, are
more often collaborators in the legislative process. Much congressional research has centered upon committee structure
and operations; another extensive focus of study has been
party leadership. Unfortunately, we have only a rudimentary
knowledge about the range of possible relationships between
party leaders and committee leaders. This paper explores several alternative, if not supplementary, mechanisms for
strengthening the party leadership and committee structure
in the House of Representatives. First, it outlines some developments taking place in the House Democratic Caucus
during the opening months of the 93rd Congress—1973 to
1974. Second, the paper speculates on the implications of
creating two new supracommittees—a Committee on the
Budget and a Committee on the Agenda—adding the party
leadership and bringing about a wholesale consolidation of
the remaining House committees. Neither House nor Senate
committee structure and jurisdiction can be analyzed in a
vacuum: what affects committee powers will obviously have
an effect on party leadership. It does not follow, however, that
relationships between party leaders and committee leaders
are a zero sum game in which the gains of one are necessarily
the losses of the other. On the contrary, it may be possible to
strengthen party leadership, to enhance the organization and
the effectiveness of the committees and, ultimately, to increase the overall powers of the Congress.

---

*Robert L. Peabody is Professor of Political Science at the Johns Hopkins Univer-
sity. A close observer of the United States Congress since 1960, he has been the
author, editor and collaborator on numerous articles and books, including*
Organizational Authority, New Perspectives on the House of Representatives, Congress: Two Decades of Analysis, To Enact a Law: Congress and Campaign Financing
and The Education of a Congressman. *An Associate Director of the American Political Science Association Study of Congress since 1965, he is currently completing a
long range study of leadership selection and operations in the House of Representatives and the Senate.*

PARTY leaders, committee leaders and rank and file members in the United States Congress, while sometimes adversaries, are more often collaborators in the legislative process. Adversary relations are primarily, but by no means exclusively, partisan matters—majority versus minority, Democrats versus Republicans. Of course, few roll call votes beyond the opening vote for Speaker in the House of Representatives are ever decided by strict partisan division. Both parties have their dissident wings—southern Democrats and liberal Republicans, in the main—and all parties have their mavericks. Moreover, conflict can, and frequently does, occur along regional, ideological, urban-rural and other cleavages. Generational resentments flare up in both the House and the Senate from time to time and may even spark organized revolt and the removal of incumbent leaders. Still, all in all, norms of accommodation and compromise are far stronger than those perpetuating conflict: to get along, go along; today's enemy may be tomorrow's ally; we are all compromisers in this body. These are the norms which are frequently voiced and, more important, practiced.

INTRODUCTION

Although few members of the House, not to mention those of the Senate, would consider themselves followers—we are all equal here and every member starts off with one vote—only a small proportion of either body could be considered leaders in any general sense of the term. Members will sometimes make estimates, such as: forty or fifty of us really run the House or there are only about twenty senators who really count. Regardless of the accuracy of these estimates, it is well to remember that leading or following are hardly independent concepts; they define one another.[1]

By and large, congressional leaders fall into four somewhat overlapping categories: (1) constitutionally designated leaders, such as the Speaker of the House and the President *pro tempore* of the Senate; (2) formal party leaders, such as majority and minority leaders and whips; (3) committee leaders, especially chairmen and ranking minority members; and (4) informal leaders, men whose intelligence, integrity, demonstrated experience or active pursuit of higher office have earned them an added measure of esteem or respect from their peers.

These categories are seldom pure for a variety of reasons. By long practice Speakers perform in a dual capacity: as the presiding officer of the House and as their party's principal leader. Since a Senate President *pro tempore* is by tradition the most senior member of the majority party, he almost inevitably chairs one of the major Senate committees as well. Informal leaders, while they may not as yet hold a committee chairmanship or position of ranking minority member, are quite likely to be high ranking on one or more committees. Thus, their influence is not unrelated to committee status. Seeking a Senate position from the House will not necessarily lead to higher prestige in that body, at least not until the aspirant is successful. However, the Senate's role as a presidential incubator in recent years has enhanced the external prestige, if

1. Cecil A. Gibb, "Leadership: Psychological Aspects," in *International Encyclopedia of the Social Sciences* (New York: Macmillan, 1968), vol. 9, pp. 92–93.

not always the internal influence, of certain of its members—a Kennedy, a Goldwater, a Humphrey or a McGovern. Even the losers who return to the Senate can occasionally convert some of their increased visibility and enhanced stature into legislative payoffs.

Ralph K. Huitt and David B. Truman, among others, have emphasized the main obstacles to central party leadership in Congress: the members' independent constituency base, the system of decentralized standing committees and the mediating and supplementary nature of American political parties.[2] Stemming from, and reinforcing, these political realities are members' expectations about what leaders can and cannot do for them and their sense of the strengths and limitations which grow up and around any given leadership position. From time to time strong legislative personalities, such as a Reed, a Cannon or a Rayburn, a Taft, a Johnson or a Dirksen, will enter into high office, infuse it with new vigor and, possibly, even succeed in altering the nature of the position. No legislative leader, no matter how strong his personality, can ever fully escape the constraints placed upon him by the collaborative demands of legislative leadership and the fundamental autonomy of his followers which flows from their independent constituencies.

Much congressional research has centered upon committee operations; another focus of study has been party leadership.[3] Unfortu-nately, we still have only a rudimentary knowledge of the range of relationships possible between party leaders and committee leaders. Lacking much quantitative data or even much systematic qualitative information, this essay will bolster what little literature there is with impressions gained from a decade of Congress watching, including an unusual opportunity to observe party leaders and committee leaders in legislative strategy planning sessions during the first session of the 89th Congress—1965.[4]

Although the subcommittee structure of both houses has proliferated rapidly since the Legislative Reorganization Act of 1946, the overall committee structure—other than the additions of several new committees—has not been drastically altered since the end of World War II. The House Select Committee on Committees, under the direction of Richard Bolling—Democrat, Missouri—and David Martin—Republican, Nebraska—held extensive

---

2. Ralph K. Huitt, "Democratic Party Leadership in the Senate," *American Political Science Review* 55 (June 1961), pp. 334–335; David B. Truman, *The Congressional Party* (New York: Wiley, 1959), p. 95.

3. The works of Richard F. Fenno, Jr., *The Power of the Purse: Appropriations Politics in Congress* (Boston, Mass.: Little, Brown, 1966)

and *Congressmen in Committees* (Boston, Mass.: Little, Brown, 1973); and John F. Manley, *The Politics of Finance* (Boston, Mass.: Little, Brown, 1970) are outstanding examples of the former; major contributors to the later literature—in addition to Huitt and Truman—would include Lewis A. Dexter, Charles O. Jones, Donald R. Matthews, Nelson W. Polsby and Randall B. Ripley. For more complete citations and an overview of this literature, see, Robert L. Peabody, "Research on Congress: A Coming of Age," in *Congress: Two Decades of Analysis*, ed. Ralph K. Huitt and Robert L. Peabody (New York: Harper and Row, 1969), pp. 1–73.

4. Many of the insights about the relationships between party leaders and committee leaders in the House of Representatives set forth in this essay stem from my earlier research on the Committee on Rules and observations made through access to the House floor during a six-month internship in 1965 in the office of the then majority whip, Hale Boggs of Louisiana.

hearings in 1973 and will presumably be bringing recommendations before the full House in the spring or summer of 1974. Resolutions introduced by Senators Brock, Mathias, Stephenson and others would create a similar vehicle for reexamining Senate committee structure, perhaps in 1974 or the following year.

Neither House nor Senate committee structure and jurisdiction can be analyzed in a vacuum; what affects committee powers will obviously have an effect on party leadership. It does not follow, however, that relationships between party leaders and committee leaders are a zero sum game in which the gains of one are necessarily the losses of the other. On the contrary, it may be possible to strengthen party leadership, to enhance the organization and the effectiveness of the committees and, ultimately, to increase the overall powers of the Congress.

To these ends, this paper explores several alternative, if not supplementary, mechanisms for strengthening the party leadership and committee structure in the House of Representatives. First, it outlines some developments taking place in the House Democratic Caucus during the opening months of the 93rd Congress—1973 to 1974. Second, the paper speculates on the implications of creating two new supracommittees—a Committee on the Budget and a Committee on the Agenda—adding the party leadership to these committees and bringing about a wholesale consolidation of the remaining House committees. Students of Congress are fond of contrasting the many differences between the House and the Senate: size, length of tenure, flexibility of rules, the nature of the constituency, prestige and visibility of members and so on. Most observers tend to play down their common features, including a similar institutional workload, an approximately parallel committee structure and a shared political culture. Without resorting to an extensive examination of the comparable and contrasting features of the two bodies, the concluding section of this paper discusses the political feasibility of some of these proposals, including their possible extension or application to the United States Senate.

DEVELOPMENTS IN THE HOUSE DEMOCRATIC CAUCUS, 93RD CONGRESS[5]

Tentative evidence for a more aggressive Democratic party leadership—one eager to create and use power—was provided in the opening days of the 93rd Congress—1973 to 1974. Once elected, Speaker Carl Albert of Oklahoma and Majority Leader Thomas P. O'Neill of Massachusetts appeared to be taking a series of steps to both consolidate and expand their institutional powers; their prime, if not exclusive, vehicle for change was the slowly awakening Democratic Caucus.[6] Instead of thwarting or uneasily acquiescing to reform proposals put forward by the leaders of the Democratic Study Group (DSG), Al-

5. The following section is based on a working paper, "Toward Centralized Party Leadership" (mimeographed, 1973), part of a forthcoming book, *Leadership in Congress: Stability, Succession and Change*, intended for 1974 publication in the American Political Science Association—Little, Brown Study of Congress Series.

6. Walter Oleszek of the Congressional Research Service and House Select Committee on Committees staff provides some answers to the question of why House party caucuses have become increasingly important in recent years; see his draft article, "Party Caucuses in the United States House of Representatives" (mimeographed, 1973).

bert and O'Neill now seemed eager to ride the crest of the congressional reform wave. Resolution of the question as to what extent the relatively new Democratic leadership initiated or merely legitimized some or all of these potentially far-reaching modifications would take this discussion rather far afield. In most instances the reforms are still unfolding; hence, evaluation in depth would be premature. It may nevertheless be useful to reexamine briefly some of these attempts at structural reform through the party caucus.

Committee on Committees

A resolution, introduced and adopted at the opening-day Democratic Caucus, added three leaders —Speaker, majority leader and Caucus chairman—with full voting rights to the Democratic Committee on Committees. The House Republican floor leader has long chaired his party's Committee on Committees, but with no vote. Heretofore, this committee, with its complete control over committee assignments and, hence, in large measure, the careers of individual Democrats, was composed solely of the Democratic members of the Ways and Means Committee. The Speaker and majority leader have traditionally been included as *ex officio* members. By and large, the leadership has been able to get what they had asked from this group, especially on a leadership committee, such as the Committee on Rules. However, leaders had no votes on the Committee on Committees and they would seldom attend its deliberations. In the 93rd Congress, Albert, O'Neill and Olin Teague of Texas not only had a vote, but they were each allocated a zone to represent the Democratic delegations of several states.

Committee on Rules

Speaker Albert used his newly acquired voting rights on the Committee on Committees to insure that the Committee on Rules, the principal scheduling body of the House, would remain loyal to his direction. All three new additions—Morgan Murphy of Illinois, Gillis Long of Louisiana and C. R. McSpadden of Oklahoma—could be expected to vote with the leadership most of the time. Thus, a revolution in leadership control of the Rules Committee, begun in 1961, had come full circle.[7] Although one or more of the ten majority members might subsequently leave the reservation, for the first time since the early 1930s all of the Democratic members would be nominally loyal to leadership requests.

Retention of the appointive whip

All but one of the four congressional parties—Senate majority and minority, House majority and minority—elect their party whips. A case can be made for the exception—House Democrats—on the grounds that the third man in the party hierarchy should be responsible to the Speaker and majority leader. O'Neill, the newly elected House majority leader, with Speaker Albert's quiescent support, argued for and kept the majority whip's position appointive at the opening caucus. The power to appoint obviously enhances the strengths of the top leadership, as well as minimizes

7. Milton C. Cummings, Jr., and Robert L. Peabody, "The Decision to Enlarge the Committee on Rules: An Analysis of the 1961 Vote," and Peabody, "The Enlarged Rules Committee," in *New Perspectives on the House of Representatives*, ed. R. L. Peabody and Nelson W. Polsby (Chicago, Ill.: Rand McNally, 1963), pp. 167–194 and 129–166.

potential conflict among them. Still, pressures to convert the position into an elective one continue; not least of the causes is the younger members' dissatisfaction with an emerging escalator pattern of moving up the leadership selection ladder—from whip to majority leader to Speaker.[8]

Toward a revitalized Steering and Policy Committee

In the opening months of the 93rd Congress the Democratic leadership also threw its support behind a reformed and reenergized Democratic Steering and Policy Committee. Albert's predecessors had been leery of such a policy body. Former Speaker Rayburn, in particular, preferred the more informal gatherings of a "board of education," late-afternoon meeting of his hand-picked associates and friends, tempered with appropriate beverages. Speaker McCormack had reactivated a Steering Committee in the middle 1960s; however, he rarely made use of it, let alone encouraged late afternoon hospitality hours. Under the initial DSG-sponsored proposal, Speaker Albert was to chair the committee with the preponderance of members selected from regions. Once the leadership decided to go along with the plan, they set about enlarging its membership so as to bring it under their dominance. The final compromise increased the size of the committee from fifteen to twenty-three members, eight of whom were to be appointed by Speaker Albert. The committee is charged with making "recommendations regarding party policy, legislative priorities, scheduling of matters

for House or Caucus action, and other matters as appropriate to further Democratic programs and policies."

Creation of a Select Committee on Committees

On January 31, 1973, with the creation of the Select Committee on Committees, the House took a major step toward what could become the most far-reaching congressional reorganization in decades. The extensive hearings of this committee are but the first step down a long and arduous road leading to recommendations, possible floor ratification and the even more difficult tasks of implementation. One observation, in passing: is it not time for Congress to maintain a continuing examination of its committee structure and work load through either the renewal of the Select Committee's life or a Joint Committee on Congressional Operations with a more broadly-based representation? The relative ineffectiveness of the latter committee's activities—created by the Legislative Reorganization Act of 1970—indicates some of the magnitude of problems ahead, no matter what the select committee proposes.

Modifications of the seniority system and committee structure

For the outsider, criticism of Congress almost uniformly begins with a cry for reform of the seniority system, however little the workings of that system are understood. In 1970 both the House Democratic and Republican parties created special committees to study the problem. At the opening of the 92nd Congress in January of 1971 both parties modified their methods of selecting committee chairmen and/or ranking

8. Robert L. Peabody, "Party Leadership Change in the United States House of Representatives," *American Political Science Review* 61 (September 1967), pp. 675–693.

minority members. Under the Hansen—Democrat, Washington—committee recommendations, any ten Democrats could demand a separate caucus vote on the nomination of a committee chairman. Furthermore, committee chairmen could no longer be chairmen of more than one of their subcommittees, and no member could chair more than one legislative subcommittee. Under the Conable—Republican, New York—committee recommendations, Republicans could now vote by secret ballot on the ranking minority members or chairmen of each standing committee, as nominated by their Committee on Committees.

In 1973 Democrats moved closer to the position already adopted by the minority party—namely, automatic secret ballot voting on committee chairmen. Although no chairman came close to losing his position in 1973, all were put on notice that their conduct would be subject to biannual examination, with at least the threat of possible caucus removal. Furthermore, some senior chairmen might decide to retire rather than risk the embarrassment of a negative vote toward the end of an otherwise distinguished—at least in terms of longevity—congressional career.

In less publicized efforts the Democratic Caucus also put into effect a far-reaching Subcommittee Bill of Rights. Building upon the major changes already brought about by the Hansen committee recommendations two years earlier, they adopted a Caucus rule on committee and subcommittee organization and procedures which required each chairman to call his Democratic members together "prior to any organizational meeting of the [full] committee," and to implement a broad range of rules dealing with the powers of subcommittees, jurisdic-

tion, staffing and the selection of subcommittee chairmen. The extent to which the Democratic members of the twenty-one standing committees met and complied with these extensive procedural and organizational changes, to say nothing of their longer range impact, awaits more comprehensive analysis.[9]

Moreover, even as these changes were being instituted, on February 22, 1973, reformers succeeded in pushing through two more restrictions of the powers of a committee chairman—namely, limitation on the use of closed rules and proposed modifications of the House rules which would open up committee deliberations to the public. This resolution was subsequently modified on the House floor to allow a majority of any committee to establish closed sessions. While experience with these reforms has been limited, they seem to represent a considerable breakthrough in efforts to dampen the impact of a strict seniority system, to open up committee deliberations and to limit the powers of an arbitrary or capricious chairman.

Yet, a word of caution is in order. Even given some slippage, any reform which reduces the powers of committee chairmen or ranking minority members would seem to strengthen the hand of the central party leaders, providing they are able to maintain the support of a majority of their colleagues in their respective party caucuses. However, it does not necessarily follow that all efforts to create more or less au-

9. For an excellent first assessment, see, Norman J. Ornstein, "Causes and Consequences of Congressional Change: Subcommittee Reforms in the House of Representatives, 1970–73" (Paper delivered at the 1973 American Political Science Association Annual Meeting, New Orleans, Louisiana, 7 September 1973).

tonomous subcommittees will, in the long run, work to ease the tasks of the party generalists or aid the leaders in bringing about more coordinated and improved legislative programs. Indeed, the proliferation of subcommittee autonomy could lead to one hundred thirty little fiefdoms, instead of the present twenty-one decentralized power centers and, thus, could further complicate the already difficult challenges of ordering priorities and scheduling legislation for floor debate and passage.

Perhaps it is time to take a bold, even audacious, look at committee structuring—a reorganization with more clear-cut lines of authority and appointment of committee chairmen in a way which would promote greater loyalty and responsibility to the central party leaders and caucuses. The proposed formation of House and Senate Committees on the Budget highlight some of the problems of committee reorganization and actual or potential power struggles between party leaders and committee leaders, in this instance, with senior members of the Appropriations and Ways and Means Committees.

PROPOSED MODIFICATIONS IN COMMITTEE STRUCTURE[10]

Committee on the Budget

Without getting overly involved in the substantive questions posed by the recommendations of the Joint Study Committee on Budget Control, the proposed creation of two suprabudget committees—one House and one Senate—leads directly into the broader problem of committee structure in the two chambers. As set forth in H.R. 7130, and its counterpart Senate bill, S. 1641, the House committee would consist of twenty-one members: seven members from the Appropriations Committee, seven members from the Ways and Means Committee and seven members selected at large. The Senate Committee would be composed of fifteen members, similarly broken down in thirds. According to the joint study committee:

Drawing on the appropriations and tax committees for two-thirds of the membership of each of the Budget Committees means that in effect these budgetary decisions at the committee level, to a substantial degree, will continue to be made by the financial committees of the House and Senate which have basic responsibilities in these areas. At the same time, the one-third representation on these committees of the legislative committees of the House and Senate means that their views also will be well represented.[11]

It hardly seems likely. In effect, the eighty members of the already elite financial committees will have fourteen spokesmen; the remaining three hundred fifty-five members of the other nineteen standing committees of the House will have seven to represent their collective interests. Decisions about national priorities will be made not at the committee

10. These proposals were first set forth in "House Leadership, Party Caucuses and the Committee Structure," *Working Papers on House Committee Organization and Operation*, House Select Committee on Committees, 93rd Cong., 1st sess. (Washington, D.C.: Government Printing Office, 1973).

11. U.S., Congress, Report of the Joint Study Committee on Budget Control, "Recommendations for Improving Congressional Control Over Budgetary Outlay and Receipt Totals," 93rd Cong., 1st sess. (Washington, D.C.: Government Printing Office, 1973), p. 18.

level, but at a supracommittee level.[12]

The overall concept of a congressional budget as a means of restoring the waning powers of Congress in an age increasingly characterized by executive encroachments has a powerful attraction, at least to this student. However, at a minimum, it requires an extended base of representation—with, perhaps, no more than three to five members from both Appropriations and Ways and Means and with a majority of members selected at large. In this age of rapidly advancing technology and increasingly scarce resources, no single committee has a monopoly on the necessary information for establishing overall priorities. A more diversified committee would be not only more representative of the House, but would probably be better prepared to develop a strong consensus behind the concurrent resolutions as they came from the Budget Committees. As experience with presidential veto messages has dem-

12. One way to minimize some of the problems of establishing new supracommittees, especially the excessive workloads of its members, would be to make them exclusive committees—that is, once a member was selected, he would be required to give up his present assignments on other committees, such as Ways and Means or Appropriations. Provisions could also be attached calling for staggered terms and rotation off the Budget Committee after four to six years. Further incentives to serve on these important committees would be guaranteed if seniority rights on original committees were maintained. In other words, a member having served on the Committee on Budget could return to Appropriations or Public Works and regain the same seniority level he ordinarily would have achieved had he never left the committee. The former provisions could be written into the original legislation; the latter could be accommodated by actions in the respective House and Senate party caucuses or conferences.

onstrated throughout 1973, only a nearly united majority, with considerable help from the minority party, has any chance of promoting its policy preferences in the face of determined executive branch opposition.

Furthermore, it seems imperative that both the majority and minority leadership be represented on any such priority-setting committee. H.R. 7130 would provide for the Speaker to appoint the seven at-large members. An alternative measure, S. 1541, introduced by Senator Ervin of North Carolina would leave selection processes the same as those for other standing committees. Should the bill survive congressional action—to say nothing of a presidential veto—the Speaker should appoint himself and/or the majority leader as well as the minority leader. Participation by the central party leadership would be useful in establishing national priorities; inevitably, they must play a major role in the implementation of whatever outcomes flow from committee deliberations. Even though time constraints may prevent them from being full time working members, majority and minority leadership perspectives need to be represented from the beginning.

Committee on Agenda

When Speaker Carl Albert testified before the House Select Committee on Committees in the spring of 1973, he urged this group to give special attention to problems of agenda setting, scheduling and legislative workloads. He outlined a number of procedures which might make the process more orderly, ensure the flow of more bills in the early months of a session and help balance out the workload before the almost inevitable legislative logjam at the end.

To any long time student of the Committee on Rules, the following proposal may sound like still further heresy. I wonder if the time has not come to set aside fears of a possible return of Cannonism to the House and to replace the Speaker as the chairman of the Rules Committee. The committee would be reconstituted as a Committee on the Agenda. A small membership would seem most appropriate—no more than nine congressmen, six in the majority and three in the minority. Preferably, the Speaker would preside over the committee and the minority leader should serve as the ranking minority member. Both should have the power to appoint their remaining party members, subject, of course, to ratification by their respective party caucuses.

The primary function of the Committee on Agenda—not unlike that of the present Committee on Rules —would be to control the flow of legislation to the floor. Testimony by floor managers of legislation, majority and minority, would be restricted to short statements about the contents of the bill and the traditional questions about the type of special order desired, the time of debate and the like. Ideally, the committee should move away from what largely preoccupies the present Rules Committee—namely, prefloor hearings on the substance of legislation; instead, it would primarily make procedural decisions. If this latter objective could be achieved, then the time demands on top leaders should not prove unduly burdensome. Present original jurisdictions over rules changes and other such matters could be reassigned to a subcommittee of a reconstituted House

Rules and Administration Committee—not unlike that of the Senate.

It can be argued that these proposals ask too much of already heavily burdened leaders—putting them on two powerful special committees, when at present they serve on none. Yet, what is being recommended is but the institutionalization of much of that which already preoccupies the Speaker and, to a lesser extent, the majority and minority leaders: setting of floor agendas, establishing legislative priorities, assisting in the coordination of the powers of taxation and appropriation and planning and implementing floor strategies for the parties. This is not to minimize other functions of the Speaker, such as presiding over the House, controlling space and representing his party and the House to the nation. Party leaders should be allocated additional professional and clerical staff to carry out their increasing responsibilities. Compared to the president or even the typical cabinet head, congressional party leaders are woefully understaffed.

Having long since abandoned a usual caution and preference for incremental change, let me conclude with an even more audacious, if not radical proposal—a proposed wholesale consolidation of the present House committee structure.

Consolidation of committees

The need to reexamine committee jurisdictions in the light of changing work loads has been stressed by any number of members testifying before the House select committee, including former Minority Leader Gerald Ford. Not surprisingly most members testified that the jurisdictions of their own committees could, and should, be expanded; few offered to relinquish currently held powers or urged the demise of their own committees. One probable approach to what is inevitably an exercise in the distribution of power would remain largely incremental. Assessments of committee work loads would be made; attempts to balance them out among the existing committees would be undertaken. Perhaps the Committee on Education and Labor would be separated; other committees might be consolidated; a committee or two might even be abolished. In a body in which committee jurisdictions are jealously protected and aggrandizement of power is inevitably the name of the game, perhaps piecemeal modifications of the committee structure are all that is politically feasible. However, if one may speculate merely to raise pertinent issues, why not at least consider a different,

far more modern committee structure? There is, after all, the precedent set by the Legislative Reorganization Act of 1946—for better or for worse, depending, as always, on one's policy preferences.

In that speculative spirit of a major consolidation of committees, then, I would like to propose retaining the two-tiered structure of committees and subcommittees, but with both rather drastically reduced in number (see chart). Overall, there would be ten House committees: two special —a Committee on the Agenda and a Committee on the Budget—and eight standing committees—

—Government Operations, including oversight, House Administration, part of Rules and the District of Columbia;
—Technology and Sciences, including Space, Transportation and so on;

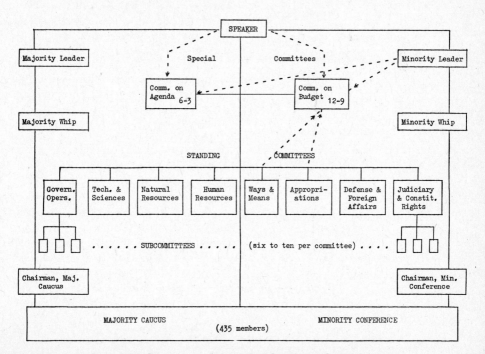

PROPOSED CONSOLIDATION OF THE STANDING COMMITTEES

—Natural Resources, including Interior, Public Works and so on;

—Human Resources, including Education, Welfare and Labor; conceivably, this might necessitate two committees;

—Ways and Means, including Revenue Raising, but, perhaps, with Welfare and Trade allocated to other committees;

—Appropriations, mainly a matter of reorganized subcommittees;

—Defense and Foreign Policy, given their inevitable interrelationship, perhaps it is time they were combined; this might also include jurisdiction over international banks and trade;

—Judiciary and Constitutional Rights.

I hold no strong brief for this particular breakdown; I think there are clear benefits in keeping the number of committees to eight or ten. These benefits include: a streamlining of authority and a reduction of the fragmentation which characterizes the existing committee structure, more effective use of members' time and better utilization of staff. No structure, no matter how designed, would ever eliminate a duplication of efforts or conflicts over jurisdiction. However, it is quite likely that a streamlined structure would simplify these problems. Any structure is outmoded even as it comes into existence.

Every member of the House would be assigned to one regular standing committee with transfers permitted whenever vacancies open up. With the exception of the two special committees, each committee would be an exclusive one and average about fifty-five members in number. Obviously, the size of such umbrella committees poses addi-

tional problems. I suspect that, as with the Appropriations Committees, subcommittees would become the prime focus of power. The chairman of each committee would be appointed by the Speaker, ratified by the majority caucus and approved by the full House. In order to spread power around, there might be a limit on the time any one member could serve as chairman—say, for five terms.

Each regular standing committee would be authorized to create six to ten subcommittees, with each member assigned to no more than two subcommittees—fifty to seventy in total. A strong argument can be made for rather tightly drawn jurisdictions for each subcommittee, tempered by the further flexibility that two or more subcommittees could meet on common problems across committee lines. In other words, subcommittees would be utilized as building blocks to form different combinations to meet different problems. When considering a bill all subcommittees with overlapping jurisdictions would be invited to meet, hold common hearings, mark-up and report out a consensus bill. Which standing committee would receive final jurisdiction would be largely determined by the predominance of the subject matter, but the Speaker would have final authority to resolve jurisdictional disputes. In the case of competing or overlapping bills, the Committee on the Agenda would be empowered to decide the form of the special order for consideration on the floor—as, for example, the procedures were worked out to consider bills from Commerce and House Administration, which eventually became the Federal Election Campaign Act of 1972.

CONCLUSIONS

I would not wish to underestimate the difficulties of bringing about even a more modest committee reorganization than has been proposed here. Nevertheless, I am convinced that the long range benefits to be gained by such a plan are substantial: a committee structure in which responsibilities can be assigned; a more effective legislative process; stronger House leadership; and an overall gain in stature for the House, both in the eyes of the citizenry and in real power vis-à-vis the executive branch. The choice is never clear cut. One path, the incremental approach, seems to lead to a furtherance of intramural struggles over who hangs on to the existing power. The alternative approach has, at least, the long range potential of restoring the House to its proper role in our system of separation of powers—that is, to a continuing parity with the other branches of government.

What of the Senate, its leadership and committee structure? I see no compelling reasons why its organization should necessarily parallel that of the House of Representatives. Unlike the clear separation of tasks and frequently built-in conflict between party leaders and committee leaders in the House, the Senate is characterized by much more informality, nonpartisanship and an unusually high degree of collaboration between and among its floor leaders, their assistants, the committee chairmen and ranking minority members. All four principal Senate party leaders participate actively in at least two standing committees and, indeed, average almost four subcommittee chairmanships or ranking minority positions. The time has long since passed when a top party leader would hold that position

simultaneously with a committee chairmanship, but as recently as 1966–1968, Senator Russell Long of Louisiana did manage to serve as both Chairman of the Senate Finance Committee and majority whip; his emphasis on the former role to the neglect of the latter contributed to his subsequent loss of that position to Senator Edward Kennedy in January of 1969.[13]

It would be misleading to conclude from the leaders' involvement in committee activities that leadership in the Senate is any less demanding than it is in the House. However, it does seem clear that the smaller size and more collegial atmosphere of the Senate allow leaders more time to pursue their own legislative interests and committee activities. On occasion, a Mike Mansfield can combine his role as leader with pursuance of a prime interest in foreign policy questions. Still, it would appear that for most leaders committee activities remain more peripheral than central.

Coupled with the size discrepancy between the two bodies, it also seems to follow that House committees are more likely to come to the floor in an adversary relationship to the rest of the body. Especially with regard to major legislation, committee leaders tend to be preoccupied with protecting their bills before the onslaughts of their colleagues, Democrats as well as Republicans. Senate committee leaders appear more tolerant of floor amendments; distinctions between committee members and noncommittee members are generally blurred. As Fenno concludes in his masterful compara-

13. "Selections of A Senate Majority Whip: Long, 1965; Kennedy, 1969," chap. 14 in Peabody, *Leadership in Congress*.

tive study of *Congressmen in Committees:*

Since the House and Senate are different institutions, it should not be surprising that their committees are also different. Senate committees are less important as a source of chamber influence, less preoccupied with success on the chamber floor, less autonomous within the chamber, less personally expert, less strongly led, and more individualistic in decision making than are House committees.[14]

A strong case can be made that the Senate should also undertake a thorough study of its committee structure and jurisdictions, although their problems seem less acute than those in the House and, thus, a more leisurely timetable would seem to be appropriate. None of the resolutions introduced at the beginning of the 93rd Congress have cleared the Senate Rules and Administration Committee as the first session is drawing to a close. Perhaps, those advocating reforms should bide their time, go to school on the findings, recommendations and results of the House Select Committee on Com-

14. Richard F. Fenno, Jr., *Congressmen in Committees*, pp. 190–191.

mittees and negotiate an agreement with their party leaders such that a Senate select committee, or a Joint Committee on Congressional Operations Study, could be launched early in the 94th Congress—1975–1976. It is quite likely that a prestigious, broad-based Senate committee could improve upon whatever final recommendations are proposed and adopted by the House. Certainly, it would have the advantage of hindsight and the benefits of a similar two-year pacing of the study and its implementation. The question of whether the Senate should attempt to modify its structure to bring it more in line with the House must remain an open one until the Bolling-Martin select committee experiment has come to full fruition. The ultimate standard for the Senate must not be what the House achieves or fails to achieve. Rather, its members must ask themselves: how can we streamline our structures and procedures so as to enable both members and staff to anticipate, not merely react to, public needs? How can we best meet the challenges which will inevitably confront the Senate, the Congress and the country as we enter into the last quarter of the twentieth century?

Towards Restructuring the Congressional Committee System

By NORMAN J. ORNSTEIN

ABSTRACT: While the standing committee structures of the House of Representatives and Senate have functioned well for their legislative systems, some endemic problems remain. Because individual legislators have different backgrounds, interests and goals, and because committees have varying attractiveness for members, a natural selection process builds a distinct bias into committee assignments, overrepresenting those with special interests in the subject matter of the committee. Thus, rural legislators dominate the Agriculture and Public Works Committees; port area congressmen, Merchant Marine and Fisheries. The problem is especially acute in the House, where congressmen have only one or two committee assignments, and reformers have recently strengthened the powers of committee caucuses and subcommittees. Several large scale reforms are suggested to make committees more representative of the larger legislative entity and, thus, to improve the formulation of national public policy. For the House these reforms include: (1) consolidating standing committees to a total of seven or eight; (2) limiting the tenure of committee chairmen to prevent long term accumulations of power by small numbers of legislators; (3) rotating committee assignments to further ensure a wider range of members on each committee and to give congressmen in-depth experience in a larger number of issue areas. Formulas are suggested to limit the turnover on a given committee at any given time to protect expertise. For the Senate, a consolidation of both committees and subcommittees is suggested to give senators more flexibility to cope with a heavy and ever expanding workload.

Norman J. Ornstein, special editor of this volume, received his Ph.D. from the University of Michigan. An Assistant Professor of Political Science at Catholic University in Washington, D.C., Ornstein is the author of several articles on Congress and editor of a forthcoming book, Change in Congress. *Professor Ornstein, Robert L. Peabody and David W. Rohde are currently working on a book on decision making in the Senate. Formerly, he served as an American Political Science Association Congressional Fellow and taught at the Johns Hopkins University School of Advanced International Studies in Bologna, Italy.*

VERY early in its existence Congress adopted a standing committee system. One hundred and eighty years later, after periodic changes in committee structures, the standing committee systems of the House of Representatives and the Senate are the most significant features of both legislative bodies. The one assumption universally shared by those who are currently focusing on reform is that standing committees are here to stay in the United States Congress; no other mode of operation is ever discussed.

No doubt, standing committees have functioned well for Congress' operations. They have permitted the two legislative bodies to cope with their increasingly heavy workload through a manageable division of labor, and they have facilitated the process of individual specialization which provides expertise necessary to cope with the resource- and talent-rich executive branch and with the complexity of contemporary issues and legislation.[1] These are problems of a technological society and a large legislative body; neither of these conditions is likely to disappear. Thus, standing committees will become more and more solidified. Suggestions for change in the committee systems must be put within this framework.

Standing committees fulfill important goals for the legislative system. Because of their central position in the legislature, committees are also objects of great significance for individual legislators and their careers. Committee assignments are vitally important to each member, whether he is primarily concerned with implementing public policy, attaining internal power and prestige or protecting his elective flanks. Because committees have varying attractiveness to members, they tend to attract members with different goals; thus, they tend to be quite unrepresentative of the larger body membership.

THE PROBLEM OF COMMITTEE UNREPRESENTATIVENESS

In the House there are twenty-one standing committees; representatives sit on either one or two. Some committees deal with major issues of national public policy, such as Armed Services and Ways and Means. Others deal with narrower policy areas—which may still be vitally important to smaller groups within the society—such as Post Office and Civil Service and Merchant Marine and Fisheries. As Fenno has detailed in his recent book *Congressmen in Committees*,[2] each of these committees offers different incentives to its members —incentives which will attract some legislators, depending on their goals and outlooks, and will not appeal to others. Ways and Means and Appropriations appeal to members who

1. The increasing role of the federal government in American society and the growing volume and complexity of governmental decisions have created great problems for Congress in gathering and evaluating information to formulate and oversee public policies. How can 535 legislators—most of them lawyers —hope to compete with a bureaucracy which today is 3.5 million strong—with countless scientists, doctors and technical experts backed up by vast resources, including 6,000 computers? The response in Congress has been the sharpening of specialization and division of labor via the committee system. The House, in particular, has tried to develop its own member specialists, offering them incentives to maintain and enhance their expertise. Thus, the seniority system is based on continuous committee service, not House service, encouraging members to stay on their committees and not to move around, thus, presumably not diluting their knowledge.

2. Richard F. Fenno, Jr., *Congressmen in Committees* (Boston, Mass.: Little, Brown, 1973).

desire influence and prestige within the House; Interior and Post Office appeal to those whose districts benefit from these committees. Internal incentives for specialization, the small number of assignments and the varying character of committees lead members of Congress to gravitate towards committees in which they have a perceived special stake or interest; thus, for example, congressmen from western areas go to Interior; those from rural areas go to Agriculture; and those from port areas go to Merchant Marine and Fisheries. Members who lack such an interest will leave these committees as rapidly as they can—a good example is Shirley Chisholm's brief encounter with the Agriculture Committee—and committees become dominated by those with an original special interest.

Some committees, such as Rules and Appropriations, do appeal to a wider range of legislators, and so an unbiased committee assignment procedure could make these universally desirable committees representative of the larger body.[3] With most other committees, however, it must be emphasized that a natural selection process is at work. Since committees have unequal attractiveness to members, then, regardless of the initial assignment process, people interested in farm problems will tend to gravitate to the Agriculture Committee and those with reclamation interests will move to Interior, even if they are first put on incompatible committees.

It follows, then, that the policy outputs ratified—or blocked—by a particular committee might well be significantly different from those which would have been formulated

if the entire body had been acting. While the full memberships of House and Senate do act on committee recommendations—although not on measures committees fail to report—the limited time available for floor consideration and the greater specific knowledge and interest of committee members give their recommendations great impact.

Moreover, the crucial importance of committees for individual legislators makes change in the committee system, especially major change, difficult to achieve. Too much is wrapped up in members' committees to allow them to easily cede jurisdictions—much less to permit committees to be abolished—and periodic reassessments of committees are infrequent. It is quite remarkable, given the tremendous changes which have occurred in America and the world in recent years, that the last time the committee systems of House and Senate were evaluated and restructured was 1946—the year before Richard Nixon first came to the House of Representatives.

In this essay, I will discuss these problems, and possible ways of reconciling the individual and system functions of committees. How can committees be responsive to the larger legislative entity, and how can future necessary change be facilitated? With fewer committee assignments, a more hierarchical structure and fewer noncommittee-based resources for members than has the Senate, the House of Representatives suffers more acutely from committee unrepresentativeness—although Senate committees are not immune—and so the House will receive somewhat more attention. In a latter section the Senate committee system will be discussed.

The proposals for reform which

3. Such an unbiased system does not, however, exist now.

will be analyzed are not minor. If enacted, they would sweepingly alter congressional structures—with no certain fashion of predicting the emerging relationships of power. It would be most difficult, if not impossible, to get Congress to restructure itself willingly in such a fashion. However, a low probability of enactment should be no deterrent to analyzing large scale reforms —indeed, it could be argued that tailoring analyses of reform to perceived probability of success helps to limit the amount of change which will occur. Furthermore, the raising and discussing of larger questions and the challenging of some of the basic assumptions underlying the contemporary committee systems in the House and the Senate can give a better understanding of the role of committee structures in the congressional process.

PAST REFORMS

Any examination of committee structures must first be put into the context of the origin and the enactment of past reform proposals. Most recent efforts at internal reforms have focused on aspects of committee operations.[4] The seniority system arose from the 1910 revolt in the House.[5] The 1946 Legislative Reorganization Act's most sweeping provision greatly reduced the number of standing committees in both House

and Senate.[6] In the Senate the most significant change of the 1950s was the Johnson rule,[7] which guaranteed each Democrat a major committee assignment. In the House the Rules Committee was the major focal point of the late 1950s and early '60s, with reformers attempting both to enlarge it[8] and to bypass it—via the twenty-one day rule. Recent reforms in the House in 1971 and 1973 have significantly altered the subcommittee system,[9] the selection of committee and subcommittee chairmen and the conduct of committee meetings.[10]

What have these reforms tried to accomplish? By examining some of them more closely one may be able to better understand how future structural changes might affect congressional behavior and legislative outputs.

POWER AND COMMITTEE CHAIRMEN IN THE HOUSE

The seniority system arose as a way of shifting power from an omnipotent Speaker of the House, whose greatest formal weapon had been his ability to appoint committee members and chairmen. The

4. There are two notable exceptions. Focus on the filibuster—Rule XXII—in the Senate points up the relative importance of floor considerations in the Senate. The recorded teller vote and electronic voting in the House may be the most significant structural reforms in Congress since 1946. See, for example, *Congressional Quarterly Weekly Report*, 25 September 1971, pp. 1967–1970.

5. See, Nelson Polsby, Miriam Gallagher and Barry Rundquist, "The Growth of the Seniority System in the U.S. House of Representatives," *American Political Science Review* 62 (September 1969), pp. 787–807.

6. See, George Goodwin, *The Little Legislatures* (Amherst, Mass.: University of Massachusetts Press, 1970), pp. 3–30; and Walter Kravitz's essay in this volume.

7. For a good account of the implementation of the Johnson rule, see, Rowland Evans and Robert Novak, *Lyndon B. Johnson: The Exercise of Power* (New York: New American Library, 1966), pp. 74–75.

8. See, for example, Tom Wicker, *JFK & LBJ* (New York: William Morrow, 1968), pp. 25–82.

9. Norman J. Ornstein, "Causes and Consequences of Congressional Change: Subcommittee Reforms in the U.S. House of Representatives, 1970–73" (Paper presented at the 1973 Annual Meeting of the American Political Science Association, New Orleans, Louisiana, 4–8 September 1973).

10. See, *Washington Post* story by Mary Russell, 5 July 1973, p. A13.

seniority custom was devised as an automatic, nonpolitical method for selecting committee chairmen and preventing a subgroup of legislative actors—in this case, a subgroup of one—from using accumulated power to dictate outcomes to the larger body membership.

The enlarging role of the federal government in American society and, to a lesser extent, the 1946 reduction in the number of committees greatly increased the importance and power of the standing committees. Much of this power went to the handful of committee chairmen. Chairmen had formal powers—control over hiring and firing of committee staff, control over formation and jurisdiction of subcommittees and appointment of subcommittee chairmen—as well as the informal influence of prestige and expertise. Most importantly, the technical operation of the seniority system in the House meant that chairmen achieved their positions automatically and retained them without being directly responsible to any larger authority. The important step, ratification of the appointment by the majority party caucus, was done by a single vote for all committee assignments and chairmanships, making it virtually impossible to challenge any particular chairman.

Working mainly through the House Democratic Caucus, contemporary reformers in 1971 and 1973 moved, through a series of changes, to rectify this latter day power imbalance in which smaller concentrations of power, rather than being eliminated, were centered in the hands of committee chairmen.[11] First, the Democrats attempted to get automatic voting by the party

caucus on each individual chairmanship. They partially succeeded in 1971 at the start of the 92nd Congress; a vote was permitted on a chairman if ten members demanded it. At the beginning of the 93rd Congress in January of 1973 an automatic vote procedure was implemented. No chairman lost his position in either of these years, but, as Peabody has noted: "all were put on notice that their conduct would be subject to bi-annual examination with the threat of caucus removal at least a possibility."[12]

At the same time vast changes have been implemented in the structure of the subcommittee system, also accomplished largely via the Democratic Caucus.[13] Subcommittee chairmanships were limited to one per member in 1971, thereby spreading out these positions to younger members. In 1973 a Subcommittee Bill of Rights was implemented by the Caucus; it enlarged and specified the powers of subcommittee chairmen, enabling them to hire their own professional staffs and to handle legislation on the floor. The selection of subcommittee chairmen was formalized, as well. All of these reforms strengthened subcommittees and subcommittee chairmen at the expense of committee chairmen. Importantly, these changes were made subject to ratification by the individual committee caucus of the majority party.

There is little question that, although the specific recommendations came from an ideologically and regionally balanced Democratic committee on reform headed by

---

11. Ornstein, "Congressional Change." It is quite interesting to see the increased importance of the party caucus, both in substantive and structural areas, in Congress.

12. Robert L. Peabody, "House Leadership, Party Caucuses, and the Committee Structure," Select Committee on Committees, Working Paper on House Committee Organization and Operation (Washington, D.C.: Government Printing Office, 1973).

13. Ornstein, "Congressional Change."

Representative Julia Butler Hansen of Washington, these changes were instigated by liberals who felt the committee system of the 1960s— especially through seniority—favored Southern conservatives. Nevertheless, an examination of them, on paper at least, shows that these 1971 and 1973 changes were sensitive to the unrestricted accumulation of power brought about through the 1910 reforms. Some power was taken from committee chairmen and spread out to subcommittee chairmen, which meant a broader distribution of power in terms of region, ideology and seniority. However, unlike the previous reforms, checks were put on committee chairmen, via the party caucus, and on subcommittee chairmen, via committee caucuses. In theory, at least, one of the major problems of the committee system in the past was ameliorated, although it will take several years before the real impact of these reforms can be assessed.[14] Nevertheless, as nearly as can be determined and as far as structural reforms can go, the House Democrats have arranged safeguards against the possibility of a substitution of one hundred fifty fiefdoms for twenty.

These safeguards can break down, especially through individual committees and their majority party caucuses. While committee chairmen have had their formal powers curbed, they and their subcommittee counterparts are now responsible to the full committee membership,

14. There are many ifs involved here. For one thing, if the Democrats should become the minority party in the House, these changes become largely academic. In addition, one must remember that there were structural barriers to an accumulation of power in 1910—primarily, the discharge petition and Calendar Wednesday—but they were little utilized and have not had the intended impact.

especially the majority party caucus. Should a committee decide to defy the full party membership there are few direct remedies. One cannot easily restructure an entire committee; thus, a problem which remains is ensuring that an individual committee does not become biased in some fashion relative to the full body membership—the representativeness problem again.

SUGGESTIONS FOR CHANGE

How, then, can committees reflect the makeup of the entire body as a microcosm of the nation without drastically affecting their capacity for knowledgeable formulation and oversight of public policy? A series of structural modifications might be able to achieve this goal, while at the same time building in an increased flexibility for future change; possible reforms are discussed below. It should again be emphasized that such changes are not likely to be implemented soon, if ever. For one thing, their inception would involve success in several separate forums. Committee assignments are handled by individual party caucuses; proposals to implement uniform criteria, such as a limitation on continuous service on a committee, would have to be accepted by each of the parties, or would not work. Other proposals, such as a reduction in the number of standing committees, could be implemented through the House as a whole, but would involve large scale changes which would encounter opposition from many sources—not the least being many of the current committee chairmen and other high ranking members.

Finally, these changes operate under the assumption that the House is attempting, first and foremost, to pass and oversee good national governmental policy. Congressmen, however, have other goals as well —some personal, such as getting reelected or having personal influence within the House, and some constituency-related, such as seeing that particular interests of one's own district are well represented. To the extent that these goals predominate, major changes which might conflict with them will have little chance of success. Nevertheless, discussing significant structural reforms is a useful method of understanding how Congress, through its committees, operates.

Consolidation of committees

The first, and greatest, step in making committees representative would be to consolidate committees in the House; the final total should be perhaps seven or eight standing committees, each with approximately fifty-five members and with each representative having one assignment. Our concern here is less with the specifics of rejurisdiction or with the problems of appropriation, taxation and authorization—questions which have been discussed in detail by others—than with the broader implications of this type of innovation. Elsewhere in this volume Robert L. Peabody outlines one system,[15] which we will utilize for analytic purposes. In a modification of this type one could consolidate committees with very different incentives and, thus, broaden the natural base of each new committee. For example, a Committee on Natural Resources could include interior, public works, environmental and agricultural jurisdictions, appealing to both urban congressmen concerned about pollution and rural

congressmen concerned about farm problems. A Committee on Human Resources could include the areas of education, health, welfare and labor. A Committee on Defense and Foreign Policy could encompass armed services, foreign affairs and international economic concerns. The other committees suggested by Peabody are Government Operations, Technology and Sciences, Ways and Means, Appropriations and Judiciary and Constitutional Rights.

House committees now range in size from nine to fifty-five; with this reform all committees would be composed of about fifty-five members. Thus, to some extent, the diffusion of workload which a committee system makes possible would be countered—it is extraordinarily difficult for fifty-five people to work as a unit, and the tendency would be strong for a greater division of labor. As was the case following the 1946 consolidation of committees down to nineteen, subcommittees would continue to proliferate. The recent House Democratic reforms which increased subcommittee chairmanships suggest that this proliferation would not necessarily be bad.[16] Giving out more subcommittee chairs can encourage congressmen to do their legislative work; furthermore, by giving each member a piece of the action, legislative activity and oversight can be enhanced. Once one reaches the point of overlap at which members must chair several different units, the effects of subcommittee proliferation become negative. Until that point is reached, more subcommittees may be beneficial. With fifty-five-member committees, the major work would be done at the subcommittee

15. See Peabody's contribution to this volume.

16. Ornstein, "Congressional Change."

level; therefore, great care would be required to make subcommittees both representative and responsive. The problem of creating one hundred fifty autonomous and autocratic subcommittee chairmen is a real one which is reduced, but not eliminated, by the principle of committee caucus review.

Limitation of chairmanship tenure

Secondly, the problem of the chairman's power must be considered—both for committees and, as indicated above, subcommittees. Committee chairmen retain considerable influence within their bailiwicks; a reduction in committees would enhance the influence of the smaller number of new chairmen, in spite of the steps which have been taken to curb the powers of chairmen. An essential corollary of committee consolidation would be limitation of the tenure of committee chairmen, for example, to six years in their House careers. Such a step would decrease the influence of chairmen and would discourage any long term individual accumulation of power. Exceptional individuals could still make significant contributions through subcommittee chairmanships and other legislative activities. Chairmanship of any single subcommittee would have to be limited in the same fashion, for the same reasons; yet, to give continuing incentives to members for legislative work, the future opportunity to chair other subcommittees should exist.

In a practical sense, this proposal —or some variation—could be implemented through the majority party caucus; the proposal could exempt current chairmen and allow them to complete their careers in order to diffuse a major source of opposition. Indeed, a similar proposal

was suggested this past year to the Democratic Caucus committee on reform by Florida Representative Charles Bennett; however, it was not acted upon.

Rotation of assignments

Another way of ensuring committee representativeness is to rotate, in some fashion, committee assignments. Currently, continuity on committees is encouraged, primarily by rewarding continuous committee seniority rather than overall seniority. Thus, when Representative Edith Green—Democrat, Oregon— moved last year from the Education and Labor Committee to the Appropriations Committee, she sacrificed eighteen years of seniority and a second ranking position on Education and Labor to become thirtieth ranking member of thirty-three Democrats on Appropriations. Lateral moves of this sort are not often taken.

On the other hand, the new House Democratic Steering and Policy Committee has built in a procedure which ensures a steady rotation of members, while limiting the overall turnover each two years to permit required continuity. A similar system could easily be adapted for the standing committee system. For example, continuous service on a committee could be limited to six years, after which a member would be required to leave the committee for four years before returning, if he desired. Ranking on each committee, and subcommittee chairmanships, could be decided by a combination of overall tenure and committee seniority—ratified by committee caucuses—as could committee chairmanships; if the most senior member had already served six years as a committee chairman, the next ranking member would be recommended to the majority party caucus. Finally, to ensure a continuing influx of fresh viewpoints, preference for some, perhaps half, of contested vacancies on desirable committees could be given to those who have never served on the committee, so long as the overall turnover on the committee did not exceed one-third for a given Congress.

A rotation system of this type would have several consequences. First, it would prevent any small group of legislators, whatever their ideologies, from becoming entrenched in the same formal power positions for extended periods of time. Also, by diluting internal vested interests, it would enable Congress to restructure itself more easily as policy areas and problems changed—legislators would have less stake in preserving their own congressional status quo.

Secondly, it would broaden the knowledge base in Congress by giving each legislator a wider range of experiences in several issue areas, without penalizing him for doing so. This would not drastically impair member expertise, for members could still spend several years during their legislative careers working on a single committee or dealing with a single problem. As most legislators would attest, a good grasp of the issues facing a particular committee or subcommittee can come after a short period of time; the outlines, if not the specifics, of policy proposals are usually quite similar from term to term. A legislator who has served on a committee for thirty years is little more expert than one who has served on the same committee for fifteen years—if they are matched in perseverance and intelligence. In fact, by allowing congressmen to examine issue areas from different perspec-

tives, a rotation system could enhance expertise. Moreover, by building in mechanisms to limit the turnover on a committee at any given time to one-third or one-half, one could prevent the admittedly improbable situation of a committee composed entirely of inexperienced newcomers.

Finally, each committee would, at any given time, more accurately reflect the overall membership of the body—regionally, ideologically and in seniority. A regularized change of membership would give each committee a wider range of legislators; rural congressmen would be spread more broadly throughout the committee system and would no longer be so concentrated in the Agriculture and Public Works Committees, while big city congressmen would no longer be as heavily represented on the Education and Labor and Foreign Affairs Committees. Policy outputs formulated by a wider spectrum of legislators would be more likely to reflect national needs and desires.

This innovation would, however, have significant side effects as well. Larger proportions of members would have served on each committee and would be less hesitant about speaking out on the floor about a committee's recommendations. All committees would become, in Fenno's phrase, more permeable, and floor debate would become more significant. Most likely, amendments would increase, and the efficiency of floor debate and decision making would decrease correspondingly. This type of environment exists to an extent in the Senate, which by virtue of its smaller size can react more flexibly; it might create chaos in the House. On the other hand, floor procedures could be created to streamline debate and deliberation, and vigorous and meaningful floor debate—if not efficient—might well produce better decisions.

Presumably, also, committee staffs—having the continuity on committees which legislators would lack—would increase in importance, particularly in crafting legislation. This is not a serious problem, however. Legislators would not become wholly dependent on their staffs; they are intelligent and capable individuals with control over the direction and substance of policy concerns. Elliott Richardson's successful administration of the Defense Department—Richardson being no expert in technical defense topics —is an example of the limitations of staffs in dictating or shaping outcomes.

Consolidation of committees deals with many of the same areas; perhaps, given its implementation, a built-in rotation of committee assignments would be unnecessary. A better solution might be merely rotation among subcommittees, limiting chairmanships and tenure in a similar fashion. This approach would check the erosion of specialization and expertise caused by committee rotation; however, it would limit the interchange of ideas and viewpoints across policy areas and would make a future rejurisdiction of committees more difficult by giving members more stake in protecting their particular committee's interests.

THE SENATE

The House of Representatives and the Senate are two very different institutions with disparate modes of operation; thus, committees and the committee system as a whole might serve quite varying functions in the two bodies.[17] The most fundamental difference between the two institutions is also the most obvious— that of membership size. The one hundred members of the Senate serve on seventeen standing committees and one hundred twenty-one standing subcommittees; comparable figures for four hundred thirty-five House members are twenty-one committees and one hundred twenty-three subcommittees. Numerically, it is obvious that senators must have either smaller committees or more committee assignments; in fact, the Senate has both. Senate standing committees average fifteen members in size; House committees, thirty. As Asher notes, in his essay in this volume, senators average 2.6 committee and 9.7 subcommittee assignments, while House members sit on an average of 1.6 committees and 3.5 subcommittees.

It is quite clear that these size differences have a direct importance for proposals of committee structural change.[18] For example, while an expansion of subcommittees in the House might be desirable—to spread the action and encourage substantive involvement by younger legislators—such an action would be highly undesirable in the Senate. Better than half the members of the House lack subcommittee chairmanships or ranking minority memberships, but ninety-seven out of one hundred senators have at least one ranking position and many senators have several. To add new subcom-

17. See, Fenno, *Congressmen in Committees,* especially chap. 5.
18. See, Norman J. Ornstein, "Information, Resources and Legislative Decision-making: Some Comparative Perspectives on the U.S. Congress" (Ph.D. diss., University of Michigan, 1972), especially chap. 6.

mittees in the Senate would spread even thinner its already overburdened members. Thus, one might at the same time call for an expansion of subcommittees in the House and a consolidation and reduction in the number of subcommittees in the Senate.

Similarly, 60 percent of the Senate is represented on the three most powerful and prestigious committees—Appropriations, Finance and Foreign Relations—while only 22 percent of the House sits on its three super committees—Appropriations, Rules and Ways and Means. The problem of committee representation and meaningful assignments for legislators is a different one in the Senate than in the House. A rotation of committee assignments would be less meaningful in the Senate, for most senators already serve on a broad range of committees. In the Senate a more major problem is that of the individual workload and division of labor. Senators have too many time commitments and assignments; they are stretched too thin, substantively. A majority of Democratic senators chair multiple subcommittees, and most senators miss the bulk of their scheduled committee and subcommittee meetings and hearings.[19]

For these reasons a consolidation of both committees and subcommittees makes sense for the Senate. The

19. For some additional suggestions and thoughts on this topic, see, Norman J. Ornstein, "Streamlining the Work of the Senate," *Washington Post*, 2 August 1973, p. A24.

overall workload will not decrease no matter what the reform, but a reduction in the number of assignments and chairmanships for each senator would enable a more efficient allocation of time and resources. Senators would have more control over scheduling; overlaps could be minimized. A consolidation plan similar to Peabody's for the House could be employed, while also limiting chairmanship tenure in the manner described. Senators would still sit on two committees and several subcommittees—they would be permitted no more than two chairmanships; thus, they could still cross several issue areas, limiting the problem of representativeness.

CONCLUSION

Standing committees are not Constitutionally mandated structures; they are congressional responses to heavy workloads and unwieldy decision making. The reforms mentioned above are an attempt to make committees and their policy outputs reflect the larger legislature membership and, thus, the nation. Enacting these changes in the House or the Senate is, to say the least, unlikely—in the near future, at any rate. Nevertheless, the implications of modifications of this type should be seriously contemplated by both scholars and legislators. At the least, by discussing them we shed light on the underlying assumptions, behavior and limitations which characterize contemporary committees.

Between Party Battalions and Committee Suzerainty

By Charles O. Jones

ABSTRACT: President Nixon's challenge to congressional authority in the early months of 1973 stimulated critical review of how Congress does its work. As Lord Bryce observed long ago, of the three methods to facilitate the operation of large assemblies, the United States has emphasized development of a strong committee system. While providing many advantages, Bryce noted that the system also tends to lessen cohesion, reduce responsibility and lower public interest in legislative proceedings. This article questions whether the committee system accommodates the new political realities of frequently split party control between Congress and the White House. It argues that changes should be made to increase the authority and visibility of party leaders so that presidential programs might be challenged more coherently in Congress. Specific changes are suggested to that end—changes which seek to maintain the advantages of the committee system, while reducing its disadvantages.

Charles O. Jones is Maurice Falk Professor of Politics at the University of Pittsburgh. He is the author of a number of books and articles on Congress, political parties and public policy. He has recently completed a book on air pollution decision making, to be published soon under the title Clean Air: The Policies and Politics of Pollution Control.

An earlier version of this paper was presented to the House Select Committee on Committees, chaired by Representative Richard Bolling—Democrat, Missouri—on June 14, 1973.

D URING the early months of 1973 the halls of Congress reverberated with cries of anguish as the administration presented bold budgetary proposals, impounded funds for programs popular on the Hill, reorganized the executive branch and proposed an expansive interpretation of executive privilege. Buoyed by an incredible victory at the polls and final settlement in Vietnam and skeptical of prospects for congressional support, President Nixon tested his authority to go it virtually alone. Before Watergate broke in late March, he clearly demonstrated that a president could go very far on his own— ignoring, though sometimes taunting, a Congress organized by the other party.

The president's actions were soon interpreted as commentary on the sad state of affairs in Congress. Many pictured Congress as immobilized —incapable of responding to presidential encroachments on legislative authority. As in the past, such direct threats to the power of Congress stimulated reform proposals both inside and outside the institution. As the media emphasized a Constitutional crisis, both the House and Senate acted to adjust the imbalance in presidential-congressional sharing of authority.

At least two broad strategies are available to Congress in any such undertaking: the essentially negative approach of reducing the power of the president and the more positive approach of increasing Congress' decision-making capacities. While no doubt satisfying, "cutting the president down to size" risks unwanted long term effects, without necessarily increasing congressional authority. It is difficult to make reforms apply only to one president at one point in time. Rather, they affect the operations of the office, itself; they change expectations of the institution; and they may influence the president's bargaining advantages in foreign and domestic policy making. Thus, "get Richard Nixon" cannot be played as a single-target game. The mark applied to his cloak of authority remains to stain that of his successor.[1]

Seeking to increase the decision-making capacities of Congress is not a risk-free endeavor, either. Institutional reform always affects more than the primary object of change, and those secondary and tertiary effects are difficult to identify and evaluate in advance. However, I judge the risks in this approach well worth taking since I continue to view Congress as the most public and representative of our national political institutions. Put another way, improving Congress' capabilities also changes expectations and bargaining advantages throughout Washington, but in a direction consistent with commonly accepted democratic principles.

Implementing this second, more positive, approach requires analysis of the centers of leadership and accountability in Congress. The committee system is a logical starting place, and in 1973 the House of Representatives wisely established a Select Committee on Committees under the chairmanship of Richard Bolling—Democrat, Missouri—"to conduct a thorough and complete study" of that important network.[2]

1. Reference here is to efforts by Congress to alter the president's budgetary authority, war powers and authority to negotiate treaties, and not to the self-imposed stain of Watergate, which also affects future presidencies.
2. See, U.S., Congress, *Congressional Record*, 93rd Cong., 1st sess., 31 January 1973, daily ed., pp. H591–H603.

Diagnosing congressional ills cannot be limited to committees, however. Political parties, in particular, also must be studied. Party and committee leaders have traditionally shared power in Congress, not always in happy accord. In this paper I will argue that the time has come to increase the authority, responsibility and visibility of congressional party leaders. Inevitably, any such increase comes partially at the expense of congressional committee leaders; therefore, opposition from that source may be expected. The proposal can be defended in two ways: (1) such reordering may, in fact, result in greater overall authority for Congress so that in absolute terms committee leaders may actually gain power; and (2) failure to make changes may jeopardize existing congressional authority and thereby may threaten the whole democratic structure in this nation.

PARTY OR COMMITTEE?

Always fearful of power, we have traditionally sought to disperse it where possible. Nor have Americans ever been fond of political parties. In fact, many attempts have been made through the years to destroy them. It should not surprise us, therefore, to find a weak party system in Congress. The rest of the world views this feature as quite curious, however. For example, in studying and observing the House of Representatives Lord Bryce concluded many years ago that the "feature . . . Europeans find the strangest" is that the House "has parties, but they are headless."

There is neither Government nor Opposition. There can hardly be said to be leaders. . . That the majority may be and often is opposed to the President and

his cabinet, does not strike Americans as odd, because they proceed on the theory that the legislative ought to be distinct from the executive authority.[3]

Yet, both the House and Senate face what Bryce identifies as "the most abiding difficulty of free government"—that is, "to get large assemblies to work promptly and smoothly either for legislative or executive purposes."[4] Bryce notes that through history three methods have been employed to overcome this difficulty:

—Leave very few and comparatively simple questions to the assembly.
—Organize the assemblies into well-defined parties, each recognizing and guided by one or more leaders . . . [which] move like battalions at the word of command.
—Divide the assembly into a number of smaller bodies to which legislative and administrative questions may be referred.[5]

It is the third alternative—a strong committee system—which is "applied . . . most of all in the United States."

Though understanding its advantages, Lord Bryce found much to criticize in the congressional committee system. He spotted three results of the system which are of particular relevance today—so much so that they can serve as orienting purposes for this discussion.

3. James Bryce, *The American Commonwealth* (New York: Macmillan, 1915), vol. 1, p. 151.
4. Ibid., p. 156.
5. Ibid. Of course, many variations are possible among these alternatives. Some have been tried in Congress—for example, the binding Caucus of the House Democrats 1911–1915. See, James S. Fleming, "Reestablishing Leadership in the House of Representatives: The Case of Oscar W. Underwood," *Mid-America* 54 (October 1972), pp. 234–250.

It [the committee system] lessens the cohesion and harmony of legislation. Each committee goes on its own way with its own bills just as though it were legislating for one planet and the other committees for others. . . . The advance is haphazard; the parts have little relation to one another or to the whole.

It reduces responsibility. . . . In the United States the ministry cannot be blamed, for the cabinet officers do not sit in Congress; the House cannot be blamed because it has only followed the decision of its committee; the committee may be an obscure body, whose members are too insignificant to be worth blaming. The chairman is possibly a man of note, but the people have no leisure to watch sixty chairmen: they know Congress and Congress only; they cannot follow the acts of those to whom Congress chooses to delegate its functions. No discredit attaches to the dominant party, because they could not control the acts of the . . . men in the committee room. This public displeasure rarely finds a victim.

It lowers the interest of the nation in the proceedings of Congress. Except in exciting times, when large questions have to be settled, the bulk of real business is done not in the great hall of the House but in this labyrinth of committee rooms and the lobbies that surround them. . . . People cease to watch Congress with that sharp eye which every principal ought to keep fixed on his agent.[6]

Of course, Congress did not settle on the third alternative—dividing "the assembly into a number of smaller bodies"—just to give Lord Bryce something to criticize. There are perfectly sound reasons for a strong committee system associated with the political realities of congressional functions, structure, authority and elections. The question before Congress today is whether the present system of strong committees-weak parties continues to accommodate political realities. I think it does not, and the creation of the Bolling committee—among other actions of Congress in 1973—indicates that the members, themselves, are also questioning the existing structure. Surely, there is a way station between party battalions and committee suzerainty.

NEW REALITIES FOR OLD PROCESSES

Perhaps the most obvious political reality today is that a Republican is in the White House while the Democrats continue to hold a majority in both houses of Congress. Furthermore, that Republican was elected by one of the greatest landslides in history. In the wake of that victory it seemed apparent that Richard Nixon intended to govern with only very limited congressional participation.

Split party control between Congress and the White House serves to set Bryce's observations in sharp relief. In the past, increased presidential authority has tended to act as a corrective to the problems of cohesion, responsibility and visibility of issues, with the president assuming the central leadership role in the national political system. With split control, however, the inadequacies of Congress are once again obvious to all. This would be less serious, perhaps, if split control were a rare phenomenon. That is, many scholars, pundits and politicians are willing to accept presidential dominance of national policy making as solving many of the problems raised by Bryce. As it is, however, split control is no longer exceptional. Between 1900 and 1946 only Woodrow Wilson had to face opposition party

6. Ibid., pp. 162–163.

control of both houses of Congress, and then for just two years—1919 to 1920.[7] Since 1946, however, split party control has prevailed 50 percent of the time—14 of 28 years. In the last twenty years—1954 to 1974—it has been the predominant pattern, occurring 60 percent of the time—twelve years. Furthermore, prospects are that it will continue at least until 1976.

Apparently, this condition is acceptable to the American public. First, they have given implicit approval by splitting their votes in huge numbers. Second, a recent Harris poll showed that 50 percent of the respondents thought that split control was a better way to govern, and another 16 percent thought it made no difference.[8]

WORK ASSIGNMENTS IN CONGRESS

It is in this context of confused responsibility that Lord Bryce's criticisms of the congressional committee system have relevance. One can make a logical argument in support of split control as an adversary process in which the public interest is ultimately served. As one of Harris' respondents observed: "Divided control keeps each branch of government in line." But how are we to determine responsibility, develop cohesion and maintain interest in Congress if power is dispersed throughout the committee system? As Bryce says: "The people have no leisure to watch sixty chairmen." How is the ordinary citizen or even the careful observer to pinpoint re-

sponsibility in Congress today? It is unreasonable to hold party leaders responsible, for they have too little authority. It is impossible to monitor the entire committee system. Although the number of standing committees was mercifully reduced by the Legislative Reorganization Act of 1946, federal government functions have increased many-fold; thus, the congressional workload is greater than ever. As a result, the total number of legislative work units continues to grow. My most recent count shows 57 standing and special committees—House, Senate and joint—and 288 standing and special subcommittees—a total of 345 congressional work units for the 535 members. In the Senate, where every-member-a-leader seems to be the dominant principle, there are 23 committees and 140 subcommittees, each requiring a chairman and ranking minority member.

Even more dramatic is the number of work assignments required for this division of labor. As indicated in table 1, a total of 4,037 slots are listed in the current directory of committees and subcommittees. Above all, these figures demonstrate the staggering workload of the national legislature. It has been found necessary to create a fantastic array of specialized units which come to be demanding of a legislator's time and talents. As shown in table 1, the 435 House members must fill 2,452 committee and subcommittee slots, an average of 5.6 per member—1.8 committee; 3.8 subcommittee. With less than one-fourth the membership of the House, the Senate has two-thirds of the committee and subcommittee positions of the lower chamber: 1,585 slots for 100 senators, an average of 15.9 per member—3.9 committee; 12 subcommittee.

7. Presidents Taft and Hoover also faced opposition party control of the House of Representatives in 1911–1912 and 1931–1932, respectively.

8. Harris Poll results, as reported in *Chicago Tribune*, 25 January 1973.

TABLE 1

TOTAL COMMITTEE AND SUBCOMMITTEE POSITIONS, 93RD CONGRESS, FIRST SESSION

	COMMITTEE POSITIONS	SUBCOMMITTEE POSITIONS	TOTALS
House of Representatives	732	1,581	
House positions on Joint Committees	61	78	
	793	1,659	2,452
Senate	328	1,113	
Senate positions on Joint Committees	61	83	
	389	1,196	1,585
Grand Total			4,037

SOURCE: Compiled from listings in *Congressional Quarterly Weekly Report*, 28 April 1973, pp. 957–1004.

This division of labor is a great strength of Congress—its way of responding to the escalating demands for government action in a modern society. Yet, dispersal of work assignments is effective in the long run for policy development only if mechanisms are available for tracking and integrating individual efforts. It is in this respect that congressional organization is weak.

THE PROBLEM OF ACCOUNTABILITY

How can the public possibly comprehend this maze of working units? Where is the accountability in this system? Each member must face reelection and, in theory, is accountable at that time. However, the typical voter is unlikely to know very much about the member's committee and subcommittee assignments. Indeed, various polls and surveys show that most voters cannot even identify their representative; senators get somewhat more recognition.[9] Furthermore, most incum-

9. One study showed that 39 percent of adults could name the congressman from their own district; 57 percent could name at least

bents are reelected—normally, over 90 percent of those who seek another term.[10] The available data from voting behavior studies do not suggest anything approaching the classic theoretical model of elections as accountability events.

What is the basis of voting in congressional elections, if it is not a weighing of an incumbent's record? Typically, in House races, it is party affiliation. Republicans vote for Republican candidates; Democrats, for Democratic candidates; and Independents tend to split in the direction of the winner. For example, in districts where there are more Republicans than Democrats, the Republican candidate is elected over

one senator. As reported in *Washington Post*, 8 July 1970. Another study showed that 46 percent of those who voted in 1958 had not read or heard anything about either congressional candidate. Warren Miller and Donald Stokes, "Constituency Influence in Congress," *American Political Science Review* 57 (March 1963), pp. 53–54.

10. See, Charles O. Jones, *Every Second Year: Congressional Behavior and the Two-Year Term* (Washington, D.C.: The Brookings Institution, 1967), p. 68.

and over again.[11] If redistricting occurs, or if a large number of Democrats move into a district, the incumbent may be defeated. But then, typically, the Democrat is elected over and over again. Overall, the trend has been in the direction of greater stability of the House, both in turnover of members and average length of terms served.[12]

A party-based vote can, of course, be an accountability vote. That is, voters may be reaffirming support for a set of broad principles which they presume to be the basis of policy action within the congressional party structure. The party's legislative record might serve as a basis for judging performance, but the voter would be hard pressed to determine what that record was or who was responsible for compiling it. That condition is unlikely to change in a Congress so dominated by its committee system that, for example, a Wilbur Mills—Democrat, Arkansas—opts for the chairmanship of the House Committee on Ways and Means rather than seeking the Speakership.

A RATIONALE FOR CHANGE

I propose strengthening political parties in Congress as a counterweight to the decentralizing tendencies of the committee system. It is the only move I can identify which will fix responsibility and promote unity and visibility for legislative issues. Surely, neither the ordinary voter nor the sophisticated analyst has the "leisure to watch" 345 chairmen. Also, as has been noted, party does seem to provide a general orientation for voters, even if many split their tickets and prefer divided party control.

No institution with exclusive power to reform itself is likely to make change simply as an artful exercise. Either there must be direct pay-offs, or it must be apparent that continuing to do business in the same way will be harmful to the membership. Why should members support changes now? In the present circumstances of split party control, the Democrats have the incentive of developing alternative proposals to those offered by the Nixon administration. However, greater cohesion, responsibility and visibility are prerequisites to any such offerings by the congressional Democratic parties.

The House Republicans have made important changes in the last fifteen years to facilitate development—or sometimes merely discovery—of party positions on policy questions.[13] Since a minority party can never count on controlling the White House for very long, changes made now—when the Democrats also have a stake in the reform—can be of long term significance by increasing the minority party's capacity to offer constructive opposition when a Democrat moves back into the White House.

This is the time to act. If the Democrats recapture the White House in 1976, there will be many fewer incentives for change. Democrats may be expected to accept the

11. Nearly 80 percent of House districts elected candidates from the same party for five straight elections between 1952 and 1960. See, Charles O. Jones, "Inter-Party Competition for Congressional Seats," *Western Political Quarterly* 17 (September 1964), p. 465.

12. See data summarized in William J. Keefe and Morris S. Ogul, *The American Legislative Process: Congress and the States* (Englewood Cliffs, N.J.: Prentice-Hall, 1973), pp. 126–127.

13. These are summarized in Charles O. Jones, *The Minority Party in Congress* (Boston, Mass.: Little, Brown, 1970), chap. 8.

leadership of their president, even in the face of further erosion of congressional authority. The rewards of increased presidential power are tempting and can be more easily shared within the majority party. Parenthetically, one might observe that the crisis of presidential-congressional relations came with a Republican in the White House—not so much because he had more power than his Democratic predecessors, but because his exercise of that power was consistently unsatisfactory to the Democratic majority in Congress.

At least one other argument in favor of reform can be offered. In the past a very persuasive case was made against any proposals which might bring more than two members of Congress of the same party into the same room. Ours are umbrella-type political parties, it is argued, and all points of view are accommodated. One cannot insist on a party line and maintain the two-party system. The Democrats, in particular, have permitted widely divergent views on fundamental issues—in part, because their traditional strength in the South provided a solid base for electing presidents and collecting majorities in Congress.

Accepting the fact that both parties still allow a broad spectrum of ideologies, there is evidence to suggest that the parties are becoming nationalized. No longer need either party feel so constrained by its base in a particular region that it can never call a meeting of the membership. As indicated in table 2, the Republicans now have sizeable representation in both the House and Senate from Southern and border states. Just ten years ago, in the 88th Congress, Republicans had but three senators and seventeen representatives from the South; most of these—all three senators and eleven of the seventeen representatives—were from border states.

The Democrats have been building strength in traditionally Republican areas in the Midwest, Northeast and West. As indicated in table 2, there are nearly as many Democratic senators from the West as from the South, and percentagewise, Midwestern and Western Democrats are capturing nearly as many Senate seats as their Southern colleagues —60 and 58 percent, respectively, compared to 67 percent in the South.

It must be acknowledged that the opportunity for reform may have already passed. One of the more de-

TABLE 2

REGIONAL DISTRIBUTION OF HOUSE AND SENATE SEATS BETWEEN THE DEMOCRATS AND REPUBLICANS, 93RD CONGRESS, FIRST SESSION

REGION	HOUSE SEATS		SENATE SEATS	
	Democratic	Republican	Democratic	Republican
East	61 (54%)	52 (46%)	9 (40%)	13*(60%)
South and border	97 (72%)	38 (28%)	28†(67%)	10 (33%)
Midwest	43 (39%)	68 (61%)	13 (60%)	9 (40%)
West	42 (55%)	34 (45%)	15 (58%)	11 (42%)
	243	192	57	43

* Includes James Buckley—Conservative, New York.
† Includes Harry Byrd, Jr.—Independent, Virginia.

pressing effects of Watergate for those interested in congressional reform is that it removed the stimulus for change. The threat to congressional policy-making authority is gone. Members of Congress may actually have been deluded into thinking that the president's catastrophe has in some fashion increased their own capacities to make decisions. However, Watergate has negated the president's earlier advantages without curing the problems of the legislative branch. One must question whether a balance of power in which the president is as immobile as Congress is in the best interests of the nation.

AN AGENDA FOR CHANGE

A brief discussion of reform goals must precede the recommendation of specific changes. It should be noted at the outset that it is emphatically not the purpose here to return to the days when Joseph G. Cannon—Republican, Illinois—and Nelson W. Aldrich—Republican, Rhode Island—ruled the House and Senate, respectively.[14] The specter of Cannonism, in particular, is almost always raised whenever anyone suggests more authority for party leaders. Proposals for change need not go that far, nor should any increase in the authority of party leaders fail to include means for holding those leaders accountable for the use of their authority. As noted earlier, the search here is for a reasonable course between Lord Bryce's second and third alternatives—between party battalions and committee suzerainty.

14. One of the best sources on the Cannon-Aldrich era is Kenneth W. Hechler, *Insurgency* (New York: Columbia University Press, 1940).

A strong and effective committee system in Congress clearly befits the operation of a strongly pluralist political system. Also required, however, are means by which Congress can reach conclusions about what actions to take on the major issues of the day. The president will certainly recommend policies on these matters. If the Congress of the future is to be something more than a ratifying body on policy, it must generate credible alternatives. Such counter proposals as a coherent program can most reasonably be expected to come from the party which does not control the White House. Thus, I am really speaking of changes to increase the likelihood that the presidential out-party will be in a position to challenge, not simply attack, the president's program. That can only happen, in my judgment, if party leaders assume enough authority to begin to shape and direct, not command, that which goes on in congressional committees.

Therefore, the changes proposed below increase the authority of party leaders, while seeking to make them and the parties they lead more publicly visible. The increased authority justifies holding them accountable for what happens in Congress. The visibility is a means to that end.[15]

15. These proposals are primarily directed to changes in the House of Representatives, although some apply to the Senate, as well. Some require formal changes in the rules. Others require changes in existing party structure. I am less certain that changes made in the Senate will, or should, alter the functions of that institution. As it stands, the Senate serves as a "hot-house for significant policy innovation," and this function is facilitated by "its organizational flexibility." Still, if it is important to do so, it ought to have the means to integrate innovations. On this matter, see, Nelson W. Polsby, "Strengthening Congress in National Policymaking," *Yale Review* 59 (Summer, 1970), pp. 481–497.

Party leaders

Party leaders should be visibly responsible for policy action by their membership. However, they cannot legitimately be held responsible without an increase in authority. The following proposals are offered as means to increase leader visibility and authority:

—Provide for more formal nomination and campaign procedures in electing party leaders, possibly holding two caucuses: the first for nominations; the second, a week later, for elections.

—Permit the Speaker to appoint the Committee on Rules—consulting the minority floor leader for filling minority party vacancies.

—Permit the Speaker to appoint the chairmen and the minority floor leader to appoint the ranking minority members of the Committees on Appropriations and Ways and Means.

—Require all privileged committee reports to be cleared through the Speaker's Office.

Party apparatus

The majority and minority parties should increase their capacities for developing alternatives to the programs of a president of the other party. Efforts should be made to see to it that these alternatives receive consideration in Congress and are visible to the public:

—Authorize policy research staffs for both political parties in the House. These staffs would support the caucus or conference and would be under the direct control of a committee appointed by the party floor leaders.

—Utilize the policy committees for developing party positions on proposals—those offered by the president, the other party and the party's own research staff—and for urging congressional committee consideration of the party's own proposals.

—Establish a separate Committee on Committees in the House Democratic Party, chaired by the Speaker, with the membership elected in caucus by region. The floor leader and whip would serve *ex officio* on the committee.

—Reduce the membership of the House Republican Committee on Committees by having the membership elected in conference by region.

—Institute an end-of-session caucus review of the party record in legislation, with reports from committee chairmen or ranking minority members and party leaders. Such a meeting would provide for debate and planning for the next session. It should be open to the press and the public.

Committees and subcommittees

Other changes—which are less directly related to party-committee relationships, but which involve the efficiency of committee operations, the potential for developing alternatives and the power of committee leaders—should be made:

—Survey existing staff functions and centralize where possible. For example, it may be feasible to establish an Office of Congressional Committee Organization and Administration which would handle routine matters, such as scheduling hearings and executive sessions, arranging for witnesses and editing the hearings and reports.

—Increase the computer-based information capability of congressional committees and hire information retrieval specialists. This function could also be centralized—possibly, in the Congressional Research Service.

—Expand the Congressional Research Service's research capability, as distinct from its daily response capability for the thousands of inquiries it receives.

Conclusion

I am conscious of the fact that Congress reforms itself. I have come to believe, however, that the 93rd Congress faces a unique opportunity. Changes made now could vastly increase Congress' decision-making capacities. I do not believe we should be forced to depend so heavily on the presidency for policy decisions—as important as that office is, and should be. Through its political parties and their leaders Congress has the potential to produce integrated alternative proposals to those offered by the executive. This can be done without a return to Cannonism and without a loss of the advantages of the most well-developed committee system in the world. It is to this end that the remarks and recommendations in this paper are directed.

Restructuring the House of Representatives

By John W. Gardner

ABSTRACT: Most organizations have a structure designed to solve problems which no longer exist. Jurisdictional boundaries within organizations tend to get set in concrete. Some potential solutions are not seriously considered because those solutions would threaten jurisdictional lines. The House of Representatives is like other organizations in this regard. In order to perform effectively its Constitutional and traditional functions, the House must update itself. However, there is no one ideal mode of organization which—if we achieve it—will spare us later reorganizations. The Select Committee on Committees of the House of Representatives is now looking into this difficult issue. Common Cause has advanced a number of proposals for the select committee's consideration and will be working to help achieve reforms designed to improve the effectiveness and the accountability of the House and its committees. Our proposals are: (1) rotation, (2) jurisdictional realignment, (3) improvement of oversight, (4) revision of budget and priorities-setting procedures and (5) strengthening of the Speakership.

John W. Gardner served as Secretary of Health, Education and Welfare from July 1965 to March 1968. Following his resignation he became Chairman of the National Urban Coalition and, in October 1970, Chairman of Common Cause. At the time of his appointment to the Cabinet by President Johnson, Dr. Gardner was President of the Carnegie Foundation of New York and the Carnegie Foundation for the Advancement of Teaching; he had joined the Carnegie Corporation in 1946 as executive associate, becoming its President in 1955. He served on President Kennedy's Task Force on Education and as Chairman of President Johnson's Task Force on Education and the White House Conference on Education. In 1964 Dr. Gardner was awarded the Presidential Medal of Freedom, the highest civil honor in the United States. He was the editor of President Kennedy's book To Turn the Tide, *and is the author of the books* Excellence, Self-Renewal, No Easy Victories, The Recovery of Confidence *and* In Common Cause.

A NUMBER of years ago I wrote an article on "How to Prevent Organizational Dry Rot."[1] I made the point that, if preventive measures are not taken, all human organizations tend to stagnate, rigidify and eventually succumb to the infirmities of age. However, preventive measures are possible. Organizations can continuously renew themselves. I set out several requirements for the organization which seeks renewal, and one of those requirements was fluidity of internal structure:

Obviously, no complex modern organization can exist without the structural arrangements of divisions, branches, departments, and so forth . . . Specialization and division of labor are at the heart of modern organization.

But jurisdictional boundaries tend to get set in concrete. Pretty soon, no solution to a problem is seriously considered if there is any danger that it will threaten jurisdictional lines. But those lines aren't sacred. They were established in some past time to achieve certain objectives . . . *Most organizations have a structure that was designed to solve problems that no longer exist.*[2]

This is the perspective from which I view the present problem of congressional reorganization.

There is no one ideal mode of organization for Congress which—if we achieve it—will spare us later reorganizations. As long as free self-government lasts, be it thousands of years, we will be correcting imbalances of power, coping with new threats to responsive government and fighting off the tendency of all human institutions to age and to become insider's games. Congress is

1. John W. Gardner, "How to Prevent Organizational Dry Rot," *Harpers*, October 1965.
2. Ibid.

process, more like the flame than the candle. It is the play of conflicting forces, the balancing out of bids for power, the constant making and remaking of what the astronauts call in-course corrections. In short, the solutions offered here speak to the condition of Congress today. They are not a ticket to Utopia.

To put it another way, the recommendations which follow are offered with a measure of humility. At the same time, it will become apparent that I do not intend to emulate those affectionate students of Congress who have come to love every quirk and oddity in its creaky functioning and would not change it for the world. Every human organization must evolve or die. Furthermore, in a swiftly changing world the only way to conserve is to innovate.

ROTATION

My first recommendation is that the House adopt a system of rotation of members among committees. Under rotation members would move from one committee to another, perhaps every six to eight years. Obviously, guidelines must be set for the manner of assignment of members to committees to ensure a balance of geographic and political representation on each committee. One approach is illustrated by the cross-sectional make-up of the Democratic Steering and Policy Committee which was established by the Democratic Caucus last winter.

One obvious advantage of rotating House members from committee to committee is that members would receive wider exposure to governmental policy and would thus be better prepared to make broad and deep judgments on the issues before them. They would bring the wisdom and perspective gleaned from service on one committee to their deliberations on another committee. Members would less frequently have to defer to some senior member whose encyclopedic knowledge of the subject matter concealed the poverty of his ideas.

A second advantage of rotation is that it would break up, or at least hamper the formation of, what I have called on other occasions the unholy trinity: the longstanding underground alliance of a committee member, a middle-level bureaucrat and a special interest lobbyist concerned with the same subject matter. Such alliances—the products of ripened acquaintance and mutuality of interest—would develop less powerfully under a system of rotation. Furthermore, under rotation, executive branch programs would more frequently be judged by persons who had no role in the initial development of those programs; therefore, no reasons of personal pride or political gain would exist to prevent objective oversight.

The third advantage of rotation is that it would strike the death knell for legislative fiefdoms presided over by aging satraps. Committee chairmen would continue to be selected by vote of the members of the majority party caucus. However, the grip of seniority would be loosened more effectively than by any of the recent measures. No doubt, there would still be a presumption in favor of representatives with the greatest tenure in Congress, but rotation would inevitably diminish the force of that criterion. Since a new chairman could look forward to only a few years tenure, his role would clearly be to organize the business of the committee rather than to consolidate a power base.

Under such arrangements merit would become more of a consideration in the emergence of leaders in the committees of the House. No longer would a promising legislator have to wait twenty years or more for a position of leadership. The result should be the attraction of persons with the highest qualifications to service in the House.

Some may object that rotation would undermine the specialization which is supposed to be a major strength of the House today. Yet, specialization is an institutional strength only up to a point, beyond which it becomes a weakness. Specialization in the House too often lulls members into uncritical acceptance of what the House experts assert. The result may be a harmonious, or at least quiet, system of reciprocity, but not necessarily a creative legislative process. A committee system is necessary to get the work of Congress done, but the system need not be so rigid or so minutely specialized as the present one. A member with only one major committee responsibility can, with reasonable diligence and in fairly short order, learn what he or she needs to know to legislate wisely. A greater burden would be placed on congressional committee staffs, but the upgrading of these staffs is long overdue and must occur in any case. Furthermore, it is critically important that adequate minority staffing be assured for each committee. The minority party should be entitled to at least one-third of the staffing allowances for each committee.

Behind all the reasons for rotation is one overpowering reason. All human institutions age; most eventually die of the infirmities of age. The arteriosclerosis of institutions involves undramatic symptoms, such as rigid internal structure, rules which cannot be changed, specialization instead of breadth, vested interests, fixed routines and hallowed customs. Rotation is a freshening device. It will loosen up stiffened joints, bring new blood to tired committees and enliven the whole system.

JURISDICTION

I hardly need dwell on the need for revising the jurisdictions of committees. Under the present committee structure, important subjects are sometimes dealt with inadequately because there is no committee to go into the matter or because there are too many committees which claim jurisdiction. Some committees are too narrow in scope; some committee jurisdictions make no sense. Some committees are too powerful.

The worst example of imbalance of power is the Committee on Ways and Means. That single, small committee handles all tax and foreign trade matters, Social Security, Medicare, health insurance, revenue sharing, pension legislation, the debt ceiling and such tax-related matters as lobbying by businesses and foundation-supported organizations. Ways and Means has a poor record of responsiveness to the public and the rest of Congress. Until October 1, 1973 it always held secret mark-up sessions, and it has no subcommittees. The fact that Democratic members of Ways and Means make committee assignments for their party further enhances the power of the committee. This function should be placed under some body directly responsible to the Democratic Caucus—preferably the Speaker.

The House should start with a clean slate in devising a proper committee structure, rather than refining the current jurisdictions by cutting and fitting. The number of committees should be sharply reduced. It follows that most of these committees—Ways and Means is an exception—will have broader jurisdictions and more power and that there will be fewer committee chairmen. In order to ensure members of ability ample opportunity to rise to positions of leadership, each committee should have an adequate number of subcommittees. It is crucial that these subcommittees have an explicitly defined jurisdiction within the committee. The authorizing, appropriating and oversight functions should be merged into a single committee with respect to each area of committee jurisdiction —I will return to this issue later.

If there is a smaller number of committees with broader jurisdictions, committees will have more subjects to cover than they have presently. Committee chairmen and members who are specialists now will become generalists. To break up the workload, to provide for a sharing of power and to provide for greater flexibility within the committee structure—since subcommittees can be added, abolished or changed more easily than full committees —every House committee should be mandated to establish a reasonable number of subcommittees with designated jurisdictions. Subcommittee chairmen should be selected in the same manner as full committee chairmen: by ballot in the caucus of the majority party.

To the extent that jurisdictions of full committees are broadened, some of the work of the Committee of the Whole House is theoretically reduced; having broader scope, the committees should begin to make some of the trade-offs between, for example, highways and mass transit—trade-offs which are now made on the floor or are not made at all. The role of the subcommittees should be to provide detailed investigation, to frame the debate and to advocate a point of view which may compete with that of another subcommittee. The role of the full committee, then, is to provide overview and synthesis.

This should not be to the detriment of floor debate. If the rotation principle is adopted, members should gradually become more knowledgeable and independent on a broad range of subjects. Floor debate should become more informed. It should reflect more serious and sophisticated questioning and analysis of issues—replacing questions designed merely to find out what is happening, which are commonplace in floor debate at present.

OVERSIGHT

Congress has the responsibility not only of writing the laws of the land, but of seeing that the executive branch carries them out. As everyone knows, Congress has not performed its oversight function adequately.

If oversight is to have a sharp edge, it must be closely linked to the appropriations function. We have already recommended that oversight, authorizations and appropriations be merged in a single committee with respect to each substantive area.

No doubt, effective performance of oversight will require strengthened committee staffs, but that is not the greatest need. Modern large scale organizations are so far-flung and complex that not even a managerial genius can know what is going on through personal observation, questioning of subordinates or inspection tours. Today, most successfully managed organizations of any size have highly sophisticated information systems designed to answer the kinds of questions a good manager might ask about the organization's performance. Neither the chairman of General Motors nor the secretary of defense could function effectively without such indices.

The Congress has never fully explored the potentialities of such information systems. Congress should require executive agencies to place before it a great deal of crucial information in precise, summary form; this will permit Congress to judge, at a glance, the agency's performance in various dimensions. In addition, oversight functions should be facilitated by the adoption of a law declaring that every federal agency charter, and the operations of each agency under its charter, are to be reviewed every five years, with a presumption that flaws in both charter and operations can be corrected by remedial legislation.

BUDGET PRIORITIES AND ECONOMIC POLICY

One of the most important, yet most neglected, functions of the Congress is legislating federal budget priorities and overseeing the management of the economy. The solution to this problem proposed by the Ullman-Whitten committee is totally unacceptable, because it would increase the power of the Ways and Means and Appropriations Committees without significantly improving the ability of the whole House to deal with budget questions.

It has been said recently that progressive legislators may want to duck the budget question because the existing piecemeal procedures have tended to favor great spending programs, such as Medicare, social security and water pollution control. I think that that time has passed; we have all witnessed the beating taken by domestic spending issues of the highest priority in recent months —largely because of the pressures on the budget caused by continued growth in defense expenditures and tax cuts made in 1969 and 1971. The budget reform issue can no longer be turned aside.

Some instrument is needed which will provide for: (1) the combined consideration of revenues and expenditures; (2) the absolutely necessary addition of a three- to five-year planning framework for federal taxes and expenditures; and (3) adequate means of overseeing the functioning of the executive with regard to monetary and fiscal policy, interest rates, the federal reserve system and antiinflation policy, as well as an ability to review overall national priorities issues.

As indicated above, it would be wrong to lodge these enormously important functions in either the already excessively powerful Ways and Means, or Appropriations, Committee or in a new committee with membership drawn from these committees. A new Committee on Budget Priorities and Economic Policy is needed to perform the three essential functions. This committee must have the power to recommend the means for reconciling expenditures and revenues; it must face the politically uncomfortable tasks of setting a budget ceiling and proposing to the House a formula for allocating budget resources among the substantive committees. The procedures established must set forth a process whereby the House and Senate can make the final determination on budget priorities unencumbered by procedural obstacles to majority rule. There must be ample time for the Congress to review the

findings and recommendations of the Budget Committee.

The basic work on priorities within substantive areas will already have been done in the other committees of the House—that is, committees which would have all authorizing, appropriations and oversight functions. With full implementation of the advance budgeting concept, authorizing functions would need to be accomplished only once every three years or so, thus, freeing time for detailed oversight work in the interim.

The Budget Committee should complete analysis of the administration's budget at least eighteen months in advance of the budget's effective date. The Budget Committee's major task should be reconciling the work of the substantive committees with spending targets and ranges, latest estimates of tax resources and any changes in priorities.

Any plan for consolidating authorizing, appropriations and oversight functions is contingent on the creation of institutional procedures for comparing revenues and expenditures and advance funding and realignment of the substantive committees. Common Cause strongly supports all of these changes.

Obviously, it will be necessary to provide exceptionally competent staffing resources for the Budget Committee. This does not mean that it has to match the executive agencies in numbers of budget personnel. Congressional staff should be allowed to sit in on specified portions of the executive budget-making process and should have access to the same data which the Office of Management and Budget has before it. This data should be public information available to all citizens and interested groups. Congress simply must be in a position to speak as the equal of the executive branch in budgetary matters. More important, the work of the congressional committees, including the mark-ups, must be done openly. Secrecy has plagued the functioning of the money committees in Congress, much to the detriment of the public interest.

Improvement of staffing resources and an end to secret committee meetings would increase the productive flow of information about budget issues among the executive, the Congress and the public. A tax expenditure budget would help legislators and the public understand the critical questions in tax policy: the purposes and costs of tax benefits. Citizens have a right to know how their tax dollars will be spent, and unless they feel that they and their elected representatives have fully participated in the taxing-appropriating process, citizens will distrust the system. Congress has to win the public's support for tax measures and public expenditure programs. The place to begin is with clear, understandable information and a budget process open to public view and participation.

THE SPEAKERSHIP

It is urgent that the office of the Speaker of the House be strengthened. This Constitutional office is vital to the efficiency of the House of Representatives. No body of 435 human beings can function effectively as a group without strong leadership. The capacity of the Speaker to provide such leadership is diminished by the rigidified committee system, by isolated enclaves of uncontrolled power and by the absence in some substantive areas of committees preestablished to accept appropriate grants of power.

Some liberals are allergic to the word and concept of leadership, and the phrase "strong leadership"—and I submit that it is so rare among legislative bodies as to be virtually unknown—gives them a terrible case of the shakes. However, total absence of leadership would be chaos. The choice is among kinds of leadership.

Anyone who has observed the Congress and state legislatures over the years and has read a little history recognizes, at the very least, the following possibilities:

—a tyrannical Speaker with all the power gathered into his hands;
—a strong Speaker accountable to a healthy caucus;
—a tyrannical caucus dominated by an oligarchical circle;
—an alliance of baronial committee chairmen, ruling by live-and-let-live trade-offs.

Another possibility observable in some state legislatures is leadership stemming from special interest representatives wholly outside the legislative body.

From the standpoint of a member of the House, the most attractive choice depends on the member's age, seniority, leadership gifts, venality and so on. From the standpoint of the citizen, the best hope of effectiveness and accountability in the House is a strong Speaker who, in turn, is accountable to a vigorous and open majority party caucus.

The strengthening of the Speakership need not diminish the independence of the individual members nor make the House into a personal czardom. The goal would be to create a power to open procedural channels, not a power to dictate policy. It would also be a shared power—one which depends on accountability to the full majority party caucus. It would not by-pass committees, but instead would make them responsible to the will of the majority caucus.

While such procedural hedges as these would guard against the abuse of the Speaker's power, the Speaker should be given considerable day-to-day authority to move the business of the House and to manage its housekeeping functions. The House as presently constituted is burdened with too many procedural hurdles which stall legislation. The Speaker and the majority party caucus should have the power to cut through this red tape and bring issues before the House as a whole. In this way the House would have the capacity to act when a majority consensus prevailed rather than being frustrated by a wholly unnecessary dispersal of authority.

CONCLUSION

Now, let me summarize some of the considerations which seem to me of paramount importance in any reorganization of the House. First, any acceptable plan must substantially reduce the number of committees and draw down the excessive concentration of power now centered in the Ways and Means and Appropriations Committees. Second, any reorganization worth supporting would have to make meaningful revisions in the way congressional budget priorities are set and overseen. Third, the jurisdictions of the substantive committees must be modernized to focus the attention of the House on contemporary problems. For example, committees might be organized around each of the following subjects: social services, natural resources, transportation policy, labor and technology and consumer affairs. Finally, for any plan to be effective, it must enhance the ability of the Speaker of the House to perform his leadership function.

Book Department

INTERNATIONAL RELATIONS

RICHARD E. BARRINGER. *War: Patterns of Conflict.* Pp. xvi, 293. Cambridge, Mass.: The MIT Press, 1972. $13.95.

Barringer represents an undivided dedication to the rigorous scientific approach, and his book is above all an exposition of an elaborate method. In his own words, he is trying in this volume: "1) to explore and, if possible, establish the various configurations of factors that condition the origin, development and termination of local conflict; 2) to determine the various empirical types of local conflict that occur at each significant stage of its development . . .; 3) to establish . . . the foundations of an early warning system." The latter is quite ambitious. Earlier attempts were made in this direction, not necessarily mentioned in Barringer's volume.

In his discussion of causation, Barringer advances a multicausal or pluralistic model, and rightly so, since a pluralistic approach suggests also an open, non-dogmatic methodological attitude. In his "Codebook" he defines as many as three hundred variables and applies them in eighteen selected conflict situations, including Algeria-Morocco, Cuba: Bay of Pigs, Cyprus, Ethiopia-Somalia, Israel-

Egypt, Spanish civil war, Malayan insurgency, USSR-Iran, India-China, to mention a few. Central to his method is the "agreement analysis." This approach differs from correlations as well, as the author and Professor Wright argue from the multifactor analysis. It seems to me, however, that Barringer's "agreement analysis" is only a variation of a multifactor approach.

The major part of the volume is filled with manipulation of data by complex methods and by development of equally complex models. However, toward the end of the book, the findings are rewarding and interesting. Here, Barringer lists various types of conflict, hostilities, escalation, de-escalation, termination and settlement. Some of the types are obvious; others are indicative of a variety of alternative situations and problem solving. Indeed, here is a section of practical significance for analysts and decision makers. But while reading the lists of those various outcomes, various types of solutions, the reader wonders whether such a long and complicated method was really necessary to arrive at those results. Do we need as many as three hundred computerized variables?

In 1947 and later, Brookings Institution organized a number of seminars on foreign policy analysis, directed by the late Leo Pasvolsky. A problem was first analyzed, and a group of knowledgeable and experienced scholars and practitioners suggested alternative answers or possibilities of courses of actions—options, as they are called today. The various types of solutions suggested were based on experience, knowledge and analytical talent. A qualitative approach in this case was faster, perhaps more appropriate than solely the quantitative one; the analysis remained humane in values and sentiments.

Using his hierarchical approach to data, Barringer moves to higher and higher levels of abstractions, more and more remote from human problems. In his "relationistic" approach, the focus is on relations between two antagonists, who become almost "antagonistic partners," partners in a game of conflict. Let us take cases not included in his study, such as the rape of Nanking by the Japanese in 1937, the slaughter of Russians at Stalingrad, the torture of the Warsaw ghetto. In a relationistic approach, the conflict situation would appear as a set of variables between two antagonists, the wolf and the sheep playing equal roles, only the sheep is weaker and in consequence a loser. The actors of the drama vanish. What remains are anonymous forces only, and killers cannot be distinguished from victims. For, in forecast and conflict analysis, the personality of decision makers and the strategy are essential. In aggressive design the actor must design his courses of action in tactical and strategic patterns, dependent again on conditions or factors. The sole analysis of the latter is necessary but not sufficient. There are only few strategies available in a given historical period. An aggressive government— such as Hitler, prewar Japan—usually reapplies a strategic design which was successful in its early stage. Thus, understanding of strategic-tactical patterns of an antagonist is important in forecast and analysis of his movements. In consequence, an "action approach" is essential and complementary to a "process" or "interactional" model.

Barringer, in his attempt of a very rigorous method, has made a contribu-

tion showing the strength, but also the limitations of such an approach. In a sense, it is a document of intellectual trends and attempts of scholars to apply science in the service of a peaceful world.

FELIKS GROSS
Department of Sociology
Brooklyn College and
Graduate School
City University of New York

SAUL S. FRIEDMAN. *No Haven For the Oppressed: United States Policy Toward Jewish Refugees, 1938–1945.* Pp. 235. Detroit: Wayne State University Press, 1973. $15.95.

The tragic Hitler era continues to evoke scholarly interest and a growing volume of increasingly valuable monographs. This process has become quite evident among Jewish scholars as well, both in the United States and in Israel, indicating perhaps that the paralytic trauma of the European Jewish Holocaust has now, with the passage of some thirty years, finally become a somewhat manageable subject to examine without searing the intellect or the psyche.

During the past seven years, three major works have appeared on the American scene, each asking the same question: What did the United States —and its allies—do during World War II to prevent the destruction of European Jewry? Arthur Morse, in his *While Six Million Died* (New York: Random House, 1967), made the United States State Department and the British Foreign Office virtual partners with the Nazi murderers in the Jewish genocide. Henry Feingold, in his *The Politics of Rescue* (New Brunswick: Rutgers University Press, 1970), less polemically, but with devastating documentation, added Roosevelt's ambivalent leadership to the roster of culprits. In this new work, *No Haven for the Oppressed,* Saul Friedman broadens the villainous realms even further, to include congressional callousness, an American public opinion heavily encumbered with undertones of antisemitism, and even the American

Jewish communal leadership, sharply divided on how to best cope with the unprecedented crisis.

Both Feingold's and Friedman's works, unlike Morse's, are the results of extensive doctoral research programs, and draw heavily on governmental and private archival materials. Friedman's new work, in addition to the sources used by Feingold, has drawn more heavily on Jewish communal records, congressional figures and labor movement publications. He gives a new importance to the personal narratives of Professor Harold W. Dodds, head of the American delegation to the 1943 Bermuda conference on refugees.

Friedman's work tends to moderate the Morse-Feingold charge of blatant antisemitism laid upon Assistant Secretary of State Breckinridge Long, who directed twenty-three of the forty-two divisions of the department, including the all important Visa Division (p. 116ff.). On the other hand, he is far less sympathetic towards Undersecretary of State Sumner Welles (p. 206), who received rather favorable treatment at the hands of Feingold and Morse. He tends to be somewhat understanding of Rabbi Stephen Wise's weak leadership in the critical weeks of August and September of 1942 when the murderous picture was emerging in all its stark clarity (p. 154), and appears to dismiss the massive American Jewish Conference of 1943 as largely unimportant (p. 147). Further, his treatment of the Peter Bergson group of organizations and militants is a more appreciative one than has generally been accorded them (p. 147).

Curiously enough, Friedman does not quote certain important documents available in the very collections he researched that might strengthen even further the contentions that he put forward. Wise, for instance, was very conscious of the dangers inherent in the middle man role he had come to play between his Jewish constituency on the one hand and the administration chieftains on the other. As he wrote to Felix Frankfurter on September 16, 1942: "Have you noted that I have kept the thing [the reports of mass murder] out of the press up to this time, thus accepting a great responsibility if the threat should be executed?" (Wise Papers, American Jewish Historical Society, Waltham, Mass.) Further, the State Department records in the National Archives are replete with accounts of separate interviews during the war years with representatives of the major Jewish organizations, most notably the American Jewish Committee and the World Jewish Congress, in which the mutual denunciations and recriminations actually encouraged the passive government officials to retard the progress of positive refugee and rescue programs.

This fine volume now takes a major place in the growing literature of Holocaust research. It will undoubtedly be supplemented continuously in the near future, since a great deal of research is currently being conducted on the enormity of the Nazi crimes and the response of the civilized world to them. Hopefully, from all this knowledge will come a more aware and refined human consciousness of evil and the necessity to deal with it with courage and determination.

HERBERT ROSENBLUM
Hebrew College
Brookline
Massachusetts

LEON GOURÉ et al. *Convergence of Communism and Capitalism: The Soviet View.* Pp. iii, 168. Washington, D.C.: Center for Advanced International Studies, University of Miami, 1973. $5.95.

FOY D. KOHLER et al. *Soviet Strategy for the Seventies: From Cold War to Peaceful Coexistence.* Pp. v, 241. Washington, D.C.: Center for Advanced International Studies, University of Miami, 1973. $5.95.

Like their predecessors in the University of Miami's Center for Advanced International Studies series, these two volumes provide useful documentation for the general student of foreign affairs. In each case, the smaller portion of the book consists of an essay discussing the significance of Soviet comments on the topic at issue, followed by a considerably longer section of excerpts from Soviet publications. No effort has been made to utilize content analysis, although the subjects are highly adapted to simple techniques and the multiple authorship should have facilitated reliability tests. Nevertheless, overall representativeness of the sample appears to be assured by the expertise of the principal authors, although, as suggested below, I have some questions about the chronological apportionment. More critical, from the point of view of utility, to social scientists is the lack of conceptual frameworks. Again, however, one must accept the works for what they are: careful compilations by area experts of useful materials on highly relevant topics, rather than social scientific analyses.

In these terms, the shorter volume on *Convergence* is the more valuable. There is no attempt to forecast the prospects for convergence, or even to analyze the works of Western forecasters. The very short introduction is essentially limited to tracing the origins and emphases of Soviet criticism of the convergence theory; it performs this limited task in a brisk, critical way. The documentary extracts consist of extended passages from relatively obscure Soviet periodicals showing how the challenge of the convergence theory has forced Soviet writers to reassess the significance of important elements of Marxism-Leninism. Considering the wide range of publications drawn upon and the skill required to identify articles substantively dealing with aspects of convergence, the collection is admirable.

The book on Soviet strategy is more routine. While the lengthier introduction necessarily covers a far longer time period, nearly all of the documentary selections are too brief to be satisfying. In the absence of content analysis, though, the very large number of similar quotations which the authors could adduce to show basic continuity in Soviet objectives does provide some assurance that selectivity was unbiased. It is harder to accept the assertion that "the current leaders are more militant and activist in

their view of what is to be done by the communist side within the framework of peaceful coexistence than was Khrushchev, and are evidently willing to take positions and to encourage and support conflicts and developments that Khrushchev appeared anxious to avoid" (p. 40). As I see it, this view lumps together two distinct phases of the post-Khrushchev Soviet policy: the relatively harsh, combative period between approximately 1965 and 1970, and the more compromising stance since 1970. Even the earlier period—I have argued elsewhere—represented, in part, a real defensive reaction to what the Soviet leaders regarded as an American offensive—elimination of Soviet client dictators in Indonesia and Ghana, strong United States reaction against North Vietnam, Israeli defeat of Arabs, "bridge-building" in East Europe. These were contrasted to the bombast—and acceptance of some very real risks—which Khrushchev had indulged in for more expansionist goals. Since 1970, some Soviet policies—unwillingness to aid North Vietnamese and Syrian clients when they used Soviet arms for unauthorized attacks—suggest a higher degree of caution than Khrushchev's. I completely agree with the authors that the record demonstrates that the Soviet leadership regards coexistence as a tactic useful for a few years rather than a basic policy change; but I must ask whether men as old as the Politburo core can realistically think—as far as their own policy direction goes—in longer terms. In other words, *Soviet Strategy*, like its companion volume, is a mine of useful and reliable raw material; each analyst will refine these materials to the best of his own abilities.

JOHN A. ARMSTRONG
University of Wisconsin

GLENN B. INFIELD. *The Poltava Affair.* Pp. xiv, 265. New York: Macmillan, 1973. $7.95.

Late in the afternoon of 21 June 1944, the first British-based United States Army Air Force shuttle-bomber force landed at Poltava, Russia. The United States hoped that shuttle raids would not only expose targets in eastern Germany that had previously been beyond the range of American bombers, but also result in similar United States-Soviet cooperation with bases against the Japanese. Within a few hours, however, the Luftwaffe imperiled these hopes by a devastating night raid on the American bombers crowding the Poltava base.

Infield provides an exciting account of this raid, based on Air Force and Luftwaffe records and on interviews with German and American participants. The author, however, goes beyond a mere description of the bombing that left over sixty B-17s destroyed or damaged. He delves into the history of the shuttle effort, the intricacies of United States-Soviet negotiations, and the reason the Luftwaffe was so successful that night over Poltava.

Concerning the factor of success, Infield argues that Stalin himself wanted the attack. Though he had earlier approved the shuttle concept, Stalin had now changed his mind. Rather than break the agreement and perhaps jeopardize the flow of United States supplies to Russia, Stalin ordered the Soviet fighter force not to defend the Poltava base. The Soviet leader reasoned that the raid would so discourage the Americans that they would cancel the shuttles on their own.

Though intriguing, Infield's case is unconvincing. Though few would argue with Stalin's capability to employ such Machiavellian maneuvers, the author fails to demonstrate clearly that the absence of Soviet air defense resulted from Stalin's complicity rather than from Soviet incompetence. He gives no treatment to the command structure or communications system of the Soviet air defense to see if the explanation might not lie there, rather than in Stalin's mind.

There are other points that are bothersome. Despite his commendable efforts at research, the author uses no footnotes. This is perhaps understandable in some "popular" histories, but they are sorely missed when the author begins dealing with Stalin's plans and motives. And there are other points: the failure to use Richard Lukas' *Eagles East*, the main scholarly study of USAAF-Soviet cooperation; the use of both military and civilian time in the same paragraph; the careless labeling of photographs and the lack of a complete index or any list of abbreviations.

Despite these weaknesses—or perhaps carping on the part of this reviewer—this is a readable book, spiced with some delightful anecdotes and likely to find a wide and ready audience among general readers.

CALVIN L. CHRISTMAN
Social Science Department
William Penn College
Oskaloosa
Iowa

HEINRICH KRONSTEIN. *The Law of International Cartels.* Pp. xiv, 489. Ithaca, N.Y.: Cornell University Press, 1973. $21.50.

This work, the basic concepts of which were first presented in *Das Recht der Internationallen Kartelle,* published in Germany in 1967, elaborates a disturbing thesis: that the modern international cartel—"a coordination of the economic behavior of independent partners, based upon their consent, which results in regulation of one or more markets" (p. 41)—has fashioned an economic order which operates beyond the control of existing, public international institutions as well as the nation-state. And it is in developing and delineating this thesis that the author uses it to describe how cartels employ existing legal institutions and influence the creation of new ones to carve, defend and perpetuate that order.

But what is the law of international cartels? Its technical nature cannot be treated here, but it concerns the genesis and development of certain legal institutions and the uses—inconsistent with their original purposes—to which cartels have put them; it comprehends rules which govern the choices of law favorable to cartels for the adjudication of potential controversies; it pertains to the employment of arbitration tribunal to avoid national courts. Furthermore, it relates to the use of industrial property and corporate law to create syndicates to effect the joint purchase and sale of specific products, the fashioning of patent-holding companies to control exclusive licenses and regulate the market, and the forming of research agencies and technological boards to pursue vast areas of research and determine if, when, and where a particular technique is to be disclosed and used.

The author also specifies some of the consequences of the cartel's activities—how they operate to frustrate the objectives of national and international agreements designed to guarantee the free flow of goods and services, procure preferential treatment for "primary customers," abort the development of potential competitors, stifle technological breakthrough in the most advanced of states and thwart growth in underdeveloped nations. In elaborating all of the above, this well-written, copiously documented book supplants all existing works—such as Kari Levitt's *Silent Surrender*—which purport to deal with the international economic order from the standpoint of multinational corporations.

Although the book was written for lawyers and other specialists in the field, this welcome contribution to the literature, which seeks to escape the limits of traditional gaze on trusts, oligopolies and their regulatory laws and focus critical attention on the phenomenon of contemporary international cartels, should be a must on the reading list of all who are interested in, or who actually aspire to influence, the behavior of men and nations.

WINSTON E. LANGLEY
Department of Political Science
Boston State College

HARALD MALMGREN, ed. *Pacific Basin Development: The American Interests.* Pp. xv, 148. Lexington, Mass.: D.C. Heath, 1972. $10.00.

Published for the Overseas Development Council, this book is largely a series of papers prepared for the ODC seminars on American interests in East Asian development during 1970 to 1971. Malmgren wrote an overall introductory chapter and a very short conclusion to reflect events after the July 15, 1971 Nixon announcement of his future trip to China, but the role of China is almost totally ignored in the five papers and two editorial contributions. Instead, the writers focus on United States and Japanese trade and investment policies toward the noncommunist nations of Eastern Asia, and generally support increased grant aid and credits by Japan, more private American economic involvement and greater regional unity especially among the Association of South East Asian Nations (ASEAN) states. Like all such seminar products, some papers are better than others, and there is a good deal of repetition throughout, but the book is a very good review of past economic relations within the Pacific basin states and makes intelligent suggestions for the future. It also recognizes some, if not enough, of the political deterrents to economic free trade and cooperation.

Malgren's introduction points correctly to the "other half of the Guam Doctrine" wherein the United States' economic role needs major review. The economic disputes between Japan and the United States have been growing since 1969, but the two capitals seem to regard them as strictly bilateral, whereas a broader regional approach by the two major Pacific powers would be better. J. Alexander Caldwell then writes about Japanese economic cooperation in Asia since 1950, making only a few errors —such as a reference on page 24 to Japan's "family-owned" trading combines "dissolved" by the Occupation —and detailing the export and raw material promotion goals of Japanese postwar aid and reparations. He notes that the Japanese government portion of economic aid has been far too small compared with other donor states, as Tokyo relied on its business community to administer most aid programs. This is changing now: another post-1971 development beyond the scope of the book. Caldwell outlines the many obstacles to more effective Japanese aid, including fears in Southeast Asia.

The third chapter is by Seiji Naya and Richard Schatz, a short one full of statistics on United States and Japanese trade, investment and aid in East and Southeast Asia. The fourth chapter, "Rhetoric and Reality in Regional Cooperation," by Bernard K. Gordon is the briefest but one of the best possible: all writers question the practicality of any Pacific Basin Free Trade Area as suggested by Professor Kojima of Hitotsubashi University, Tokyo, but Gordon raises other points to sober the more idealistic hopes of economists who ignore political realities.

The fifth chapter is on labor utilization and multinational corporations in the Pacific area by Robert D'A. Shaw and Donald Sherk, who reject the common criticism that corporations seek cheap labor sites abroad, but propose better United States and Japanese domestic programs to take care of workers displaced by capital movement abroad. Labor is more protectionist than management because the latter can always be mobile. The demands of labor in developing and donor nations are well explained, as well as the excellent example of Taiwan—and, to a lesser extent, South Korea—in balancing domestic growth with foreign investment effectively utilized. The sixth chapter, by the ex-Indonesian ambassador to Washington, Soedjatmoko, is my favorite because of its sharp style and superb commentary on "The Role of the Major Powers in the East Asian-Pacific Region." His paper was published earlier in Richard Walker, ed., *Prospects in the Pacific* (Washington, D.C.: Heldref Publications, 1972). It stands far above the level of the other papers in the book and is therefore worth publishing twice. Soedjatmoko's transfer back to Djakarta as advisor to his government's National Planning Board is another proof of Indonesia's advancement from the economic and diplomatic failures of the old Sukarno regime.

In short, this is a book which should be in every organization or university library as a good reference to the recent past and potential future of East Asian economic relations between the United States and Japan as both donors and major powers, and the developing nations. If Australia, New Zealand and China had been given more adequate coverage, and the book brought out in cheaper paperback edition, its value would have been much greater.

DOUGLAS H. MENDEL, JR.
Department of Political Science
University of Wisconsin

JOHN W. WHEELER-BENNETT and ANTHONY NICHOLLS. *The Semblance of Peace: The Political Settlement After the Second World War* Pp. xiv, 878. New York: Macmillan, 1972. $35.00.

The publication of this book is the culmination of over five years of research into documents, memoirs, correspondence and interviews. The authors hoped to "illuminate the origins and significance of the uneasy and interrupted peace which followed the defeat of the Axis Powers." They have certainly done so.

The book is organized on a topical and chronological basis. Over six hundred pages of lively text are illustrated, thoroughly documented, and indexed. Another two hundred pages of analytical appendices and documents add depth to this impressive work.

The authors provide fascinating accounts of the wartime conferences which brought Stalin, Churchill and FDR together. The outcomes of some negotiations are explained in terms of bargaining situations, bureaucratic conflicts and diplomatic logistics. Throughout, however, the clash of personalities and perspectives is evident. FDR's vision of a postwar condominium with the Soviets —enhanced by a universally endorsed United Nations—was undermined by sphere of influence considerations. Yet personal diplomacy did yield temporary rewards; FDR and Stalin shared a mutual distain for the Free French of deGaulle, a distaste for traditional forms of colonialism, and a hard-line approach on post-war Germany's future—all values that were eventually compromised. After Roosevelt's death, his successor's lack of background and need for detailed advice brought more realistic State Department policymakers to the fore.

The authors assert that important compromises were made at Yalta and that the alliance was not ruptured by disagreement over Poland's destiny. Obstinacy on the part of Polish leaders, as well as geopolitical realities of the period, sealed Poland's fate as a satellite. The authors rightly see Czechoslovakia's fall as a greater tragedy that could have been avoided in 1945. United States troops could have advanced to Prague, rather than graciously halt at the request of Soviet military commanders.

The authors boldly analyze the near inexplicable Soviet *volte-face* towards Austria, along with other historical curiosities. Inquiries into the politics of the Nuremberg trial, the unconditional surrenders of Italy, Germany and Japan, and resulting peace treaties are developed with a knack for appropriate anecdotes.

Parts of this book will undoubtedly infuriate some scholars. The authors explicitly reject claims by revisionist historians that East and West must share blame for the development of implacable and hostile policies. The authors place responsibility for the cold war on Moscow. There is little sense conveyed of an impending clash between chiliastic superpowers regardless of key political actors—many of whom seemed interchangeable. Because they do not clearly explicate the major findings and economic emphases of revisionists, the authors are vulnerable on this score.

Isolated lapses, such as confusion over twenty billions rather than millions demanded in reparations from Germany, are of little consequence. It is unfortunate, however, that simplistic cold war imagery is frequently evoked in the concluding chapters. NATO still represents the forces of "freedom-loving peoples," the Warsaw Pact, "the organized might of Communist power," and "Red China" is ominously portrayed. Some may skim such passages and erroneously conclude that the book lacks historical balance. A reading of the introductory chapter should quickly dispel such impressions and indicate the book's rich promise.

The strengths of this ambitious study far outweigh both picayune and ideological objections raised here. It is unfortunate that its inflated price will probably limit the book's readership.

PAUL CONWAY
Department of Political Science
State University College of
New York
Oneonta

ASIA, AFRICA AND
LATIN AMERICA

ALAN H. ADAMSON. *Sugar Without Slaves: The Political Economy of British Guiana, 1838–1904*. Pp. x, 315. New Haven, Conn.: Yale University Press, 1972. $12.50.

In this excellent but deeply depressing book, Professor Adamson shows how a small group of sugar planters in British Guiana kept rich and powerful throughout the nineteenth century despite the triple blows of slave emancipation, the loss of their protected British market and the world collapse of sugar prices. Accepting no moral lessons from the abolition movement, these planters continued to exploit their colored workers outrageously, while mouthing smug racist statements to the effect that they were promoting the civilization of the Blacks. Adamson credits the planters with business efficiency in mechanizing and modernizing their sugar industry, but he argues that they mainly survived by extracting heavy labor at low wages from a large dependent work force. With the termination of slavery in the 1830s, the Guyanese Negroes (Creoles) began to leave the plantations to take up peasant farming in the unoccupied land of the colony. The sugar planters, making little effort to woo them back, quickly found acceptable substitutes by importing East Indian coolies on ten year contracts. Half of the 46,514 immigrants who arrived between 1834 and 1848 were dead by 1848, but this did not stop the traffic from continuing until, by 1918, 341,491 laborers had entered Guiana, 236,205 of them Indian.

A narrow oligarchy of planters kept total political control of the colony—less than 1 percent of the population could vote in 1850—and they poured nearly 20 percent of the public revenue into paying for this immigration, thus taxing the Creole peasants to subsidize the sugar plantations. Furthermore, the colony government did its best to prevent the development of a viable peasant economy independent of sugar; it blocked Creole land purchases, broke up village communes, levied crushing taxes and offered no schools, hospitals, transportation or other public services in return. The laissez faire Liberals who staffed the Colonial Office protested these tactics, but always surrendered to the sugar lobby.

Adamson is a sober scholar with an axe to grind, and a reader with no interest in Guyanese history can find his tale compelling. He is best on the economic side of the story: the cost of immigration, wages, prices, public finance, plantation capitalization, the sugar trade, and so forth. He is less satisfactory on the social side, for his sources give little sense of how the Creoles and coolies lived, or how these rival ethnic blocs interacted with each other. Just what might have happened to this land of El Dorado had the sugar planters quit a century ago no one can say, but the planters' legacy of an oppressed plural society is the curse of independent Guyana today.

RICHARD S. DUNN
University of Pennsylvania

GIOVANNI ARRIGHI and JOHN S. SAUL. *Essays on the Political Economy of Africa.* Pp. 416. New York: Monthly Review Press, 1973. $12.50. Paperbound, $4.50.

This work is a collection of essays, all but two of which have previously been published. As the somewhat ambiguous title of the work indicates, the material included in the book encompasses a wide spectrum ranging from Nationalism and Revolution in Sub-Saharan Africa to an appendix on African Peasantries. The only real link between the essays is the common and preconceived ideological approach of the authors.

The work of Arrighi and Saul is well known to Africanists, and their Marxist views are readily apparent in this book. Envisioning themselves as an integral part of the "anti-imperialist struggle," they attempt to establish a theoretical basis upon which to build the "African revolution." To this end the authors eschew some of the techniques traditionally associated with their respective disciplines—economics and political science—and seek to place themselves on common ground with the oppressed peoples of Africa. They are only partially successful, inasmuch as their scholarship follows predictable academic patterns, but the authors' Marxist interpretations are certain to stir the controversy and discussion so dear to the radical heart.

Therein lies the book's greatest utility—as a medium well-calculated to foster contention and encourage intellectual rejoinders. Otherwise it is simply a group of essays, which incidentally vary considerably in quality, treating a number of currently popular themes on modern Africa. Loosely tied together in three sections with the nebulous headings of overviews, perspectives and case studies, the essays deal with topics such as socialism, populism and development on both a national and pan-African level. The research is sound but unexceptional, and the authors' perfunctory preface is disappointing. The value of the book would have been enhanced considerably by a substantial introduction, giving a fuller explanation of the methodological and conceptual approaches advocated by Arrighi and Saul and employed by them in their work. Still, their arguments have a cogency often missing in works tinctured by polemic, and the importance of the issues they raise in the context of contemporary developments in tropical Africa is such that all serious students of the region will want to familiarize themselves with the book.

JAMES A. CASADA
Winthrop College
Rock Hill
South Carolina

DOROTHY BORG and SHUMPEI OKA-
MOTO, eds. *Pearl Harbor as History:
Japanese-American Relations, 1931–
1941*. Pp. xv, 801. New York: Columbia
University Press, 1973. $25.00.

In July 1969, a group of American and
Japanese scholars, some established and
other newcomers, assembled at Lake
Kawaguchi in Japan to deliver papers
and discuss the workings of their respective countries in the decade after the
Manchurian Incident of 1931. The bina-
tional specialists were to avoid rework-
ing old mines by comparative study of
public and private organizations and institutions which were important in prewar decision-making. Eleven Americans
and fifteen Japanese submitted substantive essays, the American editors provided background, and Richard Leopold
supplied historiographical reflections—a
gentle critique and comparison contain-
ing the only commentary on the oral
phases. The six hundred page text is followed by 136 pages of ill-placed but
generous footnotes, plus useful glos-
saries. The book's title is catchy but misleading, for the cataclysm of Pearl Harbor is offstage and anticlimactical.

Symptomatic of its genre and multi-
plex authorship, the collection is uneven
and repetitious. Certain first-rate scholars must not have been invited or could
not attend; one thinks of Hata, Maru-
yama, Butow, and Crowley. More importantly, parallelism of the supposedly paired essays is lacking. Thus
Weigley's fine twenty-four page piece on
the United States Army and War Department overshadows Fujiwara's disappointing eight pages on the Japanese
Army—a topic described equally well by
Hayashi elsewhere in English. Good
papers by Imai and Graebner are mis-
matched, the former writing on cabinet,
monarch and elders; the latter, on
Hoover, Roosevelt and the Japanese.
Other authors slight the comparative, institutional framework; for example,
Borg's discourse on Dennett and Gris-
wold, Thomson's distraction by Horn-
beck. Nevertheless, there are path-
breaking contributions concerning the
Commerce and Treasury departments
(by Gardner), the Finance Ministry
(Yamamura) and American business
(Wilkins). Particularly noteworthy papers examine the roles of the Foreign
Ministry (Usui), the American Embassy
in Tokyo (Iriye), the two navies (Hein-
richs, Asada) and structural-functional
problems in general (Mushakoji). Ernest
May's piece on American press coverage
of Japan is interesting, but unexpectedly
thin.

The Kawaguchi papers reflect new information and mature scholarship.
Leopold correctly notes that differences
in approach may reflect Americans' contention that the Pacific War was "a mistake, one that led to many of the intracta-
ble problems confronting the United
States today, while the Japanese view
that conflict somewhat fatalisti-
cally . . . ."

Borg *et al.* have handled their editing
and translation chores admirably. As
Leopold asserts, we have long passed the
point "when specialists on either side of
the Pacific can do proper work in this
field without a command of both languages." An inexpensive paperbound
edition of *Pearl Harbor as History* is
much needed.

ALVIN D. COOX
Department of History
San Diego State University
California

DANIEL S. LEV. *Islamic Courts in Indonesia: A Study in the Political Bases
of Legal Institutions*. Pp. ix, 281.
Berkeley: University of California
Press, 1972. $11.75.

It was always easy to frame Indonesian
politics in terms of a conventional left-
right spectrum with a multitude of political parties pegged neatly from the Partei
Komunis Indonesia (PKI) on the left to
Nahdatul Ulana, Muslim Teachers Party
(NU) or Partei Sarekat Islam Indonesia
(PSII) on the right. And this was
confirmed by the parties themselves, as
they consolidated into *aliran,* and by
Soekarno's ideological nostrums, such as
Nasakom, which sought to amalgamate,
but acronymically confessed the conventional spectrum.

Students who delved further were soon mired in the reality of an incredibly complex political slough, whose bottom, which they could little more than sense, was rooted in the tangled religio-political sources of legitimate authority. The Islamic courts, continually in tension with *adat* and civil law, symbolized this puzzle of authority sources, but were a subject which was at once forbiddingly complex and dismissed by most social scientists as theoretically uninteresting, since all the axioms of modernization treated such things at best as vestigial remnants of tradition.

Dan Lev's book, product of some fifteen years' effort, cuts deeply into the confusion and looms as one of those few volumes which will stand as musts for students of Indonesian politics. The pervasive but curiously leaden quality of Islam in Indonesian politics was adequately clarified for me for the first time, perhaps because of Lev's ingenious amalgam of historical and institutional analysis, concrete accounts in the specific legal areas of divorce and inheritance, and finally a broad-gauged, thoroughly engaging discussion of political ramifications. There is the suggestion, for instance, that Indonesia's "functionally distinct legal systems [may] represent competing principles of legitimacy that are related in an overarching political order that is itself legitimate." In other words, in this inherent conflict system, there may be operating "something like a moiety structure."

Myriad confusing and overlapping relationships—such as modernist to traditionalist Islam, political Islam to nonpolitical Islam, Java Islam to non-Java Islam, Islam to nationalism, Islam to the military, Islam to the bureaucracy—are brought into some manageable perspective through the prism of Lev's examination of the court system. For this reason it must be said that this is a book which far exceeds the dimensions of its title. Not just students of legal institutions in new nations, or scholars of Islam, but all students of Indonesia, will benefit equally. Moreover, while explicitly eschewing trendy modes of political science abstraction, the analytic framework exemplifies a kind of innovative approach which assiduously holds abstraction to a level befitting the data at hand. Closely reasoned, redolent in pertinent fact material, this publication markedly augments our efforts to understand Indonesia.

ROGER K. PAGET
Department of Political Science
University of Colorado

JOHN W. DARDESS. *Conquerors and Confucians: Aspects of Political Change in Late Yuan China.* Pp. 245. New York: Columbia University Press, 1973. $12.50.

With this solidly researched and clearly organized account of central government politics in the late Yuan, Professor Dardess has met a long-standing need among Western students of Yuan and Ming history. The period emphasized begins with the restoration of the line of Qaishan in 1328, and ends with the overthrow of the minister Toghto in 1355, which set in motion the disintegration of the Yuan regime.

The author's main argument in analyzing the course of events runs roughly thus: (1) after the restoration of 1328, Mongol nobles in the steppes and their allies in the Chaghatai and Ogodei Khanates were effectively excluded from Yuan politics, and the Muslim "financial experts" who had balanced the Chinese-oriented bureaucrats were ousted from key positions. (2) Yuan emperors, deprived of the military and political resources of inner Asia, "fell captive to the conquest establishment in China"—namely, the Mongol nobility and their Turkish and other allies and dependents. (3) In coping with administrative tasks within China, the establishment faced a dichotomous choice between "violently irreconcilable" policy lines defined by two groups within the Confucianized bureaucracy: the reformist heirs of Wang An-shih, and the conservative heirs of Ssu-ma Kuang. (4) The establishment, having adopted Confucianism as the state ideology, was split by this conflict, the "Yuan institutions were inadequate to control or contain the controversy," and the empire disintegrated in warfare among rebel and loyalist regimes.

This analysis is undoubtedly useful in drawing attention to neglected issues in the decline of the Yuan, but it is also open to question on several levels. The argument depends upon the assumptions that the dismissal of Toghto was decisive in bringing about the fall of the Yuan, and that his fall was a consequence of the reformist-conservative struggle in the central government. The author appears to have overstated his case in asserting that the antidynastic rebellions had been crushed by the end of 1354 in view of the fact that, within months, they were stronger than ever. A second doubtful assumption is that the measures of administrative centralization, especially under Qoshila, had been so successful that the central government had become the decisive theater of Yuan politics. The division of north China into warring regimes under Mongol nobles after 1355 suggests that the antibureaucratic, militaristic and feudal bent of steppe culture was still alive and well among the provincial nobility. Reference to Liu Kuang-i's *Meng-ku Yuan ti feng-chien* (Taipei, 1965) might have been a useful corrective here. Finally, the relation between ideology and politics is not a simple one, but complex and possibly ambiguous: action is influenced by ideology, but ideology rationalizes action. It would be hard to prove that the ideological ghosts of Wang An-shih and Ssu-ma Kuang were in control of Yuan politics.

ROMEYN TAYLOR
Department of History
University of Minnesota

PATRICIA W. FAGEN. *Exiles and Citizens: Spanish Republicans in Mexico.* Pp. x, 250. Austin: The University of Texas Press, 1973. $8.00.

This new addition to the established Latin American Monographs series of the University of Texas provides the reader with the first full length account of the Spanish exile community in Mexico since the end of the Civil War. It has been conservatively estimated that some seven thousand to fifteen thousand educated, upward mobile and mainly middle-class Spaniards crossed the Atlantic to settle in Mexico, once the Republic's fate was sealed.

The book is divided into two distinctive sections, both in approach and in research techniques. Chapters 1 through 6 are predominantly based on published sources and a few manuscripts—in Spanish and English—and introduce the necessary historical framework for the rest of the monograph. Chapters 7 through 10 synthetize and interpret materials gathered from sixty-six in-depth interviews with Spanish Republicans in Mexico, conducted in 1966–67, and make up the most original and stimulating contribution of this pioneer study.

After a sketchy introductory chapter on the Spanish Republic, in which, among other issues, the Anarchists' role is never fully clarified—Federica Montseny and Diego Abad de Santillán were in fact Republican ministers at one time—Fagen devotes two chapters to document the defeat and rescue of the Spanish exiles and the polarization that took place between Juan Negrín's and Indalecio Prieto's factions, particularly relevant to the refugees' problems in their host country. Chapters 4 and 5 are an excellent summary of the contributions made by the exiles to academic, artistic, literary and scientific fields from the time the Casa de España was converted into El Colegio de México (1940), and also of the complex network of cafés, schools, professional and regional organizations these Spaniards created in their new surroundings, as if to reawaken past confrontations in a different setting. Especially illuminating is chapter 6, which discusses the anti-Franco tactics carried out by the refugees in international forums such as the United Nations, the vagaries of the Republican government in exile, the internecine struggles and the vain search for political unity among quarrelling groupings.

The chapter on "Hispanism and Hispano-America" does not fulfill the expectations of its title because Fagen fails to take into consideration related developments in other Latin American countries which also received Spanish exiles. One example in point would have been the reaction of the Republicans in Mexico to Perón's moves to strengthen Argentina's diplomatic and economic relations with Franco at the time of the 1946 international boycott. Chapters 8 and 9 are the most rewarding in the whole book, treating as they do the conflicts of the exiles' "dual allegiance" to the Mexico in which they lived and the Spain they wanted to see reformed. Chapter 10, besides being a summary of the investigation, draws a contrasting parallel with the politically motivated migration of European intellectuals to the United States during the thirties and forties. Perhaps the recent example of Cubans abandoning their homeland after 1959 could have been examined by Fagen as a case in reverse from the Spanish Republicans in Mexico. As a minor comment, one would still like to have some detailed information about Spanish military exiles, such as the late Colonel Alberto Bayo.

Exiles and Citizens is the best empirical study to date about "Pilgrim Spain" in the post-1939 period. The sadness of the story and its irreconcilable paradox are aptly conveyed in Fagen's appraisal of the exiles: "In over thirty years of exile they have accomplished practically nothing toward this goal [to overthrow Franco], and their Republic is nearly forgotten in Spain. When Franco ceases to rule, the exiles who then return to Spain will be essentially foreigners in that country."

ALBERTO CIRIA
Simon Fraser University
Canada

RICHARD R. FAGEN and WILLIAM S. TUOHY. *Politics and Privilege in a Mexican City.* Pp. 209. Stanford, Cal.: Stanford University Press, 1972. $8.50.

This small book will tell you everything you want to know about political processes in Jalapa, capital of the state of Veracruz, Mexico, in admirably analytical, nonencyclopedic fashion. Based upon questionnaires and laborious interviews, it is a model study of the pattern of politics in that city of approximately one hundred thousand population. The authors strictly defined their objectives and their procedures, but they treat their subject, not only in the narrow limits of a specific Mexican city, but rather in a broader national context. In their concern with municipal details they do not lose sight of the fact of a city living and functioning within both a state and a nation. Chapter 2 gives the best brief description of the overall Mexican political system that this reviewer has seen.

The *Partido Revolucionario Institucional* (PRI) governs Mexico as its domain, and it also enjoys a political monopoly in Jalapa. But its centralistic control and its authoritarian procedures are tempered by personalism—"In this country there is always a person who knows somebody who knows someone who knows the president"—by flexibility in specific cases, and by respect for the distinction between public and private affairs. The overall result in Jalapa is deteriorating local authority and ineffectual municipal administration. The authors cite with enthusiasm the example of Jalapa's Improvement Committee which functioned successfully as a locally motivated experiment in government-community cooperation for municipal improvement in the 1950s, but which ceased to be effective when converted into an agency of the state of Veracruz.

The on-site scientific investigations by the authors usually only confirmed the obvious. Their inquiries revealed, to their surprise, that the poor are generally satisfied with their lot in life. "There are no masses struggling to free themselves in Jalapa; there is no widespread sense of oppression or repression." They discovered that, in all classes of the population, educational advantage produces a more complacent attitude toward the socio-economic milieu, that is, it has a counter-reformist effect. In other words, education in Jalapa encourages the young to aspire to become "oligarchs." It would be difficult to generalize similarly about the stabilizing effects of education, either for Mexico or for Latin America as a whole, and the authors do not venture this generalization.

In this study, the task of drawing the political profile of Jalapa has been well performed, but the authors go on to judge it in terms of the criteria of "classical democratic theory," which they define as requiring citizen participation in decisions affecting himself, the accountability of rulers to the ruled, and the equitable distribution of goods and services. As a result, in face of the conflict between these criteria, eminently Yankee in character, and the accustomed mores of Mexican society, the authors heavily discount the latter and convert this study into an argument for structural reform.

"Something is very wrong in Mexico," they rightly conclude, and they attribute the wrongness to the failure of the *Partido Revolucionario Institucional* (PRI) to live by the above criteria of "classical democratic theory." It can scarcely be denied that the PRI has failed to fulfill expectations, but the authors do not face the basic doubt that Mexico can be saved from its tragedy by the criteria of democracy. Nor can it be denied that reform in Mexico along the suggested lines would only aggravate the conflict element in Mexican society.

The authors accept, uncritically, the welfare and planning function of the Mexican government, both national and state, and challenge only the way in which this function has been discharged in the past. They willingly, even joyfully, accept the logical corollary that it must use its already existing autocratic and centralized governmental mechanism not, as now, to satisfy powerful elites, but to establish an egalitarian society.

This study shows two faces—the one a model analysis of a typical Mexican city, and the other a plea for reactivation of the Mexican Revolution. Going far beyond the objective facts revealed by the study, it ends irrelevantly in emotional panegyric to the revolutionary ethic.

DONALD MARQUAND DOZER
University of California
Santa Barbara

ALAN FEINSTEIN. *African Revolutionary: The Life and Times of Nigeria's Aminu Kano.* Pp. ix, 299. New York: Quadrangle, 1973. $9.95.

Has a really mature biography of any of the leaders of the new states of Asia and Africa yet appeared? It is early in the life of these states, but the wave of charismatic men that led some of them is now for the most part over, and the best-known leaders—Nehru, Sukarno, Nasser, Nkrumah—are dead. The question is posed because biographies of some of the leaders of the second rank, like Malam Aminu Kano, the subject of this book, are now regularly appearing.

Alan Feinstein, a dentist, became intrigued by Africa and acquainted with some of Nigeria's leaders. He has written a readable, mostly undocumented, biography of one of Nigeria's most admirable politicians, a patrician northerner who pressed for reform in that country's most feudal area decades ago and who now is a commissioner—or minister—in the present military government. It is not a critical biography and it does aim to please its subject, which is not as such to its discredit. The book contributes little to political science beyond some anecdotal material on Aminu Kano's background. Aminu Kano has remained about as incorruptible as any African politician, but, for example, the author merely states that Aminu has "been able to wander in and out of nepotistic and corrupt circumstances without seeming to become either contaminated or greatly disturbed." In what social circumstances are what sort of men able to stand above corruption, defined as a societal pathology?

What political scientists need—and this is not Feinstein's problem—is more nomothetic work done on what causes charismatic leaders to rise as they have done at various points—and to disappear so suddenly: this must be related to the social structures of a country. Of all the variables of statecraft, that of personality or leadership remains the least studied in a systematic and theory-building way. A few recent volumes—Downton's and Greenstein's, for example—suggest that the draught is almost over, which is good; nowhere more than in the developing world has the assumption been more prevalent—or less examined—that leadership variables are the most potent variables, thanks to the weakness of political and social structures.

W. SCOTT THOMPSON
The Fletcher School of
  Law and Diplomacy
Tufts University
Medford
Massachusetts

PETER GUBSER. *Politics and Change in Al-Karak, Jordan: A Study of a Small Arab Town and Its District.* Pp. xiii, 189. New York: Oxford University Press, 1973. $14.50.

Peter Gubser's case study of political development and change in the Jordanian town and district of Al-Karak is the most recent of a series of monographs on the Middle East, under the editorial direction of Albert Hourani of St. Antony's College, Oxford. Although the series lacks cumulativeness and organization, its scholarship remains high. It is a welcome contribution to the understanding of society and politics in the Middle East, particularly since so much that is written about the area is concerned solely with the immediate aspects of the Arab-Israeli conflict. Gubser's work serves as a refreshing reminder of the major transformations occurring in Arab society while our attention is riveted upon the newsworthy aspects of the area.

Gubser's work, though characterized by some of the stylistic shortcomings common to published doctoral dissertations, is a first-rate example of field research. The book traces the political and social conditions and dynamics of a small town and its surrounding community in the desert kingdom of Jordan, during the period of Ottoman occupation and the Hashemite Amirate down to the present. It explains and illustrates the changes wrought upon a traditionally organized tribal society by the infusion of modern communications and education and recent infusion of local and national government institutions. The key variable in the political and social transformation of Al-Karak, argues Gubser, is the growth of an educated middle stratum, less tied to familial and tribal affiliations than other social groups. The growth of this group, along with the town's increasing interaction with the Amman regime, have weakened traditional tribal ties and altered parochial values in a modernizing direction. The creation of new local institutions and the intrusion of the national government have created new arenas of political competition and new political, social and economic goods. Change in Al-Karak, however, is gradual, and the substitution of a horizontal political and social organization for the traditional vertical divisions has only just begun. There is, of course, nothing that is startlingly new in this, but the case will provide analysts of political development with useful data for their theories.

One of the strengths of Gubser's analysis is that he does not seek to impose a single theoretical framework upon his observations. Instead, he draws upon a wide range of political, sociological and anthropological theory to explain change in Al-Karak. His conclusion is persuasive. The traditional tribal and kinship system, which operated almost in isolation, has not disappeared. Rather, it has been altered and serves new functions, but still operates alongside modern symbols of authority and rule. Indeed, as the author makes clear, the Amman government has sought to manipulate traditional symbols and work through traditional institutions in order to clothe it in legitimacy—which it has not entirely succeeded in doing—and to create a sense of social and political order and continuity. Gubser's discussion of modes of dispute settlement in Al-Karak are particularly useful in illustrating these points. In sum, Al-Karak is in the midst of transition; a transition which is slow and oftentimes painful.

The author's conclusions about the

role of the educated middle stratum and the integration of traditional and modern techniques of government are buttressed with useful examples, drawn from historical chronicles or based on personal observation and interviews. While he correctly limits the conclusions he draws, owing to the limitations of the case, his very narrowness of focus is an asset, because it provides a clear picture of what political and economic development are all about outside the capitals of the Arab world.

RICHARD W. MANSBACH
Rutgers University
New Brunswick
New Jersey

ANGUS MADDISON. *Class Structure and Economic Growth: India and Pakistan Since the Moghuls.* Pp. 181. New York: W. W. Norton, 1971. $7.95.

In his book *Class Structure and Economic Growth: India and Pakistan Since the Moghuls,* Angus Maddison analyzes the interdependence of social structure and economic performance in India and Pakistan from the Moghul period to the present. Though the author admits that, due to the complex repercussions of the social structure on economic growth, any rigorous conclusions are not possible (p. 11), his analysis lends itself to the general conclusion that in both countries social structures have been dysfunctional and governmental actions have been largely ineffective.

In the first chapter, the reader is introduced to the rest of the book as well as to the major conclusions of the author. The second chapter provides a brief account of the socio-economic framework of India during the Moghul period. In spite of the splendor and size of some of its cities, the per capita income in the subcontinent during the Moghul period was only about two-thirds of that of France and England. Tax burden was relatively heavy but most of the tax revenue was spent on ostentatious consumption and unproductive activities. Moslem and Hindu education were confined to religious instruction. The Moghul state apparatus perpetuated the caste system and the joint family system and, thus, was largely parasitic and unproductive in nature.

In chapter 3, Professor Maddison discusses the socio-economic impacts of the colonial rule on India. Though Britain's primary interest was economic exploitation of India, many of her social and political policies were aimed at westernizing the subcontinent. Having failed to westernize India, the British established themselves as a "separate ruling caste" (p. 43) which pursued a policy of "de-industrialization" (p. 54) by destroying Indian industries. Their socio-economic policies widened the gap between the rich and the poor and kept the social structure essentially the same as that in the Moghul period.

Chapter 4 deals with the social origins and ideology of the nationalist movement in India. Though four distinct branches of the nationalist movement are mentioned in this chapter, the revolutionary nationalism of Netaji Bose and his Indian National Army is conspicuously absent in any of the discussions.

In chapter five, Professor Maddison makes a brief analysis of some of the major factors of economic growth in India and Pakistan since independence. Even though India's rate of growth is better than it was under British colonialism, it is well below the average rate of growth for developing countries. Many factors, such as very low level of per capita income, low level of foreign capital, poor natural resources, as well as drawbacks in the economic policies of the government, such as inadequate land reforms and cumbersome government regulations, are cited as the major reasons.

Chapters 6 and 7 contain an analysis of the social structure and the author's findings. Professor Maddison concludes that, in spite of high sounding slogans of socialistic pattern of society, Indian society remains more or less unaffected by the social and economic policies of the government. The upper income groups continue to benefit at the expense of the urban and rural poor. The bureaucratic structure created by the British remains more or less intact and incapable of influencing social and economic outcomes in the country. In chapter 7 an analysis of the social impact of Pakistan's "functional inequality" leads the author to question the basic premise of the economic planners in Pakistan that a certain amount of economic inequality is essential for economic growth.

The book brings out more similarities between India and Pakistan than differences. In both countries bureaucracy has tremendous control over economic activities and has helped in maintaining social stratification. Both countries witnessed increases in: economic inequality, life expectancy of the people, power of bureaucracy, size of armed forces, size of professional class and basic industries.

Professor Maddison reaches the inescapable conclusion that any meaningful social and economic development in the subcontinent can be achieved only through effective reforms of the bureaucratic structure and enhanced freedom for the private sector. Though an in-depth analysis of the complex interdependence of social, political and economic factors is beyond the scope of this book, it provides a valuable contribution to the study of underdevelopment in the subcontinent by analyzing its contemporary social and economic problems in historical perspectives.

P. I. MATHEW
Department of Economics
Westfield State College
Massachusetts

ITAMAR RABINOVICH. *Syria Under the Ba'th 1963–1966.* Pp. xx, 276. New York: Halsted, 1973. $15.50.

From a historical point of view, the rise and metamorphosis of the Ba'th party in Syria may be considered among the most significant events in the entire history of the Arab Middle East. For the first time in Arab history, a group of intellectuals attempted to establish a political party based upon a well-defined secular ideology and planned to transcend the tradi-

tional political forces in the area, including the forces of personality cult and religion. The significance of the Ba'th movement, therefore, lies not so much in its eventual success or failure as a political instrument, as in the fact that it was attempted at all.

Many books have been written about the establishment, development, and transformation of the Ba'th party in Syria—some favorable, others critical, but very few analytical. This book attempts to summarize, rather discreetly, the historical background of the Ba'th party as gleaned from the available sources. According to the writer, these sources are "Ba'thi documents, memoirs and books of polemics, and the Arabic Press and radio broadcasts" (p. xii). The writer also proposes in this book to "establish the chronology of the period, to identify the issues and acting forces that shaped events, and finally, to evaluate the significance of the changes and developments that took place in Syria between 1963 and 1966" (p. xi). In my opinion, however, while the writer succeeded very well in establishing the chronology and identifying the issues and acting forces, he did not fully succeed in evaluating the significance of the changes and developments that took place in Syria. Perhaps the full impact of the rise and transformation of the Ba'th movement on Syria and Syrian politics may not be fully understood for some time to come. One might add, however, that should another group of intellectuals in Syria—or any other Arab country —attempt to establish a new political party based on a secular ideology, they would learn a great deal from the experience of the Ba'th movement.

The first two chapters of this book are devoted to the historical background of the Ba'th party from 1945 to 1963. The remaining five chapters summarize the experiences and development of the Ba'th movement within Syria itself, as well as in relation to Nasser's Egypt and neighboring Iraq. The main pitfall of the Ba'th leaders is well summarized by the writer as follows: "While they still preached a doctrine of long term revolutionary preparation and conversion as a precondition to the assumption of power, they seem actually to have become ready to do so by a short cut" (p. 14).

Twice the Ba'th leaders attempted to assume rule by a short cut and twice they failed and caused the paralysis, if not the collapse, of their movement. The first time was when they sought union with Egypt under Nasser, and the other time when they sought the support of the military in Syria itself. Had they continued to promote their ideology and waited for the right time to assume power, their movement would have certainly taken a different turn.

WILSON B. BISHAI
Harvard University

JOSEPH S. SZYLIOWICZ. *Education and Modernization in the Middle East.* Pp. xii, 477. Ithaca, N.Y.: Cornell University Press, 1973. $19.50.

The goal of this book is to analyze "how education in the Middle East has functioned both as an object of change and as an agent of change" (p. vii). In fact, the study focuses upon the relationship between education and modernization as it has developed in three societies —Turkey, Iran and Egypt. As such, it stands as one of the rare cases of a truly comparative, that is, cross-cultural, analysis of Middle Eastern society and politics. Professor Szyliowicz, one of the most imaginative scholars of the contemporary Middle East, systematically erects a conceptual framework that enables him to uncover patterns and build generalizations concerning Middle Eastern educational processes.

The basic conceptual typology divides political systems into four ideal types: the radical, the reformist, the adaptive and the competitive. The radical system, such as Egypt since 1952, is characterized by a will to transform and modernize society. The reformist type, for example, contemporary Iran, is marked by a political regime that promotes only so much change as to preserve and protect traditional authority patterns. The adap-

tive polity, such as Saudi Arabia, is one that steadfastly resists change and innovation. The competitive type, for example, contemporary Turkey, is characterized by modernity defined in terms of democratic politics. One might criticize this typology on the grounds that the categories lack adequate indices of differentiation. The distinction between reformist and adaptive types, for example, is not clear. Can one, in fact, distinguish Iran from Morocco along these lines? Also, the competitive type seems artificially appended to the scheme to provide a special category for Turkey; the criteria of classification are different here and smack of the rather parochial Western view of "democratic" politics. Despite these reservations, the classification remains a provocative one, as it leads Szyliowicz to generate a number of important hypotheses regarding education in the Middle East.

The discouraging conclusions are that:

the educational enterprise in every country has demonstrated a remarkable ability to withstand efforts at reform and to absorb the impact of major external forces without changing (p. 454);

In every country of the Middle East . . . the structure of a modern educational system has been created, but in every country the functioning of that system at all levels possesses many aspects that are dysfunctional for modernization (p. 448);

it is no exaggeration to state that education has reached a state of intellectual and financial insolvency and can only be expected to deteriorate even more (p. 452).

Indeed, Professor Szyliowicz convincingly demonstrates that these gloomy generalizations apply, regardless of whether the political system is reformist (Iran), competitive (Turkey), or radical (Egypt). The political dynamics differ, but the educational results remain the same.

This is an important book. The chapter on traditional education in the Middle East is excellent. The discussion of the Egyptian, Turkish and Iranian case studies is objective and informed. Unfortunately, the price of the volume is exorbitant. Only members of Szyliowicz's "social core group" can, therefore, obtain ready access to his book. The masses will have to either line up at the library or rely upon the good will of their friends in the elite to loan them a copy of the book. It is, in this case, worth the inconvenience.

JAMES A. BILL

The University of Texas
Austin

MALCOLM T. WALKER. *Politics and the Power Structure: A Rural Community in the Dominican Republic.* Pp. xiii, 177. New York: Teacher's College Press, 1973. $9.00.

Walker's work is concerned with "the power structure and the sources and uses of power" (p. 1) in the Constanza Valley, an important agricultural region with close economic and political ties with the capital city. The book is based on data that the author collected in the field (1967–68), while pursuing his doctorate in anthropology. Despite its title, this work is, in fact, a conventional ethnographic monograph, and therein lie its strengths and weaknesses.

Considered as a community study, this book is a welcome addition to rural Latin American ethnography. Walker presents deft descriptions of a wide variety of social groups—ranging from successful immigrant businessmen, to government police and landless peons—of the range of economic activities, and of the routines of daily life. From his concisely presented data, an intriguing portrait of the valley emerges. It is a formerly prosperous area which has been in a steady decline during this century, principally because a booming population has put unbearable pressure on available agricultural land. In response, the community has turned outward in a desperate attempt to bring new resources into the area in the form of government projects and jobs. One of Walker's main points is that the central government is viewed as the only salvation of people living in the valley, by both rich and poor alike. For its part, the government lacks the means to solve the major problems of

the valley, but does distribute a limited amount of patronage in diverse forms. The result of this impossible situation is keen competition among the local people for political contacts in the capital city that will keep them afloat for a while longer.

While Walker provides a rich ethnographic portrait of Constanza, his analysis of the power structure is inadequate because he has focused on a community, and all the major sources of power lie outside of the community; that is, they are in the capital city. In spite of his awareness of this fact, the author has no analysis whatsoever of this extracommunity source of power. Nowhere is there any explanation of why Trujillo was so interested in Constanza—or why the Cuban guerrillas in 1959, or the United States Marines in 1965, were. Constanza appears to be a political nerve center for the whole country, yet one can never learn why from reading this book. Nor can we learn why both Trujillo and Balaguer favor immigrant businessmen—Spaniards and Lebanese—over native Dominican businessmen. In a word, those people who are native to the Constanza valley are marginal to the power structure, yet this book is about precisely these people. Logically, no lucid portrait of the power structure can emerge, and it does not. In short, this book can be read with enjoyment as a community study, but with dismay as an essay on politics.

EDWARD C. HANSEN

Queens College
City University of New York

JOHN WATERBURY. *North for the Trade: The Life and Times of a Berber Merchant.* Pp. xv, 226. Berkeley: University of California Press, 1972. $10.75.

IAN CLEGG. *Workers' Self-Management in Algeria.* Pp. 249. New York: Monthly Review Press, 1972. $8.95. Paperbound, $2.95.

These two volumes portray very different aspects of reality in two neighboring North African countries, Morocco and Algeria. The differences are explained largely by the experiences the two now independent nations had with their former French rulers. Morocco, officially taken over by the French in 1912, was not fully conquered until the 1930s, while Algeria, where the French began a brutal occupation in 1830, was largely under control by the 1870s. And once conquest was accomplished, Morocco remained a protectorate with a powerless, but nonetheless present, ruler of its own and, most importantly, without receiving an overly large number of European settlers. In Algeria, by contrast, the French governed directly—at times even incorporating Algeria into the French body politic—while allowing European settlers to secure full control of nearly all sectors of Algeria's economic life. The result made Algeria one of the most harshly administered territories in the history of Western colonial rule.

Waterbury, a man with an obvious appreciation for the nuances of Moroccan life, presents the life of Hadj Brahim, a Berber merchant from the Sous region of southern Morocco. He gained his information from interviews in French with the Soussi, beginning in 1965. Throughout, Waterbury attempts to integrate Hadj Brahim's experiences into his own knowledge of Morocco and to draw generalized conclusions from this one individual's path through life. To cover sensitive matters "certain personalities," including Hadj Brahim, and "certain events" (p. x) are fictionalized by the writer. The result is a readable and informative account of a Moroccan of the Sous, a region from which men traveled to secure fortunes for a life-style denied them because of the opportunities lacking in their homeland. Hadj Brahim was born in 1914, twenty years before the French conquered his home area; he entered the retail trade business at the age of nine. The story of his progress, and that of others from the Sous, gives a vivid portrayal of one segment of Moroccan life during the period of French rule and of early Moroccan independence. Throughout his career, Hadj Brahim remains a figure of essential human dignity, striving with honor to make his mark in the world, according to the value system of his own society. Waterbury caps his absorbing rendition with a chapter analyzing Hadj Brahim's career in the tenets of the social scientist, including an attempt to compare the reactions of the men of the Sous to similar striving groups in other regions of the world.

In his very different volume, Clegg deals with the rise and fall of the worker committees of Algeria and with the ideology of the general world movement of the self-management of segments of national economies. When independence came to Algeria in 1962 after a ferocious eight-year war, the European population, justly fearing the reaction to the terror campaign carried on by some of its members, fled the country. A spontaneous takeover of European business and agricultural establishments followed, sometimes motivated by reasons of ideology, but usually for sheer economic survival. The Algerian government, however, had no clear doctrine of economic management after the long years of struggle against the French. The new rulers accepted the self-management ideas of the workers in their early rhetoric, but in resolving the personal power rivalries left over from the revolution, little time was given to encouraging the self-management concept. Once the power struggles were resolved, the government preferred to control economic development through policies issuing from its offices. Clegg clearly delineates the process by which the new bureaucracy of independent Algeria gained control over the decentralized movements by 1968. In the process, he sheds much light upon the evolution of Algerian society, and, by incisive comparisons with the still-evolving pattern of Yugoslav self-management, upon the general world problems of the tensions between decentralization and democracy.

NORMAN ROBERT BENNETT
African Studies Center
Boston University

Deutsch Treat

Kindly mention THE ANNALS *when writing to advertisers.*

WILLIAM A. CHRISTIAN, JR. *Person and God in a Spanish Valley.* Pp. vii, 215. New York: Seminar Press, 1972. $8.95.

William A. Christian, Jr. spent many months studying the impact of various aspects of the Roman Catholic religion on the people of the Nansa Valley in Santander Province, Spain. He lived among the villagers of the towns in the region, and gradually many of them were able to express their beliefs to him. Although Christian mentions he had a Protestant upbringing, he has no difficulty understanding and characterizing the beliefs of others brought up differently. His view of the inhabitants is sympathetic, and his method of dealing with the subject matter is scholarly.

Throughout *Person and God in a Spanish Valley* it is possible to recognize a trend of gradual change in the outlook of the people. Christian wrote his study of the villagers and their beliefs just in time for the reader to visualize Roman Catholic practices, utilized for centuries, on the brink of dissolution. The Second Vatican Council is humanizing the Catholic theology, sending young priests with modern ideas to combat the villagers' reliance on shrines and divine intermediaries. The priests are trying to replace the custom of making pledges to shrine images, of engaging in penitential activities, with an alternative emphasis on relationships of one human being to another.

Christian groups the inhabitants into categories according to occupation, age, sex, marital status, closeness to the patron family of the village and time spent outside the area. The most devoted of the natives are widows, women, Indianos—people who have been away from the village for years but have returned to make devotions—and the families associated with the wealthy patron family of the town. Men in general leave the religious preoccupations for the women, confident that their women will overcompensate and thus make up

for what they lack in religious activity. The men also seem more hostile to priests.

The author interviewed many people and tried to record their comments faithfully. Generally, those interviewed profess belief in specific saintly patrons or shrines in the area. It seemed to me that the most devout were those women widowed many years with grown children outside the home. They cling to the shrines and saints to relieve anxieties and to gain comfort from sorrow.

What is significant in *Person and God in a Spanish Valley* is the implicit feeling that old folk ways are being slowly and inexorably phased out. The newer beliefs and trends are not yet strong enough to replace the old, while the people sense they are expected to change with the times. Christian feels especially sorry for the older women who place such faith in their intermediaries. The conclusion that modernity is approaching these villagers too quickly arises from Christian's analogies between human and divine. The family structure can be compared to a heavenly hierarchy. The father of the family is strong and authoritative. The father is thus compared to God. The mother, who performs most religious devotions, is compared to Mary, an intermediary—as are the saints—between the people and God. There are other examples of earthly go-betweens and heavenly ones, but without detailing them, the gist of the subject is that when the analogies can no longer be drawn—what happens to the human side of the hierarchy?

Christian has strived to explore the deep beliefs of the people while he poses the problem of replacing these credos with innovative theology. He believes that the old ways will not totally die, but in the lessening of them, many will suffer confusion. The author intends to expand his study to include other regions of Spain. I am certain he will find a great disparity between these villages of Nansa and the other ones of different regions. What he has learned and what he will learn can be of great value to those interested in the question of what to do when the old value system must be supplanted with a new one.

FRANCISCO CARENAS
University of Missouri
St. Louis

RALPH DAVIS. *The Rise of the Atlantic Economies.* Pp. xiv, 352. Ithaca, N.Y.: Cornell University Press, 1973. $5.95. Paperbound.

This large paperback is the first of a new series called World Economic History. The general aim is to present broad syntheses of recent research in economic history. Thus, important work buried in obscure periodicals and known only to the cognoscente will become more accessible to scholars not specializing in economic history, and even to intelligent laymen. *The Rise of the Atlantic Economies* certainly does this most adequately; almost everyone will learn something from this wide-ranging yet detailed survey.

The book covers the economic history of Atlantic Europe—Portugal, Spain, France, England and the Netherlands —and its American colonies, from the fifteenth century discoveries to the beginnings of the Industrial Revolution in the late eighteenth century. Several general themes stand out from the mass, mostly interesting, of detail. Davis contends that there was "an Atlantic economy; but it was subsidiary to, a modification and enhancement of, the economies of the individual countries of the Atlantic seaboard that took part in it." Thus, despite the discoveries and the colonies, "the main influences on European economic development arose within the countries of Europe themselves . . . ." Two other themes concern the end of the economic dominance of the Mediterranean states and their replacement by Atlantic states, and the general importance of noneconomic factors in economic history, such as wars, people, climate and disease.

Within this general framework, there is a wealth of detail on an impressive variety of topics. Davis rightly stresses the primacy of the Portuguese in the discoveries of the fifteenth century, with

Spain very much of a lucky Johnny-come-lately. The book is sound on population trends, on the nature and effect of technological advances, on England's eighteenth century Agrarian Revolution, and in its stress on the prerequisite of a strong agricultural base for industrial development. And finally, as one example of interesting, and relevant, minutia, how many readers of this review knew that the British in the eighteenth century consumed, per head, eight times more sugar than the French?

To close on a sour note, there is, by repute, a cloth bound edition of this book. Cornell, however, has elected to be cheap and has distributed paperbacks for review. Reviewers of the world unite . . . .

M. N. PEARSON
University of Pennsylvania
Philadelphia

G. R. ELTON. *Reform and Renewal: Thomas Cromwell and the Common Weel.* Pp. viii, 175. New York: Cambridge University Press, 1973. $8.75.

Professor G. R. Elton gave the Wiles Lectures at Queen's University, Belfast, in May, 1972 on the subject of the Common Weal and Thomas Cromwell. From this series of lectures developed the book *Reform and Renewal.*

In his book, Dr. Elton endeavors to discover the reforming traits which were begun under the government of Henry VIII, following his break with the Church of Rome. He used Cromwell's reign as a governmental looking glass into the beginning of the reform influence that would hit the whole of England. Cromwell is drawn as a lucid individual without formal training, who is able to surround himself with some very formal advisors and will become a fellow scholar in the end. Though Cromwell was not the product of a university, he began early to surround himself with scholars and to use these men as the propaganda writers that were so badly needed to make all of England realize that Henry VIII's position as the head of the Church was valid. They were important because of their ability to communicate with other scholars in the rest of the world, and thereby win them to Henry VIII's cause.

As an employer of scholars, Cromwell surrounded himself with men who both wanted fame and, at the same time, were willing to work for the cause that was somewhat unpopular with many humanists, such as Sir Thomas More and D. Erasmus. One such man was Richard Morison, who can be described as a loyal Protestant and a much sought-after mediator. He later became a member of the Privy Council and eventually survived the fall of Cromwell in 1540.

Cromwell had as his instrument for work the Act of Supremacy, which set up Henry VIII as head of the Church of England. This act was the most important ever passed by an English parliament and became the means used by Cromwell to fight the Papists in England and, at the same time, the foes of Cromwell. In the book, Elton goes into great details on the act and on later acts passed by Parliament that are directly related to it.

Another phase of the work of Cromwell, as presented by Elton, related to trade, industrial activities and the agriculture of England. Cromwell became aware of the fact, which had been already stated by Wolsey, that men should not possess land which they could not maintain. Thus, he began to establish plans to limit the enclosure of land. Men were not allowed to possess more than two thousand sheep, nor to possess two leasholds worth more than 5.00. In industry, Cromwell can be credited with the idea of proposing help to Bristol, which had lost economically because of the decline in the cloth trade and because of the simultaneous decay of over nine hundred homes within the town.

Cromwell tried, also, to establish law reforms for England, but these reforms related to the differences in Church and Common Law. In most of them, one can see far reaching reforms that were never carried out because they were far advanced for their time.

The achievements of Cromwell are well recorded in the book. He can clearly be seen as a man who was interested in reform for the good of England. Many of the grey areas of his life are cleared up and carefully examined. The book is quite readily understandable and a welcome addition to this field of Tudor studies. I hope that Professor Elton will not let Mr. Cromwell rest, but will, instead, research the minor humanists who are alluded to in the work.

J. R. TINSLEY
Morehead State University
Kentucky

WALTER HALLSTEIN. *Europe in the Making.* Pp. 333. New York: W. W. Norton, 1973. $8.95.

JOHN A. ARMSTRONG. *The European Administrative Elite.* Pp. vii, 406. Princeton, N.J.: Princeton University Press, 1973. $20.00. Paperbound, $9.75.

A very recent Gallup poll indicated that more than fifty percent of a cross section of Americans had no knowledge at all about the European Community (EC). Since it is fair to cite the Common Market as one of the most far reaching postwar developments in the Western world, any attempt to introduce greater understanding about the evolution, present status and future possibilities of that institution should receive widespread attention. Yet, in one sense, it is a shame, for the former first president of the Commission of the EC and present president of the European Movement has written an extremely valuable and stimulating book which is not only aimed at, but probably will be read by, businessmen and students of contemporary political and economic affairs.

Even if it will not be widely read, this book, in a special English language edition for the United States, gives a concise accounting of the dynamic processes of integration without minimizing the setbacks or overdrawing the successful achievements. Hallstein, it must be noted, has a definite case, but it does not injure in any way those sections of the work which may be termed historical. When the feeling of urgency or the accentuation of the time element as the essential matter becomes involved in the author's assessment of the current forces and upcoming events within the EC, the entire piece has another flavor—more purposeful and subjective and less analytical and objective.

Overall, it is instructive to compare Hallstein's present perspective after the years of combat within the Community and after the softening of the classical Gaullist position in the last three or four years. Nearly ten years ago, in the Royal Institute of International Affairs Sir Stevenson Lecture, Hallstein addressed himself to the political, agricultural, monetary, tax, industrial and labor problems in the same penetrating, outspoken, urbane and aggressive manner. Little has changed in the basic orientation and thrust of the committed ones like Hallstein, yet the constitutional crisis of 1965, the fusion of the major organizations of European unity and, most significantly, the expansion of the Community from the Six to the Nine have caused reexaminations and reconsiderations in the minds of the Community advocates which the author pinpoints, mostly in chapters 5 and 6. In fact, the one hundred and forty page chapter on European economic policy, moving from competition, conjunctural and fiscal policy to social, energy, transport and regional policies, contains the cardinal tenets of the Hallstein Market, past, present and future. The Hallstein approach is to relate the progress of Europe within a limited federalist mold and to compare its historical welding with that of the United States. This is unfortunate in one way, for the dissimilarities are too many and too obvious. However, the movement toward unity in Europe contains numerous bases for rivalry and competition between states, based on individual sovereignty, which ought to be viewed by Americans with some sympathy. Nevertheless, in his search to find a comparative base which might appeal to his readers on this side of the Atlantic, Hallstein is forced to exaggerate.

This sane attempt to awaken and enlighten Americans comes from a Europe now organized to speak with a single voice. If the forthcoming Nixon round of economics talks does not make it completely obvious that the Washington-Europe-Japan economic problems are discussions among powerful equals, then the poignant and instructive argument contained in this volume will be lost, even to the elite who read it. For this is political communication of an often highly complex nature, written too privately to a select audience. George Ball puts it well when he talks about those that are "occupationally disabled" from understanding the broader implications of European drives for unity, yet it appears that he is convinced this book will be consumed by many and not just the lobbyists for labor, industrial and agricultural interests or by professional economists and businessmen.

The tale of outer enlargement and inner evolution is meant to change our thinking and attitudes, for it raises hard questions. At a time of some strain in relations across the Atlantic, when arrangements need be negotiated between the Atlantic powers, Hallstein's words may seem disconcerting to Americans. The public discussion surrounding the "Year of Europe" has only begun, and for many who want to gain an updated insight into the inextricable relationship between economic and political policy, this work will expose them to what has happened, and is happening, in Europe.

Much of the recent literature on elites, planners, bureaucrats, managers and administrators has lacked balance and reality. Students of the European public servant now have a rare insight into this world written by a first class scholar. Armstrong's work is a comparative administrative history which explores the relationship of the French, Russian, German and British public elite and economic development and modernization. The strength of the study is to be found in the systematic depiction and analysis of the political socialization process and the historical evaluation of the administrators milieu in the last three centuries. By employing an experienced and mature social science theory, particularly on role perception, class-role behavior linkage and organizational modes, the author derives major factors which cause administrative intervention and, therefore, influence economic growth.

This contribution to an eventual definitive comparative history of elite administrative roles—one yearns to see other major industrial-technological societies like the United States and Japan examined—views with great precision the impact of the changing process of socialization. Huge chunks of the volume are dedicated to specific features, such as familial background, peer group structure, adolescent training and schooling and, as one moves into the industrial era, the major areas of higher, specialized education and the recruitment and induction systems of the national governments. The Armstrong methodology—critics of it might read the convincing argument of the appendix—utilizes the conceptual framework of social psychology and a "factor-by-factor" comparative approach (p. 45). This allows Armstrong, finally, to hypothesize five constant elements in the varied experiences of the four states which have contributed to the development of "interventionism" (pp. 305–311).

Since every effort is made in this study to integrate the materials into the major themes, it might appear contradictory and irrelevant to extrapolate certain data or particular ideas from the book. Yet this process of isolating some parts of the whole gives a hint of both its overall competence and the variety of its subject matter. Three examples must suffice. Armstrong tests the administrative elites' response to challenges by investigating the only two common episodes which the four nations shared—nineteenth century railway construction and mobilization for World War I. This results in several extremely worthwhile observations, as does the probe into the emergence of the Ecole National d'Administration (E.N.A.) which Armstrong terms "the most significant innovation in elite administrative preparation which Europe has seen in many decades" (p. 199). The swiftness of the French change in recent years is amply illustrated. Finally, the subject of the engineers, and then economists, emergence as "technocrats" and their infusion into the elite is treated in a sophisticated manner, highlighting the perils of an imbalanced elite in the direction of the excesses of economic development, as contrasted to the classically trained—law and letters—earlier national elites.

While stressing the close French-Russian connections and similarities, and also the Anglo-Prussian-German linkages, Armstrong transcends a purely historical interpretation, or purely cultural variance explanation. He identifies metropolitan influences, after service entry territorial experience, administrative integration, scientific-technological education component and systematic economics training as primary factors encouraging a positive interventionist role definition. Although not dealing directly with any policymaking implications of such an inquiry, the entire work would be fruitful reading for those interested in administrative responsiveness and value orientation.

The perceptive original interpretation, the rigorous conceptualization and model building are based on solid data, derived from a far-reaching search through virtually all of the relevant historical literature. The smooth flowing exposition is only infrequently disturbed by either excessive jargon or complexity in sentence construction. The omission of any regard for the "Eurocrats" is not crucial, but it could have suggested further helpful data. Needless to say, some will be upset with Armstrong's proclivity to overdraw likenesses and underplay dissimilarities, but the real value of this exhaustive survey is to be found in its impressive amount of information judiciously used and its bold reassessment of the European public elite and their behavior formation. The virtues far outnumber any flaws, and these few disagreements will come primarily from the ultraspecialists of national bureaucracies. Even though based on already published works, this exploratory venture deserves the careful consideration and thought of those who usually start with Max Weber and then move through the voluminous and too often unrewarding pieces which probe the concept of elite.

PIERRE-HENRI LAURENT
Department of History
Tufts University
Medford
Massachusetts

LAWRENCE C. JENNINGS. *France and Europe in 1848: A Study of French Foreign Affairs in Time of Crises.* Pp. x, 280. New York: Oxford University Press, 1973. $6.50.

Here we have an impressive and intensive study of French foreign policy for the critical year, 1848. Based on archival studies in Paris, London, Vienna, Copenhagen and Turin, and on a wide use of newspapers including revolutionary papers, this monograph shows depth and pattern; it is commendable for its linking of foreign and domestic affairs.

It was radical pressures, for example, that led Alphonse de Lamartine, as foreign minister, to publish his March Manifesto promising aid for struggling nationalities; it was his realistic sense of foreign policy which led him to negate its promises of help. Under the same pressures, the government failed to stop expeditions of armed emigrees from attempting liberating invasions. Another effect of domestic affairs appears in Cavaignac's proposal to send French troops to protect the Pope, in order to extricate himself from political dangers in his campaign for the French presidency.

Even though leftist revolutionaries needled the French government to push outward by force, to support liberal national movements abroad, both Lamartine and Bastide avoided such adventures and sought traditional diplomatic goals. Jennings makes clear, as did Frederick De Luna in his study of General Cavaignac (Princeton, 1969) that the government of 1848 was neither radical nor venturesome. Though two successive foreign ministers, Alphonse de Lamartine and Jules Bastide, felt intervention into northern Italy unwise, for political reasons they talked of intervention and even made promises. Lawrence Jennings demonstrates that the prolonged negotiations with Palmerston for an Anglo-French mediation were aimed to avoid such intervention. He holds that Austrian acceptance of mediation in September staved off an intervention which neither Bastide, Palmerston, Charles Albert nor Baron Wessenberg, in fact, wanted. Indeed, Charles Albert feared a French intervention. Actually, both Lamartine and Bastide looked upon both German and Italian unification as inimicable to French interests. Both saw in Prussia's reaching for Schleswig-Holstein the potential of a German effort to wrest Alsace-Lorraine from France; but both men had territorial designs on Savoy. Although Jennings does little with ideas and ideology in 1848—Karl Marx does not appear in the index—he does indicate that the leaders of the government feared an ideological war on the historical grounds that such a conflict led the France of 1793 into dictatorship and the Terror.

Many studies have examined special phases of French policy in 1848, but to my knowledge this is the first to examine all French foreign policy for that rather special year. With good reason scholars will turn to *France and Europe in 1848* for detailed information and persuasive interpretation.

GARLAND DOWNUM
Department of History
Northern Arizona University
Flagstaff

ROBERT E. JONES. *The Emancipation of the Russian Nobility: 1762–1785.* Pp. xii, 326. Princeton, N.J.: Princeton University Press, 1973. $12.50.

During the course of the eighteenth century, in the aftermath of the death of Peter I, Russian political life was extremely confused. The numerous accessions to the throne and the violence accompanying many of these accessions is well known. Also well known is the fact that between 1725 and 1785, the Russian nobility threw off the obligations of service to the state that had been imposed upon it by Peter I. The subject of Mr. Jones' book is this very emancipation of the Russian nobility with special reference to the period 1762–1785. The year 1762 marks the promulgation of the Manifesto on the Liberty of the Nobility by Peter III, and 1785 is the date of the Charter of the Nobility of Catherine II.

In this work, which originated as a doctoral dissertation at Cornell University, the author dissects the political, economic and social position of the Russian nobility. His fundamental thesis appears to be that the successive changes in the status of the Russian nobility, culminating in Catherine's charter of 1785, were far more the result of administrative needs of the Russian state than "political accommodation or compromise between a usurping empress [namely, Catherine II] and the dominant social and economic class."

The author, in support of his argument, relies heavily on the concept of Peter III, for example, as a kind of wise and Platonic ruler during the latter's very short reign. Despite the writings of Florinsky and his followers, this reviewer finds it hard to be persuaded to such a view. One can go along far more readily with such a lofty vision of Catherine II, although massive incongruities exist here too.

The use of sources seems unbalanced and sometimes uncritical, despite the presence of elaborate citations from archival materials in Soviet Russia. To quote Aksakov as strict historical source material is dubious, as Mirsky himself suggests, in his introduction to *Chronicles of a Russian Family*. The *American Historical Review*, *Canadian Slavic Studies* and *Slavic Review* are mentioned, but no other journals in English.

The editorial composition of the book leaves much to be desired. No mention is made as to whether dates are old or new style. No system of transliteration from Russian is indicated. Errors in spelling and titles in English, Russian, and French reveal carelessness (for example, pp. 16, 20, 296, 301, 303, 304).

However, if read carefully and critically, Mr. Jones' study has value for the specialist.

DAVID HECHT

Pace University
New York

CLARA MARIA LOVETT. *Carlo Cattaneo and the Politics of the Risorgimento 1820–1860.* Pp. x, 138. The Hague: Martinus Nijhoff, 1972. 25 Guilders.

Clara Lovett, Professor of History at the Baruch College of the City University of New York, has written a very significant revisionist political biography of Carlo Cattaneo, one of the most significant intellectual figures of the Risorgimento period in modern Italian history. Based on assiduous research in archival material—especially the Cattaneo papers in Milan—published sources, and an extensive number of secondary works, Professor Lovett's monograph presents a much needed revision of Cattaneo's influence upon and role in the politics of the Risorgimento. Since Cattaneo was a Milanese publicist of liberal-democratic tendencies and a foe of the Piedmontese monarchy, it was very natural for twentieth century Italian scholars, who were disillusioned by the impact of World War I on Italy and the period of Mussolini's fascist rule and who sought to find the roots of twentieth century political decay in Italy in the working of the nineteenth century Risorgimento period, to rediscover in Cattaneo the decent, unrealized aspirations of the Risorgimento. Cattaneo became for twentieth century scholars of Italian history, especially in the late 1940s, a democratic and federalist idealist, uncompromised by the once fashionable cult of monarchy and Cavourianism.

Professor Lovett's study emphatically demonstrates that Cattaneo was neither the uncompromising democratic radical portrayed by the supporters of Cavour nor the farsighted precursor of democratic federalism portrayed by post-World War II scholars. Cattaneo's position in the Risorgimento was constantly shifting, and he was not at all a political activist. He was at heart a political reformer, quite convinced of the inherent values of political democracy and federalism, but quite inconsistent in his views on how these values could be instituted in nineteenth century Italy. Moreover, Cattaneo had a relatively minor input into the actual politics and diplomacy of the Risorgimento. In fact, his most significant influence was on the later generations of Italian and European intellectuals who, because of the exigencies and shortcomings of their own historical milieu, reconstructed a historical picture of Cattaneo's thought and works which corresponded more to their own idealized historiographical biases than to the rather ambiguous historical legacy of the great mid-nineteenth century publicist.

JOHN STANLEY WOZNIAK

Dunkirk
New York

D. BRUCE MARSHALL. *The French Colonial Myth and Constitution-Making In The Fourth French Republic.* Pp. xii, 363. New Haven, Conn.: Yale University Press, 1973. $12.50.

Having lived in Paris in 1945–46 —courtesy of the United States Army— I can attest to the fact that most Frenchmen were not then preoccupied with colonial questions. Nor, I suspect, are there but a few academicians interested in a reexamination of the parliamentary discussions of the colonial phases of that period. For those who are, Mr. Marshall has done a good job. His focus is on the French political milieu in the wake of the psychological trauma of World War II. His conclusion—France missed an opportunity to be true to her "colonial myth."

In the course of a hundred years, a tradition had emerged in which Frenchmen of varied persuasions rationalized their control of empire on grounds of grandeur, economic gain, and *la mission civilatrice*. The republican colonial myth conceived of a "worldwide community of peoples bound together into a single nation by common ties of economic and political interest . . . sharing a common cultural base" (p. 12).

This vague attitude, in which the Left participated, punctures the cliché that imperialism was solely the product of a selfish Right.

The colonial myth was put to the test as the structure of empire was shaken. To people such as De Gaulle, it was inconceivable that France could be France without being a world power, meaning, having an empire. Domestic politics dictated a coalition of the center in which Georges Bidault disappointed hopes for self-government. Out of intricate parliamentary maneuvering, the French Union was born. It "fudged" the issue. Granting neither true assimilation nor the freedom desired by Vietnamese and North Africans nor the greater self-government requested by African spokesmen, it ultimately led to colonial wars in Vietnam and Algeria. "By preserving the symbols of French power and authority in the colonial world, the constitution may have satisfied the psychological needs of some metropolitan groups for a renewed sense of national grandeur, but it did so at the cost of alienating native support" (pp. 32–33). But then again, "It is quite probable that in an era when nations around the globe were attaining formal independence from their colonial overlords no scheme for preserving unity between France and its colonies could have succeeded" (p. 314). All of which makes much of what Marshall discusses in somewhat inordinate detail rather academic.

WALLACE SOKOLSKY

Bronx Community College of the
City University of New York

NISSAN OREN. *Revolution Administered: Agrarianism and Communism in Bulgaria.* Pp. xv, 204. Baltimore, Md.: The Johns Hopkins University Press, 1973. $8.50.

GALIA GOLAN. *Reform Rule in Czechoslovakia: The Dubček Era, 1968–1969.* Pp. vii, 327. New York: Cambridge University Press, 1973. $18.50.

Ostensibly a volume on "community building and integration," the first of the two books reviewed here is in reality a thumbnail sketch of the political history of Bulgaria, focusing on developments and public policy under the agrarian regime of Stamboliisky, the subsequent royal dictatorship and the postwar Communist party-state. While the summary of these developments is concise, well written and useful as an introduction to the subject, the volume adds relatively little to what is available in existing Western sources. Nor does Dr. Oren make any significant attempt to expand on his general themes of integration and community building. Indeed, rather than building on a substantial literature on these subjects, he seems to disclaim the feasibility of generalization from "contemporary history" (p. 171). Such caution seems to be regrettable, for his three principal units of comparison—the agrarian chiliasm of Stamboliisky, the bureaucratic dictatorship of Boris, and the Communist party-state—offer sharply contrasting political models for developing societies; hence, their relevance transcends the narrow geographical and chronological boundaries of the particular case. A more careful and systematic examination of these models would not only have provided potential analogies for the student of other societies but also a more disciplined structure for the narrative at hand.

While three of the seven chapters of the study deal with the years 1919–1944, four are devoted to Communist power and policy, the principal feature of which is seen by the author as a concerted drive for economic development "through the utter degradation of the countryside" (p. 175). The various phases of this policy, orthodox Stalinism, the "great leap forward" and more recent economic experimentation are recounted, together with some other facets of Bulgarian policy, including measures aimed at rekindling nationalist sentiments. The constitution of 1971 is described in some detail. But little if any attention has been given to more subtle changes in the party's authority and identity, to recent and quite substantial changes in economic priorities, and to experiments with economic reforms. The Soviet domination of Bulgarian policy is a recurrent theme and one that few would quarrel with. But even here some significant qualifications could have been added in view of substantial Soviet economic aid in the sixties and of the country's relatively favorable treatment within the overall scheme of Soviet-East European economic integration. Inexplicably the Comecon, of which Bulgaria is one of the principal beneficiaries, does not even appear in the text or in the appended index.

Like Oren's study of Bulgaria, Galia Golan's volume lacks a clearly formulated analytical perspective, but the reader will be amply compensated for this absence by a richness of empirical detail and by the insight with which the author examines her materials. These materials relate primarily to the design of reform, though the survey is introduced by a brief discussion of the roots of liberalization and followed by two chapters on the Soviet invasion and its aftermath. In between, the reader will find separate chapters devoted to the economy, the mass organizations, the cultural scene, the party and the state, as well as to foreign policy and the federalization of the country. In these chapters Dr. Golan not only provides a comprehensive and competent description of the issues, but also examines different sides in the ongoing public debate, and in so doing points to a number of contradictions in the overall design that other, less scholarly observers have been apt to overlook in their sympathetic treatments of reform Communism. Thus, for instance, the Action Program of the party permitted members "to express and persist in dissenting views" but qualified the concession with the words "if the dissenters are not in fundamental conflict with the statutes of the party" (p. 142). Similarly, the party was stipulated to use persuasion and to "earn" its leading role, but there was little attempt to specify consequences should the party fail in its benign endeavor. Elective institutions and the normal functions of parliamentary institutions were to be restored but the question could still be posed: "What would happen if some eight million people in the country do not wish to be led by the Communist Party, but by a Monarch of the dynasty of the Přemysl-ides?" (p. 158, Jiři Hanák, *Reporter*, April 28, 1968). The conflict was, of course, between teleological and pluralistic principles of politics—one justifying power in terms of higher objectives, the other in terms of potentially fickle popular will—epitomizing a dilemma that has long haunted Marxist revisionists and the protagonists of democratic Communism in this part of the world.

While both authors have explicitly designated their studies as monographs, the reviewer and the reader of the two volumes will inevitably be drawn to make comparisons between these two polar models of Communism in Eastern Europe. The self-evident contrasts—between "administered" and pluralistic Communism—in turn will raise further questions concerning causes and correlations, the various facets of the social, economic and international context that may explain the differences. Each one of the two volumes attempts to provide such explanations—in terms of relative degrees of economic development and differences in respective political traditions. But more conclusive answers can emerge only from a more careful examination of analogies and contrasts within a more explicit frame of reference. It is in this respect that the political scientist will still find sufficient room for creative endeavor in examining both the Czech and the Bulgarian political systems at critical junctures of their development.

ANDREW C. JANOS
University of California
Berkeley

JOHN REX. *Race, Colonialism and the City*. Pp. xx, 310. London: Routledge, Kegan Paul, 1973. $13.25.

The author, a South African, presents a collection of essays based on his research in urban Britain, his readings in the social and economic history of colonialism and his experiences and memories of his home country. To some extent it is the account of a moral and intellectual pilgrimage through the badlands of racialism. Occasionally it is moving, sometimes turgid and repetitive and often perceptive and stimulating. The material is uneven: there are accounts of seminars and a letter to another academic among the chapters, as well as several reprinted articles. Even so, it does possess the dimensions of a fairly successful book.

Professor Rex's aim is to initiate a debate on the theory of racialism. The contribution of sociologists to understanding racial problems is negligible, he argues, and he condemns American sociologists especially for their diagnosis of the city-burning of the 1960s as an urban, rather than a racial, phenomenon. But British sociologists who have explained attitudes to colonial "immigrants" in terms of their cultural strangeness do not escape his strictures. It is the author's firm contention that racial prejudice underlies the treatment of black people in both these countries as well as elsewhere.

An essential part of the thesis is Professor Rex's—and Robert Moore's—now famous explanation of racialism in Birmingham, England, with the help of the concept of "housing class." Scarcity of housing, the housing policies of British local governments and urban poverty are responsible for the tension between the tenants of slum houses, who are often white, and the Asian and African tenants of multiply-occupied privately owned homes. The latter became the scapegoats for the deficiencies of the cities' housing systems. Their inability to house themselves more satisfactorily stems usually, however, from the fact of racial discrimination and not from the intrinsic harshness of city life.

When he is on such—for him—familiar territory, Professor Rex carries great conviction, and likewise with his excursion to South Africa. But when he undertakes, modestly it must be said, the more ambitious task of constructing a model for the study of race relations, his step is not so firm. In a most interesting chapter he reviews various theories and concludes that racial problems are primarily linked with colonialism. Therefore, the fundamental constraints are political rather than economic. Physical compulsion, exemplified in slavery and Bantu labor, is the essential support for commercial exploitation. Thus there is class conflict, but it is the oppression of the "under-class" by all other classes, including the white proletariat. Hence, his ultimate implications are vaguely Marcusion.

Consequently, the author's final admonitions are about the coming black revolution which, he argues, quaintly now it seems, will be supported by China. But in transferring his attention to a world scale, he moves from the city to the countryside, from black to white revolutionaries such as Castro and Che Guevara, and thus distorts his concepts. The links between national liberation movements such as the Vietcong, the Algerian National Liberation Front (F.L.N.) and the Black Power movements are surely ephemeral and superficial. Fortunately, however, only a small proportion of the book is polemical: for the most part it is an impressive attempt to be both human and intellectually rigorous about the world's greatest dilemma.

FRANK BEALEY
University of Aberdeen
Scotland

WALTER R. ROBERTS. *Tito, Mihailovic and the Allies, 1941–1945*. Pp. xii, 406. New Brunswick, N.J.: Rutgers University Press, 1973. $15.00.

The author of this volume traces the evolution of events in wartime Yugoslavia and discusses the differences in the abilities, in the personal ambitions, and in the temperaments of Tito and Mihailovic. He examines as well the relations between the Allies and the various Yugoslav factions both inside and outside the country.

In his smoothly flowing narrative, some of it based on published documentation, some on fresh sources, Mr. Roberts agrees with many earlier analysts that, between the two resistance leaders, Tito, "a product of the hard school of Communist training," was by far the more astute politically. By a skillful correlation of his struggle against the Nazis with suppression of his partisans' principal contender for post-war power, the Mihailovic Cetniks, he managed to focus world attention on Yugoslavia and even on his own importance. His first loyalty was to the Soviet Union as the world leader of Communism—even though the Kremlin made no move to supply either political or military support until the war was virtually over. Progressively Tito converted the disillusionment and frustration stemming from this apparent neglect into an attitude of independence, and "in the end it might be said that his allegiance was more to himself than to any external force."

Milhailovic, on the other hand, gambled all on his faith in an Allied victory that would deliver his country from the external enemy. In the meantime, he sought to prevent the spread of an alien ideology that threatened his conception of postwar Yugoslavia. Though he gave unswerving allegiance to the Allied cause, to King Peter II, and to the Serbian people, he was dismissed before the conflict ended, first by the Allies and then by the king.

In the course of the civil war, the struggle against the internal foe often ignored the external enemies. Mr. Roberts details the accommodation pacts made by some local Cetnik commanders with the Italians in Montenegro and Herce-govina; the German-partisan parleys in 1943 on exchange of prisoners and on cooperation in the event of an Allied landing in Dalmatia; and the shifts in Allied policy toward the two principal resistance forces. Whereas the British had originally supported the Yugoslav government in exile and Milhailovic, they turned to Tito after deciding that the military effectiveness of the Cetniks was only minimal. From the arrival of Brigadier Maclean's mission to Tito's headquarters, political and military support was transferred to the Partisans. As Mr. Roberts sees it, the partisan Communist leadership troubled Churchill little. Since he did not intend to make Yugoslavia his home after the war, the prime minister had said to Maclean at the end of 1943, "The less you and I worry about the form of government they set up the better." This view, based at the time on military considerations, changed later on political grounds, particularly toward the end of the war when Soviet designs became clearer.

Churchill nevertheless pushed the Yugoslav government in exile into one-sided agreement with Tito, hoping thereby to retain some British influence after the war.

Mr. Roberts touches only lightly on American leaders and on their part in the Yugoslav drama. Washington resolutely refused to exert any influence in Yugoslav affairs because President Roosevelt insisted that Tito-Milhailovic relations were not of crucial military importance to the grand Allied strategy. Pro-Serb and a mentor of the young King Peter II, he first advocated half-heartedly the reestablishment of a separate Serbian kingdom after the war, but Churchill later induced him to change his attitude. He retained his conviction nonetheless that events in Yugoslavia were remote from United States interests.

The Soviets for their part, in order not to disturb relations with the British and United States governments, showed little interest in Yugoslavia. They supported the Yugoslav government in exile well into 1943. Stalin rejected the plan to consider the partisan campaigns as a substitute for the second front, though in radio messages to Tito he instructed the partisan leader to put Soviet interests first. Since military operations in Yugoslavia were of little importance to Stalin, he sent a Soviet mission to join Tito only in February 1944, almost a year after the British had dropped liaison officers to the partisans. Not until after the Yalta meeting of the Big Three in 1945 did Stalin openly champion Tito as the sole contender for power in Belgrade.

Though his interpretation of events in Yugoslavia is the generally accepted one, Mr. Roberts still makes a substantial contribution. He has pulled together and distilled a staggering amount of detail, much of it from primary sources and much of it hitherto unavailable to researchers. With the Yugoslav archives incomplete or heavily weighted in Tito's favor, with the British files still closed, with American sources only partially available, and with the captured German documents of limited use, the student of Yugoslav affairs will find the Roberts work of evident value.

MILOS MARTIC
Department of Political Science
University of California
Berkeley

A. J. RYDER. *Twentieth Century Germany: From Bismarck to Brandt.* Pp. xx, 656. New York: Columbia University Press, 1973. $12.95.

Ryder, Senior Lecturer in History at St. David's University College, Lampeter, has written both a narrative and an interpretation of the past eighty years of German history. The narrative is comprehensive, and the interpretations are generally perceptive and moderate, based on a thorough acquaintance with recent scholarship.

This is seen clearly in Ryder's consideration of the origins of World War I. Although focusing perhaps excessively on Anglo-German relations, he avoids entering into a discussion of the classic war guilt issue, while making clear the lack of wisdom and moderation which characterized German policy.

Ryder displays equally good sense in his evaluation of Stresemann and his appraisal of the implications of Hindenburg's election to the presidency and his service in that office. Also noteworthy is the section on Weimar culture, which goes beyond the usual name dropping approach of the textbook.

Ryder is at his best in clarifying the "murky" and "desperate" politics that marked the end of the Weimar Republic. He identifies, first, four factors which shaped events—the growing rejection of the Republic by the moderate right, the depression, the breakdown of parliamentary government and the attitude of the army—and, second, six crucial stages —the collapse of the Müller government, the dissolution of the Reichstag and the elections of September 1930, the fall of Brüning, the dismissal of the Prussian government, the elections of July 1932, and the fall of Schleicher and appointment of Hitler. None of these events, of course, is unfamiliar to students of German history, but Ryder succeeds in achieving an orderly presentation of an disorderly era.

Beyond the customary survey of the creation of the Nazi dictatorship in 1933–1934 and Hitler's diplomacy in the 1930s, Ryder offers some insight into the Nazis' domestic program through his consideration of the economy, cultural policy and relations with the churches. Unfortunately, there is no specific treatment of the regime's anti-Semitism, although reference is made to it.

Ryder's discussion of World War II is generally satisfactory, although he displays a distinctly pro-British bias in his treatment of Allied military and political decisions, especially towards the end of the war.

In discussing the origins of the Cold War, Ryder adheres to the conventional view that aggressive Soviet expansionism was its primary cause. At the same time, he gives serious consideration to the March 1952 Soviet initiative on German reunification. Although, as he sees it, the evidence does not permit a final judgment, he admits the possibility that a real chance of agreement may have existed, and, therefore, that the Western failure to respond positively may have been "the decisive missed opportunity in post-1945 German history" (p. 528). Ryder's discussion of the development of the two Germanies is sound, especially his treatment of the Federal Republic's political evolution and economic growth and his evaluation of right-wing extremism.

One is struck by a few errors, such as a reference to Allen Dulles of the "Office of Strategic Studies" and the citation of 1949, rather than 1948, as the year of Sokolovsky's withdrawal from the Allied Control Council. The notes are extensive, and the bibliography is thorough and useful, particularly in its citation of journal articles. All in all, this is a remarkably well-balanced and well-written history.

BIRDSALL S. VIAULT
Winthrop College
Rock Hill
South Carolina

LEO VALIANI. *The End of Austria-Hungary.* Pp. xiii, 474. New York: Alfred A. Knopf, 1973. $15.00.

This is a translation of *La Dissoluzione dell'Austria-Ungheria*, first published in Italy in 1966. For this English edition, the author has added two additional appendices. One is a survey of material on peace feelers between the Entente and Austria-Hungary, as revealed in recently published German and British documents. The other covers French documents of the Ministère des Affaires Etrangères on Italy and the Yugoslav movement, which the author received permission to consult in 1968. Neither of these appendices changes in any substantial way his original account. They parallel in format a third appendix which appeared in the original Italian edition. This dealt with the activities of the American publicist G. D. Herron in respect to peace feelers with Austria-Hungary. All three are recitals of diplomatic maneuvers but do not present documents relating to the study as is usual in appendices.

The 256 pages of text and 41 pages of appendices are supported by 156 pages of footnotes. There is no separate bibliography, and the footnotes are meant to cover this omission. They attest to the wide research the author has done. He has consulted numerous archives and private papers as well as many obscure articles. Unfortunately, citations in the footnotes are not easily checked; sometimes the author refers only to a book's title with *op. cit.* or to an author who has written numerous volumes, but without indicating which title. For example, when one comes across R.W. Seton-Watson, *op. cit.*, how can one be certain to which of this author's many writings in this field he refers? To trace back to find the first citation among these voluminous footnotes is more than should be asked of any reader. There is no mention of the translator, and it is unfortunate that the publisher's stylist did not break up some of the long sentences which are more than replete with subordinate clauses. These sentences are correct enough, but do make for difficult reading.

The book contains information and detail, but it is not well sorted out. Views of important men and of lesser officials and journalists are recited with equal attention. There is mention of the Secret Treaty of London of 1915, but the actual negotiation of that agreement, with its clauses respecting territorial cessions, colonial affairs and Italy's obligation to enter the war, is not systematically discussed.

The author does give special care to Hungarian attitudes. Francis Ferdinand, he claims, would have relied upon the introduction of universal suffrage in Hungary as a means of bringing about constitutional reform in the Dual Monarchy. The steadfast opposition of Italian Foreign Minister Sonnino to the establishment of a large Yugoslavia is underlined. The emphasis in the volume is on the rise of the independence movements among the different nationality groups of Austria-Hungary and the gradual acceptance by the Entente powers of the necessity of the breakup of the Monarchy. The "national or social revolutions that convulsed and dismembered Austria-Hungary in 1918" are not gone into (p. 246) and, therefore, the historical account as proclaimed in the book's title is incomplete.

ERNST C. HELMREICH
Bowdoin College
Brunswick
Maine

UNITED STATES HISTORY AND POLITICS

ERIK AMFITHEATROF. *The Children of Columbus: An Informal History of the Italians in the New World.* Pp. 371. Boston: Little, Brown, 1973. $8.95.

Italian-Americans feel misunderstood, and rightly so, according to Amfitheatrof. "Their record in this New World . . . remains opague, confusing. In the days of the Sacco-Vanzetti trial, Italian workmen were regarded as subversives. Now, to suspicious liberals, they are angry flag-waving hard-hats" (p. 5). This book aims to challenge the stereotype that "Italian-Americans are all blue-collar workers, gardeners, fish peddlers—and *Mafiosi*" (p. 8).

Amfitheatrof succeeds in highlighting the diversity of Italians who have come to America—navigators, explorers, middle-class expatriates from the north, peasants form the south—as well as the diversity of their experiences in America—rich and poor, conservative, anarchist, and labor organizer, law abiding and not so law abiding. In attempting to balance the image of Italians in America, however, he does not provide a completely representative picture. Only two short chapters are devoted to the lives of those immigrants from southern Italy who crowded into Mulberry Bend and the other urban ghettos. Equal space, for example, is given two seventeenth century Italian explorers. But he cannot be criticized too strongly for this, because his purpose is to challenge stereotypes, not to provide a view of the modal life style.

In support of his contention that "nothing is clear about the Italian-Americans that does not take into account their past in Italy" (p. 314), Amfitheatrof provides an account of the unification of modern Italy precipitating the exile of Italian patriots in the United States. He also reviews the economic, political and social history of south Italy and Sicily, from the Greeks to the time of the mass migration from that area at the turn of the century. This chapter, in particular, contributes greatly to an understanding, not only of that exodus, but of the behavior of Italians in America—the padroni system, the lack of political participation, and the Mafia. In keeping with this view, the author points out the continuing ties Italian-Americans have had with Italy—for example, perpetuation of cultural traditions and how events in Italy, the rise of Mussolini in particular, have affected and divided Italian-American communities.

The author's skills as a professional writer (Time-Life) are readily apparent. *The Children of Columbus* is a most interesting book. The story of Italians in America is frequently personalized through biographical sketches of historically important individuals, from Christopher Columbus to Joseph Colombo, Sr. For example, he describes Garibaldi's political career in Italy and exile in the United States; La Guardia's successes and failures; Giannini's career from son of an immigrant farmer to chairman of the Bank of America Board and president of Transamerica Corporation; the Italian-Swiss Colony—utopian dream for an immigrant cooperative—and the beliefs and activities of Sacco-Vanzetti, leading to an apparently unjustified death sentence. Most readers will find their stereotypes challenged, and most will learn something of the forces, largely cultural and economic, which shaped the lives of immigrants, including those in the ghettos.

The social scientist will add interesting historical data to his probably generalized picture of Italian-Americans, but is unlikely to gain much sociological insight.

ANN BAKER COTTRELL
Sociology Department
California State University
San Diego

MARK L. BERGER. *The Revolution In The New York Party Systems 1840–1860.* Pp. 172. Port Washington, N.Y.: Kennikat Press, 1973. $8.50.

Mr. Berger's book is a welcome guide through the labyrinth of New York politics, 1840–1860, where one might easily lose his way among Barnburners, Hunkers, Free Democrats, Hard Shells, Soft Shells, Adamantines, and National Democrats; among Silver Grays, Sewardites, and Old Line Whigs; among Know-Nothings, Know Somethings, and Americans; and finally among the elements of the fusion forming the Republi-

can party. For the shift in issues during the twenty years before the Civil War from the tariff, money, and internal improvements, to slavery and slavery extension, nativism, religion, and temperance, did indeed effect a revolution.

One thing conspicuously missing in this work is any substantial evidence of high principle or idealism held by anything like a majority of New Yorkers and other Northerners on issues of free soil and antislavery extension. These issues seem to have been significant to them largely in economic and political, not in moral, terms. For this reason, one is somewhat taken aback at the statement: "The Northern response in opposition to the Kansas-Nebraska bill was almost unanimous" (p. 6). Actually, northern votes in Congress in 1854 could easily have defeated the bill, and although the northern fall elections went overwhelmingly against Nebraska men, this degree of hostility was short-lived. In the presidential election of 1856, when Kansas horrors were widely known, election statistics show that the Republican, anti-Nebraska candidate, Frémont, won only forty-five percent of the northern popular vote, whereas his opponents, Buchanan (Democrat) and Fillmore (American) won fifty-five percent. Further, in this area where opposition to the Kansas-Nebraska Act was said to be "almost unanimous," Buchanan won the electoral votes of California, Illinois, Indiana, Pennsylvania and New Jersey. In light of these data, and after making allowance for the lack of absolute precision between parties on issues, the author's statement as to northern attitude seems unsustainable.

The conclusion that the election of 1856 "revealed that the people of the Empire State had had enough of acquiescence" and that "what they wanted now was resistance" (p. 137) appears equally questionable. If this was their wish, they showed it in a strange way: they gave Frémont, who won the state by a plurality, only forty-six percent of the vote, whereas they gave Buchanan and Fillmore fifty-four percent. It is this reviewer's belief that, old as the theme is, the political upheaval in New York and the north shortly before the Civil War is still in need of research in depth.

JENNINGS B. SANDERS

Kensington
Maryland

ORVILLE H. BULLITT, ed. *For the President, Personal and Secret: Correspondence Between Franklin D. Roosevelt and William C. Bullitt.* Pp. 655. Boston, Mass.: Houghton Mifflin, 1972. $12.50.

This fine book divides itself into two parts; the introduction to each of the six divisions by the editor, Orvill Bullitt, and the correspondence between his brother William and the president. The editor did his homework well; the list of references consulted is significant. The correspondence in all of the thirty-two chapters was placed in its proper perspective by the meticulous efforts of the editor.

The book begins with William Bullitt's appointment in 1918 to the American Commission to Negotiate Peace. In Paris, however, he became *persona non grata* with President Wilson and was sent on a mission to Russia. When Wilson ignored Bullitt's report, he appeared before the Senate Foreign Relations Committee and urged rejection of the Treaty of Versailles.

In the early 1930s, Bullitt made pre-inauguration trips to Europe for Franklin Roosevelt and helped prepare for the diplomatic recognition of Russia. As a result, President Roosevelt named him the first ambassador to Soviet Russia, after he had served briefly as assistant to the secretary of state. By 1935, Bullitt was disillusioned in Russia and recognized the forthcoming war. He urged FDR to "say nothing, do nothing, and to carry a large cannon" (p. 106).

In 1936, Bullitt became ambassador to France and soon informed FDR that "within 3 years, England will have to choose between making war on Germany or permitting Germany to dominate all Eastern Europe" (p. 144). In Paris, Bullitt was held in great respect and confidence. As the war clouds gathered, he and FDR talked almost daily over a direct phone. Repeatedly, the president was told that many peoples of Europe desperately wanted him to intervene constructively to prevent war. "The curse of the Germans is that they have swallowed *Nieberlungenlied* and do not recoil even from the *Gotterdammerung*" (p. 230).

From 1938 on, Bullitt warned that Hitler would not stop, that he, Bullitt, was disgusted at England's refusal to invoke a draft at her rejection of Russia's offer of a triplicate alliance among Russia, England and France. He urged repealing of the Neutrality Act and supplying of France and England with all weapons of war which we could produce (p. 373). Repeatedly, Bullitt returned to make personal extended reports to FDR. When war came, however, Bullitt remained at his ambassadorial post in Paris.

When the French Republic was abolished in 1940, Bullitt returned home. The president sent him on an extended mission to the Near East. From early 1942 throughout 1943, Bullitt remained unemployed. He presented an extended peace plan to FDR and protested when FDR rejected it. Having earned the president's disfavor, he joined the staff of General de Gaulle. At the end of the war he was highly decorated by the French government.

In spite of his unusual talents, Bullitt apparently could not build abiding friendships. He lost his friendship with Wilson and with Roosevelt. Moreover, he was married and divorced several times.

This is an excellent book and will be widely read for a long time.

GEORGE OSBORN

Department of History and Social
    Sciences
University of Florida
Gainesville

GLEN GABERT, JR. *In Hoc Signo?* Pp. vii, 139. Port Washington, N.Y.: Kennikat Press, 1973. $6.95.

In Hoc Signo?, subtitled *A Brief History of Catholic Parochial Education in America*, suffers primarily from its brevity. A big story, it is told in a fashion too restricted to do justice to the subject. This is doubly unfortunate, because the author exhibits a knowledge of his topic and his discussions produce some insights and comments worthy of his expertise. One feels that, had he written more fully—the text is barely one hundred pages—a more valuable commentary probably would have been generated. Perhaps the rising costs of book production are the most satisfactory explanation, after all, of this limited description *cum* analysis of Catholic parochial education in America.

The book follows a chronological order of development, superimposed onto which are the distinctive contributions made to Catholic parochial education by the English, the Irish and the Germans, whose work is discussed in three separate chapters. This takes the story down to 1919. The fourth chapter deals with the "golden era"—1919–1958 when the system stood at its zenith and the motivations supporting the system were unquestioned. Since 1958 Gabert records the doubts, the uncertainties, in short the fading of the "golden era." In the course of the discussion, the author reviews the reasons why a parochial system of education became an objective of the Church in America by reciting the familiar arguments. He rehearses the controversy over lay trusteeship from a school's perspective; retells the Know-Nothing episodes of the middle of the nineteenth century, retraces the various steps taken by the American Plenary Councils; relates the growth of the schools to vicissitudes within the Church in general and the Papacy in particular, thereby recapitulating much Catholic Church history.

One important contribution which Gabert makes is his insistence that it was the Germans, and not the Irish, who should be given the greater share of the credit for building the system after the Civil War. While part of the reason for this is to be associated with a general growth in education at that time, the unique role of the Germans needs to be singled out. It also deserves a more thorough statement than is made in this book. The author has done a better job of demonstrating that these church schools grew as they did, in part at least, in response to papal attitudes and papal directives. The correlation between what the Popes wanted and what the American Church was able to do is, in fact, a fascinating glimpse into the effects of papal authority.

The author has included several tables which are of marginal value and a bibliographical essay very much worthwhile.

DAVID H. BURTON
Saint Joseph's College
Philadelphia
Pennsylvania

HERBERT KAUFMAN. *Administrative Feedback: Monitoring Subordinates' Behavior.* Pp. x, 83. Washington: Brookings Institution, 1973. $5.95, Paperbound, $2.50.

ROBERT N. KHARASCH. *The Institutional Imperative: How to Understand the United States Government and Other Bulky Objects.* Pp. x, 258. New York: Charterhouse Books, 1973. $7.95.

A book under the auspices of the Brookings Institution usually offers interesting data and thoughtful suggestions. This one about administrative feedback to higher level officials in several agencies of the national government, from their subordinates in central and field offices and from both their clientele and communications media, is no exception. On the other hand, Robert N. Kharasch, a Washington attorney, has written a book about bureaucracies in general—but with special attention to the federal government—that is semiserious, insightful, sometimes cynical and much lighter reading.

The Brookings analysis, conducted under the leadership of Herbert Kaufman, senior fellow, is a specialized work principally useful to students of public administration. He and his associate Michael Couzens made soundings (p. 18) in federal regulatory and service bureaus administering (a) their own programs or (b) intergovernmental programs with wide geographical impact. They found feedback through the echelons useful, even generally adequate, in assuring administrative *esprit de corps* and program compliance. They were astonished to find feedback from clients and communications media "at a much lower level of intensity" than anticipated. There were signals of danger in the system, however—perhaps chief among them (p. 54) the levels of tolerance set by the leaders. Some of the concluding suggestions, notably the proposal (pp. 76–79) for survey research conducted by independent organizations about the effectiveness of agency policies and services, could have been written even before the study began.

The suggestion of outside studies of governmental action, persumably financed by government, is based on the rationale of independent objectivity intended to improve the effectiveness of programs. Mr. Kharasch would undoubtedly offer a more simplistic observation: that a governmental agency would want or would use an independent study only if it reinforced an ongoing institutional program.

In developing *The Institutional Imperative* Mr. Kharasch propounds a series of axioms—summarized in pages 251 through 253—that he regards (p. 6) as the "few simple and inescapable laws of institutional behavior," whether governmental or corporate. A cardinal axiom is the third (p. 13): "Whatever the internal machinery does is perceived within the institution as the real purpose of the institution (i.e., function is seen as purpose)." All else, to him, is virtually a defense of that principle.

Filled with anecdotes of frustration, many of them wryly humorous, Kharasch's volume is at first glance a fun book, but it is also a journeyman's analysis of the malaise which amounts to "a profound distrust of the workings" of institutions. No statistical evidence is offered to document that malaise, and no measure is afforded to estimate the prevalence of popular disenchantment. Yet no literate American is unaware of the currency of the mood. No institution is exempted from Kharasch's analogies, and none is exempt from his strictures against the institutional self-occupation and self-justification and against the institutional irrelevance of truth, morality or purpose. The focus of his book is negative; if he is partly and incisively right, he is also largely mistaken.

FRANKLIN L. BURDETTE
Director, Bureau of Governmental
Research
University of Maryland

MATTHEW HOLDEN, JR. *The Politics of the Black "Nation."* Pp. vii, 235. New York: Chandler, 1973. $5.95.
The White Man's Burden. Pp. v, 284. New York: Chandler, 1973. $5.95.

In these companion volumes of essays, Professor Holden weighs the rationality and irrationality of black-white relations, past, present and impending, in the United States. *The Politics of the Black "Nation"*—the term is meant to emphasize the economic and cultural distinctiveness of the races today—deals with the internal and external politics of the black community, and *The White Man's Burden*, with racial policy and politics in the white community. Professor Holden's premise is that the races are interdependent, for better or for worse. They cannot turn their backs on one another for long. Their options are misunderstanding or understanding; mutual destruction or reconciliation.

The Politics of the Black "Nation" examines a historical succession of external strategies. Booker T. Washington's acceptance of a role of client to influential whites is treated sympathetically; the labors of W.E.B. DuBois and Martin Luther King, Jr., and others to induce whites to live up to their principles, warmly; and separatism, from Marcus Garvey to Stokely Carmichael, icily.

In a number of respects Professor Holden is an heir of the early DuBois—an elitist black intellectual addressing both races, straightforwardly critical of misguided members of both, eclectic, and hopeful. He expects leaders in the struggle for black liberation to emerge as they have in the past from the black bourgeoisie, and equally unfashionably insists that they can and must forge links with white ethnics rather than spend themselves on proven friends and enemies among whites.

Professor Holden's unsentimental pragmatism is not designed to comfort anyone, least of all militants. He regards most efforts to bolster black power and pride as self-defeating: college students learning to man barricades win short-lived gratification at the expense of scientific and bureaucratic training; elementary school students in community-controlled schools, absorbing the philosophy of Malcolm X, remain innocent of mathematics. Morale is important, he concedes, but hardly as important as coping with politics and the economy. In its pure form it is an irrational "politics of collective psychiatry"—a spectator sport. It is no substitute for the acquisition and use of skills suited to a technological multiracial society.

Black culture, like black power, has its obstructive qualities, he argues. Its defiance, cynicism and fear, moralism, and Dionysian independence discourage a sustained, coordinated attack on the problems of blacks in an unfriendly environment. The work to be done is undramatic: in education, capital formation, income support, employment and equal treatment before the law, to begin with, supported by a black information network, black think tanks and a growing complement of black elected officials.

In *The White Man's Burden* Professor Holden assesses the capacity of whites to contribute to racial peace. In this volume, as in *The Politics of the Black "Nation,"* there is a balance of description and prescription, censure and praise, and pessimism and optimism, along with a fresh look at white liberals and college activists, white police, reparations for blacks, urban statehood and the danger of insurrection, to mention a few subjects.

Neither volume is light reading. They are recommended to friends and skeptics alike for their breadth and thoughtfulness.

ROBERT SICKELS
University of New Mexico
Albuquerque

EMMETT JOHN HUGHES. *The Living Presidency.* Pp. 377. New York: Coward, McCann and Geoghegan, 1973. $10.50.

I have always felt that presidential memoirs, collected papers and biographies contained the most essential ingredients for understanding the American presidency. This is not because little else of value has been written on the presidency and certainly not because personalized accounts are an infallible guide to the actual facts of presidential conduct. It is, rather, because biographical, and autobiographical accounts particularly, are as close as we are ever likely to get to the facts as the presidential personalities perceived them. And there is nothing clearer in Emmett John Hughes's remarkable book than the message that the presidency is a highly personalized office, whose energizing force lies in the personalities of its occupants, the opportunities they see for the exercise of presidential initiative and power, and their own predilections for shaping the office and their conduct within it.

The everlasting virtue of this book —conveyed so well by its title—is that it comes alive with the presence of men who have occupied the presidential office. In its pages they are all represented; those who adroitly guided the nation through crises, as well as those who artlessly plunged the nation into them. Hughes has combined a broad historical overview of the presidential office with a penetrating analysis of many of its occupants to produce an unmatched treatment of the American presidency.

The book's most significant contribution is its treatment of the scope of contemporary presidential power, particularly the president's war powers, once called by Charles Beard, "the unexplored and dark continent of American government." The territory has now been skillfully explored, with an effect that is at once both illuminating and absolutely chilling. Not only does a president have the opportunity to be "as big a man as he can," as Wilson said, but he can also be, to use a contemporary expression for belligerence, as bad a man as he can. Hughes recounts FDR seizing upon a relatively harmless incident between an American ship and a German submarine in September, 1941, to deliver a sabre-rattling address he had prepared months before, the effect of which, according to Samuel E. Morrison, was to pit the United States against Germany in *de facto* naval war on the Atlantic. Truman, convinced he was saving the world from its third conflagration, committed American troups to Korea and informally advised a group of congressional leaders three days later. And Lyndon Johnson, emulating Roosevelt, used the flimsiest of pretexts and, it turned out, misrepresentation of facts, to extract the fateful senatorial resolution which delivered him the war in Vietnam he yearned to wage, even while campaigning in 1964 as the candidate of peace.

Much though the citizenry may be appalled by the unwise or wrongful use of presidential power, or driven to scorn politics by the spectacle of scandal in the White House heaped upon a terribly costly and ignoble war provoked and prolonged by the White House, we nevertheless cling to both the symbol and substance of a vigorous presidency as the chief hope for progress, prosperity and national greatness. In point of fact, it is hard to fault this judgment. Periods in American history of presidential eclipse offer no evidence of superior judgment or performance by other political institutions, either national, state or local. Nor does human history offer evidence that personal rights and liberties can be safeguarded adequately by an enfeebled government, or that a nation can long endure in a vacuum of leadership. We may be the victims of occasional exploitation by our own leaders, but the alternative is eternal exploitation by someone else's leader. Hughes is quite correct when he says that the most powerful weapon against abuse in the arsenal of a democratic citizenry is their own capacity and will not to place, uncritically, their fates into the hands of anyone who happens to possess presidential authority; not to surrender, unconditionally, control over their own government. The price of liberty, indeed, is eternal vigilance, and we need more books like *The Living Presidency*, which makes that point perfectly clear.

EVERETT F. CATALDO

Florida Atlantic University
Boca Raton

MARTIN E. MANTELL. *Johnson, Grant, and the Politics of Reconstruction.* Pp. xi, 209. New York: Columbia University Press, 1973. $9.00.

Historians once treated the Reconstruction following the Civil War as a melodrama in which the blacks and their friends were the villains and the advocates of white supremacy were heroes. During the past few decades, revisionists have caused new interpretations to prevail with respect to practically all phases of the story. Until recently, however, two important topics have remained almost completely unrevised—the role of Ulysses S. Grant, both as general in chief from 1865 to 1869 and as president thereafter, and the impeachment of Andrew Johnson. Grant has continued to be viewed as a rather confused and easily put-upon soldier who joined the Radicals out of anti-Johnson pique, and as an ineffectual president who deserves his classification, along with Warren G. Harding, as an outright failure in the White House. Johnson's impeachment is still presented all too often as a vindictive move against an executive already reduced to powerlessness.

That Grant is due for a startling rehabilitation is suggested by the tenor of a Northern Illinois University conference, in April 1973, devoted to his career. Reinterpretation of the impeachment has been given impetus by Michael Les Benedict who, in *The Impeachment and Trial of Andrew Johnson* (1973), argues that the action was justified because of

Johnson's obstruction of the congressional program.

Martin E. Mantell of the University of Arkansas, Pine Bluff, now furthers the reinterpretation of both themes in *Johnson, Grant, and the Politics of Reconstruction*. In contrast to Benedict—who stresses Grant's conservatism as a reason for his 1868 nomination—Mantell, on the basis of confidential correspondence, describes Grant as inwardly a convinced Radical from 1866 on, and attributes to him an important part in the shaping, as well as the enforcing, of the Reconstruction Acts. Like Benedict, Mantell sees impeachment as a success despite the acquittal, since the trial had the effect of lessening, if not eliminating, Johnson's obstructionism.

This rather slim volume, derived from the author's doctoral dissertation on the election of 1868 and written under the supervision of Eric McKitrick at Columbia University, amounts to an interpretive essay or series of essays pointing the way to further study. As such, it is a worthwhile contribution and a conclusive, though not a fully buttressed, monograph. Careful editing would have saved the author from numerous and sometimes distracting gaucheries of style.

RICHARD N. CURRENT
University of North Carolina
Greensboro

WILSON CAREY MCWILLIAMS. *The Idea of Fraternity in America*. Pp. xiv, 695. Berkeley: University of California Press, 1973. $14.95.

This is a history of the United States—not America—considered in terms of the conflict between liberalism and pluralism. Professor McWilliams holds that there is such a thing as human nature and that humans cannot be satisfied by the individualism that the liberal tradition permits. Humans require fraternity, and this is an essentially social term in a way that liberty and equality are not—these last two have physical analogues. He argues that fraternity requires ". . . intense interpersonal affection . . . is limited in number of persons and social space . . . involves shared goals . . . considered more important than 'mere life' . . . implies a tension with loyalty to society at large. . . ." McWilliams gives impressive psychological historical analyses, and does this in a rich and exciting style. He has considered an enormous amount of material, and we are treated to an original study of most of the major periods and movements from the Puritans to the Black Panthers. The dominant interest is the matter of fraternity, *gemeinschaft*; the dominant delight is in seeing the limits and frustrations of the effort to reduce the good life to the merely rational individual. "Rarely if ever has social science concerned itself with the positive role which groups or emotions can play in individual perception" (p. 56). Discussions of the matter frequently ignore ". . . the possibility that the individual himself, not the group, is the greatest distorter of reality. . . ."

One particularly valuable part of McWilliams' book is the way in which he combines literary criticism with political, religious and social history. He analyzes Hawthorne, Melville, Whitman and Mark Twain as well as John Winthrop, Jonathan Edwards, Jefferson, Emerson, Bellamy, the Roosevelts, Henry A. Wallace, and so forth. He stops for an extended study when he finds an author saying something like: " . . . man works only for his fellow man . . . " (Thurman Arnold). And he never takes "mass" goals as substitutes for "fraternal instincts." Of course, his standards are so rigorous that he finds almost no successful examples of fraternity in our history. When we seem to have it, as with the Black Panthers, we learn that their community feelings come from the need to oppose outsiders and not from purely fraternal, internal objectives.

There are unsupported snap judgments along the way. "Dresden, Hiroshima, the Cold War: these are the natural children of the New Deal." Children, natural or otherwise, are not inevitable; when they occur we want to know the mechanism and the parentage. McWilliams' history ends pessimistically because while "fraternity is a need of man . . . there is no simple tactic which can produce brotherhood . . . under modern conditions" (p. 93). I have some petty complaints about his concept of human nature and the role of fraternity. He is vague and impressionistic, but no one is any better at this stage. An exciting and useful history.

SIDNEY AXINN
Department of Philosophy
Temple University
Philadelphia

HOWARD N. MEYER. *The Amendment That Refused To Die.* Pp. ix, 252. Radnor, Pa.: Chilton, 1973. $7.95.

This book provides a good account of the struggle for civil rights in the United States. Mr. Meyer's thesis is that the Constitution has been twice made: first, in Philadelphia in 1787 and including the first eight amendments; second, in 1868 with the adoption of the Fourteenth Amendment. "The original Constitution," the author holds, "was the fruit of a revolution . . . the second American constitution [Fourteenth Amendment] was an attempt to consolidate" the revolution engendered by the war between the states.

The second constitution, however, was subject to betrayal by the United States Supreme Court—the *Civil Rights* cases, the *Slaughterhouse* cases, *Palko* v. *Connecticut*, and the like. Hence a third revolution, "begun by blacks, and often the burden was carried by them alone," became necessary, the aim being "to bring about a return to the [second] constitution." Mr. Meyer writes: "The third American revolution has been won on paper; it seems remote from accomplishment in deed. The question that every American must ask himself is whether or not the return to the Constitution has taken place too late."

Overlooking certain of Mr. Meyer's pronouncements regarding the rebellion of the colonies and the adoption of the Constitution, my chief complaint is his uncritical acceptance of Mr. Justice Black's history of the framing of the Fourteenth Amendment, to support the incorporation of the entire Bill of Rights as restraints upon the States. Mr. Meyer declares: "Never has a Supreme Court opinion been freighted with such a convincing array of historical evidence as that which was offered by Justice Black in the appendix to his 1947 dissent in the case of *Adamson* v. *California.*" Mr. Justice Black's view was challenged by Charles Fairman, one of America's outstanding constitutional historians, in the December, 1949, issue of the *Stanford Law Review.* After a long and detailed study of the sources, Professor Fairman concludes: "In his [Mr. Black's] contention that Section I [of the Fourteenth Amendment] was intended and understood to impose Amendments I to VIII upon the states, the record of history is overwhelmingly against him." I wish that Mr. Meyer had devoted at least a chapter to an attempt to answer Professor Fairman.

Though I agree that the recent court decisions regarding race relations were long overdue, their base might well have been other than a possibly questionable reading of history.

There are a few minor objections. The title is confusing. When I was invited to review this book I had no inkling as to which amendment Mr. Meyer had in mind. After all, there are many amendments and, other than the Eighteenth Amendment, they appear to be alive, some of them kicking.

Mr. Meyer has provided the reader with no footnotes precisely indicating his sources. Also, there is no index and this omission limits the book's usefulness. At the risk of revealing a cranky side to an otherwise compassionate nature, I object to calling the Fourteenth Amendment, "Big Fourteen."

C. GORDON POST
Wells College
Aurora
New York

JAMES C. MOHR. *The Radical Republicans and Reform in New York during Reconstruction.* Pp. xv, 300. Ithaca, N.Y.: Cornell University Press, 1973. $12.50.

In this book, Professor Mohr has undertaken a commendable task. Dissatisfied with the excessive attention paid by historians to the effect of Reconstruction on the South and southern states, Professor Mohr turns the historical spotlight on the North, specifically New York state. He sets out to answer the pertinent question: What were the Radicals' policies at home?

His treatment of Reconstruction politics in New York is not the first, however. In 1913, Homer A. Stebbins, a Dunning student, published *A Political History of the State of New York, 1865–1869.* Although more than half a century old, this work is still useful. But Mohr decidedly improves on it by showing that Governor Reuben Fenton and his radical-reform coalition were not merely Republican precursors of the Democratic Boss Tweed, but initiated significant civil and institutional reform during the immediate post-Civil War period. New York Radical legislators, for example, studied penal reform, created the Board of State Commissioners of Public Charities, worried about proper housing and fire protection and began various metropolitan changes. Their lack of success, claims Mohr, was not flagging zeal or crumbling idealism but loss of legislative control after 1867 and the emergence of the Tweed element. It was then, and only then, argues Mohr, that the New York Republican party— including its Radical remnants— turned to business for support and money, avidly sought federal patronage and gradually came under the control of Roscoe Conkling.

There will be those who will claim that Mohr exaggerates the importance of general societal and political reform as a factor in Radical politics between 1865 and 1867, and that he makes too neat a distinction between the radical reform coalition of Fenton and what follows. Others will be skeptical of Mohr's emphasis on the racial issue—mainly involving suffrage—as the critical issue in the Radical coalition's ultimate defeat. Even so, Mohr has unquestionably made a sound contribution to Reconstruction history and to an understanding of New York state politics.

ROBERT K. MURRAY
Pennsylvania State University

BERNARD W. SHEEHAN. *Seeds of Extinction: Jeffersonian Philanthropy and the American Indian.* Pp. xii, 301. Chapel Hill, N.C.: University of North Carolina Press, 1973. $11.95.

In 1791 Timothy Pickering remarked to a tribal gathering: "There are some white men who do not love you" (p. 267). Though the understatement undoubtedly shocked none of his listeners and is as appropriate today as it was then, it does capsulize a major theme in the sordid chapter of white American-Indian relations. If anything, the ever-increasing number of scholars devoting their energies to native American scholarship has reinforced this truism by re-evaluating past myths, researching topics long neglected and broadening understanding of the lengths to which white Americans went to eradicate Indianness. And yet, along the way from 1492 to 1973, there were influential people who tried to stem the tide of Indian degeneration by offering integration and then separation, as a civilized alternative. It is these people, at least those who lived during the Jeffersonian era, who intrigued Sheehan and earned his scholarly attention.

It is difficult to bring a new and fresh approach to a subject that has provoked thousands of published words by a myriad of previous historians, but Sheehan has done just that and more. He approached his task as if no historian before him had offered a clear picture of the strivings of Jeffersonian philanthropists to raise Indians from barbarism to civilization by forcing them to abandon the hunter-warrior culture, forsake their tribal order and renounce communal ownership of land. The end result is a masterpiece that will stand for decades to come, not because it is without defect but because it adds new dimensions to a topic that heretofore has been used to explain American benevolence or to ridicule the idiocy of closet philosophers. But Sheehan proves that the utterances and efforts of the philanthropists were significant and should be contemplated by thoughtful scholars. Also, he shows clearly the impact of Comte de Buffon's environmental utterances on America's first generation of political leaders. Buffon, and other Europeans, cut the Jeffersonians to the quick by predicting that whites would fail to prosper in America because of a "mysterious flaw" in the continent. To prove their case, the Europeans used the savage Indian as a prime example of what an unsuitable environment does to human beings. No self-respecting American intellect could fail to accept Buffon's challenge and, among other things, the Jeffersonians intensified their efforts to civilize native Americans. Though they failed miserably to achieve the goal, Sheehan did not fail in his effort to examine the topic and to explain the extent of the failure. For that reason, above all others, the book deserves to be read and contemplated.

The bibliography in *Seeds of Extinction* is less than useful; it does not contain most of the better secondary sources on the subject. On the other hand, Sheehan's footnotes are impressive and show full use of available major and minor collections and contemporary publications, and he is eminently fair in his handling of this material. After all is said and done, he is not sure what the Jeffersonians achieved in Indian affairs. He readily admits that their efforts were doomed to failure, not because they lacked sincerity or vigor but because most whites refused "to accept the Indians, civilized or not, as part of the white man's world" (p. 241), and because "tribesmen never quite lost perception of themselves as Indians" (p. 267). The first reason is shameful; the second is not.

ARTHUR H. DeROSIER, Jr.
Department of History
East Tennessee State University
Johnson City

SYDNEY NATHANS. *Daniel Webster and Jacksonian Democracy.* Pp. 249. Baltimore, Md.: Johns Hopkins University Press, 1973. $10.50.

Daniel Webster, long dormant in historiography's graveyard, has been the subject of several recent monographic studies. This new-found interest in Webster may be the result of a fascination with what Professor Nathans offers as

a basic theme: Webster was a genuine "misfit" in the politics of the Jacksonian period. An antagonist toward political parties and a believer in government by gentlemen, Webster was compelled, so Nathans argues, to accommodate himself to the changing currents in American politics. He was not altogether successful in this regard; and thereby hangs a tale.

The author sympathetically traces Webster's career from 1828 through the defeat of Henry Clay in 1844. Nathans' efforts to connect Webster with Jacksonian democracy are best seen in the first two chapters in which the Webster-Jackson flirtation during the nullification controversy and Webster's dreams for a constitutional union party are discussed. As Nathans points out, the unusual alliance between these two men was short-lived, because Van Buren was anxious to break it up and because the bank issue served as an obstacle to any sort of permanent entente.

In the remaining eight chapters, the focus shifts to the Webster-Clay partnership and rivalry. The author notes the irony of Webster, who had little faith in political parties, being forced to embrace partisan politics in order to advance his own presidential aspirations. The unpleasant fact that both Webster and Clay were denied the Whig nomination on the 1840 ticket merely compounded this irony. Whig successes in 1840, followed by the sudden death of Harrison and elevation of Tyler in 1841, generated additional Webster-Clay antagonisms.

There is a noticeable tinge of pathos in Nathans' story of Webster's Cabinet days. Webster bravely embarked upon the unrewarding task of reconciling his party to Tyler's program, once more demonstrating his desire to minimize party feelings. Meanwhile, Clay busily fanned the flames of resentment against the president and also nurtured the seeds of his own political ambitions. Webster stubbornly clung to his Cabinet post, only to be rebuffed by the Whigs and eventually by Tyler himself. Such were the rewards of a peacemaker in the Whig family.

The book closes somewhat somberly,

Webster's achievements in diplomacy affording the only relief to an otherwise bleak picture. By concluding with 1844 rather than 1852, Nathans perhaps over-emphasizes the Webster-Clay rivalry and the Webster-as-a-political-anachronism themes. Moreover, this well-written and sound book suffers from an unfortunate title, since the Webster-Jacksonian democracy connection receives relatively minor attention.

PAUL H. BERGERON
Department of History
University of Tennessee
Knoxville

HAROLD ORLANS. *Contracting for Knowledge.* Pp. 286. San Francisco: Jossey-Bass, 1973. No price.

This book is an outcrop of earlier groundwork done by Orlans in 1966, when he conducted a staff inquiry for proposed governmental subcommittee hearings to be held by the Research and Technical Programs Subcommittee on Governmental Operations, chaired by Representative Henry S. Reuss of Wisconsin. The original data base for some of the content of the present volume is contained in an earlier four volume work entitled: *The Use of Social Research in Federal Domestic Programs* (1967), direct result of Orlan's earlier efforts for the subcommittee which subsequently disbanded in 1969.

Orlans states forthrightly the central purpose of the volume; but conceivably there are also other purposes, purportedly less central, that intrigue him. He states that the central purpose of the book is to assess the "value and limitations of the knowledge yielded by *applied* social research . . . [and] . . . an additional purpose is to subject the claims of social scientists to the same critical scrutiny which they are accustomed to apply to others." This purpose—or these purposes—is also bound up with the social scientists' unconvincing position on objectivity, as well as the contention by Orlans that "a fundamental function of social science is not to attain an unattainable certainty but rather to foster a sense of confidence in the midst of uncer-

tainty." Therefore, while subscribing to the distinction between basic—others call it pure: knowledge for the sake of knowledge—and applied research, Orlans states that his objectives lie with the latter, yet often enough spends his time writing about issues closely aligned with the former. Those who read the preface of this book too closely would perhaps not be encouraged to proceed further: to be candid, it is theoretically muddled and obscure.

Some of the rest of the volume is related to Orlans' stated central purposes, and some of it is not. Part 1, which discusses the political views of social scientists, associations and the "unimpressive" efforts of the latter to develop codes of ethics, is theoretically related to the objectivity/subjectivity dilemma rather than the value and limitations of applied research. In part 2, using the Reuss data, Orlans concludes that scholars conclude that they have little responsibility to governmental funding agencies. Part 3 examines who gets funds, what freedoms—to publish—are associated with them, and what attempts have been made to assess the quality of research. This part is tangentially related to the preface's stated central purposes. The theme of part 4, on the "Uses of Social Research," hinges on the political attitudes of researchers in implementing research results or on practical observations concerning the organization of knowledge. This latter chapter (chapter 12) is, in this reviewer's estimation, one of the more thought provoking in the book. The last chapter attempts to bridge the gap between public policy and "good empirical and theoretical research:" the latter's excellence, if it continues to be "subjectivized," turns "feeble knowledge into reeds of belief."

To say that this book "subject[s] the claims of social scientists to the same critical scrutiny which they are accustomed to apply to others" is to overstate the case. The data and the theoretical framework of this book are much too slipshod for that. This is not to say that there are not insightful and polemically provocative suggestions to be found here. But they would have perhaps found a more ready audience had they been published individually in journals of opinion.

EDWARD L. SUNTRUP
Department of Sociology
University of Minnesota

GEORGE N. RAINSFORD. *Congress and Higher Education in the Nineteenth Century.* Pp. xi, 156. Knoxville, Tenn.: University of Tennessee Press, 1972. $6.95.

GEORGE Z. F. BEREDAY. *Universities for All: International Perspectives on Mass Higher Education.* Pp. xv, 158. San Francisco, Calif.: Jossey-Bass, 1973. $8.50.

We are approaching an age of mass college attendance for the world's most advanced industrial nations. Rainsford focuses on one aspect of the subject—the development of federal support for higher education in this country, particularly during the nineteenth century. Bereday's stage is much broader, girdling the earth's northern hemisphere. He addresses himself primarily to burgeoning advanced education in four industrial countries—the United States, Canada, the USSR and Japan—contrasting their growth patterns, and the problems arising out of that growth, with those of industrial Western Europe.

Both authors offer impressive credentials as authorities in their respective areas of endeavor. A trained historian, college professor and college administrator, Rainsford manifests considerable skill in locating relevant information, analyzing its significance and placing it in proper context. A former Polish cavalryman and British paratrooper, Bereday earned advanced degrees here and in England. Now a professor of comparative education at Teachers College, Columbia University, he has taught in Japan, the USSR and Canada, and he boasts an extensive background of writing and editing in that area. In *Universities for All* he has brought to bear much of his first hand knowledge in a crossnational appraisal of the "reverberations and consequences of [growths in enrollments] within North America, the USSR,

and Japan in contrast to Europe." He has also made extensive use of recent research in this area, sponsored by the Organization for Economic Development and Cooperation (OEDC). Bereday originally sought to learn how other industrial nations were adapting American precedents in mass education to their own needs, but the pivot of comparison often swings to the USSR, Japan and Canada as well.

Limitations of space foreclose the possibility of offering more than brief glimpses of the contents of either volume. In general, Rainsford has addressed himself to two problems: how federal aid to advanced education in this country started, and where it is going. He concentrates chiefly on the disappointments of early American statesmen, who envisioned a genuinely national system of education, growing support for locally controlled education from the proceeds of land sales, gradual conversion of that support into annual, tax-based grants, the establishment of land grant colleges following the Morrill Act of 1862 and the vast impact of these colleges on American life, and the origins of categorical grants in the Hatch Act of 1887 and the Morrill Act of 1890. Historians usually date the first categorical grants about a quarter of a century later. Rainsford presents a persuasive case for placing these earlier measures in this category.

Bereday places major emphasis on the impact of mass admissions on institutions of advanced education. He is primarily concerned with expanding opportunities for the culturally disadvantaged, raising a broad spectrum of postsecondary institutions to equal status and equal curricular levels with traditional universities, converting university "republics" into "democracies"—recognizing "junior staff power and student power"—and university responsiveness to public opinion.

Both books may make substantial contributions to their respective spheres of interest. One reason has been indicated above. Their authors have disclosed a liberal rather than a narrow interpretation of the scope of their subject matter; both place the subjects of their inquiries into a broad historical context. Rainsford, for example, does not confine his narrative to the enactment of national laws, or to Congressional debates that preceded their passage. He also reveals the forces that impelled Congress to act on these measures, such as sectional interests, which often clashed, and the activities of pressure groups. He also provides a rich array of background materials, probing such subjects as the English system of higher education in the sixteenth century, the modifications of that system that arose out of the colonial experience, the progress of science in nineteenth century America, the influence of science on the founding of the land grant colleges, and the interaction of science, technology and those colleges on American agriculture.

History illuminates the past, helps explain the present and takes us to the threshold of the future. Rarely, if ever, does it offer a full and clearcut guide to that future. It is not surprising, then, that Rainsford's exposition of the past record of federal aid is much fuller and more explicit than his projections of things to come.

Bereday is not nearly as inhibited, partly because his predictions about the future course of higher education tend to reflect his political and social views. When he advocates "open admissions" to colleges, for example, he espouses one side in a vehement debate now taking place on the results of a policy of this kind in the City University of New York. Bereday is justifiably proud of the insights he offers in this area, based on "comparative evidence." Others might argue, however, that direct, first-hand evidence of the results of open admissions could be more cogent than analogies with the experience of nations across the seas. In any event, a scholar's first duty is not merely to proclaim eternal verities, but to set forth his views, regardless of the possibility of adverse criticism. That is the path that eventually discloses new truths.

FREDERICK SHAW
Bureau Head, Bureau of
    Educational Program Research
Board of Education of the
    City of New York

JAMES L. SUNDQUIST. *Dynamics of the Party System: Alignment and Realignment of Political Parties in the United States.* Pp. x, 388. Washington, D.C.: The Brookings Institution, 1973. $8.95.

In his third major probe of relationships between aspiration and practice in vital dimensions of the American governmental system—his earlier studies were of *Making Federalism Work* (1969) and *Politics and Policy: The Eisenhower, Kennedy, and Johnson Years* (1968)—James Sundquist has synthesized comprehensive historical data within rational and sophisticated theoretical contexts, in order to evaluate and predict directions of political party realignment.

As in the earlier works, Sundquist makes superb use here of the formidable research resources available through Brookings. This project was assisted, also, by data from The Inter-University Consortium For Political Research at the University of Michigan. It is far more, however, than a compilation and explication of material gathered by others; Sundquist thinks, writes and challenges with trenchancy, precision, and originality.

As the title of the first chapter, "Party Realignment: What? When? How?" makes clear, his desire to reach to the core of political reality has a Lasswellian ring in its invocation of gut questions. Sundquist intersperses chapters on theory with distillations of relevant data, as he reviews alignments and realignments over a 140 year span. Scholarly depth, factual precision and careful documentation in citing the extensive literature and preparing illustrative charts and tables make this 388 page volume an invaluable new reference source for students of politics.

The primary strength of the book is not as an analytical museum with modern decor for exhibiting the past, but rather as an interpretive resource center correlating trends and patterns from the past in order to develop predictive guidelines for the future. Ten chapters deal with historical essences, such as the realignment of the 1850s, agrarian revolt and the rise of populism and the "aftershocks of the New Deal earthquake." The three opening chapters establish Sundquist's diagnostic framework and develop five "hypothetical scenarios" keynoting struggles for power that can produce realignment within the major parties. Chapters 13 and 14 then amplify his historical findings through formulation and discussion of sixteen hypotheses about realignment, along with reemphasis on the dynamic and multidimensional qualities of the party system.

All of these can be considered preludes to the last three chapters that lead the reader, in some sixty-seven pages, through the post-New Deal "crosscutting issues" and into today's and tomorrow's realignment potentialities. Despite the growth of independent voter attitudes reflected in voters' self-identification and in ticket splitting since the 1960s, including the exodus of some ten million eligible voters from formal identification with the major parties, Sundquist believes that "the headlong march toward decomposition that marked the late 1960's will be checked and even reversed," at least in the short run, and that "most of those who ceased identifying with one or the other major party in the recent turmoil will re-identify."

The one oversight in the volume from a reviewer's vantage point, as the surrealism of Watergate pervades recent politics, is its pristine rationality. Sundquist obviously sees policy issues as the key factors in party alignments. Psychological manipulation, dirty tricks and outright falsehoods perpetuated through mass infusions of unrecorded money are alien to his analytic repertoire. In short, Sundquist posits continuity of a political party system molded by and responsive to the concerns of the American people rather than to the "end justifies the means" machinations of a reelection committee cabal. The author's neglect of this sleazy realm serves as a hallmark of his commitment to an open and democratically responsive party system.

VICTOR G. ROSENBLUM
Northwestern University
Chicago

POLITICAL THOUGHT

GERRY D. BREWER. *Politicians, Bureaucrats, and the Consultant.* Pp. 291. New York: Basic Books, 1973. $12.50.

Gerry D. Brewer's book, *Politicians, Bureaucrats, and the Consultant,* is, like many scholarly books, misnamed. Instead of exploring the broad and somewhat vague subject of its title, this book focuses quite narrowly on the uses and abuses of simulation techniques and model-building as means for solving contemporary urban problems. Not all consultants are model-builders, and certainly not all social science model-builders wish to try to earn their livings by applying simulation methods to day-by-day urban problems. Yet, as Brewer notes, there is a strong tendency to believe that a model without practical applications must not be very successful and that a community not using the latest techniques to solve its diverse problems must not be very up to date.

The first ninety-six pages contain a truly outstanding discussion of simulation. Brewer begins with a general analysis of models as "views of the world." Then, he takes up four areas of evaluation: theoretical appraisal, technical appraisal, ethical appraisal and pragmatic appraisal. The material is presented in a very clear, succinct manner, and the substantive questions raised and discussed penetrate to the very heart of the model-building enterprise. This reviewer would like to urge the author and publisher to make this section of the book available in a low cost paperback edition for classroom use immediately.

The second half of the book presents two examples of simulations gone wrong—the attempts by the cities of San Francisco and Pittsburgh to generate urban decision models as part of their respective Community Renewal Programs. Though the particulars of the case studies are different in several important ways, the message from each is essentially the same—the community was sold a bill of goods by a consulting firm, and the consulting firm and its distinguished array of academic advisors failed to produce. Unfortunately, these case studies are somewhat difficult to follow in their complexity and detail due to the author's rather choppy style and disjointed organizational pattern. Perhaps the problem is merely the contrast between the highly successful presentation of the general or theoretical material in the first part of the book and the more descriptive character of the second part.

In sum, *Politicians, Bureaucrats, and the Consultant* ought to be added to the list of required reading for all students and practitioners of urban planning and for all social science methodologists.

JOSEPH ZIKMUND
Albion College
Michigan

RICHARD E. FLATHMAN. *The Practice of Political Obligation.* Pp. xxvii, 334. New York: Atheneum, 1972. $12.95.

What particularly distinguishes Flathman's work—as well as his previous book, *The Public Interest,* (John Wiley and Sons, 1966)—is his combination of careful language analysis in the Oxford tradition with a serious substantive concern with certain normative aspects of political theory. He steers a middle course between those who would reduce problems raised by propositions about political obligation to verbal or, at best, cognitive issues about reason and intention, on the one hand and, on the other hand, the positivists with their inevitable tendency to study phenomena of human interaction as if they merely amounted to regularities in behavior.

This book is a critical study of the practice of political obligation, which operates, writes Flathman, "only if men *choose* or *decide* to do or refrain from doing certain *actions* because they believe that there are *good reasons* for accepting and obeying or rejecting and disobeying *rules* that require or forbid those actions" (p. xv; his emphases). Flathman tells us that Plato, Hobbes and other great theorists of the past have been concerned with how to bring about political stability by promoting obedient behavior, namely, nonreflective, habitual obedience, by way of myths and authority. But he argues that such behavior is apt to lead not to stability but to static, and therefore brittle, precarious social orders.

The author's substantive position evolves through a careful analysis of concepts of "rule" and of types of rules governing political action in contrast to rules governing behavior, and rules that do both (chaps. 2–4); and, of course, by way of a thorough investigation of "consent," "obligation," and "freedom," as well as types of practices referred to by alternate uses of these key concepts (chaps. 5 and 6). The two concluding chapters outline a general rule-utilitarian position, in qualified opposition to the long tradition of theories of implied consent as justification for political obligation.

Space limitations make it impossible to convey the full dimensions of Flathman's achievement; neither can I properly develop my disagreements with him. The concluding chapter includes an illuminating exposition of and commentary on the Socratic argument in the *Crito,* the essence of which is contrasted to Hobbes's interest-based obligation theory. Socrates comes out the winner. To Flathman, the *Crito* still provides the most satisfactory argument to justify the practice of political obligation in reasonably well-ordered states.

What I miss most in the book is a clear humanist vision, as well as a sense of the real world in which we live. Flathman defends principled civil disobedience, but in the interest of stability rather than the humanity of the oppressed. His position is cogently critical, even of the argument in the *Crito*—Flathman ends up a step or two to the left of Socrates—but strikes me as profoundly uncritical in the larger sense, in that he has little to say to those of us who care deeply for justice but have shed the democratic illusion, and indeed have come to see the American political-economic system as the principal obstacle to justice in the modern world. Is there no higher ground for political obligation than the alleged requirements of that deceptive mirage, the modern democratic state?

CHRISTIAN BAY
University of Toronto

CATHARINE HUGHES. *Plays, Politics, and Polemics.* Pp. xv, 194. New York: Drama Book Specialists, 1973. $7.95.

In order to have any real influence and in order to be an instrument for political change, political theater must lead and not follow. Although she is not at all sure that the theater can fill this role, Catharine Hughes argues in this new book that contemporary American and European protest theater, by ignoring any possibility of doubt, has consistently failed; failed as polemic in that it has failed to change minds, and failed also as good theater.

Ms. Hughes is drama critic for the New York weekly, *America,* and American Theater Critic for *Plays and Players* (London) as well as contributor to a number of prominent publications.

To present her argument, the author has organized her book into three parts, with a brief introduction and a brief concluding chapter. Each part consists of a series of critical essays, and each essay, with the exception of the first, deals with a single political play. In all, some twenty-two plays are discussed.

The plays covered in part I all concern American domestic controversies such as McCarthyism; the J. Robert Oppenheimer affair; the Rosenbergs' trial, and civil rights. Plays evaluated include Feiffer's *Little Murders, God Bless,* and *The Whitehouse Murder Case;* Arthur Miller's *The Crucible;* Donald Freed's *Inquest;* Heinar Kipphardt's *In the Matter of J. Robert Oppenheimer;* Richard Wesley's *The Black Terror;* Charles Gordone's *No Place to be Somebody,* and Arthur Kopit's *Indians.*

Part 2 discusses plays with a war theme. For these critiques, Ms. Hughes has chosen Sean O'Casey's *The Silver Tassie;* David Rabe's *The Basic Training of Pavlo Hummel;* Daniel Berrigan's *The Trial of the Cattonsville Nine;* Peter Weiss's *Viet Nam Discourse;* Joseph Heller's *We Bombed in New Haven;* Stanley R. Greenberg's *Pueblo,* and Ralph Hochhuth's *Soldiers.*

Part 3 is miscellany entitled "Other Controversies," which also examines plays dealing with controversial figures such as Pius XII, Hammarskjöld and Bertolt Brecht. The plays considered are Ralph Hochhuth's *The Deputy;* Peter Weiss's drama of the atrocities of Auschwitz, *The Investigation;* Robert Shaw's *The Man in the Glass Booth;* Peter Weiss's *Trotsky in Exile;* Conor Cruise O'Brien's *Murderous Angels,* and Gunter Grass's *The Plebians Rehearse the Uprising.*

It is Ms. Hughes's thesis that most playwrights in the contemporary theater of controversy lack either the genius or the vision to transform their protests into art—that they speak only to the converted with the "oversimplification of the propogandist rather than with the power of illumination possessed by the true creative artist. . . ." By excluding even the possibility that there may be another side to a question dealt with in a play, the potential to convince and change minds is lost. And by exluding doubt, too often the very conflict that is the essence of good drama is also excluded. Of the plays discussed, only in *The Basic Training of Pavlo Hummel* does the author find a play that really "works—has impact—not through a denunciation of the American role in Viet Nam, but because it recognizes that war *does* have a lure for men, that they kill and are willing to kill for complex and varied reasons."

Ms. Hughes is a good drama critic, and she makes her case effectively, insofar as the dramatic failures are concerned. Social scientists may be less satisfied, in that little attempt is made to provide hard external evidence that these plays have failed to convince anyone or even have impact. Her case rests more upon definition of what a good polemic should be. While the same analytic points are made with each play examined and some cross references are included, the social scientist will also be disappointed that overall analytic continuity is sparse and that no developmental transitionals connect one critical review to the next. One is left with the impression that the book's organization came about quite by chance and that it would have made little difference in which order any of the parts or essays appeared. Nevertheless, each essay is well worth reading for its own sake.

THOMAS M. WATTS
Dean, School of Behavioral
Sciences
California State College
Bakersfield

LUTHER P. GERLACH and VIRGINIA H. HINE. *Lifeway Leap: The Dynamics of Change in America.* Pp. 332. Minneapolis, Minn.: University of Minnesota Press, 1973. $12.50.

This work is an attempt to explain social change in contemporary America in terms of a social-evolutionary, rather than a simple linear model. To this end, a series of distinctions between developmental and revolutionary change is introduced. Developmental change, understood on an almost Spencerian model, is fundamental and can come about only through a considerable passage of time. In distinction to this, revolutionary change is seen as an only momentary overturning of given existing situations; to be correctly understood it must be fit into a long-term developmental movement. While revolutionary action attempts to effect changes in the patterns of human existence, only developmental or evolutionary change can actually be successful in this regard. Thus it is the latter which is the real fruition of the former's aspirations.

Through a series of examples, of which those dealing with the ecology movement are especially interesting, the authors attempt to show that change, while possibly initiated by antiestablishment groups, is most often taken over by the establishment in reaction to initial protests. The end result is that, while both protestors and those protested against work together to bring about essential modifications in the system, in the long run change is to be credited primarily to the conservative or middle of the road groups who really control the social apparatus. While there is little that is theoretically new in this thesis, the au-

thors' detailed examples in specific limited cases do shed some light on the actual workings of such processes in the realm of practice.

The authors' claim to having created "conceptual tools which can be used to interpret what is happening and to form a basis for the uniquely human capacity to evaluate and choose" is, however, another matter. The equation of social evolution (development) with vague renderings of the theories of biological evolution is, while often repeated, never adequately justified. And while it appears that the basis of the proffered theory is a simple assertion of a cause and effect chain, no firm grip on the fundamental causes is ever established. Also quite questionable is the authors' decision to limit their discussion of revolution to simple agitation and the realm of immediate political action—a move which naturally makes revolutionaries either idle dreamers or actors in the realm of the irrelevant. Two rather shocking examples of this are the exclusion from consideration of Communist revolution—certainly no simple action in the immediate—and of Marx's conception of human nature. While the purpose of the book is not the analysis of Marxism, it and other theories of social change must at least be examined before one can relegate revolution to the wastebin by asserting the preeminence of an ill-defined theory of evolutionary development.

JOSEPH BIEN
Department of Philosophy
University of Missouri
Columbia

FRANK MACKINNON. *Postures and Politics: Some Observations on Participatory Democracy.* Pp. ix, 275. Toronto, University of Toronto Press, 1973. $12.50. Paperbound $3.75.

ALFRED DEGRAZIA. *Politics for Better or Worse.* Pp. 377. Glenview, Ill.: Scott, Foresman, 1973. No price. Paperbound.

MacKinnon's major theme is man's dependence on politics and postures, the "flourishes [that] make our communications more agreeable to ourselves and acceptable to others." The book is, in effect, a long essay on postures and human relations as these affect such matters as power, leadership, bureaucratic administration and participation. He accepts participation democracy as the central principle of modern constitutional government, but rejects the naive assumption that any kind of participation is *ipso facto* desirable. Men are too often inclined to substitute nonnegotiable theoretical principles and their allegiance to institutions that presumably embody such principles in the place of individual postures by which their actions may be assessed and their characters judged. The case of a churchman who supports his political views by appeals to his religion is a familiar illustration. MacKinnon quotes Cardinal Cushing: "It's great to live with saints in heaven, but it's hell to live with them on earth." The doctrinaire Marxist or the simple advocate of unrestrained participatory democracy who thinks in terms of nonnegotiable principles illustrates a similar problem.

The doctrinaires are closely related to the larger group of meddlers—always eager to mind other people's business —to whom the recent popularity of participatory democracy has been an open invitation to get into things, especially when through incapacity or lack of interest they will not be called upon to carry through their proposals. Such meddlers, attracted by ego-satisfying band wagons, turn up in all types of institutions—political, educational, social and professional—where they invariably contribute to the difficulty of rational decision-making and to the excessive bureaucratization of administration. "The great majority contribute little more than unproductive activity. And almost all of them hinder the work of others" (p. 112). The characteristics of men that complicate and weaken government, especially in administration, are egoism, excessive delegation of power, and individual eccentricity. The second, which tends to dissipate

and obscure responsibility, can only be contained by limiting the centralization of power. All three can be contained by encouraging nongovernmental outlets for man's natural tendency to posture: participation in sports, dramatics, music, and "other colorful and cultural outlets."

Democracy need not be drab, even for those whose participation in government is minimal. Ceremonies, traditional rituals, public acknowledgement of well-known rules of the game can still play an important role in reminding people of all ranks, opinions and interests that they too are part of a complex but intelligible community. If a democratic system fails in this respect, a simpler, less honest, more brutal system is likely to take its place. More generally, MacKinnon argues that culture is a major strand in the fabric of a nation and in the bonds that hold people together, since men need more than food and clothing. "They must also create, express themselves, relieve their emotions, and entertain, amuse, impress, and inspire one another" (p. 225).

MacKinnon's book is a readable, sophisticated comment on some of the present problems of democracy. The author draws upon his own extensive experience and shrewd observation, with little reference to recent empirical research. Criticism will no doubt come from some impatient social scientists whose science, while depriving them of humor and blunting their common sense, has endowed them with more certainty about men and affairs than the author has the audacity to assume.

Alfred DeGrazia, author of *Elements of Political Science* and numerous other professional books, has written a breezy elementary textbook in which, moving from empirical propositions, he states twelve principles and twelve policies relating to democratic politics or, as he prefers to call it, *"kalotic* politics." He summarizes his general argument in one sentence: "The society of the future should be moved: 1) to develop polyvalent (multi-valued) and benevolent (open-hearted) persons, 2) to organize all authorities by representative systems, 3) to produce goods by scientific methods, and 4) to distribute them without vicious discrimination" (p. 87). Clearly, much remains to be done, but the honest reformer must have hope and be radical. "Weak measures will not work" (p. 182). The book includes some thirty pages of comic cartoons, along with many pages of imaginary conversations designed, by further simplication, to explain the argument. What educational purpose the book may serve remains something of a mystery.

JOHN D. LEWIS
Professor Emeritus
Oberlin College
Ohio

YVES SIMON. *Work, Society and Culture.* Pp. 234. New York: Fordham University Press, 1971. $7.50.

It is hardly news that academic philosophy in the United States is in bad shape. People have asked themselves why this is so. This is obviously not the place to enter into a discussion of the causes of the chronic weakness of American academic philosophy, but reading this post-humous work of Yves Simon, one is struck by yet another symptom of that weakness. For here is a philosopher with unusual intellectual powers and moral dedication, deep and wide culture, and striking originality, who has a profound influence upon small groups at the universities of Notre Dame and Chicago—where he taught—but who might as well have written and taught in some inaccessible foreign language, considering the attention academic philosophers in this country have paid him.

The book under review consists of six chapters dealing with the concept of work, work and society, man at work, the working class, work and wealth, work and culture. The volume has been edited by Vukan Kuic of the University of South Carolina. One of the author's sons has added a complete bibliography, spanning the years 1923–70.

Reading this book, one is struck by one quality which distinguishes the whole of Simon's work: the combination of a profound understanding of the basic insights of Western philosophy with a vivid experience of the philosophic problems of the contemporary world. It is the interaction of these two factors which is at the root of Simon's originality and importance for contemporary philosophy. It must also be said in favor of this book that, while it is closely reasoned, it is easily accessible to the reader. Since the author is telling us something which is worth listening to, he does not need to resort to a jargon, which only too often fills an intellectual void with the appearance of inaccessible profundity.

HANS J. MORGENTHAU
Political Science Department
City College of New York

BEN WHITAKER, ed. *The Fourth World: Victims of Group Oppression.* Pp. 342. New York: Schocken Books, 1973. $10.00.

ROLAND MOUSNIER. *Social Hierarchies: 1450 to the Present.* Pp. 206. New York: Schocken Books, 1973. $9.00.

The introductory essays and the eight field reports in this book emphasize again the tremendous complexities of group oppression. Few in the world are neither victims nor oppressors, and the rationalizations for being an oppressor are as varied as are the adjustments of the oppressed.

These reports are sponsored by the Minority Rights Group, an independent and international nongovernmental body centered in London. According to Whitaker, this group is dedicated to "investigating and publishing facts. . . to help the position of persecuted or disadvantaged ethnic, religious or cultural minorities (or majorities) in any country." Thus it hopes "to develop an international conscience with regard to minorities' treatment and human rights." Just how it can accomplish this by being "concerned with the problems, not the politics," is not clear. The problems have a very heavy politico-economic component that cannot be ignored.

Four of the reports deal with blacks in Africa and in Brazilian society. As Mason observes in his introduction, "a list of the U.N.'s ideal 'rights' corresponds very neatly with what an African has *not* got. He has virtually no legal *rights* in six-sevenths of the sovereign territory of which he is a subject." The other four reports describe problems of the "double minority" in the two Irelands, among the religious and some national minorities in the Soviet Union, and among the Burakumin in Japan.

As one reads the reports, one has a growing sense that the group views minorities of the world from an Anglicized perspective. This is suggested at many points in dealing with the blacks and the Soviet minorities, but especially in the chapter on the two Irelands. Mason sets the tone when he contends: "Legal *rights* are won by force or bargaining or persuasion and in Britian have been won gradually, piecemeal, one at a time. To distinguish them from ideal 'rights' might possibly help minority leaders to think of them as attainable step by step, while to say that everyone has [ideal] 'rights' (which are taken to mean [legal] (*rights*) when they patently have not is surely to encourage intransigence." And intransigence is the last thing that the entrenched would wish to observe in those they oppress. An intellectual American southern segregationist would fully agree. The British have been saying that to their exploited minorities in the British Isles and around the world for generations. With regard to the two Irelands, Harold Jackson—a reporter for the London *Guardian*—neglects to mention in his analysis the use British employers have made of Irish Roman Catholics as a means of splitting their workers against themselves and of frustrating union organization. For him, as for other rationalists of the Englishman's "civilizing" burden, the British are merely trying to create law and order among unreasonable hot heads. He thinks the time may come when the British will "ask themselves why they should remain in a situation which offers no visible advantage to them." He does not tot up the profits from full Protestant employment, disciplined by high Roman Catholic unemployment.

Social Hierarchies is an effort to classify societies made up of what the author calls orders but which social scientists generally designate social classes. He bases his analysis principally on the Catholic League of France in 1585–1599, the French Republic of 1793, the Italian Fascists, the German Nazis and the Soviet Russians. For the future, he predicts a "technocratic society of orders in which the scientists and technicians enjoy the highest rank," as conceived by Saint-Simon and Auguste Comte.

Much ado is sometimes made of interchanging a few terms, citing historical justifications for this momentous act, and thus presumably upsetting key existing social theory. Mousnier has done this by giving a restricted and idealized definition to "class" and by resurrecting and expanding more realistic notions of stratification under the headings of "order" and "estate," an exercise not to be unexpected from a French specialist in French history.

The book was apparently written to discourage the current Maoist agitations among Mousnier's Sorbonne students. He thus claims that the only alternative to his "technocratic society of orders" with its totalitarian tendencies is a "society of direct, egalitarian and democratic workers' management, but which seems unable to remain so expect by rejecting marxist-leninist planning, rapid industrialization, a substantial rise in living standards, and an age of plenty." Even if his students should insist upon working for such a nonaffluent future as he pictures this Maoist one to be, he sees little chance for them to succeed. I suspect that his students project other possible futures for their society.

ALRED MCCLUNG LEE
Brooklyn College
The City University of New York

SOCIOLOGY

BORIS I. BITKER. *The Case for Black Reparations*. Pp. vii, 191. New York: Random House, 1973. $7.95.

JOHN R. FRY. *Locked-Out Americans: A Memoir*. Pp. x, 174. New York: Harper and Row, 1973. $5.59.

The dramatic appearance of militant James Forman before the congregation at Riverside Church in New York City on a Sunday morning in May, 1969 and his interruption of the service with a reading of the "Black Manifesto," can be viewed in retrospect as one of the peakings of the by now largely passé Black Power movement. Forman, at that time a leader in the Student Non-Violent Coordinating Committee, presented his document under the heading "Total Control as the Only Solution to the Economic Problems of Black People" and in it, as well as in a later elaboration at the National Black Economic Development Conference, called for $500 million in reparations, from the Christian and Jewish religious groups in the United States. This money, based on a per capita assessment of fifteen dollars per black person, was to be used for the acquisition of land, media outlets, support for welfare organizations, the construction of a black university and the like, having the ultimate goal of providing blacks with complete control over their economic and social destinies in the United States. The reaction of white liberals and moderate black and white organizations to this startling demand was divided, with some elements within various religious bodies scrambling to provide funds to implement some of Forman's demands, while moderate black spokesmen, such as Bayard Rustin, and such citadels of white liberalism as the *New York Times* lambasted the manifesto and its rationale. Very few individuals and groups, however, explored the actual legalistic basis for a demand for black reparations, as Boris I. Bitker has sought to do in the present work.

Bitker, a lawyer and Sterling Professor of Law at Yale University, presented in two lectures at Ohio State University in January, 1971, the case for the legal possibilities of reparations to blacks for crimes inflicted upon them by the white community. This book is an expanded version of these lectures, with further reflections and amplifications. It should be stated at the outset that at the time the lectures were delivered, the author assumed that Forman's demands would receive some sort of serious hearing by American public opinion, but in the period between the book's gestation and the present, the Black Manifesto has fallen into the media discard file along with the plethora of other demands, declarations, posturings and the like that marked the heyday of the manifestation of Black Power in the late 1960s.

The rationale for the payment of reparations to blacks lies, in Bitker's view, in that, although indemnities are ordinarily paid only for violations of generally accepted legal principles, it is not terribly unusual to adopt the procedure of redressing injuries incurred by acts thought to be legal at the time, but later changed through different legal and constitutional interpretation. Thus, he feels that certainly compensation for the effects of school segregation could be paid, as well as for violations of the separate but equal doctrine, especially since these violations were legally wrong, even when committed.

Bitker does indicate, however, that there would be manifold problems involved in the allocation of funds among present-day blacks, including the possibly undesirable establishing of a government code of racial identification and the problem of whether to pay black organizations or individuals, let alone the tremendous backlash on the part of the nonblack element of American society that would ensue, given the adoption— or even serious consideration—of such a procedure. Bitker's analysis provides an interesting legal and intellectual situation, but, as for providing the basis for the reality of political action, its effect will almost certainly be nonexistent.

John R. Fry's memoir of his association with the Black P. Stone Nation youth gang of Chicago in the 1960s also has a somewhat dated air about it. The recent savage attacks on whites by black youth gangs in Boston, along with continued depredations by other gangs in Philadelphia and Chicago, have probably eliminated a great deal of the sympathy, exhibited by white liberals in the past —sympathy for these elements of the *lumpen proletariat* which, at times, even involved financing, by foundations and whimsical philantropists, of these groups' presumed efforts to go straight. Fry's First Presbyterian Church in Chicago gained a considerable degree of noteriety in the media during the late 1960s as a headquarters for the Black P. Stone Rangers, with consequent close scrutiny by the police, Mayor Daley's investigators and even a senate committee. The author is, as might be expected, extremely sympathetic to the situation of these rejected elements of American society and seeks to find meaning and even justification for their banding together into a huge youth gang defying any and all authority, from whatever source, outside their own ranks. Much of what Fry states is true, especially in regard to the hopelessness of the future of lower socio-economic strata blacks in the Chicago, and other, ghettos; but this does not take into sufficient consideration those significant portions of the black population, striving desperately to maintain some sort of decent existence in the face of the constant brutalities and savagery perpetrated upon them by the Black P. Stone Nation and other youthful criminal elements.

NORMAN LEDERER
Administrative Director
Menard Junior College
Merrill
Wisconsin

LEONARD BLUMBERG, THOMAS E. SHAPLEY, JR. and IRVING W. SHANDLER. *Skid Row and Its Alternatives: Research and Recommendations from Philadelphia.* Pp. xxxv, 309. Philadelphia, Pa.: Temple University Press, 1973. $10.00.

Philadelphia's Skid Row Project—a joint enterprise of the Greater Philadelphia Movement (community activists dedicated to civic good), the Redevelopment Authority, and Temple University—opened its Diagnostic and Relocation Center in 1963. This is both a report of the center's activities and a vehicle for the statement of the authors' recommendations about how communities should deal with the Skid Rows of the nation.

The center was geared to viewing Skid Row as a social welfare problem, amenable to casework treatment. Each client had an "anchor" counselor who made diagnoses, made referrals and received feedback from them. The center's treatment procedures are described in the book and illustrative biographies of its clients are included.

Several chapters are devoted to a description of Skid Row inhabitants and their problems, the data for which derive from a variety of sources: a 1960 survey of residents of the area, the records and responses of those residents who became clients of the center and/or who became involved with particular agencies, such as police, courts and hospitals. Included are such topics as their alcohol use, downward class mobility, relationship to the police and courts (the operations of which are characterized as oppressive and denigrating), housing (in cubicle hotels, rooming houses, bar hotels and missions, the latter characterized as "mutual exploitation"), employment, health, morbidity and mortality and how its residents feel about Skid Row. The authors' value judgments aside, the information contained therein—when added to the work of Bogue, Dunham, Spradley, Wallace, Wiseman and others—contributes to our knowledge of the problem.

Other chapters describe research that was conducted on some rehabilitation efforts. A group therapy treatment program in a correction facility was assessed: recidivism declined in both the experimental and control groups, though the change was not statistically significant in either. A halfway house experiment was attempted, but the usefulness of its findings was limited by the small numbers involved. An evaluation research on intensive counseling was also conducted; of sixty clients in an original caseload, data are presented on thirty-seven who were found three years later—"20 were better and 17 were not."

The authors also offer recommendations, including one that comprehensive service centers providing intensive casework programs for rehabilitation of Skid Row residents be established. To critics who might charge that such a recommendation, though possibly based upon their predilections and experience, need not follow from their research findings, the authors answer: "What looms as important is that our program was successful with some men. . . . " That quotation seems to characterize this book quite well.

LAWRENCE PODELL

Office of Program and
  Policy Research
The City University of
  New York

ROBERT T. BOWER. *Television and the Public.* Pp. v, 205. New York: Holt, Rinehart and Winston, 1973. No price.

Eighty percent of this book consists of tables with comment on television audiences and their attitudes towards TV in 1960 and 1970. The remainder embodies the author's comment on changes that have taken place in this period. This survey, like a previous one on 1960 findings, was financed by Columbia Broadcasting System (CBS), and this book is published by a subsidiary of that company. The field work was carried out by the Roper Organization under the direction of Carolyn W. Crucius, who admirably completed the task.

Levels of approval have not changed greatly in the ten years under consideration, although some excitement of the medium for the public has worn off. Some changes are indicated. The polls show that the public views news programs more than they did. They show that the public places more reliance on TV as a news source than on other media. TV has become the dominant news source for the American people, according to this study. There is some comment by the public that there is bias in news coverage and some rather vocal displeasure at the disruptive events shown on the TV screen.

The book is disappointing on two counts. Technically the grey printing on white paper makes reading a minor debacle. Second, the shortcomings of programs on TV are only lightly touched upon. From a corporate standpoint, investment by CBS in the survey and book may bring more profits to the company. The book is a tool for advertisers. Study the tables and you can synthetically construct a show or pick a program to please the audience you want. Audience predispositions, areas of ignorance, apathy or knowledge are spelled out. Advertisers will scan the tables to find compelling determinants of programming—a common denominator of interest to the largest potential buying public. Leadership in a democratic society and social responsibility are lost in this pandering to the lowest common denominator.

The decade brought quantitative change, if not much qualitative change. Today 31 percent of United States families have two or more TV sets. Color TV's are in a third of our homes. VHF television commercial stations have increased from 440 to 508, UHF commercial stations from 75 to over 800. Viewing time has increased from five hours three minutes daily in 1960, to five hours and fifty-six minutes in 1970.

The public can only judge performance of a medium by its own frame of reference. It can only judge what it hears and sees, not what it might hear and see. People cannot judge what they are not getting or have not experienced.

From a broad standpoint, this book is cash register tape and reflects on the social control of CBS.

EDWARD L. BERNAYS

Cambridge
Massachusetts

IAN BUDGE and CORNELIUS O'LEARY. *Belfast: Approach to Crisis. A Study of Belfast Politics, 1613–1970.* Pp. vii,

396. New York: St. Martin's Press, 1973. No price.

Violence in Northern Ireland today, continues a history of rioting which has erupted periodically since the early nineteenth century. By means of a detailed historical study, and of a survey they conducted in Belfast in 1966, Budge and O'Leary attempt to specify the conditions which led to the present crisis.

A particularly useful source of insight is the systematic comparison throughout the book of Belfast with Glasgow. The two cities are remarkably similar, including similar religious compositions, but have had distinctly different political histories. This comparative perspective provides a control to more clearly delineate those attitudes, or behavior, which contributed to political instability in Belfast.

As a major conclusion, the authors reject the popular economic explanation, linking religious intolerance with rioting. After stating that religious loyalties are widespread and intense, while class consciousness is at a low level in contemporary Belfast compared with other British cities, the authors argue: "Historical analysis shows clearly that there was nothing in the basic nature of Irish religion to link it irreversibly with party conflict. . . . The connection was fostered by politicians for their own advantage. . . after 1798." The successful use of the religious appeal by Conservatives and later by Unionists gave them an inbuilt Protestant and electoral majority in Belfast, from the mid-nineteenth century until the late 1960s. At no time during that period was the Catholic minority associated with the ruling of the city. From this "developed a complete hiatus in communication between minority and majority politicians, a feeling of alienation on the part of minority politicians and a general distrust of parties and of party competition" (pp. 373–374).

This, and other conclusions reached by the authors, are based essentially on historical developments. The 1966 survey is used for a detailed analysis of the modern situation, and an appendix explicitly details the procedures used in taking the survey. The fact remains, however, that the total sample size of the Belfast resident survey was only 229 completed interviews. Many of the detailed cross-tabulations of this survey data, on which much of the second half of the book is based, are not definitive, but, rather, suggestive.

The book is consistently well written, and is recommended for those who wish a better understanding of the present strife in Belfast.

ROBERT E. KENNEDY, JR.
Department of Sociology
University of Minnesota
Minneapolis

NORMA EVENSON. *Two Brazilian Capitals: Architecture and Urbanism in Rio de Janeiro and Brasilia.* Pp. xiv, 225. New Haven, Conn.: Yale University Press, 1973. $19.50.

DAVID S. EPSTEIN. *Brasilia, Plan and Reality: A Study of Planned and Spontaneous Urban Development.* Pp. xiii, 206. Berkeley, Cal.: University of California Press, 1973. $10.00.

Dr. Evenson, professor of architectural history, wrote her doctor's thesis on Chandigarh, capital of the Punjab. She speaks of Chandigarh and Brasilia as the two notable undertakings in this century to create a capital city *tout à coup.* Dr. Epstein, professor of anthropology, wrote his study of Brasilia as his doctoral thesis.

The selection of the plan for Brasilia came from one of the most curious architectural competitions ever devised. It was limited to Brazilians. The submissions were signed: no practice of anonymity or code numbers. I was told at the time that there were so few Brazilian architect-urbanists that every one in the profession knew who was involved. An "international jury" made the award, that is, three Brazilians and Holford, United Kingdom; Sive, France; and Papadaki, United States of America. They spent three days considering twenty-six submissions. The award was made to a submission consisting of five cards revealing free-hand sketches and a brief statement.

The creation of an inland capital to unite the south and the north was contemplated in the original constitution at the time of the independence of Brazil. It was Kubitschek who determined to build it within his one term of office as president—no reelection. Oscar Niemeyer, who had worked with Papadaki in Le Corbusier's atelier as a young man, was his technical adviser. It was reported at the time of the competition that the president and Niemeyer had determined that Lúcia Costa should win.

I heard Lúcia Costa explain his plan at the Pan American Union in Washington soon thereafter. The inspiration had come to him at lunch. He drew a bird on the tablecloth, with its head, body, tail and wings. Dr. Everson quotes Lúcia Costa as saying that the pattern has also been compared to a cross. Costa explains that the monumentality of the great boulevards shows that man has made the automobile his tool and has learned to live with it. The residential areas of Brasilia are called superquads, with dead-end internal streets excluding through-traffic, and the neighborhood center in the middle with schools, playgrounds and shops.

Neither of our authors asks the source of this designation. Their bibliographies are wide-ranging, but I see no reference to Radburn, New Jersey—the United States adaptation of the British garden city—"The Town for the Motor Age," with its superblocks, commenced in 1925. Dr. Evenson saw them also in Chandigarh, the basic plan for which was created by Albert Mayer of New York, one of the Radburn team. Only later was Le Corbusier called in, and he adhered to the basic superblock design.

In Brasilia—as in Chandigarh—there promptly developed a shack town, originally justified as a temporary expedient to house unskilled construction workers. This phenomenon is Dr. Epstein's chief concern, the reality as opposed to the plan. His bibliography shows his awareness that the *favella*, the *barrio*, the *ranchito*, is a permanent element in every Latin American metropolis. He seems unaware of the *Wildsiedlungen* that rim Berlin and Vienna. Social studies have shown that the spirit of mutual aid is stronger in these spontaneous communities than in well planned public housing. Dr. Epstein's difficulty is that he cannot decide which typology of Brazilian society to follow to explain the freetown. The cultural anthropologists who have studied Brazil come up with conflicting theories of dyadic or assymmetrical social groups.

The simple fact is that no country in the world has discovered how to provide clean, sanitary housing for the unskilled and the unemployed. This fact makes the sessions of the United Nations Committee on Housing, Building and Planning so depressing for the delegates: none can boast of significant success.

As for Rio as capital, Dr. Evenson traces for us its European antecedents. Only last year I asked officials, urbanists and municipalists in Rio whether they would pick that site for a great metropolis today, with its peaks everywhere, through which vehicular tunnels must be pierced for communication. The answer was, widely, no.

The greatest defect in Brasilia—as in Chandigarh—is the failure to make it a social community. One superquad is assigned to workers in the Ministry of Finance, another to the Defense Ministry, and so forth. I commented on this to the editor of the independent liberal newspaper in Brasilia. He said, "I have a column about this in my paper nearly every week." It is the next generation, he said, who have grown up together in Brasilia, who are expected to achieve this integration. Why do architectural historians and urban anthropologists not bring these elements to their purview in these days of the interdisciplinary approach?

CHARLES S. ASCHER
International Representative
Institute of Public Administration
New York

LUDWIG L. GEISMAR. *555 Families: A Social-Psychological Study of Young Families in Transition.* Pp. vii, 267. New York: E. P. Dutton, 1973. $9.75.

The central city lower class family has long been characterized as failing. From the literature on immigrants to contemporary discussions of black and white poor, the themes of immorality, disorganization and brutality have been predominant in discussion, both scholarly and popular, of the urban poor. In part, of course, this is simply a reflection of reality—the poor are disproportionately represented among the divorced, do have higher rates of illegitimacy than the nonpoor, and do encounter more than their share of difficulties with their children. Two problems, briefly, are involved in the interpretations of these and related facts. First, though disproportionate shares of troubles are clear, focus on troubles often obscures the fact that the majority somehow cope with their poverty and stigma well within the limits embraced by the term "normal." Second, there is considerable controversy over the causes of disorganization. Some argue that the poor are implicated in a subculture that perpetuates misfortune and ill prepares the poor for participation in the mainstream of the society. Others argue that the poor are different only in that they have less money.

Ludwig L. Geismar's 555 Families is the report of a study of largely lower class young families who had just given birth to their first child. A subgroup of the 555 families was interviewed several times over the course of roughly three years to gather information on the changes that families experience as they cope with the contingencies of job, child-rearing and husband-wife or mother-lover relationships. The major findings are not surprising, though they are important and deserve reiteration. Geismar found that most families, including families composed of an unwed mother and her child(ren), function adequately—children are at least adequately cared for, parents support one another and most unmarried mothers maintain themselves and their children without pathological results. To be sure, the poor, black or white, are less likely than those more comfortably situated to achieve and maintain satisfactory levels of family functioning but, still, even the majority

of the poor do function adequately. Geismar also introduces some evidence suggesting that the malfunctioning of the poor is created more by inadequate facilities and opportunities than by subcultural traits.

Though the subject matter of 555 Families is of obvious general interest, this is not a book I would recommend to the general reader. The findings are reported in the prose equivalent of monotone, and the discussion of family life is both abstract and opaque, mediated by correlation coefficients, factor loadings and averaged means that put the stuff of life at some considerable remove. The combination of deathless prose and lifeless respondents will be a deterrent to all but the specialist.

Specialists, too, will find 555 Families a disappointment. Discussion of controversial issues is schematic and remains within the boundaries of well worn argumentation. Geismar's analysis of the changes in family functioning is largely descriptive, and changes were anything but dramatic. Even the absence of change—for better or worse—is, of course, important to record, but the shortness of the time span over which the families were observed limits the impact of the findings. All in all, 555 Families lacks conceptual richness and fails also to provide data that highlight the subtleties and texture of urban family life.

JAN DIZARD
Amherst College
Massachusetts

HERBERT JACOB. *Urban Justice: Law and Order in American Cities.* Pp. 145. Englewood Cliffs, N.J.: Prentice-Hall, 1973. $6.95.

LEONARD RUCHELMAN, ed. *Who Rules the Police?* Pp. 288. New York: New York University Press, 1973. No price.

The civil rights struggles and other urban riots and violence of the last decade severely wracked American cities and brought their political systems and administration of justice under attack. Among their consequences was a flood of books—of which these two are creditable additions—by scholars and others who investigated these conflicts and described how public officials and the courts dealt with them.

Within this context, Jacob has analyzed urban judicial systems in a slim, compact book that says a great deal about them. While he surveys the formal organization of urban courts at city, county, state and federal levels, he is mainly concerned with their informal organization, that is, with the politics of police, judges, prosecutors, lawyers and other judicial personnel who are active in the courts.

Jacob's major conclusions may be summarized as follows: according to him, the urban courts do not function as much to dispense justice as to dispose of cases. Through negotiation, bargaining or haggling, prosecutors and lawyers, sometimes with judges present, agree to have defendants plead guilty to lesser charges of law breaking and to accept milder sanctions to avoid court trials. This is especially true of criminal cases, but civil cases also are more often settled out of court. While judges and lawyers revere adversary proceedings as the best way to learn the truth in court cases, they find trials inconvenient, time consuming and expensive, and avoid them when possible. The courts, always overloaded with cases, would be utterly clogged, were every man to have his day in court.

Another conclusion is Jacob's recognition of the central role the police play in involving citizens in the criminal process. Police exercise considerable discretion, or freedom of decision, in making arrests, collecting evidence and testifying in courts. Police departments, more largely, determine the criminal activities they choose to enforce, and display different degrees of professionalism in performing their duties. Even when citizens are freed after arrests by police, they are never extricated from the criminal process without some penalty.

A third observation is that justice, if not blind, is at least class-conscious. Upper class or richer defendants, whether individuals or corporations, hire lawyers to defend them, negotiate settlements and use the law for their own purposes. Poor defendants are often poorly defended, and more likely to cop pleas and suffer sanctions, even when these do not involve imprisonment.

Finally, the police, prosecutors and courts are challenged to administer justice equitably because of the number and varieties of crime, political demonstrations and other forms of violence that appear endemic today.

Ruchelman augments Jacob's treatment of the police by considering public and other controls over the police in his book, which is a collection of readings intended for classroom use. Who rules the police is a crucial matter, not only because police have discretionary power to arrest or dismiss violators, but also because the police are organized in their own unions and exhibit considerable militancy and political activism in protecting their self-interests. To a large extent, police are governed by their own officials and organizations; they have closed their ranks to recruits they do not approve of, and they resist civilian control boards which appear threatening to them.

Ruchelman's selections reveal the range of studies of police departments made by social scientists in recent times. With greater knowledge of the police available, solutions to the problems they cause or experience, it may be hoped, may also be available.

JOHN SIRJAMAKI
Department of Sociology
State University of New York
at Buffalo

BRUCE D. JOHNSON. *Marijuana Users and Drug Subcultures.* Pp. vii, 290. New York: John Wiley and Sons, 1973. $12.95.

Based on detailed statistical analyses of questionnaires completed by 3500 men and women at twenty-one colleges and universities, this work grapples with some thorny questions surrounding the increased use of marijuana by America's student population. In 1967, surveys showed 5 percent of college students had tried marijuana; by the end of 1971 the percentage had risen to 51, and it is believed to be higher today.

People familiar with the drug scene will hardly be startled by the author's findings. Among many facts, his data shows that users are introduced to marijuana by friends; that a large percentage of regular smokers become occasional sellers; that it does not lead to harder drugs like heroin; that there is little causal relationship between its use and juvenile delinquency, crime, political militancy or sexual promiscuity.

The key to increased usage is seen in the growth of a youth subculture with its own norms, one of which is the social smoking of marijuana. This leads to an ingenious argument which turns the official wisdom upside down. A widespread demand for an illegal substance has created a large drug subculture in which marijuana is economically central. Since this subculture helps to expose young people to more dangerous drugs, the way to combat the problem of harder drugs is to legalize marijuana. With no marijuana sales, the entire drug subculture will wither away, reducing the chances of students coming in contact with health-destroying drugs.

While such a proposal, backed by a mass of data and much sophisticated analysis, is sensible, the book is hardly designed to be convincing. Its prose turgid, its pages a thicket of tables, graphs and formulas, its ponderous academic approach would seem to preclude reaching just those lawmakers the author hopes to influence, leaving as an audience only a small number of social scientists interested in the development of their own subculture's intellectual techniques.

By focusing strictly on statistical manipulation, the author's vision remains narrow. One can accept his findings and proposals, and yet know he has touched only a small segment of reality. The increased use of drugs and stimulants in recent years has been by all segments of society, and it is certainly connected to historic changes in value systems and life styles. It is difficult to entertain seriously the idea that legalizing marijuana will significantly affect such emerging behavior patterns of a post-industrial society.

ROBERT A. ROSENSTONE
California Institute of Technology

KEVIN LYNCH. *What Time Is This Place?* Pp. vi, 277. Cambridge, Mass.: The MIT Press, 1972. $10.00.

The author of this fascinating book, Kevin Lynch, is professor of urban planning at MIT. Its subject matter is the change of time in relation to architecturally occupied space.

To those willing and philosophically prepared to come to grip with the facts of history and human society under the aspects of philosophy of science, its reading will be a delight. This publication abounds in methodology and logical structure of scientific theory and linguistic-logical analysis of meaning and emotive evaluation. This writer who, twenty-five years ago introduced philisophy of science to engineering and architecture students at Georgia Institute of Technology, found here justification for his pioneer work.

In view of space limitation, it is impossible to discuss a philosophical treatise in detail. Even naming the chapter headlines would not throw light on the subject. Its gist is spatial and temporal aspects of ecological organization, the perceptual and behavioral responses to change in space and time. It is the fixation of internal time—time as it is in our mind defined as the interval between "tick and tick." For instance, what spatial change concerns in time would be, according to Lynch, that colonies in a new world tend to be reactionary replicas of the social system from which they came. Consequently, how American or Soviet the first moon colony will be!

The fundamental factors inducing city planning are obvious. Disaster and migration are just two cases of rapid marked environmental changes. Lynch postulates that a stunning environmental disaster may destroy a society, or cause it to revert to a more primitive level. Post-

Nazi West Germany and her destroyed cities are hardly mentioned by Lynch; otherwise, he would not have made such a statement.

Of definitely practical interest to city planning instructors is the appendix: "Asking Questions." Here, experimental questionnaires had to be answered by students. The questionnaires focus on one general location, namely the central business district of Boston. As a result, interesting links rose to the surface. The form of this questionnaire and the various answers will certainly stimulate adoption of similar lists of questions and inquiries, followed by interrogative statements to be investigated or discussed. Of specific value is a thorough bibliography, useful to city planners.

ROBERT SCHARF
Georgia Institute of Technology
Atlanta

MARCELLO MAESTRO. *Cesare Beccaria and the Origins of Penal Reform.* Pp. xii, 179. Philadelphia: Temple University Press, 1973. $7.50.

FRANKLIN E. ZIMRING and GORDON J. HAWKINS. *Deterrence: The Legal Threat in Crime Control.* Pp. xiv, 376. Chicago: University of Chicago Press, 1973. $13.50.

The most intellectually exciting part of Maestro's book is chapter 2, a fourteen-page synopsis of Becarria's classic essay *On Crime and Punishment,* an eighteenth century masterpiece which still is an incisive analysis of both empirical and ethical issues in deterrence. This is accompanied by an interesting account of the antecedents and consequences of the essay in Western sentencing policy. In addition, there are many details on the intricacies of Becarria's family life, but the most impressive biographical material is the brief information on his many innovations in the thirty years of his lifetime which followed his writing the famous essay at age twenty-six. These innovations included a metric system of measurement, a population theory which anticipated Malthus, theories of eco-nomics—as an Italian Adam Smith—and one of the first schools of veterinary medicine. Unfortunately, the book gives little insight into the reasons for this fantastic creativity.

Criminal justice would advance tremendously if the Zimring and Hawkins book became the greatest influence on sentencing since Becarria's work. This advance would not be a rapid and precisely predictable change, however, for these authors do not offer glibly confident directives in the style of classical criminal law theorists. Instead, they raise more profound questions, assess relevant knowledge, and suggest the kinds of research which would enhance our comprehension and control of deterrent effects.

Zimring and Hawkins show, essentially, that the question of whether punishment deters crime is unanswerable unless one specifies the situation, the offense, the penalty, the way in which the threat of penalty is communicated and the audience of the communication. The deterrent effect itself, they indicate, is not absolute; it has complex variations. Furthermore, changes in statutes to alter penalties in order to achieve a change in deterrence often do not result in the alteration of sentences anticipated by the lawmakers, for enforcement and adjudication are always selective and negotiated. Therefore, the average penalties of judges tend to be highly stable, although they are affected much more by legislation which alters the minimum sentence that can be imposed than by changes in the maximum possible penalty.

On a few issues Zimring and Hawkins omit some important considerations. Their apt assessment of fines (p. 175ff.) neglects the potential of fines as a percent of income—a Scandinavian method—of installment payment of fines and of variations in what Eglash called "creative restitution" related to the offense. While they refreshingly supplement individualistic views of risk assessment and behavior by a section on "group processes and group morality" (p.

209ff.) that draws on delinquent gang research, and they cite Werthman's Goff-
manesque analysis here, they neglect the
insights on risk-taking behavior as
"character building" in Goffman's essay,
"Where the Action Is." When appraising
survey methods in deterrance research,
they appropriately criticize queries of
knowledge or attitude on penalties, but
they are unappreciative of the survey's
potential as a source of information independent of police data on rates of vic-
timization by predatory crimes, or rates
of participation in victimless crimes.

Finally, those who rely on the index of
this book to locate where a particular author is cited will be disappointed; although the index mixes some proper
names with its topical references, many
of the authors mentioned in text or footnotes are not indexed.

DANIEL GLASER
Department of Sociology
University of Southern California
Los Angeles

HARVEY LUSKIN MOLOTCH. *Managed
Integration: Dilemmas of Doing Good
in the City.* Pp. 250. Berkeley: University of California Press, 1973. $8.95.

This engrossing and inventively researched volume, while dealing with
matters of broad concern to America's fast
changing cities, focuses on the efforts of
the South Shore area in Chicago's inner
city to check advancing black invasion
and build "a stable, integrated community" where whites could continue to
dwell in large numbers. South Shore is
delineated in precise detail in relation to
surrounding areas.

Terming his study "an attempt to
evaluate in the light of the actual determinants of racial change the potential for
community action to prevent the reseg-
regation of urban areas," the author
reviews—in an introductory section on
the racial change process—the theory
and research on the invasion-succession
cycle. Furthermore, using data from interviews with 177 real estate dealers, he
shows how the dual market and other
economic considerations affect decisions
which speed racial transition. He thus

points out some of the obstacles with
which intervention programs must contend.

Molotch made a searching investigation of the work of the South Shore
Commission in the mid-sixties when it
was one of the largest community organizations in the country, running a vast
array of programs. Most of these were of
the community improvement type—to
reduce crime, upgrade public schools
education, plan physical improvements
and so forth—designed to strengthen the
area's appeal for white residents, but
make it attractive to blacks as well. Employing more direct means was an ambitious Tenant Referral Service which,
through a network of contacts, strove to
draw whites to South Shore while discouraging black applicants and placing
those accepted "where they would do
the least harm." Having attended some
one hundred meetings, Molotch describes the work of the commission in
intimate detail: its leadership, organization, the dominant role of whites, and the
euphemisms used to smooth dissension
and cloak its sometimes questionable
strategies.

During the study period, the commission was still growing, and confidence
prevailed concerning the outcome; but
when Molotch used ingeniously com-
puted racial change rates 1960–67 to
measure its effectiveness, he found it
was failing. South Shore's black population was increasing as rapidly, propor-
tionately, as those of other nearby changing areas where no intervention programs were under way. Like the rest, it
was moving through the classic
invasion-succession cycle, a point
confirmed by a 1970 revisit which found
South Shore nearly all black. In line with
the ecological view, he concludes that
"racial change patterns are determined
by forces beyond the local community,"
and only under unusual circumstances
—such as in Hyde-Park-Kenwood,
studied by Rossi and Dentler, which had
strong external supports—can citizens'
intervention win success.

Throughout his research, Molotch
forged an independent course, with
stimulating results. Rather than cleaving

to a "worked-out study design," he adopted, as his study progressed, various research approaches offering significant insights. Weaving his diverse materials into a well-organized book, he presents a penetrating, multifaceted view of South Shore and its commission, within a framework of closely reasoned discussion and analysis.

Arresting are his honestly expressed doubts about the enterprise he studied. He is not sure that community organization is necessarily "doing good" just because it involves many citizens. He questions, too, whether residential integration is worth fighting for, even if achievable, when existing status-power differences circumscribe black-white interaction. Biracial equality, eliminating disparities, is the goal earnestly to be sought.

CAROLYN ZELENY
Department of Sociology
Wilson College
Chambersburg
Pennsylvania

CHARLES G. OAKES. *The Walking Patient and the Health Care Crisis.* Pp. 432. Columbia, S.C.: University of South Carolina Press, 1973. $9.95.

CHARLES SANDERS. *Black Professionals' Perceptions of Institutional Racism in Health and Welfare Organizations.* Pp. 203. Fair Lawn, N.J.: R.E. Burdick, 1973. $9.50.

Charles Oakes's book is concerned with policy making, planning, regionalizing and organizing ambulatory medical care programs. He gives special consideration to medical records evaluation and research and to continuity of care. A last chapter discusses medical power structure, proprietary hospitals, licensure of paraprofessionals, regulation of quality, and disaster planning.

It is difficult to understand how anyone can devote 432 pages to the subject of ambulatory care without sizeable, coherent sections concerning: (1) the financing and economics of ambulatory care, and (2) the politics of medical care. A section on financing would contain information concerning the rationale behind current financing of ambulatory care and the pros and cons of alternative methods. The section on politics or interest groups in medical care would analyze the forces constraining or propelling physicians and managers in restructuring the medical care system. Oakes's emphasis on consumer participation in generating effective medical care systems is unjustified by research findings. This Oakes admits, without softening or clarifying his position. The author has assembled a vast literature on ambulatory care, which he cites incessantly, including several useful case studies. Of particular interest is analysis of appointments by four thousand low income patients at the Thomas Gailor Clinics in Memphis.

Charles Sanders analyzes the perceptions of thirty leaders of two newly formed black professional organizations of social workers and health administrators. Perceptions concern racism in professional organizations. Sanders does not validate the extent of racism which actually exists in the professional organizations; rather he deals with the characteristics of perceived racism and the tactics and strategies of the newly formed groups in stimulating changes in the professional organizations and providing alternatives to black professionals.

Sanders found that the social workers were more concerned with a strong black base and hence encouraged coalition building among blacks, while the health administrators emphasized developing white coalitions or alliances with the power structure. Social workers made greater efforts to build and strengthen their home communities, encouraged consumer input and welcomed members lacking professional credentials. Health administrators were older, and Sanders indicates they showed more vested interest in their jobs, the profession and the white, health professional associations. The health administrators did not perceive racism with the same degree of intensity as did the social workers. Characteristics of institutional racism specified by Sanders include: staffing, role and function, organization values, membership pattern, goals, program activity, publications, conferences, scholarships, awards and grants, recruitment, education and training, funding source, evaluation of programs, official position on social issues, and coalition and alliance to deal with the problems facing minority groups.

ANTHONY R. KOVNER
Department of Health Care
  Systems
University of Pennsylvania
Philadelphia

ALICE SCHLEGEL. *Male Dominance and Female Autonomy: Domestic Authority in Matrilineal Societies.* Pp. xiv, 206. New Haven, Conn.: Human Relations Area File Press, 1972. $8.00. Paperbound, $6.00.

STEVEN GOLDBERG. *The Inevitability of Patriarchy.* Pp. 256. New York: William Morrow, 1973. $6.95.

Women's Liberation has entered anthropology, but anthropology offers little comfort to Women's Liberation. It is only novelists who equate matriliny with an idealised matriarchy. Alice Schlegel's problem is the correlation, in matrilineal systems throughout the world, of other factors with control over women respectively by their husbands and their brothers. An elaborate statistical exercise leads to the unsurprising conclusion that the crucial variable is residence. Where a man takes his wife to live in his home, as happens in a good many matrilineal societies, her brother cannot exercise much authority over her; and where, as used to be the Nayar rule, husbands never live with their wives, they must be under a brother's guardianship.

Discussing unilateral cross-cousin marriage, Dr. Schlegel observes that, since in societies where this is the preferred form, young men seldom initiate their own marriage arrangements, theories which base the preference for one side or the other on a young man's sentiments towards his senior kin are unconvincing. But her idea that a "function" of cross-cousin marriage is to enable old men to hold on to authority through their ability to bestow brides is not very convincing either; their position is strengthened in just the same way by their control of property in a system of generalised exchange with bridewealth.

As the argument proceeds, the word "dominance" comes to be used more often than "authority." Yet in discussing descent systems, what we are concerned with is authority in specific fields, not some generalized, quantifiable dominance which pervades a total relationship. Another unconvincing argument is that which offers an explanation of the relative disapproval of father-daughter and sibling incest in terms of the locus of authority. Primate females are attracted by dominant males—meaning here leaders in a band. So perhaps women try to seduce the men under whose authority—to use my term—they are. Where husbands are dominant, cowives are jealous; where brothers are dominant, they are not—I wonder whether there is any reliable ethnographic evidence on this point. So daughters have to be insulated from their fathers in "husband-dominated" societies; sisters from their brothers in "brother-dominated" ones.

Dr. Goldberg tells us why male dominance—using the word in a more acceptable way—is universal and cannot be explained away by the argument that the anthropologists who have observed it have often been men. He ascribes it, not to a conspiracy of men to keep women in their place, but to a biological determinant which differentiates the sexes, even before birth. This is the greater capacity for aggression—or dominance assertion—which is engendered in the central nervous system of males by testicular secretions before birth and at puberty. Men seek dominance in personal relationships, and achieve it with women because the women's aggression is not strong enough to resist theirs. They are all the time in competition for high status positions, and in the contest, whoever wins, women again must lose because of their lower level of aggression. Therefore, whatever roles carry high status, men will seek them and will achieve them to the near exclusion of women. It is logically conceivable that a society might cease to attach high status to political leadership. Such a society might be nonpatriarchal, but whatever roles became the object of emulation, women would be underrepresented in them. General medical practice in the Soviet Union, he remarks in an interesting illustration, may well come to be regarded as "women's work" because it does not confer high status. And in France all the famous cooks, even if they are not the best, are men.

In a useful appendix, Dr. Goldberg gives excerpts from books that have been quoted as evidence for the absence of male dominance in primitive societies. An anthropologist who has read any of them will be astonished that they could have been used in that way.

LUCY MAIR

London
England

NIGEL WALKER and SARAH MCCABE. *Crime and Insanity in England: New Solutions and New Problems.* Vol. 2. Pp. 316. Chicago: Aldine, 1973. $12.50.

Previous critics have described the first volume of this two-volume work as an authoritative study of the changing attitudes of the English courts to the culpability of the disordered offender. Way stations in the first effort involved such issues as fitness for trial and a history of the concept of mercy from old Saxon times, both dotted with train stops at such familiar names in crime and punishment as Bracton, Hale, and McNaghten. The new book deals with what the authors call "the utilitarian revolution" in the trial and disposal of the disordered offender, a movement which has resulted in the diminishing of insanity as a legal defense in Great Britain.

Beginning with the story of the first attempts to treat "criminal lunatics" in Bethlem Prison, Walker and McCabe describe the stratagems used by the prisons over several hundred years to relieve themselves of emotionally disturbed inmates. The retrograde nature of these effects led finally to the 1959 act, an entitlement which forms the central theme of this volume.

The first volume described the courts interest in finding ways to answer three questions: "Is the prisoner fit to be tried?" "Is he to be blamed for what he did?" and "Is he nevertheless too insane to punish?" The essence of the second volume is to be found in the author's effort to answer what may well be a more important fourth question: "Is a psychiatric or penal measure more suitable?" The word suitable in this context is meant to convey the notion of humaneness and effectiveness, in contradistinction to the terminology of the 1948 act which used instead the concept of expedient. The main theme of both volumes is the detention and treatment of the offender, who is officially recognized as mentally disordered, and the problems which he poses, not only for the traditional moralist, but also for the utilitarian reformer.

The book concludes with an interesting discussion about whether the "disordered offender has a stronger claim to humanity than other offenders." In a fashion both provocative and poetic, the authors contend with Modestinus that "his [the prisoner's] madness is punishment enough."

In summary, Walker and McCabe have written a worthwhile book, chock-full of facts about crime and insanity in England and in a style which is pleasantly understated in the traditional English manner.

MORTON LEVITT

University of California
Davis

ECONOMICS

JOHN HICKS. *Capital and Time: A Neo-Austrian Theory.* Pp. v, 213. New York: The Oxford University Press, 1973. $10.00.

Most modern growth theory assumes that the distinguishing characteristics of factors of production, such as capital, are physical and qualitative. Output results from the contemporaneous combination of these inputs in the production process. The capital intensity of production can then be measured by, say, the ratio of capital to labor inputs. An older—and competing—view is the Austrian theory in which the distinguishing characteristics of factors of production are the dates at which they are applied. Output at a point in time results from the combination of previous inputs, with the intertemporal complementarity of previous inputs determining the relationship between input and outpur. A central feature of this view is that the capital intensity of production can be measured by the degree of "roundaboutness"—or time taken—in production. Other things being equal, capital intensity can be increased only by increasing roundaboutness.

By the early 1930s, the Austrian theory had largely been abandoned in favor of the modern view because of one insurmountable difficulty: it could not handle the case of fixed capital. Capital, in the Austrian view, is essentially working or circulating capital, not durable goods. By virtue of being durable, fixed capital does not simply contribute to output at a single date, but to a flow of outputs at a sequence of dates.

Professor Hicks attempts to resurrect the Austrian view and, in part, to reconcile it with modern growth theories by adopting its fundamental notion that production is a process involving a time stream of inputs. However, he drops the Austrian view that the output of the production process occurs at a point in time, replacing it with the notion of a time-stream of outputs, which allows the model to handle the case of fixed (durable) capital and, therefore, overcome the fundamental objection to the Austrian theory. However, with this seemingly simple change, most of the basic features of the Austrian theory disappear. For instance, very early in his book, Professor Hicks is able to show that the whole notion of "roundaboutness" as a measure of capital intensity, which is central to the Austrian theory, collapses. In fact, for the most of part I (chaps. 1–6) of the book,

Professor Hicks's neo-Austrian view bears a closer resemblance to modern growth theory than it does to the old Austrian theory, particularly with respect to the study and comparison of steady states. While many of the results presented in part I will seem old hat to many readers, the neo-Austrian approach to the derivation of such results is particularly novel. At least with respect to steady-states, Professor Hicks has successfully reconciled the (neo-) Austrian with the modern view of capital.

Of somewhat more interest to economists are parts 2 and 3 of this book. The potential strength of the neo-Austrian view appears to be the light it may shed on the analysis of disequilibrium processes. Unfortunately, Professor Hicks is able to say very little, in general, about the characteristics of such disequilibrium processes. This is recognized by the author and he contents himself, in part 2, with a fairly full solution to a very special case involving the traverse of the economy from one steady-state to another, as a result of an exogenous technological change. Nonetheless, this section is suggestive of the possible wide application of the model to disequilibrium problems with respect, for instance, to unemployment. At the moment, however, the model is not sufficiently developed to properly handle such questions, in the general case. Finally, in part 3, Professor Hicks turns his attention to the twenty-year old controversy concerning the measurability of capital and the existence of a "production function." Professor Hicks demonstrates that his neo-Austrian view may shed much light on the controversy. However, his results are, again, predominately suggestive.

While the concepts and notions with which Professor Hicks is dealing are extremely technical, the material is presented in a very lucid and nontechnical manner. The text uses little more than elementary algebra and some simple diagrams. Mathematical appendices are provided for those who desire more rigorous treatment of the results presented in the main text. Readers interested in Professor Hicks's neo-Austrian view of capital will find a briefer and much more technical presentation of its main features in the June, 1970 issue of the *Economic Journal*.

JON P. HARKNESS
Northwestern University
Evanston
Illinois

MAURICE M. KELSO, WILLIAM E. MARTIN, and LAWRENCE E. MACK. *Water Supplies and Economic Growth in an Arid Environment*. Pp. 327. Tucson: The University of Arizona Press, 1973. $8.50. Paperbound.

The book is a case study of water supplies in Arizona. It is a highly analytical study, testing the hypothesis that water scarcity need not restrain the economic growth of Arizona. The research delineates the climate and physiography of the state, the volume and withdrawal of water supplies, and the economic pattern of development as it relates to present and future water requirements.

The analysis includes the use of marginal value productivity theory, which reveals the inefficiency of water use in the state. The existing users of water in the state have created a draft—3.0 to 3.5 million acre-feet per year—on the underground supplies, equal to approximately three times the annual recharge of the ground water stock. Under existing water law in Arizona, the rights to the use of natural water as to location, nature, and timing are not associated with the economic costs involved, but determined by nonmarket administrative rules and regulations. In most cases, water allocations have ignored the opportunity costs entirely, or administrative methods have allocated water supplies at less than their socioeconomic efficiency.

In a detailed investigation of state agriculture, it was concluded that to maintain the present agricultural sector an additional 906 thousand acre-feet of water would need to be developed over the next fifty years, at a price low enough to allow irrigation of such low-value crops as grains and forages. More realistically, there would have to be higher costs, forcing a decline in cropped acreage devoted to the production of such crops. In an estimation of the costs of agricultural adjustment, the authors employed a complete study of the direct and indirect costs, including forward and backward linkages in the economy. They have concluded that the state should delay entrance into large-scale water development schemes. "Arizona would be better off merely to absorb the cost of agricultural adjustment, concentrating on development of alternative nonfarm growth and intrastate transfers that would make that growth possible."

The study developed a set of five alternative trade patterns, illustrating the agricultural adjustments based on the projections generated by the representative-farm linear-programming models. While conventional wisdom—Trade Pattern I—would suggest that the existing agricultural users ought to be insulated against pressures for change due to declining groundwater availability, water shortages would be so severe by 1980 that increasing the water supply would not be feasible. In Trade Patterns III and IV, however, water policies would be modified to facilitate transfers of water resources involving the encouragement of the nonagricultural sectors in which water would generate high values per unit of water input. Patterns III and IV differ in the amount of reduction of low income agriculture. Pattern III would yield a viable economy for Arizona through the year 2000; after that the economy would need to move toward a pattern of trade somewhere between III and IV.

The authors come to the conclusion that, "Currently, the water problem is a management, an institutional, a policy problem—a problem of demands for water more than one of supplies—a problem of man-made restraints." They suggest that the state should pursue policies shaping demand, including the expenditure of public funds to encourage and subsidize industrial, commercial, and consumer immigration and to facilitate the transfer of water resources out of low return uses in agriculture.

The book is certainly a well documented work of analytical research.

While other arid environments may not correspond exactly to the situation in Arizona, the tools and techniques of the study will have considerable applicability in water scarcity studies.

RUSSELL P. BELLICO
Department of Economics
Westfield State College
Westfield
Massachusetts

ROGER G. NOLL, MERTON J. PECK and JOHN J. MCGOWAN. *Economic Aspects of Television Regulation*. Pp. 342. Washington, D.C.: The Brookings Institution, 1973. $8.95.

This book is a well-written, interesting analysis of the effects of the major regulations of the Federal Communications Commission (FCC) on the television broadcasting industry, and a strong criticism of those regulations. It concentrates on five key issues that have confronted the FCC and the industry:

1. The economic viability of Ultra High Frequency broadcasting
2. The future of noncommercial public television
3. The criteria for granting and renewing television station licenses
4. The role of subscription or pay television
5. The future of cable television, domestic satellites and video cassettes

The authors use economic analysis to bolster their arguments that the FCC has been guided in its regulation philosophy by four quite conflicting objectives: establishment of as many local stations as possible, diversity in program content, fulfillment of broadcasting's role as a public servant and the maintenance of an acceptable level of competition. They assert that regulatory policies promulgated thereunder have, instead, failed to increase local programming. The rules have interfered with the expansion of the television industry, its willingness and ability to adopt new technologies, and have only resulted in shielding the industry oligopoly from competition.

The approach of the book is scholarly and well structured, yet written in a very readable style. The technical statistical and econometric analyses, for instance, are fortunately presented in two appendices at the end of the volume, so that the thesis of the authors is not cluttered with economic jargon and is quite convincing.

The book has two main faults. First, it hits at only certain selected aspects of television regulation and thus is not truly the comprehensive economic analysis of the entire television industry that is described in the fly leaf. More important, perhaps, is the fact that much of the empirical evidence used by the authors to back their arguments is based on small samples and meager data. The authors admit this, but it is certainly better than nothing, and they allege government policy decisions in this field are also based on just as inconclusive, conjectural information.

By and large, the book is an impressive work by equally impressive authors and a true contribution to the body of knowledge of the television industry. It should indeed cause those involved with establishing the policies and regulations of the FCC to re-examine their thinking on the subject.

SIDNEY I. SIMON
Department of Economics
Rutgers University
New Brunswick
New Jersey

WILLIAM and ELIZABETH PADDOCK. *We Don't Know How: An Independent Audit of What They Call Success in Foreign Assistance*. Pp. 331. Ames, Iowa: Iowa State University Press, 1973. $4.95.

The objective of this book is important—to evaluate the success of our foreign aid programs in Mexico and Central America. William Paddock is a specialist in tropical agriculture, and the authors have a thorough knowledge of the Central American area. They report on about twenty-five projects sponsored by the United States Agency for International Development, the Rockefeller Foundation, the Peace Corps, the Inter-American Development Bank and private missionaries. Although the projects they examine had been recommended by their sponsors as highly successful, the authors conclude that almost all of them were either failures or had results different from those intended. Although this book will be resented by administrators of foreign aid programs, follow-up evaluations of attempts to help other countries should be welcomed. The book is written in a popular style, and the authors vigorously present their point of view.

The technique of the authors—field observations of what had been done, combined with interviews with persons concerned—has some shortcomings compared to statistical and economic analysis, but was probably not unsuitable for most of the projects they visited. They found that the various efforts to promote small peasant agriculture through land reform, government subsidized loans, and agricultural extension services were failures. Also, contrary to the claims made by officials in Washington, an energetic peace corps volunteer had not revolutionized tomato farming in El Salvador. They also found that the twenty-eight cent charge per patient at mobile health units in Nicaragua had not raised the revenues needed to finance the expected community development projects. In addition, the Rockefeller Foundation had exaggerated the contribution of the work of Nobel Peace Prize winner Norman Borlaug in increasing wheat output in Mexico. On the other hand, the authors' conclusion that the Central American Common Market is not only a failure, but contributed to the war between El Salvador and Honduras in 1969, needs more detailed analysis and documentation than that afforded by on-the-spot observations and interviews.

The authors do not make the mistake of failing to appreciate the economic progress that has occurred in Mexico and Central America during the past thirty years. The book includes accounts of the successful industrial development in Monterrey, Mexico, and in San Pedro (Sula), Honduras. The authors' basic theme, however, is not optimistic. They are modern propagators of the dismal Malthusian prediction that population growth will exceed the growth of food supplies. They see little hope for Latin America with its limited natural resources unless populaion growth is effectively limited.

COLIN D. CAMPBELL
Department of Economics
Dartmouth College
Hanover, New Hampshire

ARNOLD W. SAMETZ, ed. *Financial Development and Economic Growth: The Economic Consequences of Underdeveloped Capital Markets.* Pp. vi, 257. New York: New York University Press, 1972.

Are developed capital markets—a complex of financial institutions and financial instruments by which savings are transferred from the original savers to the ultimate users—a sufficient or necessary condition for real economic growth? Does the absence of developed capital markets necessarily, or usually, operate to frustrate real development? Is sustained and substantial real development possible without concomitant financial development! These are questions of importance both to our understanding of the process of economic growth and in the formulation of efficient development strategies. The work under review is to be welcomed, for it directly faces these important questions and, from the experience of carefully selected countries, attempts to formulate some preliminary answers.

Unlike the recently published works by McKinnon (*Money and Capital in Economic Development*) and Shaw (*Financial Deepening in Economic Development*), which attempt to argue theoretically that financial reform is of central importance in the growth process, the studies edited by Sametz are empirical, and it is the stated position of the editor that "there is no royal financial road to economic growth: each system works; it is the particular mix of costs and benefits associated with each that differs among financial systems" (p. 1). We find this approach stimulating, for the individual studies are not mere recitation of facts, but rather the available facts of financial and real development are variously examined to explore possible relationships. Unlike McKinnon and Shaw, who advocate basically a single path to development, the studies edited by Sametz evidence a multiplicity of possibilities. Of course, this does not provide simple and easy answers; but it does help to avoid *simpliste* and facile policy prescriptions.

Symposia are, like the proverbial curate's egg, of mixed quality and of differing interest to different readers with the consequence that they are notoriously difficult to review fully. To me, the articles by Sametz, Hawkins and Patrick were especially interesting.

Sametz discusses in rapid compass the financing of American investment in Europe and demonstrates—shades of de Gaulle!—that such investment was largely financed by local (European) borrowing. Unfortunately, the most provocative and interesting part of his essay, that dealing with welfare implications, is all too briefly handled: for instance, he concludes (p. 22) that Europe's welfare would be improved if it restrained American direct investment, but this is a position that requires amplification, especially since he believes that the underdeveloped countries of the world should not so exclude such investment. Why? Surely a small and weak underdeveloped country is less able to protect itself from exploitation and manipulation, so that it should be all the more careful about allowing a massive multinational behemoth within its doors. As the Japanese have demonstrated, methods of importing technology without abandoning equity control can be devised.

Hawkins examines how the French have used imperfections in their capital markets to implement and, indeed, reinforce their "indicative" planning. This is an extremely stimulating approach to the problems of plan implementation and demands elaboration. One especially wishes to know how technological innovation and the growth of new enterprises and processes are affected by such imperfections and the planning process.

Patrick shows that pronounced economic development in postwar Japan has taken place in the context of a rather primitive financial system, thus demonstrating that financial innovation is not necessary—either as a precondition or as a concomitant—for real growth. It is not clear from the essay, however, whether Patrick believes that the pace of real development, however high in actuality, would have been different under different financial arrangements. A stimulating essay would have been better had it engaged in more speculation.

Other essays can only be mentioned in passing. Ben-Shahar examines Israel as a case study of a dual financial market; this raises the interesting question of whether or not financial dualism exaggerates or ameliorates dualism in other sectors of the economy. Rangarajan restricts himself to an examination of the government securities market in India and so, perforce, presents a one-dimensional view of the financial system. Engberg's essay on the operation of central banking in the context of underdeveloped financial markets is, however, very disappointing. It is so panoramic in its coverage that it can be accused of being superficial. Moreover, it neglects to consider the increasing literature and detailed case studies that have appeared in this area within the past ten or fifteen years.

Despite these minor reservations, however, and the fact that the empirical data are somewhat obsolete since they do not extend beyond 1968, this volume of studies deserves a wide audience, for it raises important questions and examines them in a nondoctrinaire fashion.

JAMSHED K. S. GHANDHI
The Wharton School
University of Pennsylvania

JOHN G. SIMON, CHARLES W. POWERS, and JON P. GUNNEMANN. *The Ethical Investor: Universities and Corporate Responsibility.* Pp. vii, 208. New Haven, Conn.: Yale University Press, 1972. $9.50.

HENRY G. MANNE and HENRY C. WALLICH. *The Modern Corporation and*

Social Responsibility. Pp. 106. Washington, D.C.: American Enterprise Institute for Public Research, 1972. $5.75.

These are two contrasting books dealing with the general subject of corporate social responsibility. The Simon, Powers and Gunnemann—hereafter referred to as SPG—volume, however, concentrates on universities and their investment policies. Both books were born from debate and dialogue. SPG were influenced by a cross-disciplinary seminar at Yale on social investment policy, while the Manne-Wallich book—MW hereafter —is one of the rational debate series of the American Enterprise Institute.

The SPG book is by far the more scholarly and innovative of the two. It clarifies significantly the meaning of social responsibility and the nature of the university. Its authors distinguish between social responsibility as eliminating social injuries which may accompany economic activity, and as affirmative actions taken by firms to attain particular social goals. At a minimum, business firms have the obligation to reduce any social injury which they may cause. Universities in the administration of their portfolios should encourage the application of this basic definition. They should seek the highest return on their investment portfolios, but subject to the constraint of reducing any social injuries generated by companies in which they are stockholders.

SPG engage in successive layers of analysis. First they look at corporations, then turn to shareholders as investors in enterprises, and finally to universities as investors in corporations. They recognize that the dilemmas confronting universities are acute, but nonetheless frame concrete guidelines by which universities can sort through the complex investment issues which face them.

SPG have universities as restrained, limited battlers in the ring of corporate social policy. They should seek a diminution of social injury rather than achievement of grand causes. Advocates of a more positive and affirmative stance may be disappointed in these conclu-sions. However, in the words of the authors, "The application of negative injunctions, to be sure, will not rebuild cities or make deserts bloom, but it can limit or halt the destruction of life, of opportunity and of beauty. This may not be enough, but it is a great deal."

The MW book, on the other hand, is essentially pedestrian in style and coverage. Manne, in his attack on social responsibility, presents a discussion polemical in tone on occasion and based on conventional economic theory. He shows little awareness of multiple-goal models of the firm or of the impact of the cultural context on business decision making. The business enterprise is a production machine with a profit orientation, to be certain, but this machine operates in a particular environment which shapes not only constraints on the enterprise, but its objectives as well. Executives are not mechanical robots immune from the social milieu in which they have grown up. Their utility functions as well as the constraints which face them are given a social definition. Conventional economics ignores the implications of a sociological input into micro theory.

Wallich presents the interesting hypothesis that diversification of shareholdings by many corporate owners requires that firms engage in programs which do not pay from their point of view, but which benefit their industry or the corporate system at large. He joins his Yale colleagues in proposing that stockholders should take an active interest in the development of corporate social policy. Stockholders should stay and fight through proxy battles and with communications with managers rather than opt out via the "Wall Street rule" of selling your stock if there is disagreement about company policy.

While Manne and Wallich generally take opposing positions concerning corporate responsibility, there is some agreement. Manne, for example, accepts the necessity of government action to eliminate various negative spillovers on others of business activities. However, he holds that the extent to which such negative externalities exist has been exaggerated. From his standpoint, most "do-gooding" programs of business are carried out as long-run profit maximization. Wallich, on the other hand, wants corporations to engage in widened pursuit of profits so that a decentralized pluralism is fostered in America. Such policies, in addition, advance the profit position of stockholders who hold shares in a wide range of corporations.

HAROLD L. JOHNSON
Department of Economics
Emory University
Atlanta
Georgia

BARRY WEISBERG. *Beyond Repair: The Ecology of Capitalism.* Pp. 201. Boston, Mass.: Beacon Press, 1971. $6.95.

WILLIAM LEISS. *The Domination of Nature.* Pp. vii, 242. New York: George Braziller, 1972. $6.95.

I shall give Mr. Weisberg's *Beyond Repair* only a little more attention than it warrants, in order to move on to Leiss's provocative argument. Weisberg, co-director of the Bay Area Institute in San Francisco, is persuaded that the environmental crisis "is rooted in the social division of labor and the formation of classes." "The suffering and death of war, racism, sexism, and ecological imbalance indeed stem from the same fundamental sources." It is an interesting thesis and one, therefore, regrets that Weisberg does not argue it, but simply posits it as dogma. Looking hard for merit in his pop-Marxist diatribe, I can report that he is on target in indicting the elitist and frequently reactionary character of much of organized conservationism and he sees through the alarmingly regressive politics of the more passionate population controllers. In short, he understands that environmental problems and their solutions must be considered in light of larger questions of social justice. Such insights, while no longer novel, are important; it is unfortunate they are so deeply buried under Mr. Weisberg's rantings.

Corporate capitalism is depicted as a conspiracy theory with a vengeance. The author is not too sure of his philosophical underpinnings, however. At one point we are told that, since the capitalist system is a result of conscious conspiracy, it is amenable to change if only "the people" will to be liberated. Later we are assured that "individuals can no more be held responsible for our present peril than the first dinosaur who walked into a tar pit." Questions of the relationship between political will and historical determinism aside, Weisberg never deviates from his conviction that capitalism is the root of all evil. Any reinforcing connection between the existing order and some manner of evil—or even a state of coexistence between the two—is proof positive that capitalism is a causal agent. Mr. Jones is an alcoholic and a banker, therefore capitalism induces alcoholism.

There is no sentiment platitudinous enough to embarrass Mr. Weisberg. "The corporate organization of profit directs the society, instead of society democratically directing the means and ends of corporate organization. We must struggle toward a society in which human beings as such are sovereign —not consumers, producers, or managers." When he is not writing a catechism for radicals who discovered the class factor yesterday, the author offers lengthy lectures on the obvious, such as page upon page about how unsafe the automobile is, why it is not an ideal form of urban transportation, and the various ways in which carbon monoxide is not good for breathing. Most egregiously, Weisberg blithely walks into a trap that more thoughtful Marxists carefully avoid. He assures the reader that socialist societies such as China, the Soviet Union and North Korea have discovered the happy balance between production and environmental protection. Innocent of the knowledge that the Soviet Union has this year proudly chalked up its 250 millionth citizen and boasts of having 275 million by 1988, Weisberg asserts that "the Soviet Union maintains a declining birth rate [because] socialist society considers ecological and social balance as inseparable." Weisberg makes no effort to restrain his enthusiasm for North Korea as "a potent lesson in the viability and superiority of socialist development." Together with the radicals of yesteryear and the Henry Kissingers of today, his admiration for all things Chinese approaches religious reverence.

William Leiss, a young political scientist at the University of Saskatchewan, offers, in *The Domination of Nature*, one of the most thoughtful and potentially important arguments set forth, so far, in the continuing debate about the relationship between "man and nature." It is a frankly theoretical work, a study in the history of an idea, and among its chief merits is the author's refusal to bid for immediate relevancy by identifying with any of the myriad parties in the pro- or antitechnology, pro- or antigrowth, controversies. Being relatively free of dogmatic tenets, Leiss weaves a complex and frequently scintillating theme that sometimes poses old questions in new ways and also raises new questions that might provoke a measure of lucidity in a discussion, now deeply obfuscated.

Although his historical reach is encompassing, Leiss knows he is himself part of the intellectual history he discusses, and he tentatively associates himself with the Frankfurt School, connected with Jürgen Habermas and others. The starting point of his investigation is the late Georg Lukacs' remark that nature must now be understood as a "social category." That is, it becomes increasingly implausible to posit man or society over and against nature. There is, he implies, a symbiotic and inseparable connection between society and nature that almost makes the use of the distinction simply an heuristic device, not to be mistaken for empirical description. Beginning with this hypothesis, Leiss moves back historically to examine the various alternative ways in which man and nature metaphors have been conceived.

Eschewing the rhapsodic and fanciful reverence for the East that mars so much discussion in this area, Leiss knows that publicly significant study of his subject neither can, nor should, escape the burden of an emphatically western intellectual history. In examining the ancient Greek and Biblical roots of the idea of the

"domination of nature"—later, for reasons that are not entirely clear, he prefers the phrase "mastery of nature"—Leiss offers an important correction of Lynn White's famous essay on the religious origins of the environmental crisis. "White's argument must be qualified to this extent, namely, that Christian doctrine sought to restrain man's earthly ambitions by holding him accountable for his conduct to a higher authority." Leiss's caveat is crucial to his overarching argument that the future requires a human moral assertion which challenges all forms of the doctrine that nature contains its own inherent logic to which man and society, having once discovered the logic, need offer only obedience.

He believes the axis of the history of the idea of nature is Francis Bacon, and a large part of the book is, I believe rightly, devoted to the ways in which Bacon successfully synthesized the "arts" of magic, alchemy and "scientific method" with the prevailing Christian worldview. "No outstanding thinker after Bacon devoted comparable attention to the concept of mastery over nature. . . . So definitive was his work that the history of all subsequent stages in the career of this idea down to the present can be arranged as a set of variations on a Baconian theme." At the heart of Bacon's influence was the belief that nature could and should be mastered by art—what would later be termed technology—rather than by morality. Leiss contrasts this with an earlier Christian vision, in which the saints tamed the wild animals by virtue of, and in witness to, their holiness. Leiss notes that Bacon's *New Atlantis*, the vision of a utopia gained by the mastery of nature through science, is devoid of any mention of moral progress or restructuring of values. Unlike the political and moral spheres, said Bacon, science and the arts "never harmed any man, never burdened a conscience with remorse. Its blessing and reward is without ruin, wrong or wretchedness to any. For light is in itself pure and innocent; it may be wrongly used, but cannot in its nature be defiled." The assertion of science's innocence was probably necessary to secure the legitimation of alchemy and its cousins in Bacon's seventeenth century Christian world, but it represents a naivete that we can clearly no longer afford.

Leiss is—for reasons not, I think, essential to his argument—excessively kind to Marx and Engels and their hopes for a classless society in which, for the first time, men will become "true masters of nature, because and insofar as they become masters of their own process of socialization." The other thinkers receiving major attention are Max Scheler, Edmund Husserl and Max Horkheimer, the last also associated with the Frankfurt School. The focus on Scheler's idea of science as *Herrschaftswissen,* "knowledge for the sake of domination," helps illuminate one possible conceptualization of the problem.

Leiss's own hope seems to lie with a socialist projection of a "framework of collective rational control." When that is established, "technology will be liberated from its all-too-effective service in the cause of human conflict. Until that time, however, we remain victims of a dilemma whereby every outstanding victory in the scientific and technological mastery of nature entails the real possibility of an equally great catastrophe." The impression is conveyed that things are going to have to get a lot worse before they get better. The gap between "the rational organization of labor and instrumentalities on the one hand, and the irrational uses to which that organization is put on the other" will continue to widen toward that point at which "the objectives themselves are called into question." Giving in, somewhat, to the antitechnological bias now so fashionable in our culture, Leiss at times seems to make exaggerated claims about the horrors unleashed by the technological monster, without coming clean about the indices of human misery and well being, which alone can serve as criteria in deciding the pros and cons of technological society. Here is at least one point at which dogma seems to distort the author's powers of observation and analysis. One suspects that he very much wants the gap to widen more rapidly, the better to facilitate the radical social re-

structuring he envisions; thus it is strategically necessary to raise the level of discontent against technology under its present controls.

It is not possible in this space to trace the full richness of Leiss's argument, and perhaps I have emphasized my misgivings at the expense of my enthusiasms about the book. Others have observed that Mao has turned Marx on his head by asserting the primacy of consciousness over social reality. In a similar way, Leiss suggests a revolution by which moral assertion defies the various orthodoxies premised upon "the laws of nature." The content and sources of that moral assertion remain frustratingly unclear. But that is, perhaps, another book. The great achievement of the present work is to drive us back to reconsider Bacon's fatal choice and to entertain the possibilities inherent in the legends about the saints and the beasts.

RICHARD J. NEUHAUS
Lutheran Church of St. John the
  Evangelist
Brooklyn
New York

OTHER BOOKS

ADORNO, THEODOR W. *Philosophy of Modern Music.* Pp. vii, 220. New York: The Seabury Press, 1973. $8.95.

ALTBACH PHILIP G. and DAVID H. KELLY *American Students: A Selected Bibliography on Student Activism and Related Topics.* Pp. 192. Lexington, Mass.: Lexington Books, 1973. $25.00.

AMBROS, STEPHEN E. and JAMES ALDEN BARBER, JR., eds. *The Military and American Society.* Pp. ix, 322. New York: The Free Press, 1973. $2.95. Paperbound.

The American Revolution 1775–1783: An Atlas of 18th Century Maps and Charts. Theatres of Operation. Washington, D.C.: Naval History Department of the Department of the Navy. 1973. No price.

ARONSON, ROBERT L., ed. *The Localization of Federal Manpower Planning.* Pp. iv, 102. Ithaca, N.Y.: New York State School of Industrial and Labor Relations, Cornell University, 1973. $6.00. Paperbound, $4.50.

ASHMORE, HARRY S. *Fear in the Air. Broadcasting and the First Amendment: The Anatomy of a Constitutional Crisis.* Pp. 180. New York: W. W. Norton, 1973. $6.95.

AZAR, EDWARD E. *Probe for Peace: Small-State Hostilities.* Critical Issues in Political Science. Pp. iii, 89. Minneapolis, Minn.: Burgess, 1973. $1.75. Paperbound.

BACHRACH, BERNARD S. *A History of the Alans in the West: From their First Appearance in the Sources of Classical Antiquity through the Early Middle Ages.* Pp. xi, 161. Minneapolis, Minn.: University of Minnesota Press, 1973. $11.50.

BAER, HAROLD and AARON J. BRODER. *How to Prepare and Negotiate Cases for Settlement.* Revised ed. Pp. 291. New York: Law-Arts, 1973. $17.50.

BARRY, BRIAN. *The Liberal Theory of Justice: A Critical Examination of the Principal Doctrines in "A Theory of Justice" by John Rawls.* Pp. ix, 168. Oxford, England: Clarendon Press, 1973. No price. Paperbound.

BARRY, MARY J. *A History of Mining on Kenai Peninsula.* Pp. v, 214. Anchorage, Alaska: Alaska Northwest Publishing, 1973. $7.20. Paperbound.

BARSTON, RONALD P., ed. *The Other Powers: Studies in the Foreign Policies of Small States.* Pp. 341. New York: Barnes and Noble, 1973. $21.50.

BAUMAN, ZYGMUNT. *Culture As Praxis.* Monographs in Social Theory. Pp. 198. Boston, Mass.: Routledge and Kegan Paul, 1973. $10.00.

BECKER, ERNEST. *The Denial of Death.* Pp. 320. New York: The Free Press, 1973. $7.95.

BIANCO, LUCIEN. *Origins of the Chinese Revolution, 1915–1949.* Pp. vii, 222. Stanford, Cal.: Stanford University Press, 1973. $2.95. Paperbound.

BLEVINS, LEON W. *The Young Voter's Manual: A Topical Dictionary of American Government and Politics.* Pp. ix, 366. Totowa, N.J.: Littlefield, Adams, 1973. $3.95. Paperbound.

BOOTH, PHILIP. *Social Security in America.* Policy Papers in Human Resources and Industrial Relations 19. Pp. 180. Ann Arbor, Mich.: Institute of Labor and Industrial Relations, The University of Michigan —Wayne State University, 1973. No price. Paperbound.

BOOTH, PHILIP, ed. *Social Security: Policy for the Seventies. Proceedings of the Seventh Social Security Conference.* Pp. vii, 229. Ann Arbor, Mich.: Institute of Labor and Industrial Relations. $8.00.

BOTTOMORE, TOM, ed. *Karl Marx.* Makers of Modern Social Science. Pp. 188. Englewood Cliffs, N.J.: Prentice-Hall, 1973. $6.50. Paperbound, $2.45.

BRAGER, GEORGE and HARRY SPECHT. *Community Organizing.* Pp. v, 363. New York: Columbia University Press, 1973. $10.00.

BOURGUIGNON, ERIKA and LENORA S. GREENBAUM. *Diversity and Homogeneity in World Societies.* Pp. ix, 194. New Haven, Conn.: HRAF Press, 1973. $8.00. Paperbound, $5.00.

BRANDT, WILLIAM J. *The Shape of Medieval History: Studies in Modes of Perception.* Pp. ix, 196. New York: Schocken, 1973. $2.95. Paperbound.

BRASS, PAUL R. and MARCUS F. FRANDA, eds. *Radical Politics in South Asia.* Pp. xiii, 449. Cambridge, Mass.: The MIT Press, 1973. $15.00.

BROOM, LEONARD and PHILIP SELZNICK. *Sociology: A Text with Adapted Readings.* 5th ed. Pp. 653. New York: Harper and Row, 1973. $10.95.

BROWN, HARRY JAMES and FREDERICK D. WILLIAMS, eds. *The Diary of James A. Garfield, 1875–1877.* vol. 3. Pp. 599. East Lansing, Mich.: The Michigan State University Press, 1973. $22.50.

BROWN, TRUESDELL S. *The Greek Historians.* Pp. 208. Lexington, Mass.: D. C. Heath, 1973. $2.95. Paperbound.

BRUS, WODZIMIERZ. *The Economics and Politics of Socialism: Collected Essays.* Pp. vii, 117. Boston, Mass.: Routledge and Kegan Paul, 1973. $8.00.

CAIN, GLEN G., RICHARD B. FREEMAN and W. LEE HANSEN. *Labor Market Analysis of Engineers and Technical Workers.* Policy Studies in Employment and Welfare no. 18. Pp. v, 88. Baltimore, Md.: The Johns Hopkins University Press, 1973. $1.95. Paperbound.

CAIRNCROSS, ALEC. *Control of Long-Term International Capital Movements.* A Staff Paper. Pp. vii, 104. Washington, D.C.: The Brookings Institution, 1973. $2.50. Paperbound.

CALDWELL, OLIVER J. *A Secret War: Americans in China, 1944–1945.* Pp. ix, 218. Carbondale, Ill.: Southern Illinois University Press, 1973. $2.65. Paperbound.

CAPORASO, JAMES A. and LESLIE L. ROSS, JR., eds. *Quasi-Experimental Approaches: Testing Theory and Evaluating Policy.* Pp. ix, 368. Evanston, Ill.: Northwestern University Press, 1973. No price. Paperbound.

CARNEGIE COMMISSION ON HIGHER EDUCATION, THE. *Continuity and Discontinuity: Higher Education and the Schools.* Pp. vii, 116. New York: McGraw-Hill, 1973. $2.95. Paperbound.

CARR, STEPHEN. *City Signs and Lights: A Policy Study.* Pp. 272. Cambridge, Mass.: The MIT Press, 1973. $10.00. Paperbound.

CATCHLOVE, DONALD. *Romania's Ceausescu.* Pp. 120. Tunbridge Wells, England: Abacus Press, 1973. £ 2.50.

CHAPLIN, GEORGE and GLENN D. PAIGE, eds. *Hawaii 2000: Continuing Experiment in Anticipatory Democracy.* Pp. vii, 497. Honolulu: The University Press of Hawaii, 1973. $9.95.

CHRISTENSON, REO M. *Challenge and Decision: Political Issues of Our Time.* 4th ed. Pp. 227. New York: Harper and Row, 1973. $2.95. Paperbound.

COFFMAN, TOM. *Catch a Wave: A Case Study of Hawaii's New Politics.* Pp. ix, 211. Honolulu: The University Press of Hawaii, 1973. No Price. Paperbound.

COHEN, ROBERT, JOHN MCMANUS, DAVID FOX and CONNIE KASTELNIK. *Psych City: A Simulated Community.* Pergamon General Psychology Series. Pp. vii, 328. New York: Pergamon, 1973. No price. Paperbound.

COHEN, SAUL B. *Geography and Politics in a World Divided.* 2nd ed. Pp. v, 334. New York: Oxford University Press, 1973. $3.95. Paperbound.

COLEMAN, JAMES S. *The Mathematics of Collective Action.* Pp. vii, 191. Chicago, Aldine, 1973. $9.75.

COLLETTI, LUCIO. *From Rousseau to Lenin: Studies in Ideology and Society.* Pp. 240. New York: Monthly Review Press, 1973. $8.50.

CONGRESSIONAL QUARTERLY SERVICE. *Current American Government, Fall 1973.* Pp. 140. Washington, D.C.: Congressional Quarterly, 1973. $3.00. Paperbound.

CONGRESSIONAL QUARTERLY SERVICE. *Future of Social Programs.* Pp. 92. Washington, D.C.: Congressional Quarterly, 1973. $4.00. Paperbound.

CONGRESSIONAL QUARTERLY SERVICE. *Watergate: Chronology of a Crisis.* Pp. 291. Washington, D.C.: Congressional Quarterly, 1973. $6.00. Paperbound.

CORWIN, EDWARD S. *The Constitution and What it Means Today.* Revised ed. Pp. ix, 601. Princeton, N.J.: Princeton University Press, 1973. $20.00.

CRANSTON, MAURICE. *What are Human Rights?* Pp. 170. New York: Taplinger, 1973. $6.95.

CROZIER, MICHEL. *The World of the Office Worker.* Pp. vii, 224. New York: Schocken, 1973. $3.75. Paperbound.

CULLINAN, GERALD. *The United States Postal Service.* Pp. vii, 271. New York: Praeger, 1973. $10.00.

DAVIDOFF LEONORE. *The Best Circles: Society, Etiquette and the Season.* Pp. 127. Totowa, N.J.: Rowman and Littlefield, 1973. $12.00.

DAVIS, ALLEN F. and MARK H. HALLER, eds. *The Peoples of Philadelphia: A History of Ethnic Groups and Lower-Class Life, 1790–1940.* Pp. ix, 300. Philadelphia; Temple University Press, 1973. $9.95.

DE ARMOND, DALE. *Juneau: A Book of Woodcuts.* Pp. 50. Anchorage, Alaska: Alaska Northwest, 1973. $10.20. Paperbound.

DE GRAZIA, ALFRED. *Kalos: What Is To Be Done with Our World?* Pp. v, 532. New York: Kalos Press, 1973. No price.

DE GREENE, KENYON B. *Sociotechnical Systems: Factors in Analysis, Design and Management.* Pp. ix, 416. Englewood Cliffs, N.J.: Prentice-Hall, 1973. $12.95.

DERRY, T. K. *A History of Modern Norway 1814–1972.* Pp. xii, 503. Oxford, England: Clarendon Press, 1973. £ 5.50.

DE SOLA POOL, ITHIEL, ed. *Talking Back: Citizen Feedback and Cable Technology.* Pp. vii, 325. Cambridge, Mass.: The MIT Press, 1973. $9.95.

Developing Social Policy in Conditions of Rapid Change: Role of Social Welfare. Proceedings of the 16th International Conference on Social Welfare, The Hague, Netherlands August 13–19, 1972. Pp. 249. New York: Columbia University Press, 1973. $12.50.

DISHON, DANIEL. *Middle East Record.* Vol. 4, 1968. Pp. vii, 889. New York: Halsted Press, 1973. $55.00.

D'OMBRAIN, NICHOLAS. *War Machinery and High Policy: Defence Administration in Peacetime Britain 1902–1914.* Oxford Historical Monographs. Pp. vii, 302. New York: Oxford University Press, 1973. $14.50.

DRABBLE, JOHN. *Rubber in Malaya 1876–1922: The Genesis of the Industry.* Pp. vii, 256. New York: Oxford University Press, 1973. $19.25.

DREYER, PETER. *The Future of Treason.* Pp. 177. New York: Ballantine, 1973. $1.50. Paperbound.

DUGARD, JOHN. *The South West Africa Namibia Dispute: Documents and Scholarly Writings on the Controversy Between South Africa and the United Nations.* Pp. 605. Berkeley,: University of California Press, 1973. $28.50.

EDEN, LYNN. *Crisis in Watertown: The Polarization of an American Community.* Pp. 218. Ann Arbor: The University of Michigan Press, 1973. $2.95. Paperbound.

EDITORIAL RESEARCH REPORTS. *The Women's Movement.* Pp. v, 184. Washington, D.C.: Congressional Quarterly, 1973. $3.95. Paperbound.

EDWARDS, STEWART, ed. *The Communards*

of Paris, 1871. Documents of Revolution. Pp. 180. Ithaca, N.Y.: Cornell University Press, 1973. $6.95. Paperbound, $2.95.

EVANS, R. J. W. *Rudolf 11 and His World: A Study in Intellectual History 1576–1612*. Pp. vii, 323. New York: Oxford University Press, 1973. $24.00.

EVERS, TILMAN TÖNNIES. *Militarregierung in Argentinien: Das Politische System der "Argentinischen Revolution."* Pp. 288. Hamburg, Germany: Institut Für Iberoamerika-Kunde, 1973. No price. Paperbound.

FALK, RICHARD A. and SAUL H. MENDLOVITZ, eds. *Regional Politics and World Order*. Pp. vi, 475. San Francisco: W. H. Freeman, 1973. $12.00. Paperbound, $5.95.

FALLS, CYRIL. *The Birth of Ulster*. Reprint. Pp. vii, 272. New York: Barnes and Noble, 1973. $16.00.

FEIT, EDWARD. *The Armed Bureaucrats*. Pp. vii, 199. Boston, Mass.: Houghton Mifflin, 1973. $3.95. Paperbound.

FITCH, JAMES MARSTON. *American Building: The Historical Forces that Shaped It*. 2nd ed. Pp. vii, 350. New York, Schocken, 1973. $4.95. Paperbound.

FLACKS, RICHARD. *Conformity, Resistance, and Self-Determination: The Individual and Authority*. Pp. 350. Boston, Mass.: Little, Brown, 1973. $4.95. Paperbound.

FRASER, ANTONIA. *Cromwell: The Lord Protector*. Pp. xiii, 774. New York: Alfred A. Knopf, 1973. $12.50.

FREDERICKSON, GEORGE, ed. *Neighborhood Control in the 1970s: Politics, Administration, and Citizen Participation*. Pp. vii, 290. New York: Intext Educational Publishers, 1973. $8.50.

FRISCH, MORTON J. and RICHARD G. STEVENS, eds. *The Political Thought of American Statesmen: Selected Writings and Speeches*. Pp. 374. Itasca, Ill.: F. E. Peacock, 1973. $10.00. Paperbound, $4.95.

GAGNON, JOHN H. and WILLIAM SIMON. *Sexual Conduct: The Social Sources of Human Sexuality*. Pp. ix, 316. Chicago: Aldine, 1973. $8.95.

GANS, HERBERT J. *More Equality*. Pp. xi, 261. New York: Pantheon Books, 1973. $7.95.

GEIGER, THEODORE and FRANCES M. *Tales of Two City-States: The Development Progress of Hong Kong and Singapore*. National Planning Association Studies in Development Progress, no. 3. Washington, D.C.: National Planning Association, 1973. $3.50. Paperbound.

GOTTLIEB, DAVID, ed. *Youth in Contemporary Society*. Pp. 384. Beverly Hills, Cal.: Sage, 1973. $10.00.

GROSS, FELIKS. *Violence in Politics: Terror and Political Assassination in Eastern Europe and Russia*. Studies in the Social Sciences 13. Pp. 139. The Hague, The Netherlands: Mouton, 1973. 28 Guilders.

HALLMAN, HOWARD W. *Government by Neighborhoods*. Pp. iii, 67. Washington, D.C.: Center for Governmental Studies, 1973. $1.00. Paperbound.

HANDEL, MICHAEL I. *Israel's Political-Military Doctrine*. Occasional Papers in International Affairs no. 30. Pp. 101. Cambridge, Mass.: Harvard University Center for International Affairs, 1973. $3.00. Paperbound.

HANNINGTON, WAL. *Unemployed Struggles 1919–1936*. Pp. vii, 328. New York: Barnes and Noble, 1973. $12.50.

HELMREICH, WILLIAM B. *The Black Crusaders: A Case Study of a Black Militant Organization*. Pp. vii, 186. New York: Harper and Row, 1973. No price. Paperbound.

HILTON, RONALD. *The Latin Americans: Their Heritage and Their Destiny*. Pp. ix, 253. Philadelphia, Pa.: J. B. Lippincott, 1973. $7.50. Paperbound, $3.25.

HISTORICAL OFFICE, BUREAU OF PUBLIC AFFAIRS. *Foreign Relations of the United States 1948*. vol. 2, *Germany and Austria*. Pp. iii, 1575. Washington, D.C.: United States Government Printing Office, 1973. $8.75.

HOCHSCHILD, ARLIE RUSSELL. *The Unexpected Community: A Stimulating Study That Shows the Alternatives to Isolation and Loneliness for Old People*. Pp. 193. Englewood Cliffs, N.J.: Prentice-Hall, 1973. No price.

HOUGHTON, D. HOBART. *The South African Economy*. Pp. v, 297. New York: Oxford University Press, 1973. $9.75.

HOUN, FRANKLIN W. *A Short History of Chinese Communism, Completely Updated*. Pp. 278. Englewood Cliffs, N.J.: Prentice-Hall, 1973. No price.

HOYLE, B. S., ed. *Transport and Development*. Pp. 230. New York: Barnes and Noble, 1973. $15.00.

HUFF, ANNE S. and SAMUEL I. DOCTORS. *Minority Enterprise and the President's Council*. Pp. xi, 201. Cambridge, Mass.: Ballinger, 1973. $12.50.

HURSTFIELD, JOEL. *Freedom, Corruption, and Government in Elizabethan England*. Pp. 368. Cambridge, Mass.: 1973. $11.00.

HYAMS, EDWARD. *A Dictionary of Modern Revolution*. Pp. 322. New York: Taplinger, 1973. $9.95. Paperbound, $4.95.

JONES, ALAN M., JR. *U.S. Foreign Policy in a Changing World: The Nixon Adminis-*

tration. Pp. ix, 379. New York: David McKay, 1973. $8.95. Paperbound, $4.95.

JUDD, JACOB and IRWIN H. POLISHOOK, eds. *Aspects of Early New York Society and Politics.* Pp. vi, 150. Tarrytown, N.Y.: Sleepy Hollow Restorations, 1973. $7.50.

KIEV, ARI. *Transcultural Psychiatry.* Pp. xi, 223. New York: The Free Press, 1973. $2.95. Paperbound.

KIM, YOUNG C., ed. *Major Powers and Korea.* Pp. 164. Silver Spring, Md.: Research Institute on Korean Affairs, 1973. $2.95. Paperbound.

KINTNER, WILLIAM R. and RICHARD B. FOSTER, eds. *National Strategy in a Decade of Change: An Emerging U.S. Policy.* Pp. xv, 298. Lexington, Mass.: D.C. Heath, 1973. $15.00.

KIRSCH, A. THOMAS. *Feasting and Social Oscillation: Religion and Society in Upland Southeast Asia.* Data paper no. 92. Pp. ii, 49. Ithaca, N.Y.: Southeast Asia Program, Cornell University, 1973. $3.00. Paperbound.

KAPLAN, MORTON A. *The Rationale for NATO: European Collective Security —Past and Future.* Pp. 94. Washington, D.C.: American Enterprise Institute for Public Policy Research, 1973. $3.00. Paperbound.

KAPLAN, MORTON A., ABRAM CHAYES, G. WARREN NUTTER, PAUL C. WARNKE, JOHN P. ROCHE and CLAYTON FRITCHEY. *Vietnam Settlement: Why 1973, Not 1969?* Rational Debate Series. Pp. 208. Washington, D.C.: American Enterprise Institute for Public Policy Research, 1973. $5.75.

KENNEDY, MICHAEL L. *The Jacobin Club of Marseilles, 1790–1794.* Pp. ix, 245. Ithaca, N.Y.: Cornell University Press, 1973. $12.50.

KENNY, A. J. P., H. C. LONQUET-HIGGINS, J. R. LUCAS and C. H. WADDINGTON. *The Nature of Mind.* The Gifford Lectures 1971/2. Pp. 155. Chicago: Aldine, 1973. $5.75.

KNAPP, JOSEPH G. *The Advance of American Cooperative Enterprise: 1920–1945.* Pp. 645. Danville, Ill.: The Interstate Printers and Publishers, 1973. $9.95.

KNUTSON, JEANNE N., ed. *Handbook of Political Psychology.* Pp. vii, 542. San Francisco: Jossey-Bass, 1973. $25.00.

KNUTSON, JOHN F., ed. *The Control of Aggression: Implications from Basic Research.* Pp. vii, 310. Chicago: Aldine, 1973. $12.50.

KOHNSTAMM, MAX and WOLFGANG HAGER, eds. *A Nation Writ Large? Foreign-Policy Problems Before the European Community.* Pp. vii, 275. New York: Halsted Press, 1973. $17.00.

KÖNIG, RENÉ. *Soziologie und Psychiatrie.* Kolner Zeitschrift für Soziologie und Sozialpsychologie 2. Pp. 497. Opladen: Westdeutscher Verlag, 1973. No price. Paperbound.

KONVITZ, MILTON R. *Bill of Rights Reader: Leading Constitutional Cases.* 5th ed. Pp. vii, 747. Ithaca, N.Y.: Cornell University Press, 1973. $19.50.

LADD, EVERETT CARLL, JR. and SEYMOUR MARTIN LIPSET. *Academics, Politics, and the 1972 Election.* Domestic Affairs Study 15. Pp. 99. Washington, D.C.: American Enterprise Institute for Public Policy Research, 1973. $3.00. Paperbound.

LADD, EVERETT CARLL, JR. and SEYMOUR MARTIN LIPSET. *Professors, Unions, and American Higher Education.* Domestic Affairs Studies 16. Pp. vii, 124. Washington, D.C.: American Enterprise Institute for Public Policy Research, 1973. $1.75. Paperbound.

LAFFIN, JOHN. *Fedayeen: The Arab-Israeli Dilemma.* Pp. vii, 171. New York: The Free Press, 1973. $5.95.

LANHAM, URL. *The Bone Hunters.* Pp. ix, 285. New York: Columbia University Press, 1973. $12.95.

LASCH, CHRISTOPHER. *The World of Nations: Reflections on American History, Politics and Culture.* Pp. 348. New York: Alfred A. Knopf, 1973. $8.95.

LASZLO, ERWIN, ed. *The World System: Models, Norms, Variations.* International Library of Systems Theory and Philosophy. Pp. v, 215. New York: George Braziller, 1973. $7.95. Paperbound, $2.95.

LIEBERMAN, FLORENCE, PHYLLIS CAROFF and MARY GOTTESFELD. *Before Addiction: How to Help Youth.* Pp. vii, 131. New York: Behavioral Publications, 1973. $7.95.

LISKA, GEORGE. *States in Evolution: Changing Societies and Traditional Systems in World Politics.* Studies in International Affairs Number 19. Pp. v, 184. Baltimore, Md.: The Johns Hopkins Press, 1973. $8.00. Paperbound, $3.45.

LLOYD, HOWELL A. *The Rouen Campaign 1590–1592: Politics, Warfare and the Early-Modern State.* Pp. vii, 215. New York: Oxford University Press, 1973. $16.00.

LOUCKS, WILLIAM and WILLIAM G. WHITNEY. *Comparative Economic Systems.* 9th ed. Pp. ix, 411. New York: Harper and Row, 1973. $12.95.

MALONE, JOSEPH J. *The Arab Lands of Western Asia.* Pp. ix, 269. Englewood Cliffs, N.J.: Prentice-Hall, 1973. $8.95. Paperbound, $4.95.

The Management and Financing of Colleges.

Pp. 95. New York: Committee for Economic Development, 1973. $1.50. Paperbound.

MANDELKER, DANIEL R. and ROGER MONTGOMERY. *Housing in America: Problems and Perspectives*. Pp. v, 527. Indianapolis, Ind.: Bobbs-Merrill, 1973. No price.

MARTIKAINEN, TUOMO. *Political Activity Structure, Determinants and Dynamics*. Commentationes Scientiarum Socialium 6. Pp. 117. Helsinki, Finland: Societas Scientiarum Fennica, 1973. 15 Markka. Paperbound.

MARTIN, F. X. and F. J. BYRNE, eds. *The Scholar Revolutionary: Eoin MacNeill 1867–1945*. Pp. 429. New York: Barnes and Noble, 1973. $13.50.

MASTERMAN, C. F. G. *The Heart of the Empire: Discussion of Problems of Modern City Life in England*. Pp. vii, 415. New York: Barnes and Noble, 1973. $18.00.

MAY, RONALD J., ed. *Priorities in Melanesian Development*. Sixth Waigani Seminar. Pp. v, 470. Canberra, Australia: Australian National University Press, 1973. $9.00. Paperbound.

MAYHEW, ALAN. *Rural Settlement and Farming in Germany*. Pp. 224. New York: Barnes and Noble, 1973. $14.00.

MCGARVEY, PATRICK. *C.I.A.: The Myth and the Madness*. Pp. 240. Baltimore, Md.: Penguin Books, 1973. $1.65. Paperbound.

MCLANE, CHARLES B. *Soviet-Middle East Relations*. vol. 1 of *Soviet-Third World Relations*. Pp. 126. New York: Columbia University Press, 1973. $15.00.

MEIER, AUGUST, ed. *Black Experience: The Transformation of Activism*. 2nd ed. Transaction/Society Book Series 7. Pp. 193. New York: E. B. Dutton, 1973. $7.95. Paperbound, $2.95.

MERTON, ROBERT K. *The Sociology of Science: Theoretical and Empirical Investigations*. Pp. ix, 605. Chicago: The University of Chicago Press, 1973. $12.50.

MILLER, SALLY M. *Victor Berger and the Promise of Constructive Socialism 1910–1920*. Contributions in American History, no. 24. Pp. ix, 275. Westport, Conn.: Greenwood, 1973. $11.50.

MODELL, JOHN, ed. *The Kikuchi Diary: Chronicle from an American Concentration Camp*. Pp. 258. Urbana, Ill.: University of Illinois Press, 1973. $8.95.

MOOD, ALEXANDER M. *The Future of Higher Education: Some Speculations and Suggestions*. Pp. xii, 116. New York: McGraw-Hill, 1973. $6.95.

MORGAN, W. B. and J. C. PUGH. *West Africa*. Pp. v, 788. New York: Barnes and Noble, 1973. $20.00. Paperbound, $9.50.

MORRIS, BERNARD S. *Imperialism and Revolution: An Essay for Radicals*. Pp. vii, 81. Bloomington: Indiana University Press, 1973. $5.00. Paperbound, $1.95.

MORRISON, JACK. *The Rise of the Arts on the American Campus*. Pp. xiii, New York: McGraw-Hill, 1973. $8.95.

MOUNT, FERDINAND. *The Theatre of Politics*. Pp. 288. New York: Schocken Books, 1973. $7.95.

MY. *Observations for the Treadmill*. Pp. vii, 290. New York: The Viking Press, 1973. $12.95. Paperbound, $4.95.

NEUCHTERLEIN, DONALD E. *United States National Interests in a Changing World*. Pp. ix, 203. Lexington, Kentucky: The University Press of Kentucky, 1973. $8.00.

NICHOLS, DAVID. *Financing Elections: The Politics of an American Ruling Class*. Pp. vii, 191. New York: New Viewpoints, 1973. $9.95. Paperbound, 3.95.

NOVACK, GEORGE. *Humanism and Socialism*. Pp. 159. New York: Pathfinder Press, 1973. $6.95. Paperbound, $2.25.

NÚÑEZ DEL PRADO, OSCAR. *Kuyo Chico: Applied Anthropology in an Indian Community*. Pp. 162. Chicago: The University of Chicago Press, 1973. $9.50.

OLNEY, R. J. *Lincolnshire Politics 1832–1885*. Oxford Historical Monographs. Pp. vii, 284. New York: Oxford University Press, 1973. $13.00.

O'SHAUGHNESSY, JOHN. *Inquiry and Decision: A Methodology for Management and the Social Sciences*. Pp. 200. New York: Barnes and Noble, 1973. $11.50.

PADFIELD, HARLAND and ROY WILLIAMS. *Stay Where You Were: A Study of Unemployables in Industry*. Pp. xi, 282. Philadelphia: J. B. Lippincott, 1973. $7.50. Paperbound, $3.25.

Pakistan: From 1947 to the Creation of Bangladesh. Keesing's Research Report 9. Pp. v, 143. New York: Charles Scribner's Sons, 1973. $6.95. Paperbound, $2.95.

PAPPENFORT, DONNELL M., DEE MORGAN KILPATRICK and ROBERT W. ROBERTS, eds. *Child Caring: Social Policy and the Institution*. Pp. 333. Chicago: Aldine, 1973. $9.50.

PEARMAN, JEAN R. *Social Science and Social Work: Applications of Social Science in the Helping Professions*. Pp. 224. Metuchen, N.J.: Scarecrow Press, 1973. $6.50.

PELLETIER, H. PAUL and ENRIQUE OLLIVIER. *México, País Encantador*. Pp. 62. Jericho, N.Y.: Exposition Press, 1973. $4.50.

PERKINS, E. RALPH, ed. *Foreign Relations of the United States 1948*, vol. vii, *The Far East: China*. Pp. iii, 887. Washington, D.C.:

United States Government Printing Office, 1973. $6.50.

PHILIPP, EMANUEL L. *Political Reform in Wisconsin: A Historical Review of the Subjects of Primary Election Taxation and Railway Election.* Abr. and ed. by Stanley P. Caine and Roger E. Wyman. Pp. vii, 197. Madison, Wis.: The Society Press, 1973. $12.00.

PRASAD, BIMAL. *Indo-Soviet Relations 1947–1972: Documentary Study.* Pp. v, 494. Bombay, India: Allied, 1973. Rs. 50.00.

PRESSER, HARRIET B. *Sterilization and Fertility Decline in Puerto Rico.* Population Monograph Series, no. 13. Pp. v, 211. Berkeley, Cal.: Institute of International Studies, University of California, 1973. $3.25. Paperbound.

PROXMIRE, WILLIAM. *Can Congress Control Spending?* AEI's Town Hall Meeting. Pp. 62. Washington, D.C.: American Enterprise Institute, 1973. $2.50. Paperbound.

PYNOOS, JON, ROBERT SCHAFER and CHESTER W. HARTMAN, eds. *Housing Urban America:* Pp. ix, 597. Chicago: Aldine, 1973. $25.00.

RAHEJA, B. D. *Urban India and Public Policy.* Pp. vii, 319. Bombay, India: Somaiya Publications. 1973. Rs. 50.00.

RAINWATER, LEE, ed. *Soul: Black Experience.* 2nd ed. Transaction/Society Book Series 6. Pp. 256. New York: E. P. Dutton, 1973. $7.95. Paperbound, $2.95.

RANDOLPH, LILLIAN L. *Third-Party Settlement of Disputes in Theory and Practice.* Pp. 335. Dobbs Ferry, N.Y.: Oceana, 1973. $18.50.

RHODES, GERALD, ed. *The New Government of London: The First Five Years.* Pp. vii, 562. New York: International Arts and Sciences Press, 1973. $15.00.

RITTER, GERHARD A. *Vom Wohlfahrts ausschuss zum Wohlfahrtsstaat.* Pp. 188. Köln, Germany: Markus-Verlag, 1973. DM 18. Paperbound.

ROBINSON, JOAN, ed. *After Keynes.* Pp. ix, 202. New York: Barnes and Noble, 1973. $13.50.

ROCHE, GEORGE S. *Entitlement to Unemployment Insurance Benefits.* Studies in Unemployment Insurance. Pp. 99. Kalamazoo, Mich.: The W. E. Upjohn Institute for Employment Research, 1973. $1.25. Paperbound.

ROE, DAPHNE A. *A Plague of Corn: The Social History of Pellagra.* Pp. ix, 217. Ithaca, N.Y.: Cornell University Press, 1973. $11.50.

ROOS, J. P. *Welfare Theory and Social Policy. A Study in Policy Science.* Commentationes Scientiarum Socialium 4. Pp. 251.

Helsinki, Finland: Societas Scientiarum Fennica, 1973. No price. Paperbound.

ROSENBERG, HAROLD. *Discovering the Present: Three Decades in Art, Culture and Politics.* Pp. ix, 336. Chicago: The University of Chicago Press, 1973. $10.00.

ROSITZKE, HARRY. *Left On! The Glorious Bourgeois Cultural Revolution.* Pp. vii, 200. New York: Quadrangle, 1973. $6.95.

ROSENAU, JAMES N. *International Studies and the Social Sciences: Problems, Priorities and Prospects in the United States.* Sage Library of Social Research 2. Pp. 147. Beverly Hills, Cal.: Sage, 1973. $9.00. Paperbound, $5.00.

ROSSI, ALICE S., ed. *The Feminist Papers from Adams to de Beauvoir.* Pp. ix, 716. New York: Columbia University Press, 1973. $12.95.

ROTTENBERG, SIMON, ed. *The Economics of Crime and Punishment.* A Conference Sponsored by American Enterprise Institute for Public Policy Research. Pp. 232. Washington, D.C.: AEI, 1973. $4.00. Paperbound.

RUSSELL, CONRAD, ed. *The Origins of the English Civil War.* Pp. vii, 286. New York: Barnes and Noble, 1973. $12.00.

RYAN, ALAN, ed. *The Philosophy of Social Explanation.* Oxford Readings in Philosophy. Pp. 228. New York: Oxford University Press, 1973. $2.93. Paperbound.

SAHLEIN, WILLIAM J. *A Neighborhood Solution to the Social Services Dilemma.* Pp. 128. Lexington, Mass.: Lexington Books, 1973. $10.00.

SAMPSON, R. V. *The Discovery of Peace.* Pp. vii, 205. New York: Pantheon Books, 1973. $6.95.

SCHMITTER, PHILIPPE C., ed. *Military Rule in Latin America: Function, Consequences and Perspectives.* Sage Research Progress Series on War, Revolution, and Peacekeeping vol. 3. Pp. vii, 336. Beverly Hills, Cal.: Sage, 1973. $12.50. Paperbound, $7.50.

SCHOENFELD, C. G. *Psychoanalysis and the Law.* American Lecture Series. Pp. v, 285. Springfield, Ill.: Charles C. Thomas, 1973. $13.75.

SCHRAM, STUART R., ed. *Authority Participation and Cultural Change in China.* Contemporary China Institute Publications. Pp. vii, 350. New York: Cambridge University Press, 1973. $17.00. Paperbound, $4.95.

SCHROYER, TRENT. *The Critique of Domination: The Origins and Development of Critical Theory.* Pp. 282. New York: George Braziller, 1973. $8.95.

SEARS, DAVID O. and JOHN B. MCCONAHAY. *The Politics of Violence: The New Urban*

Blacks and the Watts Riot. Pp. vii, 244. Boston, Mass.: Houghton Mifflin, 1973. $4.95. Paperbound.

SEATON, E. E. and S. I. MALITI. *Tanzania Treaty Practice.* Pp. vii, 200. New York: Oxford University Press, 1973. $10.50. Paperbound.

SEIFERT, WILLIAM W., MOHAMMED A. BAKR and M. ALI KETTANI, eds. *Energy and Development: A Case Study.* MIT Report no. 25. Pp. xv, 300. Cambridge, Mass.: The MIT Press, 1973. $11.00. Paperbound.

SHAW, G. K. *An Introduction to the Theory of Macro-Economic Policy.* 2nd ed. Pp. vii, 209. New York: Barnes and Noble, 1973. $9.50.

SIMPSON, GEORGE EATON and J. MILTON YINGER. *Racial and Cultural Minorities: An Analysis of Prejudice and Discrimination.* 4th ed. Pp. vi, 775. New York: Harper and Row, 1973. $12.95.

SIMPSON, GEORGE EATON. *Melville J. Herskovits.* Leaders of Modern Anthropology. Pp. 199. New York: Columbia University Press, 1973. $10.00. Paperbound, $2.95.

SINGER, PETER. *Democracy and Disobedience.* Pp. v, 150. New York: Oxford University Press, 1973. $6.50.

SKRINE, C. P. and PAMELA NIGHTINGALE. *Macartney at Kashgar: New Light on British, Chinese and Russian Activities in Sinkiang 1890–1918.* Pp. vii, 282. New York: Barnes and Noble, 1973. $15.50.

SMITH, F. B. *Radical Artisan: William James Linton 1812–97.* Pp. ix, 254, Totowa, N.J.: Rowman and Littlefield, 1973. $14.50.

SMITH, THELMA E. *Guide to the Municipal Government of the City of New York.* Revised ed. Pp. 360. New York: Law-Arts, 1973. $4.95. Paperbound.

SPECTER, GERALD A. and WILLIAM L. CLAIBORN. *Crisis Intervention.* vol. 2. Topical Series in Community-Clinical Psychology. Pp. x, 210. New York: Behavioral, 1973. $9.95. Paperbound, $4.95.

STARR, JOHN BRYAN. *Ideology and Culture: An Introduction to the Dialectic of Contemporary Chinese Politics.* Pp. xi, 300. New York: Harper and Row, 1973. $3.50. Paperbound.

STEPAN, ALFRED, ed. *Authoritarian Brazil: Origins, Policies, and Future.* Pp. vii, 265. New Haven, Conn.: Yale University Press, 1973. $10.00.

SUBRAHMANIAN, K. K. *Import of Capital and Technology: A Study of Foreign Collaborations in Indian Industry.* Pp. v, 248. New Delhi, India: People's Publishing House, 1972. Rs. 25.00.

Surveys of African Economies. Botswana, *Lesotho, Swaziland, Burundi, Equatorial Guinea and Rwanda.* vol. 5. Pp. v, 471. Washington, D.C.: International Monetary Fund, 1973. $5.00.

THOMAS, HUGH. *John Strachey.* Pp. ix, 319. New York: Harper and Row, 1973. $8.50.

THURBER, CLARENCE E. and LAWRENCE S. GRAHAM, eds. *Development Administration in Latin America.* Pp. vii, 453. Durham, N.C.: Duke University Press, 1973. $13.75.

TOYNBEE, J. M. C. *Animals in Roman Life and Art.* Aspects of Greek and Roman Life. Pp. 431. Ithaca, N.Y.: Cornell University Press, 1973. $17.50.

TREGASKIS, RICHARD. *The Warrior King: Hawaii's Kamehameha the Great.* Pp. xix, 320. New York: Macmillan, 1973. $10.00.

TROTSKY, LEON. *Problems of Everyday Life and Other Writings on Culture and Science.* Pp. 352. New York: Pathfinder Press, 1973. $8.95. Paperbound, $3.45.

TSURUTANI, TAKETSUGU. *The Politics of National Development: Political Leadership in Transitional Societies.* Pp. 193. New York: Chandler, 1973. $5.00. Paperbound.

TWINING, WILLIAM. *Karl Llewellyn and the Realist Movement.* Pp. vii, 574. South Hackensack, N.J.: Fred B. Rothman, 1973. $25.00.

VELASCO, GUSTAVO R. *Labor Legislation From an Economic Point of View.* Pp. v, 65. Indianapolis, Ind.: Liberty Fund, 1973. $3.00.

WADDINGTON, C. H., ed. *Biology and the History of the Future.* Pp. 72. Edinburgh, Scotland: Edinburgh University Press, 1973. 50p. Paperbound.

WADDINGTON, C. H., ed. *Towards a Theoretical Biology 4. Essays.* An IUBS Symposium. Pp. 299. Chicago: Aldine, 1973. $17.50.

WALKER, CHARLES E. and HENRY S. RUESS. *Major Tax Reform: Urgent Necessity or Not?* Rational Debate Series. Pp. 78. Washington, D.C.: American Enterprise Institute for Public Policy Research, 1973. $5.75.

WARREN, W. L. *Henry 11.* Pp. 710. Berkeley, Cal.: University of California Press, 1973. $20.00.

WASBY, STEPHEN L. *American Government and Politics: The Process and Structures of Policy-Making in American Government.* Pp. vii, 676. New York: Charles Scribner, 1973. $14.95.

WATANABE, HITOSHI. *The Ainu Ecosystem: Environment and Group Structure.* Pp. 164. Seattle, Wash.: University of Washington Press, 1973. $9.50.

WATT, D. C. and J. MAYALL, eds. *Current British Foreign Policy 1971*. Pp. v, 1322. Bloomington, Ind.: Indiana University Press, 1973. $28.00.

WEINSTEIN, FRED and GERALD M. PLATT. *The Wish to Be Free: Society, Psyche, and Value Change*. Pp. 330. Berkeley: University of California Press, $3.85. Paperbound.

WILSON, GLENN D., ed. *The Psychology of Conservatism*. Pp. v, 277. New York: Academic Press, 1973. $13.50.

WILSON, LEGRAND J. *The Confederate Soldier*. Pp. 232. Memphis, Tenn.: Memphis State University Press, 1973. $7.00.

WITHEY, STEPHEN B. et al. *A Degree and What Else? Correlates and Consequences of a College Education*. Pp. 147. New York: McGraw-Hill, 1971. $5.95.

WOLF, MARGERY. *Women and the Family in Rural Taiwan*. Pp. vii, 235. Stanford, Cal.: Stanford University Press, 1973. $8.50.

WOLFF, KURT H., ed. *From Karl Mannheim*. Pp. xi, 393. New York: Oxford University Press, 1971. $12.50. Paperbound, $3.95.

WOLMAN, BENJAMIN B. *Victims of Success: Emotional Problems of Executives*. Pp. ix, 160. New York: Quadrangle, 1973. $5.95.

WOOSTER, WARREN S., ed. *Freedom of Oceanic Research: A Study Conducted by the Center for Marine Affairs of the Scripps Institution of Oceanography University of California, San Diego*. Pp. 255. New York: Crane, Russak, 1973. $14.00.

WRIGHT, ARTHUR F. and DENIS TWITCHETT, eds. *Perspectives on the T'Ang*. Pp. vii, 457. New Haven, Conn.: Yale University Press, 1973. $15.00.

WRIGHT, BENJAMIN F. *5 Public Philosophies of Walter Lippmann*. Pp. 171. Austin: The University of Texas Press, 1973. $6.75.

WYNER, ALAN J., ed. *Executive Ombudsmen in the United States*. Pp. v, 315. Berkeley, Cal.: Institute of Governmental Studies, 1973. $5.50. Paperbound.

ZENTNER, HENRY. *Prelude to Administrative Theory: Essays in Social Structure and Social Process*. Pp. v, 205. Calgary, Alberta: Strayer Publications, 1973. $9.95. Paperbound, $4.95.

Mathematical Applications in Political Science VII

Edited by JAMES F. HERNDON *and* JOSEPH L. BERND, *Virginia Polytechnic Institute and State University. 84 pp.* $9.75

This latest volume of *Mathematical Applications in Political Science* once again presents a variety of applications of mathematics to political research. The subject matter includes primary elections, congressional voting, judicial behavior, and the analysis of aggregate data. The methods used are decision theory, measure of correlation, discriminant function analysis, and regression. It is hoped that these papers will lead both to the further application of the methods described here and to the development of still more useful mathematical techniques of political research.

Toward a Philosophy of the Seas

By HORACE M. KALLEN, *1973 recipient of the John Dewey Award for Humanist of the Year by the American Humanities Association. ix, 44 pp.* $1.50

These two essays present an enlightening interpretation of the significance of the ocean in man's perspective of life. They establish a philosophic foundation for an oceanic discipline by revealing the sea's intricate relationship to man's present actions and his goals for the future. Dr. Kallen's essays emphasize the need for innovative world leadership dedicated to the protection and preservation of the World Ocean.

University Press of Virginia   Charlottesville

INDUSTRIAL AND LABOR RELATIONS REVIEW

Volume 27   Number 2   January 1974

ARTICLES

RECENT PUBLICATIONS   RESEARCH NOTES

BOOK REVIEWS

Published quarterly by the New York State School of Industrial and Labor Relations, Cornell University, Ithaca, New York 14850

Annual subscription: $10.00 (domestic) $11.00 (foreign)
Single issues: $2.75   (domestic) $3.00   (foreign)

Kindly mention THE ANNALS *when writing to advertisers*

INDEX

Kindly mention THE ANNALS *when writing to advertisers*

MODERN CHINESE SOCIETY

An Analytical Bibliography

1. Publications in Western Languages, 1644-1972
   Edited by G. William Skinner

2. Publications in Chinese, 1644-1969
   Edited by G. William Skinner & Winston Hsieh

3. Publications in Japanese, 1644-1971
   Edited by G. William Skinner & Shigeaki Tomita

This pioneering research aid places over 31,000 works on traditional, Republican, and Communist China in all languages within a single frame of reference. Prepared specifically for social scientists and institutional historians, the volumes provide both retrospective and current bibliographic control of the secondary literature on Chinese society, the Chinese economy and polity, and personality and culture in China from the beginning of the Ch'ing dynasty to the present. Each entry is coded as to topic, time period, geographic region, type of local or regional system to which the work refers (village, market town, city-centered system, etc.), and the kinds of research on which it is based. In all volumes, headings are in English, Chinese, and Japanese. Chinese and Japanese publications are cited in characters as well as romanization, and all non-English titles are given an English rendering. Cross-tabulating the codes for all entries, computer programs have prepared a subject index by historical period, a subject index by geographical area, and a local-systems index. In addition to the three analytical indexes that are this bibliography's most distinctive feature, conventional author and subject indexes are included.

Vol. 1. 880 pages, 13,057 entries, $35.00
Vol. 2. 880 pages, 11,215 entries, $38.00
Vol. 3. 608 pages, 7,169 entries, $32.00

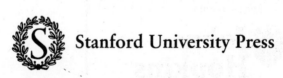 Stanford University Press

THE BENCH AND THE BALLOT

Southern Federal Judges
and Black Voters

By Charles V. Hamilton

Concentrating on the crucial
years between the Civil
Rights Act of 1957 and the
Voting Rights Act of 1965,
the author delineates the
accomplishments and the
limitations of legal and judicial power in strengthening
the southern Black vote. He
discusses the political and
economic environment, and
he looks also at the Nixon
Administration's recent record in this area. "Hamilton
brings to this study a thorough grasp of the judicial
process...combined with
a sense of social dynamics
coming from first-hand
observations and interviews
in the field."—Benjamin
Quarles. "The book is unique,
comprehensive, and crea-
tive."—Hanes Walton, Jr.
Cloth $7.95 • Paper $2.95

THROUGH DIFFERENT EYES

Black and White
Perspectives on
American Race
Relations

Edited by Peter I. Rose,
Stanley Rothman, and
William J. Wilson

Twenty social scientists,
educators, and journalists
— black and white — give
diverse and challenging
views of the current racial
crisis in the schools and
colleges, welfare bureaucracies, police depart-
ments, and electoral
politics. Included are
essays on the percep-
tions of the poor, of
black immigrants and
white ethnics, of integra-
tionists and nationalists.
With introductory dis-
cussion and summary
epilogue.

Cloth $12.50
Paper $3.95

**OXFORD
UNIVERSITY
PRESS**
200 Madison Avenue • New York, N.Y. 10016

Kindly mention THE ANNALS *when writing to advertisers*

The American Academy of Political and Social Science

3937 Chestnut Street   Philadelphia, Pennsylvania 19104

Origin and Purpose. The Academy was organized December 14, 1889, to promote the progress of political and social science, especially through publications and meetings. The Academy does not take sides in controverted questions, but seeks to gather and present reliable information to assist the public in forming an intelligent and accurate judgment.

Meetings. The Academy holds an annual meeting in the spring extending over two days.

Publications. THE ANNALS is the bimonthly publication of The Academy. Each issue contains articles on some prominent social or political problem, written at the invitation of the editors. Also, monographs published from time to time, numbers of which are distributed to pertinent professional organizations. These volumes constitute important reference works on the topics with which they deal, and they are extensively cited by authorities throughout the United States and abroad. The papers presented at the meetings of The Academy are included in THE ANNALS.

Membership. Each member of The Academy receives THE ANNALS and may attend the meetings of The Academy. Annual dues for individuals are $15.00 (for clothbound copies $20.00 per year). A life membership is $500. All payments are to be made in United States dollars.

Libraries and other institutions may receive THE ANNALS paperbound at a cost of $15.00 per year, or clothbound at $20.00 per year. Add $1.00 to above rates for membership outside U.S.A.

Single copies of THE ANNALS may be obtained by nonmembers of The Academy for $3.00 ($4.00 clothbound) and by members for $2.50 ($3.50 clothbound). A discount to members of 5 per cent is allowed on orders for 10 to 24 copies of any one issue, and of 10 per cent on orders for 25 or more copies. These discounts apply only when orders are placed directly with The Academy and not through agencies. The price to all bookstores and to all dealers is $3.00 per copy less 20 per cent, with no quantity discount. It is urged that payment be sent with each order. This will save the buyer the shipping charge and save The Academy the cost of carrying accounts and sending statements. Monographs may be purchased for $4.00 by individuals and $5.00 by institutions, with proportionate discounts.

All correspondence concerning The Academy or THE ANNALS should be addressed to the Academy offices, 3937 Chestnut Street, Philadelphia, Pa. 19104.